GLOBALIZATION FROM BELOW

Social Movements, Protest, and Contention

Series Editor: Bert Klandermans, Free University, Amsterdam

Associate Editors: Ron R. Aminzade, University of Minnesota
David S. Meyer, University of California, Irvine
Verta A. Taylor, University of California, Santa Barbara

For more books in the series, see page 296.

GLOBALIZATION FROM BELOW

Transnational Activists and Protest Networks

Donatella della Porta,
Massimiliano Andretta,
Lorenzo Mosca, and Herbert Reiter

Social Movements, Protest, and Contention
Volume 26

 University of Minnesota Press
Minneapolis • London

Published by the University of Minnesota Press
111 Third Avenue South, Suite 290
Minneapolis, MN 55401-2520
http://www.upress.umn.edu

Library of Congress Cataloging-in-Publication Data

Globalization from below : transnational activists and protest
networks / Donatella della Porta ... [et al.].
    p.   cm. — (Social movements, protest, and contention ; v. 26)
    Includes bibliographical references and index.
    ISBN 13: 978-0-8166-4642-5 (hc) — ISBN 13: 978-0-8166-4643-2 (pb)
    ISBN 10: 0-8166-4642-2 (hc : alk. paper) — ISBN 10: 0-8166-4643-0
(pb : alk. paper)
    1. Anti-globalization movement.   I. della Porta, Donatella, 1956–
II. Series.
    HN17.5.G582 2006
    303.48'4—dc22
                                                              2005035683

12 11 10 09 08 07 06   10 9 8 7 6 5 4 3 2 1

Contents

Acknowledgments

This volume is the result of a long-lasting collaboration that has already produced two other books on the "new global" movements, in particular on the anti-G8 demonstrations in Genoa in 2001: *Global, Noglobal, New Global* in Italian (Andretta et al. 2002) and *Global No Global* in German (Andretta et al. 2003). We are grateful to those who helped us produce those two books. Although some of the ideas developed in those previous works are reported in this volume, here we analyze a new set of data on the first European Social Forum in 2002.

Our research is based in part on two surveys, which would have been impossible to carry out without the collaboration of almost three thousand activists we interviewed at two transnational protest events. About thirty activists participated in Florence in focus groups, providing us with a lively picture of the movement and their hopes and worries. We also had several occasions to discuss the results of our work with other larger and smaller groups of activists. We thank them all for their time and especially for their trust in our work.

Previous results of our research were discussed at several conferences and workshops, including the international conference "La Toscana e la globalizzazione dal basso" in Regione Toscana, Florence, May 2003; the graduate conference "Globalizzazione, conflitti, movimenti sociali" at the University of Trento, June 2003; the general conference of the ECPR (European Consortium for Political Research), Marburg, Germany, September 2003; the international conference "Transnational Social Movements" at the Rockefeller Foundation Center in Bellagio, Italy, July 2003;

the international conference "The Europeanization of the Public Sphere" at Wissenschaftszentrum für Sozialforschung, Berlin, June 2003; the international conference "Debating the Democratic Legitimacy of European Union" at the Mannheim Center for European Social Research (MZES), November 2003; the "Three Countries Conference" organized by the Swiss Society of Political Science in Bern, Switzerland, November 2003; the international conference "Political Change and Globalization" in Crete, November 2003; the international conference "Anti/Altermondialisation: Anti/Alter globalization" at Fondation Nationale des Sciences Politiques, Paris, December 2003; the international conference "Conflitti, teorie dei conflitti, e mondializzazione" at the University of Naples, December 2003; the international conference "Internet and Governance: The Global Context" at Oxford Internet Institute, January 2004; and the international conference "The Policing of Protest after Seattle" at the University of Gothenburg, Sweden, May 2004. We are grateful for the many comments, stimuli, and ideas we received on those occasions. In particular, Mario Diani, Bert Klandermans, Olivier Fillieule, Hanspeter Kriesi, John McCarthy, Doug McAdam, Clark McPhail, Kathryn Sikkink, Abby Petersen, Richard Rose, Dieter Rucht, and Sidney Tarrow offered us precious comments.

We discussed our work frequently and in depth in two collegial settings: in formal and informal meetings of the research group that the authors belong to, the Gruppo di Ricerca sull'Azione Collettiva in Europa (GRACE) at the University of Florence; and in various workshops and seminars at the European University in Florence. At various times we discussed our ideas with Alessandro Pizzorno and Philippe Schmitter.

Research in the field needs committed collaborators. For their participation in different phases of our work, we wish to thank Maria Fabbri, who assisted us with data analysis; Elena Del Giorgio and Fiammette Benati, who helped with the focus groups; Claudius Wagemann, for his consultancy on statistical analysis; and Anna Carola Freschi, for her suggestions for research on the Internet. Simone Baglioni, Chiara Baldi, Lucia Baldi, Silvia Bolgherini, Stefania Bonura, Matteo Borzoni, Manuela Caiani, Lorenzo Campoli, Erica Cellini, Caterina Chirici, Elena Del Giorgio, Claudia di Muro, Maria Fabbri, Letizia Franciolini, Riccardo Franciolini, Anna Carola Freschi, Filippo Lenzi, Marco Lombardi, Francesco Manaresi, Francesco Mosciatti, Maria Francesca Nonne, Umberto Pascucci, Claudia Ranfagni, Camilla Smeraldi, Tania Spagnoli, and Duccio Viani helped us during the interview campaigns.

Finally, research also needs material help. Several sponsors have financed parts of our research. We are particularly grateful to the European

Community for the support given to four research projects related to our work: TEA (Transformation of Environmental Activism), EUROPUB (Europeanization of the Public Sphere), UNEMPOL (Project on the Contentious Politics of Unemployment), and DEMOS (Democracy in Europe and the Mobilization of Society). We also thank the Italian Ministry of Public Education for sponsoring our research on "Movimenti sociali e democrazia deliberativa: I social forum in Europa" as part of a larger project on discursive democracy, coordinated by Massimo Bonanni.

First versions of several chapters were translated by Donald Bathgate and Ioin Fraser.

Abbreviations

AFL-CIO	American Federation of Labor and Congress of Industrial Organizations
AI	Amnesty International
AN	Alleanza Nazionale (Italian Post-Fascist Party)
APC	Association for Progressive Communication
ARCI	Associazione Ricreativa e Culturale Italiana (Italian Cultural and Recreational Associations)
ATTAC	Action for a Tobin Tax to Aid Citizens
BB	Black Bloc
CGIL	Confederazione Generale Italiana del Lavoro (Italian General Confederation of Workers—left-wing trade union)
CI	Caritas Internationalis
CIRM	Centro Internazionale Ricerche di Mercato (International Market Research Center)
CISL	Confederazione Italiana Sindacati Lavoratori (Italian Confederation of Labor Unions—Catholic trade union)
CMC	computer-mediated communication
COBAS	Comitati di Base (Grassroots Trade Unions)
COCER	Consiglio Centrale di Rappresentanza dei Carabinieri (Central Council of Representation of the Carabinieri)
COISP	Coordinamento per l'Indipendenza Sindacale delle Forze di Polizia (Italian police trade union)
CONGOS	Conference of Nongovernmental Organizations

DIGOS	Divisione Investigative Generali e Operazioni Speciali (local political police unit)
DS	Democratici di Sinistra (Democrats of the Left)
EC	European Community
ECN	European Counter Network
ECOFIN	Economic and Financial Affairs Council of the Council of the EU
ESF	European Social Forum
ETUC	European Trade Union Confederation
EU	European Union
FG	focus group
FIOM	Federazione Impiegati Operai Metallurgici (Italian Metalworkers Trade Union, CGIL Branch)
FoE	Friends of the Earth
GATT	General Agreement on Tariffs and Trade
GdP	Gewerkschaft der Polizei (German police trade union)
GM	genetically modified
GOM	Gruppi Operativi Mobili (Police Special Units)
GR	Globalise Resistance
GSF	Genoa Social Forum
IC	International Council (WSF)
IGC	Institute for Global Communication
IGOs	International Governmental Organizations
IMF	International Monetary Fund
INGOs	International Nongovernmental Organizations
IPOS	international political opportunity structure
LISIPO	Libero Sindacato di Polizia (Italian police trade union)
MAI	Multilateral Agreement on Investment
MERCOSUR	Mercado Común del Sur (Southern Common Market, Latin America)
MPs	members of Parliament
NAFTA	North American Free Trade Agreement
NATO	North Atlantic Treaty Organization

NC	ATTAC National Council
NGOs	nongovernmental organizations
NOA	Nucleo Operativo Antisommossa (Experimental Squad of the State Police Public Order)
NOCS	Nucleo Operativo Centrale di Sicurezza (Central Operative Unit for Security of the Carabinieri)
OECD	Organization for Economic Cooperation and Development
PCF	Parti Communiste Français (French Communist Party)
PCI	Partito Comunista Italiano (Italian Communist Party)
PDS	Partei des Demokratischen Sozialismus (Party of Democratic Socialism; successor of East Germany's Communist Party)
PKK	Kurdish Communist Party
POS	political opportunity structure
PSOE	Partido Socialista Obrero Español (Spanish Socialist Workers' Party)
RC	Rifondazione Comunista (Italian Communist Party)
SAP	Sindacato Autonomo di Polizia (Italian independent police trade union)
SDI	Socialisti Democratici Italiani (Italian Democratic Socialists)
SILP-CGIL	Sindacato Lavoratori Polizia (Italian Police Workers' Union, CGIL Branch)
SISDE	Servizio per le Informazioni e la Sicurezza Democratica (Italian Civil Secret Service)
SIULP	Sindacato Italiano Unitario Lavoratori Polizia (Italian police trade union)
SMOs	social movement organizations
SPD	Sozialdemokratische Partei Deutschlands (German Social Democratic Party)
TRIPS	Trade-Related Aspects of Intellectual Property Rights
TSMOs	transnational social movement organizations
UCIGOS	Ufficio Centrale Investigazioni Generali e Operazione Speciali (Italian Central Political Police)

UIL	Unione Italiana del Lavoro (Italian Labor Union)
UN	United Nations
UNESCO	UN Educational, Scientific, and Cultural Organization
WB	World Bank
WCC	World Council of Churches
WEF	World Economic Forum
WSF	World Social Forum
WTO	World Trade Organization
WWF	World Wildlife Fund

1

Globalization and Social Movements

November 30, 1999. In Seattle, a city that, thanks to Microsoft, has become emblematic of the New Economy, some fifty thousand demonstrators protest against the third World Trade Organization (WTO) conference that had assembled to launch the Millennium Round, a new series of negotiations aimed at increasing market liberalization, in particular in investment and public services. A few months before, in Geneva, a coalition of organizations from various backgrounds, which had already (successfully) mobilized to prevent the signing of the Multilateral Agreement on Investment (MAI), called for the protest in Seattle. As with the MAI, the WTO negotiations were accused of restricting individual states' power to intervene on social and environmental issues in the name of free trade. No fewer than 1,387 groups (including nongovernmental organizations [NGOs], trade unions, environmentalists, and a number of religious organizations) signed the call to demonstrate against the Millennium Round. The protest events were prepared in thousands of meetings in many countries and by a global campaign of information. The demonstrators marched to slogans such as "our world is not for sale"; "no globalization without participation"; "we are citizens, not only consumers"; "WTO = capitalism without conscience"; "trade: clean, green, and fair."

From the morning of the very first day, a series of sit-ins, coordinated by Direct Action Network, stopped most of the three thousand delegates from 135 countries from reaching the inaugural ceremony. Organized into "affinity groups," only loosely linked with each other, some ten thousand demonstrators sat on the ground tied together in chains using the lock-down

1

and tripod techniques that made removing the blockages more difficult. When the police arrived to clear the streets leading to the summit site, the demonstrators did not resist but applied the tactics they had learned during courses in nonviolence. In the streets of Seattle, thronged with musical bands and theater groups, Greenpeace activists appeared with gigantic condoms bearing the legend "Practice Safe Trade," while French farmworkers went about giving away some 250 kilos of Roquefort cheese that was subject to customs duties in the United States in a tit-for-tat measure against restrictive legislation introduced by the European Union (EU) against "hormone beef." Activists of Jubilee 2000, a coalition of groups (including many religious-based ones) whose aim was to cancel third world foreign debt, linked up in a human chain. A massive march was called by the AFL-CIO (American Federation of Labor and Congress of Industrial Organizations) mobilizing over twenty thousand workers, in particular longshoremen and public service employees, demanding worldwide application of workers' rights. Farmworker organizations banded together with consumer activists and environmentalists to demand keeping food products out of liberalization agreements on the principle of precaution.

Over two hundred demonstrators dressed up as turtles—an endangered species—and wandered through the crowd with the task of troubleshooting any violence. Ben White, the designer of the colorful costumes and an activist of the Sea Turtle Restoration Project, explains: "Since the dawn of time, turtles have always been a symbol of wisdom. They never fight, they don't use violence. We represent them and we must be their voice. . . . Anyone who acts aggressively, even if it's only vocal, has to take his costume off. . . . We're not only nonviolent ourselves, we're also against the use of violence by others. Wherever the turtles come across violence they try to make peace" (in Reimon 2002, 73). On the fringes of the demonstrations, however, there were small groups that turned violent, smashing the windows of shops dealing in products of transnational corporations, such as Nike, Levi's, and McDonald's, that have been accused of using child labor or unhealthy products. In any case, the police stepped in en masse against the nonviolent blockages, deploying tear gas and pepper spray, *before* the anarchists started to get violent (Smith 2001, 13; also Morse 2001). Although a curfew was declared, blockages and police charges went on day and night for three days until the intergovernmental summit broke up without any agreement having been reached. Among the six hundred people arrested were activists from Global Exchange, an NGO, who used their passes to enter the inaugural ceremony and to make a speech to the few delegates who had managed to get in criticizing the WTO from the podium. A petition was circulated over the Internet in protest against the lack of transparency of the talks. In twenty-four hours, signatures from 1,700 groups of various kinds, many from the south of the world, were gathered (Kaldor 2000, 112).

Seattle's chief of police resigned the week after. The battle of Seattle was to come under the scrutiny of four commissions of inquiry held by the American Civil Liberties Union, the Seattle National Lawyers Guild–WTO Legal Group, the Committee for Local Government Accountability, and the WTO Accountability Review Committee; the first three are civil rights associations, and the fourth is a semiofficial Seattle local government body (Seattle Police Department 2000).

July 19–22, 2001. The G8 summit was held in Genoa. A year earlier, at the World Social Forum in Porto Alegre, Brazil, the international meeting of the movement for globalization "from below" (misleadingly termed "no global" by most of the Italian press), it had been decided to mobilize on an international scale against the neoliberal version of globalization. About eight hundred organizations came together in the Genoa Social Forum (GSF) that, together with other groups, organized the protest.

Given that many international summits over the previous two years had been met with protests that were sometimes violent, the Italian government prepared for the G8 by concentrating on keeping demonstrators away from the summit site and violent activists well away from the city itself. In addition to installing high barriers to protect the so-called red zone of the summit site, the airport, railway stations, and motorway exits were closed. In his testimony to the parliamentary investigative commission, national chief of police De Gennaro spoke of 140,000 identity checks made and more than 2,000 people turned back at the Italian borders. Internal expulsion orders were used to keep certain Italian militants from entering Genoa. With the city center closed, the port and airport sealed off, and the railway stations and motorway exits tightly controlled, Genoa emptied: two days before the start of the summit, electrical consumption and waste disposal had dropped by 40 percent.

Despite the tension caused by some terrorist incidents before the start of the summit, as well as by alarmist information from the secret services—in the parliamentary investigative commission (IPIC 2001f, 66), the former head of the national political police, La Barbera, spoke of a "multitude of information, in the bulk of cases without any basis"—the July 19 march of fifty thousand people for migrants' rights remained peaceful. The situation changed radically the following day due to what the newspapers described as the provocations of the radical Black Bloc (BB), followed by indiscriminate police actions in response. According to press estimations, between four hundred and one thousand BB members were involved, while the police spoke of five hundred Italians and two thousand foreigners. Ignoring the red zone, the morning of July 20 they attacked banks, shops, the prison, and public buildings without being challenged by the police. For the entire day, events followed a similar pattern: after the BB's attacks, the police responded by indiscriminately charging (with water cannons, tear gas, and batons) the crowd, which included peaceful protesters, doctors, nurses, paramedics, photographers, and journalists. This happened at Piazza da Novi, where the federation of grassroots trade unions COBAS and some social centers were concentrated, and at Piazza Manin, where the police attacked peaceful Rete Lilliput demonstrators (who were engaged in nonviolent intervention intended to hinder the BB). After the apparently unprovoked attack of the police against the march of the so-called Disobbedienti (Disobedients), some groups of demonstrators reacted. A *carabinieri* (Italian police) jeep became stuck and its occupants were attacked. One of the carabinieri inside opened fire, killing a twenty-three-year-old Genovese activist, Carlo Giuliani. At the perimeter fence delimiting the red zone, the police used water cannons laced with chemicals against demonstrators from the transnational organization ATTAC (Action for a Tobin Tax to Aid Citizens), the metalworkers' union FIOM, the cultural association ARCI, and other groups close to the institutional left, who were banging on the fences and throwing cloves of garlic. The mayor of Genoa, Pericù, of the Democrats of the Left (DS), who had tried to negotiate with the organizers, complained about the absence of negotiators from police headquarters. Police charges and fighting continued after the demonstration had been declared closed by the GSF spokesman, Vittorio Agnoletto. In the evening, the movement's spokespersons were careful to distance themselves from the BB but criticized the police actions. According to the center-right government of Berlusconi, the GSF was responsible for the disorder. The DS, the main opposition party, withdrew its support for the following day's demonstration, (unsuccessfully) instructing its members not to go to Genoa.

At the July 21 demonstration—whose organizers had expected one hundred thousand people, and the police chief no more than forty thousand—between two hundred thousand and three hundred thousand demonstrators gathered. Again, there were attacks by the BB, which the demonstrators tried to prevent. The police this time relied more on tear gas, fired from helicopters and armored cars, to keep themselves at a greater distance from the demonstrators. The first police charge at 2:25 p.m. took place while the procession was about to set off; similar charges took place at

2:50 p.m. and 5:35 p.m. The daily papers—and not just those supporting the movement—reported numerous attempts by the movement, which had formed its own rudimentary security force, to push back violent protesters and to rescue demonstrators and lawyers being beaten by the police. The three days of Genoa ended with 411 people treated in public hospitals—328 demonstrators (79 were admitted to a hospital), 67 policemen (5 were admitted), and 16 journalists (3 were admitted)—while the estimates of the total number of people injured ran to more than 1,000 (Gubitosa 2003, 177ff.). Out of a total cost of 240 billion lire (125 million euro) for the summit, 15 billion lire (8 million euro) had to be allocated to cover the damages (461).

Police actions after the protests ended and far from the demonstration sites further highlighted the problem of respect for demonstrators' rights at transnational protest events. The GSF, its legal advice team, the Indymedia press group, and a dormitory for protesters were based at the Diaz-Pertini school. On the evening of July 21, the police burst in with the ostensible purpose of searching for weapons. The press described the behavior of the police as particularly brutal—a description that members of Parliament (MPs) who were present concurred with. Of the 93 persons detained and arrested in the building—altogether 302 people were arrested in connection with the Genoa protests, 49 of them in the days and weeks following the events (Gubitosa 2003, 173)—62 were injured during the police action, some of them seriously. The two Molotov cocktails confiscated, together with items like cameras, mobile telephones, swimming goggles, and Swiss Army knives, were apparently brought to the school and deposited inside by police officers. The arrested demonstrators were charged with conspiracy to commit acts of plunder, but 92 of the 93 detainees were immediately released by magistrates. In the part of the school used by the Genoa Legal Forum and by Indymedia, computers were destroyed and video and printed materials were taken away. In the following days, various testimonies were published recounting the mistreatment of arrested demonstrators in the Bolzaneto barracks, where a center for identifying detainees had been set up. According to witnesses, a large number of them non-Italians, the guards used spray cans with irritants, wielded truncheons, forced detainees to stay on their feet for hours, and compelled them to repeat fascist and racist slogans.

The police handling of the demonstrations raised protests in Italy and abroad. On July 24, in various Italian cities one hundred thousand demonstrators protested peacefully against the Genovese repression. The reaction in international public opinion—and also by many foreign governments—was heavily critical. Starting July 21, there were many demonstrations, often in front of Italian embassies and consulates, in numerous European countries and beyond. While even moderate journalists denounced the violence of the Italian police, puzzlement and requests for clarification came from the consular officials of many friendly nations, not least the United States.

November 6–9, 2002. Florence hosted the European Social Forum (ESF). After the violent repression of the anti-G8 countersummit in Genoa in July 2001, many demonstrations followed in Italy as well as in other European countries and remained without incidents. Unsuccessful attempts were made by center-right governments and by some center-left politicians to stigmatize the movement for globalization from below as violent and antipolitical. Since the events in Genoa, although there have been ups and downs, local social forums have mushroomed in many Italian cities, networking organizations and individuals who criticized neoliberal globalization and advocated global justice. These networks coordinated national demonstrations on issues such as the rights of migrants and the defense of public schools, protection of labor rights as well as opposition to wars and terrorism. In particular, three hundred thousand took part in a special edition of the annual March for Peace between Assisi and Perugia, called after the terrorist attacks of September 11. After Genoa, the Italian local social forums were able to increase support for what started out as a movement for global justice (or a globalization of rights or a globalization from below). It was, in fact, in recognition of the strength of the Italian social forums that the coalition of European associations present at the annual World Social Forum (WSF) in Porto Alegre decided to hold the first ESF in Italy.

Notwithstanding the tensions before the meeting—with center-right politicians but also with many opinion leaders expressing a strong fear of violence in a city considered particularly delicate because of its artistic value (to the point of suggesting limitations to the right of demonstration in the "città d'arte")—the ESF in Florence was a success. Not only was there not a single act of violence, but participation went beyond the most optimistic expectations. Sixty thousand participants—more than three times the expected number—took part in the 30 plenary conferences, 160 seminars, and 180 workshops organized at the Fortezza da Basso; even more attended the 75 cultural events in various parts of the city. About one million took part in the march that closed the forum. The international nature of the event is indisputable. More than 20,000 delegates of 426 associations arrived from 105 countries—among others, twenty-four buses from Spain, a special train from France and another from Austria, and a special ship from Greece. Up to four hundred interpreters worked without charge in order to ensure simultaneous translations. A year later, as many as a thousand Florentines went to Paris for the second ESF.

The protests in Florence were seen as a consolidation of a social movement. The document approved by the assembly of the ESF stated, "We have come together to strengthen and enlarge our alliances because the construction of another Europe and another world is now urgent. We seek to create a world of equality, social rights and respect for diversity" (European Social Movements 2002). The press described the events as the expression of "A movement, with various souls and no recognized leader" (*La Stampa*, October 17, 2002): the no global, for critical observers; the new global, for more sympathetic ones. After the ESF, opinion polls signaled growing support for the movement's demands and the expectation that the movement would produce a split in the main center-left party, the DS (*Corriere della Sera*, November 11, 2002). Fausto Bertinotti, general secretary of the neo-communist party Rifondazione Comunista (RC), stated that "the movement of movements" "erupted in the Left," "putting in circulation an enormous quantity of politics" (*Avvenire*, November 7, 2002).

Seattle, Before and After

The three episodes we have presented are important for the history of a movement variously defined as a global justice movement, a movement for a globalization from below, or a movement for a globalization of rights. Seattle has been called a turning point and the high point of an aggregation process involving groups and social movement organizations (SMOs) active in countries all over the world: blue-collar workers and farmworkers, consumers and environmentalists, churches and feminists, pacifists and human rights associations. In fact, even before Seattle, heterogeneous and initially loosely connected groups had mobilized together, mainly against international organizations.

Environmentalists targeted the WTO because it had censured countries for breaching free trade agreements: the United States, for prohibiting the importation of prawns caught in nets without a turtle excluder device (which allows sea turtles to escape); Japan, for excluding products treated with pesticides; the European Union, for its laws against importing meat from animals fed with hormones; and Canada, for banning petrol containing a methanol additive. In 1990, Indian farmers had demonstrated against the WTO-favored patenting of seeds and organisms. Consumer protection organizations had mobilized against supranational agreements such as the North America Free Trade Agreement (NAFTA), the General Agreement on Tariffs and Trade (GATT), and the WTO for allegedly lowering consumer protection standards in the name of free trade. At the UN conferences on women's rights, feminist groups from the north of the world had met their counterparts from the south. Development NGOs pressed for a rise in aid to third world countries and even called for reparation for the historical, social, and environmental debts the north of the world imposed on the south. Supported especially, but not only, by religious groupings, the Jubilee 2000 campaign called for poor countries' foreign debts to be canceled. Pacifist and human rights organizations added their voices to these demands calling for freedom of movement for migrants or denouncing land mines.

One common theme of these campaigns was criticism of the developments that market economics had undergone since the eighties when neoliberal economic doctrines had become hegemonic. In particular, these critics accused governments of strengthening market freedom at the expense of social rights that, in the north of the world at least, had become part of the very definition of citizenship rights. In addition, while many economists were still pointing to the advantages for the south of the world in abolishing protectionist barriers, counterexperts mobilized in the protest focused on the overall negative effects of these measures in developing countries. Protests were thus targeted against what Susan Strange, an expert in international relations, called a "corporation empire," an imperial bureaucracy headed by the U.S. Treasury and transnational corporations that, together, controlled the leadership of the international financial organizations: "Authority in this nonterritorial empire is exercised directly on people—not on land. It is exercised on bankers and corporate executives, on savers and investors, on journalists and teachers. It is also of course exercised on the heads of allied and associated governments, as successive summit conferences have clearly shown" (Strange 1989, 170).

Furthermore, a factor common to all the campaigns is seeing market deregulation not as a natural effect of technological development but as a strategy adopted and defended by international financial institutions (World Bank [WB], International Monetary Fund [IMF], and WTO) and by the governments of the most powerful nations (in particular through the G7 and the G8) to the advantage of transnational corporations.

This is one of the reasons why movement organizations have often spurned the term "no global," preferring instead terms like "movement for global justice," "new global," "altermondialiste," or "Globalisierungskritiker." They maintain that they do not oppose globalization either as the intensification of cultural exchanges or the development of supranational governmental structures. They do, however, challenge the specifically neoliberal policies followed by international institutions and by national governments and call, instead, for a *different* form of globalization. After Seattle, especially, criticism of neoliberal forms of globalization and demands for "another globalization" entered the public sphere. The American magazine *Newsweek* (December 13, 1999, 36) wrote, "one of the most important lessons of Seattle is that there are now two visions of globalization on offer, one led by commerce, one by social activism."

After Seattle, ever more frequent mention was made of a *global* movement. Although the majority of demonstrators at Seattle were North American (some estimated twenty to twenty-five thousand from Washington State, fifteen to twenty thousand from elsewhere in the United States, and an additional three to five thousand from Canada), the international nature of demonstrations is confirmed by the parallel initiatives organized in more than a hundred cities in the world's north and south for Global Action Day. In addition, after the WTO clashes, protest on the issue of globalization continued in dozens of countries and went on to gain increased visibility. From Seattle onward, every international summit of any importance was accompanied by countersummits and protest demonstrations that often got wider press coverage than the official agenda did: for example, at the World Economic Forum (WEF) in Davos in January 2000, at the IMF and WB meetings in Washington, DC, in April, at the UN summit on poverty in Geneva in June, at the IMF and WB meetings in Prague in September, and at the EU summit in Nice in December. Nor did the demonstrations diminish the following year, with protests in February 2001, again in Davos, at the WEF; in April in Quebec City against the Free Trade Area of the Americas; in June in Gothenburg at the EU summit; and in July at the Genoa G8 summit. The number of countersummits and transnational protests continued to rise in 2002 and 2003 (Pianta and Silva 2003), while the threat of an armed conflict in Iraq led to an additional wave of demonstrations, culminating in a global day of protest against war on February 15, 2003.

After Seattle it was said that protests, if nothing else, had had the immediate success of bringing international summits out from the shadowy world of reserved agreements between diplomats and technocrats and into the media spotlight: "Never before had the beginning of multilateral trade negotiations been at the center of the international public sphere" (Pfeil 2000, 16).

The movement organized not only transnational protests and countersummits, but also its own global events. Another possible globalization was discussed at the WSFs in Porto Alegre (Schönleitner 2003), growing from the 16,400 participants of the first meeting in January 2001 to 52,000 in 2002 and 100,000 in 2003. In thousands of seminars and meetings, proposals of a more or less realistic and original consistency were hammered out for a globalization from below; alternative politics and policies were debated, and some of them already tested (including the participatory budgets that, among others in Porto Alegre, involve citizens in public decision making). From 2002 onward, especially, the experience of the social forums as a place to meet and engage in debate has been extended to local and macro-regional levels. In particular, in the autumn of that same year, Florence hosted the first ESF with three days of seminars attended by 60,000 participants. Debates on alternative development models—building sustainable societies—were held in Bamako, Mali, at the African Social Forum, in Beirut at the Middle East Social Forum, in Belém, Brazil, at the pan-Amazon version, and in Hyderabad, India, at the Asian Social Forum. In November 2003, a second ESF was held in Paris, in January 2004 a fourth WSF was held in Mumbai, India, and in October 2004 a third ESF took place in London.

Unexpected Protest

The emergence of a global protest movement was not expected either by scholars or commentators. Initially, many analyses on globalization tended to pessimistically forecast the demise of the movements. The limits that globalization phenomena had set on the development of collective action were emphasized the most.

Concentrated in the north of the world and focusing on the processes of institutionalization (or normalization) of the movements, social sciences were late in seeing the emergence of a global protest movement. The "end of history" was even identified with the "end of reason," "giving up on our capacity to understand and make sense, even of nonsense. The implicit assumption is the acceptance of full individualization of behaviour, and of society's powerlessness over its destiny" (Castells 1996, 4). Globalization itself was blamed for hindering the formation of collective subjects able to alter the course of history toward its termination so that "social movements tend to be fragmented, localistic, single-issue oriented, and ephemeral, either retrenched in their inner worlds, or flaring up for just an instant around a media symbol" (3).

This forecast resonated, in particular, with the more technological interpretations of globalization, considered as a product of the mobility of capital that the use of Internet and other new technologies facilitated. While the process of global interdependence has its roots in the distant past (Wallerstein 1979, 1990), the technological revolution of the eighties contributed to intensifying "both the reality of global interdependence, and also the awareness of the world as one single unit" (Robertson 1992, 8). As Manuel Castells notes, "a technological revolution, centered around information technologies, is reshaping, at accelerated pace, the material basis of society. Economies throughout the world have become globally interdependent, introducing a new form of relationship between economy, state, and society, in a system of variable geometry" (1996, 1).

In the *economic* system, growing interdependence has meant production being transferred to countries with lower wages (economic theory talks about the "delocalization of production processes"), a strengthening of transnational corporations, and especially the internationalization of financial markets to the extent that some speak of an "economy without borders." Economic global interdependence has been a factor in pushing large numbers of people from the south and east of the world to its north and west, and also in transforming the international division of labor by deindustrializing the north (where the economy is increasingly service-oriented) and industrializing some areas in the south (in particular in Latin America and Central Asia and now, also, in East Europe) where the economy used to be based on the export of raw materials. In this sense, economic globalization has questioned not only the role of the nation-state, ever less capable of governing within its own borders, but also, in more general terms, the capacity of politics to intervene in the economy and regulate social conflict. As Ulrich Beck (1999, 83) and Ralf Dahrendorf (1995), among others, have noted, global capitalism has breached the long-consolidated historical alliance among capitalism, the welfare state, and democracy. To prevent hemorrhages of capital, even left-wing governments have espoused the liberal concepts of making the workforce more flexible and cutting social spending.

Economic globalization has also raised specific problems that actors both old and new have mobilized around. In the north, it has brought unemployment, a decrease in job security, and an increase in unprotected working conditions, with frequent trade union mobilization in both industry and agriculture. Also in the south of the world, the negative social effects of the neoliberal policies imposed by the major international economic organizations, forcing developing countries to make substantial cuts in social spending, have triggered fierce protests. Already weak political regimes have allowed private exploitation of natural resources as well as development projects with major environmental impact. Native populations have mobilized against the destruction of their physical habitat (Passy 1999). A main claim of the movement, which is now finding new support from unexpected quarters, is the perniciousness of neoliberal policies for economic development.

The globalization that the movement criticizes is, first and foremost, the neoliberal variety. However, the widely accepted maxim of the nineties that capital mobility favored by technology eroded the political capability to govern markets has been questioned, not least thanks to the efforts of organizations that developed all over the world in protest against neoliberal *politics*. There is widespread feeling within the movement, which is the source of the belief that "an other world is possible," that lower state interventionism in market policies, lower taxation, and the consequent dismantling of the welfare state are not inevitable. Liberalization of trade and, in particular, of the financial markets was pushed both by political actors within single states (and in particular within the most powerful one, the United States) as well as by international actors, first and foremost international financial institutions, the WB, the IMF, and the WTO, which are main targets of the protest.

Globalization, therefore, is not only a matter of new technologies and modes of production but also of the *political* tools set in place to regulate and reproduce this social structure through, among other means, the proliferation of international governmental organizations (IGOs) and NGOs (Beck 1999; Boli and Thomas 1999). From this perspective, the international system based on the nation-state seems to be mutating into a political system composed of overlapping multilevel authorities with low functional differentiation and scanty democratic legitimacy. In the political system, globalization has brought a transnationalization of political relationships. While the national political context still filters the impact on national politics of international shifts, growing economic interdependence goes hand in hand with "a significant internationalization of public authority associated with a corresponding globalization of political activity" (Held and McGrew 2000, 27). In fact, recent research in international relations has highlighted a pluralization of relevant actors (Nicholson 1998, 131 ff.). Since the Second World War, and especially in recent years, there has been an increase in the number of IGOs with a worldwide scope of action (for example, the United Nations) or with a regional scope of action (for example, the EU, the Mercosur in Latin America, and NAFTA in North America), with military objectives (for example, the North Atlantic Treaty Organization [NATO] or the now-defunct Warsaw Pact), or with the declared aim of fostering economic development (for example, the IMF, the WB, or the WTO). This enhancement at the international level can be seen in the number of international organizations, which rose from 37 to 309 between 1909 and 1988 (Princen and Finger 1994, 1). As can be seen in Figure 1, while the growth

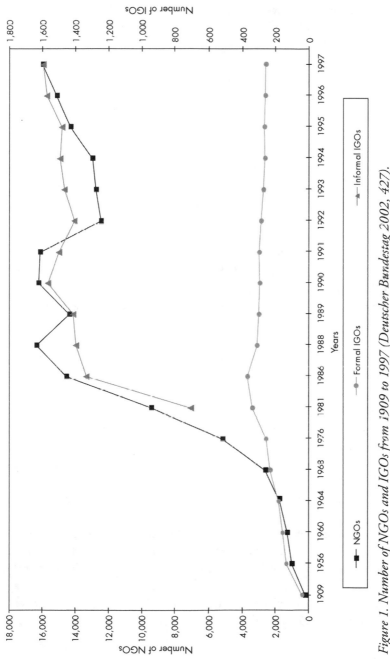

Figure 1. Number of NGOs and IGOs from 1909 to 1997 (Deutscher Bundestag 2002, 427).

of conventional intergovernmental organizations has leveled out in the last decade, there has been an increase in the number of other international organizations of a more informal character, from 702 in 1981 to 1,592 in 1997 (Deutscher Bundestag 2002, 427).

International organizations have contributed to the spread of international regulations and norms that in some cases supersede national sovereignty. As has often been pointed out, "no official authority controls states in the contemporary world system, but many are subject to powerful unofficial forces, pressures and influences that penetrate the supposed hard shell of the state" (Russett and Starr 1996, 62). Furthermore, while the majority of intergovernmental organizations function as meeting places and discussion forums where decisions are made unanimously and need to be ratified by national organs, there is a growing number of supranational organizations within which decisions binding for all member states are made, sometimes on a majority basis, not unanimously (ibid.).

IGOs have been both tools for economic globalization through policies liberalizing trade and the movement of capital, and expressions of an attempt to govern processes that can no longer be handled at a national level. In this sense, globalization has not just weakened the power of politics over economics, but has also generated transnational conflicts on the policies of the international institutions producing different results depending on the organization and field of intervention involved. In particular, opposition has arisen to the neoliberal policies of the so-called international financial institutions that wield strong coercive power through the threat of economic sanctions and conditionalities on international credit. More generally, parallel to the acquisition of power by these largely nonrepresentative, nontransparent bodies, criticism centered on their manifest "deficit of democracy."

Globalization has also produced significant *cultural* changes, the fundamental point being that there is growing interdependence in today's world: social actions in a given time and place are increasingly influenced by actions that occur in distant places. As Giddens suggested, globalization implies the creation and intensification of "worldwide social relationships which link distinct localities in such a way that local happenings are shaped by events occurring miles away and vice versa" (1990, 64). The shortening of space and time in communication processes affects the production and reproduction of goods, of culture, and of the tools for political regulation. Indeed, globalization has been defined as "a process (or set of processes) which embodies a transformation in the spatial organization of social relations and transactions—assessed in terms of their extension, intensity, velocity and impact—generating transcontinental or interregional flows and networks of activity" (Held et al. 1999, 16).

One of the dangers perceived in globalization is the predominance of a single way of thinking, which apparently emerged triumphant from the defeat of "real" socialism. The international system had been tied to a bipolar structure in which each of the two blocs represented a different ideology; the fall of the Berlin Wall, which symbolically marked the demise of the Eastern bloc, made capitalism seem the only, dominant model. The lack of a concurrent world power has certainly curtailed, at least in the short term, the need for the United States and its allies to mitigate the capitalist model through policies reducing inequalities, and has also limited the number of strategic options open to countries in the south of the world. In cultural terms, modernization processes promoted by science and the leisure industry have paved the way for what Serge Latouche has called "the westernization of the world" (1989), i.e., the spread on a global scale of Western values and beliefs (Strang and Meyer 1993, 500ff.). Although the scenario of a single McDonaldized world culture (Ritzer 1996) is an exaggeration, there is an undeniable increase in cultural interaction with the exportation—albeit filtered through local culture—of Western cultural products and values (Robertson 1992). The new channels of communication lead us to a global village in which we are targeted in real time by messages sent from the most faraway places. The spread of satellite TV and the Internet has made instantaneous communication possible, easily crossing national boundaries.

While territorial identities do not fade, the impact of values from other cultures and the growth of interaction between cultures increase the number of identifications that interweave into and compete with those anchored in the territory. Globalization is not only "out there" but also "in here" (Giddens 1990, 22): it transforms everyday life and leads to local resistance in order to defend cultural traditions against the intrusion of foreign ideas and global issues. The resurgence of forms of nationalism, ethnic movements, religious mobilizations, and Islamic (and other) fundamentalism are in part a reaction to this type of intrusion. At the same time, solidarity-based movements are mobilizing proactively on distant issues that are not immediately connected with their own national context. While cultural globalization risks causing a loss of national identity, new technologies provide a formidable array of tools for global mobilization, easing communication between worlds once distant via new media that defy traditional censorship. Increased perception of issues as global also heightens people's willingness to mobilize at a transnational level. Local traditions become delocalized and readapt to new contexts through the presence of transnational networks of ethnocultural communities (J. Thompson 1995). Besides, as can be seen in Figure 2, globalization is subjected to ever wider public debate in many countries.

Ten years after the fall of the Berlin Wall, the different actors engaged in the conflicts mentioned so far have become increasingly networked, spawning common mobilizations. A world-scale mobilization questions the "single way of thinking" of market sovereignty that had seemed without alternative, as testified for by the spreading of the conviction "that there is little we can change—singly, severally, or all together—in the way the affairs of the world are running or are being run" (Bauman 1999, 1). If globalization is the challenge, it also seems to be the resource of protesters who, as we have said, do not oppose it absolutely but aim at changing its content. Indeed, globalization has consistently transformed the conditions for collective action and, along with limits, has brought occasions and resources for protest. In economic, political, and cultural systems, the growth of interconnections has generated new conflicts as well as opportunities for expressing these conflicts at multiple territorial levels.

The various dimensions of globalization have fostered the emergence and development of a global civil society—a civil society that "increasingly represents itself globally, across nation-state boundaries, through the formation of global institutions" (Shaw 1994, 650).[1] The shift of decision making to a supranational level has, in turn, encouraged the birth of international nongovernmental organizations (INGOs) whose numbers, members, and material resources have grown.[2] The organization of a global civil society can be defined as "the social dimension of globalization" (Leonardi 2001), inevitably linked to globalization processes in economy, culture, and politics. The concept of transnational social movement organizations (TSMOs) was coined to define the INGOs active within networks of social movements (Smith, Pagnucco, and Romeril 1994; Sikkink 1993; Chatfield, Pagnucco, and Smith 1997). While social movements developed as national politics grew, the formation of TSMOs can be seen as a coherent response to the growing institutionalization of international politics (Smith 1995, 190). Over the last few decades, transnational protest campaigns have multiplied, in particular on issues such as environmental protection, gender discrimination, and human rights (della Porta and Kriesi 1999). Studies on INGOs highlighted that many of them had become increasingly institutionalized, both in terms of acquired professionalism and in the forms of action they employ (more lobbying than marching) (Kriesi 1993; Jordan

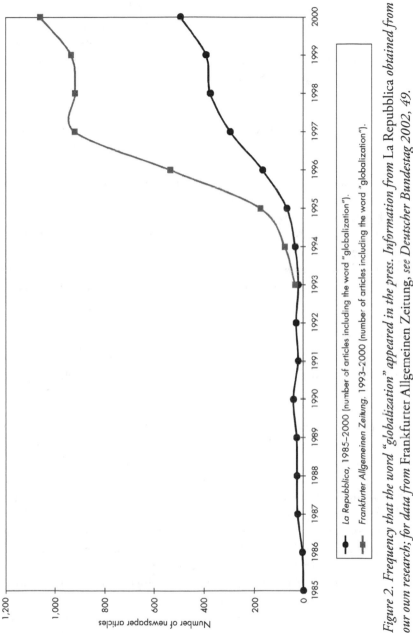

Figure 2. Frequency that the word "globalization" appeared in the press. Information from La Repubblica *obtained from our own research; for data from* Frankfurter Allgemeinen Zeitung, *see Deutscher Bundestag 2002, 49.*

- ● La Repubblica, 1985–2000 (number of articles including the word "globalization").
- ■ Frankfurter Allgemeinen Zeitung, 1993–2000 (number of articles including the word "globalization").

Number of newspaper articles

and Maloney 1997; Diani and Donati 1998; della Porta and Diani 2004). However, the global movement that emerged in Seattle managed to involve these organizations—via informal, flexible networks—in highly visible mass demonstrations. A global civil society provided the structure, the means, and the cognitive tools to mobilize recent global protest before and after Seattle (McAdam, McCarthy, and Zald 1996).

It has become increasingly clear since Seattle that the various phenomena grouped together somewhat haphazardly under the definition of "globalization" produce new conflicts as well as creating a complex framework of opportunities and constraints. As was confirmed in Prague, Porto Alegre, Gothenburg, and Genoa, the various actors engaged in the protests on global issues are more and more linked with each other in multiple, loosely structured networks. Activists and especially observers and scholars are asking, "Is this a confluence of movements, or is it just a collection of separate movements?" (Brecher, Costello, and Smith 2000, 15). If it is certain that we are dealing with new waves of mobilization in both the north and the south of the world, is it proper to use the term "global social movement"?

Global Social Movement: A Definition

To attempt to provide an answer, although not a definitive one, to this question (which also contemplates expectations of continuity or, vice versa, the ephemerality of the mobilizations), it is necessary to start from a definition of "global social movement." First of all, what are social movements? Conceptually, social movements are mainly informal networks based on common beliefs and solidarity that mobilize on conflictual issues by frequent recurrence to various forms of protest (della Porta and Diani 2006, ch. 1). Accordingly, *global* social movements are supranational networks of actors that define their causes as global and organize protest campaigns that involve more than one state. In Sidney Tarrow's definition (2001, 11), transnational social movements are "socially mobilized groups with constituents in at least two states, engaged in sustained contentious interactions with power-holders in at least one state other than their own, or against an international institution, or a multinational economic actor." In order to address the issue of the existence of a global social movement (as we propose to do in this volume) we have therefore to investigate all mentioned conditions: global identity, nonconventional action repertoires, organizational networks.

The fundamental characteristic of a social movement is its ability to develop a *common interpretation of reality* to nurture solidarity and collective identifications. The movements develop new visions of the world and systems of values alternative to the dominant ones. New conflicts emerge over the new values. In particular, since the seventies, "new" movements began to be seen as the actors of new conflicts, in contrast to the "old" workers' movement that was by then perceived as institutionalized. While Marxist analyses have traditionally upheld the centrality of the struggle between capital and labor, post–World War II changes have increased the importance of certain social stratification criteria—such as gender and generation—that were not based on class status. Contemporary societies are usually described as highly differentiated systems that invest increasing resources in order to make individuals into autonomous centers of action but that also need increased integration, extending control to the very motivations of human action (Melucci 1989). Within these societies, new social movements attempt to resist state and market intervention in daily life, claiming the right for individuals to decide on their own private and affective lives against all-pervasive manipulation by "the system." Gender difference, defense of the environment, and cohabitation among different cultures are some of the issues around which social movements have been formed in the last three decades. The establishment of a global movement requires the development of a discourse that identifies both a common identity (the us) and the target of the protest (the other) at a supranational level. As we shall see, however, observers' opinions differ: some see the beginnings of global identities, and others speak of an (almost opportunistic) adjustment by mainly national actors to a territorially multilevel government; some see mobilization on globalization as a leftover from the past, and others see it as the movement of the future. In general, the social, generational, and ideological heterogeneity that was already evident in Seattle is considered by some as proof of the strength of the mobilization, able to connect different identities, and by others as a sign of fragmentation and an indication of weakness.

Furthermore, social movements are by and large typically unusual in their forms of political participation. Many scholars see a fundamental difference between the movements and other political actors in the use the former make of *protest* as a means of pressure on institutions (e.g., Rucht 1994). By performing an unconventional form of action that breaks up daily routine, protesters address the public opinion before addressing elected representatives or public bureaucracy. Protest actions were concentrated at a national level, but globalization may be expected to generate protest at a transnational level against international actors. However, results of empirical research are unclear. First, the protests that get national press coverage still target the state or substate level of government (Imig and Tarrow 2001; Rucht 2002a); this has been confirmed for varying types of movements from environmental (Rootes 2002) to antiracist ones (Giugni and Passy 2002). It has often been emphasized that organizations active at a transnational level also adopt conventional types of action, oriented more toward discreet lobbying than street protests. On that basis, mobilizations such as those in Seattle or Genoa could be considered episodic events, with collective action still dominated by increasingly institutionalized NGOs and "normalized" action repertoires. In our research we will ask, on the contrary, whether the mobilizations of the movement for a globalization "from below" constitute a new trend with a spread of transnational protests and more disruptive action repertoires contaminating more traditional organizations.

Last, social movements are *informal networks* linking a plurality of individuals and groups, more or less structured from an organizational point of view. While parties or pressure groups have somewhat well-defined organizational boundaries, enrollment in a specific organization normally being ratified by a membership card, social movements are instead composed of loose, weakly linked networks of groups and individuals who feel part of a collective effort. Although there are organizations that refer back to movements, movements are not organizations but rather networks of relationships linking various actors, which encompass organizations (also but not only) with a formal structure. One distinctive characteristic of social movements is the possibility of belonging to them and feeling involved in collective action without necessarily having to be a member of a specific organization. It follows, therefore, that a global movement should involve organizational networks active in different countries. In fact, social scientists have increasingly adopted the term "transnational" to emphasize the presence of supranational actors other than the national governments that are traditionally considered the only relevant subjects in international relations. Globalization has enhanced the power of some of these actors (such as transnational enterprises), but it has also fostered the emergence of a "global civil society." Recent surveys point to an increase in the number of transnational organizations linked to social movements, from 110 in 1963 to 631 in 1993 (Smith 1995), a trend that is particularly vigorous in the south of the world (Smith 2001). The greater influence wielded by these organizations is beyond doubt, but opinions vary on the extent to which they are able to network more than just sporadically. For example, a study on protest in Europe spotlighted "consistent evidence for temporal contagion effects with respect to European contentious collective action" (Reising 1999, 333), assessing that "the presence of these patterns of increasing interaction among citizens in different countries of the EC/EU also supports the notion of the emergence of cross-national networks of social actors in the realm of protest" (338). Others have questioned the stability of these networks (e.g., Fox and Brown 1998; on immigration, Guiraudon 2002). A highly flexible organizational structure, with demonstrations organized via Internet by ad hoc coordination committees, is seen by some as the best solution for adapting to global society, while others perceive it as the sign of an inability to build a durable organization.

Globalization and Protest: Our Model of Analysis

While social movements became national actors with the formation of the nation-state, the institution of macroregional or global politics has produced transnational collective actors (della Porta and Kriesi 1999, 17–18). In fact, "globalization has provided social movements with new, possibly significant opportunities and resources for influencing both state and nonstate actors" (Guidry, Kennedy, and Zald 2000, 1). The forms and aims that the new global mobilization have taken on, however, still have to be analyzed: To what extent have the various fragments of protest managed to acquire a reticular organizational structure? What are the communication channels along which nodes become part of a network and interact with the outside? How can we define the aims of actors who have often rejected the negative "no global" tag, affirming that they are not fighting globalization as a whole but struggling to change its direction? Finally, what repertoires of action are deployed in the struggle for a globalization from below?

In Figure 3, the organizational model, means of communication, frames of identification, and repertoires of action are explained on the basis of combinations of variables traditionally used in research on social movements. We shall concentrate especially on the transformation of the political opportunity structure (POS) at the international level (international POS), i.e., the channels of access available to social movements at a formal institutional level and through the building of alliances (Tarrow 1994). Another dimension that emerged during demonstrations at international summits and was particularly significant for a movement that asks for bottom-up globalization is protest policing (della Porta and Reiter 1998b). The characteristics of the external environment are filtered through the resources available for the mobilization—first and foremost within the family of social movements that constitutes a basic point of reference for the protest.

As we shall see, organization, communication, frames, and repertoires

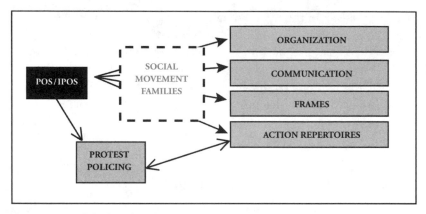

Figure 3. Model of analysis.

mainly come from earlier protest cycles but are adapted, at least in part, to the new global challenges. The cycle of protest that made its first high-profile appearance in Seattle certainly shows continuity—often visible in the histories of the activists and their organizations—with the movements of the past on labor, peace, human rights, women's liberation, and environmental protection. However, it introduces a number of new elements that transform the image of social movements that emerged in the nineties. Especially after the decline of the broad wave of peace protests of the early eighties, scholars of social movements noted a tendency toward institutionalization of the movements' organizational structures with the creation of formalized (and often rich) associations, their specialization on single issues with a certain degree of pragmatism, and a declining emphasis on protests as well as a preference for less visible lobbying strategies or voluntary action. This tendency of the movements to become more "civilized" had been explained by institutional politics adopting more inclusive strategies, even co-optation, together with a negotiated protest policing (della Porta and Reiter 1998b). In Seattle, an at least temporary interruption of this apparent trend became evident with the emergence of a highly reticular model of interaction that included more structured associations as well as smaller affinity groups; the identities shifted from single-issue to global concerns, linking, within the criticism of neoliberal globalization, the issues of exploitation of women and protection of the environment, the defense of peace and social justice. Finally, activists have gone back to occupying the streets, often clashing with the police who follow strategies based on widespread use of physical force, while the center-left seemed united with the center-right politicians in denouncing the unrealistic ambitions of the protesters and their presumed antipolitics.

The Research and the Book

We shall explore these themes and present the results of a research project that focused mainly on two events of transnational protest that happened in Italy: the G8 protests in Genoa in July 2001 and the ESF in Florence in November 2002. We shall locate these two events within the dozens of similar, transnational protests that developed especially after Seattle through secondary references to a growing body of research (in English, but also in French, German, and Italian).

The analysis will address three dimensions of the movement: a *micro*-dimension referring to the characteristics of the activists, a *meso*dimension involving the organizational networks and their activities, and a *macro*-dimension concerned with the interaction between the movement and its environment. Concepts and hypotheses are taken from the rich literature on social movements that has developed in sociology and political sciences, in particular from the seventies onward, with particular reference to the construction of collective identities, the mobilization of resources, and the structure of political opportunities (della Porta and Diani 1999, 2006).

The tools of empirical measurement we used are many and varied. The first, rarely adopted in research on movements (but see Van Aelst and Walgrave 2001), is the survey. During the days of the G8 in Genoa we distributed some 800 questionnaires to Italian demonstrators at various initiatives (such as "theme-based squares," debates, campsites), so as to be able to construct a representative sample of the various sectors of the movement. We did likewise in Florence where we gathered some 2,400 questionnaires, which in this case had been translated into English, French, Spanish, and German and distributed to Italian and non-Italian activists (in Genoa we interviewed only Italian activists).[3] Both surveys, through mainly semiclosed questions, touched on associative experiences, forms of political participation, confidence in the institutions, and identification with the movement.[4]

In both cities, we were able to monitor the representativeness of our sampled interviewees. In Genoa, we confronted the composition of our sample by organizational areas with the estimates of number of participants from the different networks provided by the organizers on the eve of the protests. Since the figures were used for logistical purposes (such as finding lodging for the incoming activists), they are quite reliable. In Florence, we compared the distribution of our sample according to nationality with that of those enrolled at the forum. In both cases, our sample was well balanced and maintained an equilibrium between male and female. From the ESF full sample we excluded the Tuscans (863 participants) because they had a different profile from other participants in terms of sociodemographic dimensions (gender, age, education, social condition): geographically close to the event, Tuscans needed a lower commitment than Italians from other regions in order to participate in the ESF. We will refer to this sample to test hypotheses without referring to the countries of origin. However, for cross-national comparisons, we weighted the responses in order to compensate for having oversampled the Italian population, randomly extracting a reduced sample of the Italian activists.[5]

In our analysis we have used standard correlation indexes (Pearson). In the case of nominal data (cross tabulations), Cramer's V is used, which is a standardization of the more commonly known phi coefficient in order to get values between −1 and 1 and to make results comparable to each other. Respecting the ordinal character of most of the variables, we have also used Mann-Whitney U tests (for dummy independent variables). As for the significance test, following the usual convention in statistics, we labeled values having a significance level less than 5 percent with an asterisk, values having a significance level less than 1 percent with two asterisks, and values having a significance level less than 0.1 percent with three asterisks.

The analysis of the questionnaires was supplemented by both participatory observation during the days of the protests and six focus groups held with Florentine activists divided into age categories.[6] In the course of this type of group interview we especially tackled issues concerning the concept the activists have of politics and how they see the aims and strategies of the movement.

In order to reconstruct the development and strategies of the protest organizations, we conducted a systematic content analysis of the Web sites of the various networks that promoted the two events and collected material on the main organizations of the protests against globalization active in Italy and abroad. From the Internet, we obtained and analyzed the documents pertinent to the main international protest events. Research into the response strategies adopted by the institutions is based on the parliamentary investigation into the events that occurred at the G8 in Italy, as well as on material from independent inquiries into police conduct during clashes in the periods of international summits (in particular Seattle and Gothenburg). Material was downloaded from the Web sites of police trade unions (in Italy and Germany), and published interviews with police officers conducted after Genoa were also consulted. With regard to the policing of the ESF in Florence, we conducted interviews with movement organizers and state officials. In addition, we examined the material on globalization and the movements present on the Web sites of European left-wing parties (besides Italy, in France, Germany, Great Britain, and Spain).

Material on the reaction to the movement by parties and other actors was obtained from a review of the Italian daily *La Repubblica* for the period stretching from the demonstration in Seattle to that of Florence, and from six other national dailies (*La Stampa, Il Corriere della Sera, L'Unità, Il Giornale, Il Manifesto,* and *Liberazione*) as well as some foreign newspapers for the days of the demonstration in Genoa and the week immediately following it. Again, with regard to the demonstrations in Genoa and Florence, we analyzed the press documentation available online on the Web site of the Chamber of Deputies. We also carried out a systematic analysis of the coverage of international protest events by the French daily *Libération,* the German daily *Die Tageszeitung,* and the Italian daily *Il Manifesto* in order to get an idea of how the movement was presented in the sphere of public mass media most significant for the base of reference of the protests. This material will be used throughout the book, seeking to reconstruct the events of Genoa and Florence from national and international perspectives.

The second chapter is dedicated to the organizational level: How is the movement structured? How does it act? Here we shall present the main networks that organized the protest events and the most important organizations within them, focusing attention on their organizational structure and democratic practices.

In the third chapter we shall seek to outline the identity of what has been incorrectly called a "no-global" movement. Who are the activists of this movement? What are their aims, their ideas, and their demands? To understand what holds such a heterogeneous movement together, we shall use sociographic information on the Italian activists in Genoa and Florence as well as on the various organizational sectors that converged in the movement. Looking at the activists' frames, we shall describe the development of a complex, multiple, and fluid collective identity.

In the fourth chapter we shall see how the movement communicates internally and externally, paying particular attention to the use of the Internet. Within the analysis of the forms of communication used by the networks and their activists, the role of the new media in the processes of mobilization, organization, and information will be emphasized, together with how alternative ideas and proposals are developed.

Chapter 5 focuses on the strategies of the movement. Starting from previous experiences of political participation gained by activists, we shall look at continuity and innovation in the protest repertoires. Countersummits and transnational campaigns will be presented as the main forms peculiar to the new mobilization. We shall also examine how activists perceive violence and underline the pronouncedly nonviolent nature of the movement.

Chapter 6 will analyze the interactions between activists and police. What models of crowd control are developed by the forces of law and order for international summits? Here we shall look at the policing of protest, a specific form of interaction that emerged as particularly significant in the sixties and seventies and that then apparently became normalized (della Porta and Reiter 1998b).

The seventh chapter is dedicated to one of the classic issues of social movement studies, the interaction between the challengers and the establishment, especially the government and the parliamentary opposition. We shall highlight the growing role of international actors and the interaction between the movement and the public sphere, which takes on a supranational dimension. Looking at globalization especially in terms of a growing interdependency, we shall single out the challenges for multilevel governance and for protest mobilization that it brings about.

The conclusions in chapter 8 will emphasize the new features of the movement for a globalization from below and discuss to what extent concepts and hypotheses of the social movement literature remain valid heuristic instruments for the analysis of contemporary transnational protest.

2

The Development of a Global Movement: Network Strategies, Democracy, Participation

Social Movements and Organization: An Introduction

Studies on social movements have stressed the role of organizations in mobilizing protest. The likelihood that an individual will commit to collective action for the common good is lessened by the tendency of an individual to avoid the costs of actions whose benefits would extend to all (Olson 1963). Only an organization capable of distributing selective incentives—information, knowledge, symbols, material resources, social spaces—can increase collective commitment to political mobilization.

Beginning with Olson's insights, scholars of social movements have developed a specific approach focusing on analysis of organization, organizational resources, and interorganizational relations (McCarthy and Zald 1973, 1977). While organizations are not the sole factor capable of explaining collective action, they undoubtedly remain an important information and mobilization channel in the movement for globalization from below. Organizations offer useful resources for coordinating protest activity, handling transport of demonstrators, developing routes of marches in cooperation with each other, setting up street protests, running workshops, and so on. Additionally, by producing documents and press releases, they grab media attention and seek to enlarge the potential for mobilization. The networking capacities of organizations are particularly advantageous for protests involving different movement sectors because they allow bloc recruitment of already mobilized groups (Obershall 1973, 117; Jenkins 1983, 62). Analyses of the organizational structure of social movements have often emphasized their network nature: "composite," "flexible," and "acephalous" have been the adjectives most often employed.

Since the sixties, then, studies on social movements have identified three specific features of the organizational structure of social movements: it is *segmented,* with groups arising, mobilizing, and declining continually; it is *multicentric,* for the presence of multiple nodes linked horizontally and the absence of a single dominant leadership; and it is *networked,* with groups and individuals connected through multiple ties (Gerlach 1976, 2001). By comparison with past movements, however, the "movement of movements" is marked by still more pronounced network features (emphasized by definitions like "network of networks"), which allow a galaxy of heterogeneous groups that maintain differentiated organizational structures to connect through weak ties. The very copresence of differing organizational models renders more rigid and structured forms of coordination obsolete.

Social movement organizations (SMOs) can be conceived of as units interacting within a social movement. The chief characteristic of the movement against neoliberalism has been its capacity to create opportunities for contacts among groups, associations, networks, organizations, and individuals with very different histories, forms of action, and social and cultural backgrounds. In this sense not only does the movement present itself as a network of networks, but within it very different organizations interact: from trade unions and parties, with their bureaucratic, hierarchical structure, to NGOs becoming increasingly professionalized, down to grassroots groups, social centers, and the local associations typified by a weak structure, horizontality of relations between individuals, and volunteer activism. Cooperation among differently organized bodies has been fundamental for the success of the movement.

The network structure also typifies the various sectors joined to the movement, where cooperation among different organizations is equally fundamental. We thus see first and foremost an integration of networks by political, ideological, or simply thematic affinity. As we shall see, the movement's various sectors have clustered particularly around religious and secular associations active on issues of peace, the environment, and women's liberation; around the organizations of the more traditional left, more sensitive to issues of labor and of political control over the economy; and around the social centers[1] and organizations mobilizing mainly in defense of the most marginalized groups, also within the advanced-economy countries (the "losers" of globalization).

In addition, the networks link together through coordinating structures made up of their spokespersons and/or delegates. The GSF acted as a coordinating structure for the various networks preparing the protest against the G8. The ESF organizing committee held meetings in all European countries in order to involve the various national movements in organizing the forum in Florence. In Italy, the ESF committee acted as a continuity group to coordinate initiatives at the national level, and other intergroup structures were set up to prepare specific campaigns, like the Stop the War Committee in the recent mobilization for peace. Though chiefly determined by decision of the various organizations, cooperation in networks and among networks is also the outcome of interorganizational interactions sparked off by various mechanisms.[2]

Within the networks, the organizations influence each other, seeking to affect the positions of related, allied, and third groups. One mechanism that can change organizational strategies and identities is competition. Organizations that feel they represent the same interests of a social base (such as the trade unions, for instance), or are dealing with the same issue (e.g., the environment, peace, and so on), interact, and often compete, with each other. Competition can emerge between different groups belonging to the same organization, especially within an umbrella structure. This can happen even in recently formed organizations.

Organizations are also conditioned by their contact with the social reference base. Particularly during periods of high mobilization, the most structured organizations lose control of the protest. In some cases the base manages to "reappropriate" the organizations as instruments for mobilization. This mechanism has recently been highlighted by Doug McAdam, Sidney Tarrow, and Charles Tilly, who talk of "social appropriation of existing organizations," stressing that "challengers, rather than creating new organizations, appropriated existing ones and turned them into vehicles of mobilization" (2001, 44).[3]

However, if the challengers manage to find the necessary resources and have the opportunity, sometimes organizations are created *ex novo*. This was the case for many groups of the extraparliamentary left in 1968 in Italy, a number of civil rights organizations in the United States, many associations, in some cases parties during ecologist mobilizations throughout Europe, and so on. The antineoliberalism mobilization, too, has seen the emergence of new organizations and new, sometimes transnational, networks of movements.

In periods of intense mobilization, competition, social appropriation, and network cooperation may reinforce each other. Through competition, the most radical groups attract the attention of a constituency they share with more structured ones. When the phenomenon becomes so visible as to threaten their representative capacity, the structured organizations start to alter their strategies and redefine their interpretation of reality in order to regain their relation with their reference base. Additionally, rank-and-file members of more institutionalized organizations pressure their leaders to join the protest. Competition thus impels the social appropriation of the organizational structures, which become vehicles of mobilization. Once the more structured organizations redefine their strategies and their identities and decide to mobilize, they find themselves cooperating with less structured groupings in specific protest campaigns or social movements. Cooperation does not resolve the competitive tensions among the organizations, but enables spaces to be created for dialogue between different actors who together redefine objectives and identities.

In the past, social movements had already tried out autonomously run spaces for political communication in small cohesive groups (consider the feminist consciousness-raising collectives or the pacifist affinity groups in the 1970s, or today the social centers), which coordinated with other groups for specific campaigns or on more general themes (della Porta 1996). In the movement for globalization from below, the importance of public spaces is indicated by the creation of social forums at local, national, continental, and world levels, acting as multipurpose places for different social and political identities to come together. As we shall see, the success of the movement is also due to the mobilization of individuals who do not belong to any of the organizations that formally join it, who are attracted by its very heterogeneity and the practices of negotiation and cooperation among open and tolerant identities (della Porta 2004).

Another aspect of the organizational dynamics to be considered is the way decisions are made. The movement against neoliberal globalization criticizes IGOs for a lack of democracy (see chapter 7 in this volume), yet internal democratic practices are the object of continual discussion. One of the movement's challenges is the search for innovative decision-making models aimed at overcoming the limits of decision in public assemblies or through delegation. These models combine limited and controlled recourse to delegation with consensus-based instruments appealing to dialogue, to the transparency of the communicative process, and to reaching the greatest possible consensus. In this chapter we shall see how these principles are applied at the various levels of the movement network and in the various sectors belonging to it.

In the next section, we shall describe the networks making up the movement, highlighting their way of interpreting the mobilization against neoliberalism and their interorganizational processes, and show how the network structure is the product of mechanisms of cooperation, competition, and social appropriation of the organizations. Then we will focus on the activists and look at which networks have mobilized, comparing the Italian, French, Spanish, German, and British networks. We shall see how the activists and participants themselves, with their experience of multiple organizational affiliations, have created informal networks that allow for circulation of information. We shall attempt to tackle the delicate problem of the internal democracy of the networks by looking at their organizational structure and decision making, highlighting both formal aspects (constitutions or declarations of principle), and substantive ones (internal debates). Finally, we will summarize the most important findings and sketch out a few conclusions on the relationship between networks, participation, and democracy in the movement against neoliberalism.

The Networks in the Network

The network is an organizational structure that facilitates the emergence of transnational movements. In the case of the movement for global justice, the network structure typifies the various sectors forming part of it, albeit with sometimes considerable diversity in organizational strategies. This is immediately apparent if one considers the Italian organized components that joined the mobilization against the G8 in Genoa in 2001. Heterogeneous organizations of the movement aggregated into thematic sectors, notably the ecopacifist sector (Rete Lilliput, Catholic and secular solidarity and voluntary associations); the antineoliberalist sector (ATTAC and organizations of the more traditional left); and the anticapitalist sector (White Overalls social centers and the Network for Global Rights). As can be seen from Figure 4, however, the GSF, the umbrella organization coordinating and preparing the protest, did not represent the whole spectrum of groups challenging the G8. Some more radical groups chose to remain autonomous, sharply criticizing the GSF's attempt to present itself to public opinion as the representative body of the movement and to lay down which forms of action are acceptable and which are not (see chapter 5 in this volume). Outside the GSF, transnational networks of anarchist (among them the Black Bloc) and anti-imperialist inspiration criticized the WSF charter of principles, regarded as too moderate and reformist in its positions. They gave rise to transnational networks that locate themselves outside the social forum movement but have as their main objective a radical critique of globalization. As we shall see, competitive and cooperative dynamics within the networks and among them impel a continual reconfiguration of the movement, formalizing new networks and breaking up others. We shall endeavor to show that this organizational flexibility represents the strong point of a movement based on differing identities, which are valued rather than being suffocated.

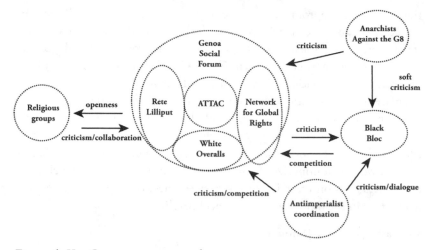

Figure 4. Key Genoa protest networks.

While our analysis starts from the Italian GSF networks, we shall seek to broaden the focus to the networks compounded at the transnational level that went on to take part in the first ESF in Florence. At the same time, we aim to bring out the differences in sectorial frames that will find a synthesis in the construction of the master frame of the movement (see chapter 3 in this volume).

ATTAC and the Antineoliberalist Left: Controlling the Market through Politics

One of the organizations created *ex novo* for the antineoliberal mobilization, and undoubtedly the most influential at the transnational level, is ATTAC. This association was set up in France in 1998 with the aim of exercising democratic control over the supranational institutions that guide the process of economic globalization. It was particularly important because it blazed the trail for other organizations committed to the fight against globalization. The principles and objectives on which the association was set up are indicated in a well-known editorial by the editor of *Le Monde Diplomatique,* Ignacio Ramonet, titled "Disarm the Markets." Ramonet proposed the creation of a "nongovernmental organization of Action for a Tobin Tax to Aid Citizens (ATTAC)" with the aim of altering the dynamics of the prevailing economic system through a number of technical measures like the Tobin tax (*Le Monde Diplomatique,* December 1997), a tax on financial transactions proposed by economics Nobel prizewinner James Tobin in 1972. The Tobin tax subsequently became one of the better-known movement claims, recently entering national and supranational parliamentary arenas. Today ATTAC is present in many European countries, North Africa, Latin America, and Canada. Present in Genoa and then in Florence, ATTAC–Italy began forming in 2001 (concluding the process in early 2002 with the first national assembly) as a national network incorporated in a wider international network covering several states. It is supported by the left-wing daily *Il Manifesto* and includes various associations—among them is the Lega Italiana per la Lotta contro l'AIDS (Italian League for the Fight against AIDS, http://www.lila.it, of which Vittorio Agnoletto, GSF spokesperson, has been national president). Also close to ATTAC is ARCI (Associazione Ricreativa e Culturale Italiana), the historic recreational and cultural association born from the Italian Communist Party (PCI) in 1957 and refounded in 1994 as an autonomous new association (http://www .arci.it).

In Italy, as in other European countries, associations traditionally close to the left tended to congregate around ATTAC: social democratic and communist or postcommunist (like Rifondazione Comunista in Italy) parties (see also chapter 7 in this volume) and also trade unions, which feel particularly close to the idea of political control of the market. In the last decade there has been a resumption and transformation of trade union action, connected with the consequences of globalization for the labor market. After the end of the Fordist-Keynesian compromise lasting half a century between trade unions, employers, and governments (Crouch 1999), in Europe the large workers' organizations had accepted as inevitable neoliberal policies (privatizations and deregulations of the labor market) implemented even by progressive governments. This, along with the growth of social dialogue practices, had reduced conflicts among trade unions.

But in the second half of the 1990s an opposition began to emerge, both inside and outside the more institutionalized trade unions (see O'Connor 2000; Shoch 2000). The protest against policies for privatizing public services like transport, schools, and health arose in most European countries (Moody 1997). In these sectors, in countries with pluralist industrial-relations patterns (marked by the presence of multiple representative organizations in competition with each other), new trade unions heavily critical of privatization, outsourcing, and public management arose (particularly against the introduction of balanced-budget principles).

These waves of protest affected the union system. In France the 1995 protests were supported by trade unions that emerged in the eighties and nineties, like Coordonner, Rassembler, Construire (Crc) and Solidaire, Unitaire, Démocratique (Sud-Ptt), which joined in with the antineoliberal movement, deploring the neoliberal turn taken by the other trade unions and adopting new models of internal democracy (based on rotation of leaders and on decisions made unanimously or by qualified majority) (Béroud, Mouriaux, and Vakaloulis 1998). In Italy the grassroots unions (COBAS)—which appeared in the early eighties and subsequently joined the Italian movement—went through a similar evolution, sharply criticizing the policies for agreements between employers and the large confederal unions (CGIL, CISL, and UIL)[4] that were accused of not protecting the weakest workers' groups, of not representing the new labor identities, and of confining themselves to defending unionized workers. In Spain a strong anarchist trade union, the Confederación Nacional de los Trabajadores (Cnt), managed to concentrate the dissent that had emerged in relation to the bigger unions (associated with the parties of the institutional left like PSOE and Izquierda Unida).

In countries with a neocorporate-type structure of representation (with representation of an industrial sector going to a single trade union), primarily public-service trade unionists have taken more critical positions, like Öffentliche Dienste, Transport, and in Germany Verkehr (Ötv) and later Vereinte Dienstleistungsgewerkschaft (Ver.di). In the United Kingdom, where 90 percent of the trade unions are in the Trades Union Congress (TUC), the labor movement umbrella organization (Allum 1995), some unions promoted and supported campaigns against privatization in such areas as health service, railways, education, and postal service; motions criticizing the "New Labour" were debated at many trade-union congresses, and some unions decided to reduce the size of their donations to the party (Lawrence 2004). Criticism developed also within the traditionally most combative occupation groups of workers in the large factories, such as the metalworkers of IG-Metall in Germany and the Italian Federazione Impiegati Operai Metallurgici (FIOM), which took part in the Genoa demonstrations against the G8, and the longshoremen who had mobilized transnationally (Levi and Olson 2000).

In recent years, traditional trade union confederations have begun to criticize neoliberal economic policies that encourage unrestrained competition among nations based on reducing the cost of labor and deregulating employment and thus rendering it precarious. In Seattle many of the demonstrators were mobilized by the AFL-CIO, which in the nineties had gone through a radical transformation in an antineoliberal direction. Significantly, on the occasion of the May 1, 2002, traditional demonstrations for workers' rights, the German trade union federation DGB chose globalization as the main theme of the event. In Italy the relations between the movement and the CGIL (the major left-wing union) intensified on the occasion of the general strike called in spring 2002 against the reform of the workers' charter, culminating in full adherence by the CGIL to the Florence ESF. In France, a major role in the *altermondialistes'* mobilizations of the nineties was taken by the CGT, which progressively distanced itself from the French communist party (PCF), adopting more participatory internal structures.

With increasing frequency the trade union organizations began to link up and cooperate at the transnational level: for instance, the Canadian, U.S., and Mexican unions mobilized together after NAFTA; the Belgians, French, and Spaniards participated in the Eurostrike of Renault workers; employees of United Parcel Service, one of the world's leading private postal agencies, carried out transnational strikes. Especially, rank-and-file transnational networks developed together with the creation of formal IGOs concerned with labor issues (Moody 1997). The main European confederated unions joined in the European Trade Union Confederation (ETUC), which was among the promoters of the ESF, along with the Trade Union Advisory Committee (TUAC). The European forum also saw the presence of the new workers' unions that set up spaces for coming together in the "Euromarches against unemployment, insecure work and exclusions," a continental network that since 1997 has been promoting demonstrations against unemployment. The European ATTAC network has guided the traditional left associations of Europe into the ESF, which has been joined by other political organizations like the International Union of Socialist Youth (IUSY) and the European Young Socialists (ECOSY).

More or less everywhere, competition and tensions between institutional and more radical unions have shifted into cooperation and to dialogue in the ESF. How is this to be explained? We may say that the competition generated a radicalization of the conflict around labor issues that involved many workers, who in turn appropriated the most institutionalized trade union structures as vehicles of mobilization. The Italian case is emblematic.

In July 2001 in Genoa, the confederated unions (CGIL, CISL, and UIL) decided not to take part in the days of mobilization. The CGIL dissociated from the violent fringes; the call from CISL was "not to join initiatives of the GSF" (*Il Manifesto,* July 24, 2001). However, FIOM, which organizes the CGIL metalworking sector, fully joined the initiatives, and many of those demonstrating on July 21, 2001, carried the CGIL flag. The unions' rank and file had already shown their desire to join the movement initiatives in an anti-free-trade direction even before the Genoa days, when "the Augustus cinema, chock full of Italian and foreign trade unionists called on by the CGIL, CISL and UIL a few yards away from the red zone to take their distance from the no-global movement, had exploded in long, liberatory applause" for Vittorio Agnoletto, GSF spokesperson (*Il Manifesto,* February 9, 2002). Subsequently, not just FIOM but also a group within the confederated union, Cambiare Rotta (Change Course), convinced the CGIL of the importance of a global movement for workers' rights. In February 2002, Agnoletto was in fact invited and heard with sympathy at the congress of the largest Italian union (ibid.). From that time on, the CGIL was present at antiwar demonstrations, and the new global movement took part in various strikes called by the confederated union. At Barcelona the three Italian unions paraded under the banners of the ETUC against the European Summit (*Il Manifesto,* March 14, 2002). At the general strike called by the CGIL on March 23, 2002, in Rome, Secretary Sergio Cofferati declared he was on the side of the young people fighting "in the globalization" for peace and the environment (*Il Manifesto,* March 24, 2002). In Florence, at the march against the war that concluded the proceedings of the ESF, Guglielmo Epifani, the new CGIL secretary, said: "A movement with these features ought really to meet everyone. It is not important to put on some hat, acronym or control over it. No one could manage that, and it would be offensive vis-à-vis the movement itself" (*Il Manifesto,* November 10, 2002).

Between Ethical Commitment and Nonviolence: Ecopacifism

In the last few months of 1997, some of the Italian organizations that, since the late eighties, had coordinated to promote joint campaigns against the imbalances brought by globalization, decided to give rise to periodic meetings with an eye to avoiding "repetition of similar initiatives that disperse the scarce energies of each organization/campaign, whereas encounter and dialogue might produce a multiplier effect" (Bologna et al. 2001, 9). The campaigns begun in the late eighties were aimed mainly against transnational corporations regarded as chiefly responsible for environmental pollution or the exploitation of labor, children's and otherwise (among the biggest targets were Nike and Nestlé).

Setting up an intercampaign table, a place for coordinating organizations engaged in campaigns focusing on different issues but with the same general objectives, enabled representatives of the various Italian organizations to meet, get to know each other, and compare and define work methods based on a process of consensual decision and common pathways. In 1999 a proposal to set up a network to enhance the level of local action spread throughout the national territory. As missionary Alex Zanotelli recalls, the idea of linking up Italian associations goes back to when "in the midnineties, I traveled Italy, finding a beautiful, rich reality, but with no visibility or political significance" (2001, 76). The project to create a network called Lilliput was launched officially in July 1999, and its organizational structure was later to prove particularly serviceable to the objectives of mobilization. Lilliput, in the form of a network of local nodes, took its first steps before the Seattle protests, although it gained some visibility only after the failure of the WTO summit. The drafting and ensuing dissemination of the manifesto in the first months of 2000 began a process that led to the active involvement of local groups in the project.

The network's name derives from Jonathan Swift: the idea of the little Lilliputians immobilizing the giant Gulliver symbolizes the strategy of uniting the strength of many tiny groups to block the giants of neoliberal globalization. The Lilliput network consists of dozens of local nodes, with a few internally more homogeneous elements, such as the environmentalist area represented by the Italian section of the World Wildlife Fund (WWF), an association founded in Switzerland in 1961, and established in Italy in 1966. Though not an integral part of Lilliput, other environmentalist (Legambiente) and animal rights (Lega Anti-Vivisezione) organizations gravitate around the ecological area of the nonviolent network.

Another component of the network is the Catholic-inspired associations, well represented by Mani Tese (Outstretched Hands) and Pax Christi. Mani Tese, born in 1964, is a lay association dealing with consciousness-raising and development cooperation as well as political pressure actions like the Global March against Child Labor, held in over a hundred countries throughout the world. Pax Christi is an international movement for peace created in 1945, which has spread to nineteen countries, has associated groups in another seven, and has ten affiliated bodies throughout the world. The Italian section, founded in 1954, changed radically in the late seventies, becoming involved in annual peace marches. In 1983 the international movement was awarded the prize for peace education of the United Nations Educational, Scientific, and Cultural Organization (UNESCO). Often critical of the ecclesiastical hierarchies, Pax Christi defines itself as "a leaven within the church" and regards the G8 as a "structure of sin" (interview with Fabio Giunti, in Marradi and Ratto 2001, 31). These organizations actively promote political consumerism, organizing boycotts of transnational corporations violating the rights of workers and not adopting production standards that respect the environment. The Lilliput network includes many NGOs operating in the world's south, which are often committed to promoting fair, solidarity-based trade with peasants and craftspeople in poor countries. Before the Genoa demonstrations, the Vatican invited the G8 leaders to "listen" to the peaceful demonstrations of the young people. Important Catholic associations met in Genoa a month before the G8, approving a manifesto from Catholics to the G8 leaders that, while not meaning those organizations were joining the protests, presented demands similar to those of the anti-G8 demonstrators, encouraging convergence (albeit not identification) between the fight against globalization and Catholic solidarism on economic questions (cancellation of poor countries' foreign debt, imposition of the Tobin tax, access to medicines, reform of intellectual property) and environmental ones (ratification of the Kyoto protocol).

The commitment of religious and ecologist groups to the mobilization against neoliberal globalization is not a purely Italian phenomenon. The Lilliput organizations coordinate in often transnational campaigns against the international-trade-liberalization policies promoted by the WTO and the environmental damages of IMF- and WB-sponsored projects, for solidarity with the peoples of Africa, and for the cancellation of poor countries' foreign debt.

International and transnational environmentalist organizations like the WWF, Greenpeace, and Friends of the Earth (FoE) participate in diverse ways and on various bases in demonstrations against neoliberalism, inverting the tendency to institutionalization that typified the environmental movement in the eighties and nineties in various European countries (Rootes 2003; TEA 2000; Diani and Donati 1998; della Porta and Diani 2004). Especially in the nineties, the institutionalization of the most visible environmentalist associations was challenged by more radical organizations mobilizing in protest campaigns against urban pollution and private traffic, for animal protection, and so on. In Italy, for instance, associations like Legambiente, WWF, and FoE were severely criticized by local citizens' committees mobilized against the implementation of a high-speed railway project (della Porta and Andretta 2002). In Britain, "from 1991 a new wave of direct action was initiated . . . by a new generation of radical activists who were critical of organizations like Greenpeace, WWF and FoE, not to mention old-guard conservation organizations like the National Trust and RSPB [the Royal Society for the Protection of Birds]" (Rootes, Seel, and Adams 2000, 11). In Germany, the organizational growth and the institutionalization of relations between the biggest environmentalist organizations and the complex German political system did not prevent less-structured organizations from displaying their dissent through more direct forms of action (Rucht and Roose 2000). In France and Spain, the progressive involvement of environmentalist associations in various forms of concertation did not bring abandonment of protest strategies or participatory organizational models (Fillicule and Ferrier 2000; Jiménez 2000). The tension between protest and institutions and the competition between groups defending the environment have certainly not diminished since then, but in addition well-organized, environmentalist organizations have come together, cooperating and talking with radical ecologist groups with few resources, in the movement against neoliberalism.

The religious component, bearer of a discourse typified by a constant call for solidarity, ethics, and values, has also gained transnational visibility with some successful protest campaigns. Nowadays, interfaith initiatives and religious organizations are more involved in international as well as national politics, cooperating with different sectors of local and global civil society.[5] According to John Clark, "many religions have experienced declining membership and mounting questions of relevance. In response, they increasingly engage in issues of morality and society beyond narrow questions of faith" (2003, 12). Thus, not only have interfaith initiatives accelerated, but "religious leaders are increasingly willing to join networks with secular organizations" and "inter-faith activities today tend to concentrate on issues of peace, sustainability, human rights, poverty, education and—more recently—economic globalisation" (13). Most of the religious international activism has so far been based on human rights and environmental protection (Livezy 1989; Keck and Sikkink 1998; Gadner 2002).

Three important religious actors are part of the International Council of the WSF: the World Council of Churches (WCC), Caritas Internationalis (CI), and the Jubilee Campaign for Debt Relief. The WCC is a global network of Christian organizations often cooperating with the Catholic Church, which in 1999 created a program to lobby both NGOs and IGOs to reorient the economy toward a more sustainable model. WCC underlines the domination of market values and asks for more solidarity and human values. Its main reference is the Bible, and its frame puts human beings at the core of social relationships. In order to oppose neoliberal globalization, this network of churches calls for a "Spirituality of Resistance." CI is a confederation of 162 Catholic relief, development, and social service organizations working in over two hundred countries and territories. The Caritas approach is based on the social teachings of the Catholic Church, and its main objective consists in spreading charity and social justice in the world. The confederation devoted its seventeenth general assembly, held in Rome on July 7–12, 2003, to "Globalizing Solidarity." The issue of globalization is a main concern of CI; in fact, as it claims in a booklet printed after the assembly, "economic globalization without the globalization of solidarity is suicide for the poor and thus for the majority of humanity" (Rodríguez 2003, 16). The participation of CI in the International Council of the WSF is a logical consequence of its commitment "to develop close working relations with Catholic and other Christian, inter-faith and secular organizations which share our vision" (Caritas Internationalis 2003).

These and other religious groups played a crucial role in the transnational campaign known as "Jubilee 2000": "Based on a biblical reference for debt relief as a new beginning, Jubilee provided a spiritual message for the millennium" (Grenier 2003, 86). Originally formed by a coalition of organizations active in 69 countries and with individual membership in 166 countries, under the leadership of Jubilee 2000 UK, the network achieved some substantial results: "commitments to bilateral and multilateral debt relief totaled US$110 billion" (87). According to the idea of the original coalition, the campaign should have lasted only until the year 2000, but its success convinced many organizations to continue the mobilization by building another network, Jubilee Research. In 1999, a relatively autonomous subnetwork (Jubilee South) was established by organizations from poor countries, which radicalized the original Jubilee 2000's claims.[6]

Religious organizations and campaigns have become more and more involved on secular issues such as environment, social justice, and human rights: "the churches themselves are changing and undergoing transformations, particularly with respect to the definition of their mission, both spiritually and temporally" (Crahan 1999, 57–58). As Gadner noticed, "In the 1990s, interactions between environmental and religious groups increased in frequency and importance. International meetings, national networks of interreligious activism, religiously sponsored environmental advocacy and education programs, collaborations between religious and environmental groups and grassroots religious and environmental advocacy are examples of the many initiatives that blossomed over the decade" (2002, 5–6).

The green, religious, and development-cooperation currents were massively present at the ESF: large environmentalist organizations like WWF International and Friends of the Earth Europe, organizations for the defense of human rights like the Fédération International Droits de l'Homme, important NGOs like Frères des Hommes Europe, Oxfam, and Oneworld. In addition to Caritas Europe, the forum was promoted by national networks for cancellation of poor countries' foreign debt active in Belgium, Switzerland, Spain, France, Germany, and Italy.

Within the religious world, as within the environmentalist movement, mechanisms of organizational appropriation were particularly visible. Active members and rank-and-file associations with more radical identities and repertoires persuaded more-structured organizations to participate in, or at least to sympathize with, the movement. Cooperation and competition within transnational mobilizations transformed the organizational structure of the movement.

Against Capitalism: The Area of Social Centers

A third area that has joined the GSF is that of the social centers, which are typified by a low level of internal coordination. While today the Italian social centers are numerous (over two hundred), they are also very heterogeneous in cultural background, objectives, and forms of action (Dines 1999). A pioneering study in the early eighties on social centers in the Milan area identified relationships with institutions (negotiation or confrontation/refusal/distance) as a particularly problematic point, observing processes of institutionalization and professionalization through transfer of resources to some social centers by institutions in exchange for carrying out sociocultural activities (Grazioli and Lodi 1984; see also della Porta 1996). In the last decade a sizable proportion of Italian social centers has undergone an organizational evolution that might be interpreted as a process of commercialization, whereby some organizations put growing emphasis on offering services paid for by member-users (della Porta and Diani 1999). This process, though not implying renunciation of activity of a political and social nature (Berzano, Gallini, and Genova 2002), is marked also by increasing interaction with the political system and adoption of more institutional action repertoires.

An evolutionary process of this type characterizes the social centers of the Carta di Milano, which in 1998 decided to coordinate action on certain campaigns concerning amnesty and decriminalization for the use of drugs, a citizenship income, and total recognition of self-management of social spaces (White Overalls 1998). These social centers, from which the Tute Bianche (White Overalls) came, are notable for moderation in action repertoires as well as their abandonment of a classical revolutionary vision. As one militant of the Bologna White Overalls said: "There are many ways of practicing revolution. . . . If by revolution we mean a classical scheme of taking power, I believe that in this sense Zapatism, but also our experience, is a further move. Foucault explained that the palace is empty . . . the problem is not to take power. The problem is to try to send messages. Here, we often live in something dirty that persists in calling itself democracy, but doesn't resemble it at all. If dreaming of a possible different world containing many worlds is a revolution, then definitely we are revolutionaries."[7] One of the main differences between the White Overalls and more radical social centers concerns relations with institutions. Some members from social centers close to the White Overalls have in the past participated in municipal elections (and in some cases been elected) or supported individual candidates. Some of the social centers that mobilized in the White Overalls have gradually become legally recognized by institutions (their occupations tolerated or legalized through the payment of symbolic leases) and have established and maintained good relations with parties such as the Greens and RC. Among the groups that participated in creating the White Overalls is the Ya Basta association, founded in 1996 after the first intercontinental meeting against neoliberalism, held in the Lacandona forest in Mexico.

Other social centers have dissociated themselves from a process of legalization and institutionalization they stigmatize as a "reformist drift" (Berzano and Gallini 2000). Starting from the Naples mobilization against the global forum on e-government (organized by the United Nations) in March 2001, the Network for Global Rights (a coordination between the COBAS confederation and some social centers mobilized on labor, the environment, and immigration) began to be formed. Differently from previous mobilizations, when the radical social centers did not join forces with the more moderate groups, the Network for Global Rights participated in the GSF, although with internal tensions (some social centers linked with it claimed independence).

After Genoa, the White Overalls decided to dissolve in order to promote the birth and consolidation of a broader entity, aiming to coordinate both moderate and radical social centers and involving the student collectives. The ex–White Overalls and part of the Network for Global Rights joined the Disobedients. The Laboratorio dei disobbedienti was also joined by the Ya Basta association against neoliberalism; the left-wing Radio Sherwood, founded in the seventies (http://www.sherwood.it); and the Giovani Comunisti (Young Communists), the youth organization of RC—born in the late nineties—which has ten thousand members. The Giovani Comunisti constituted "one of the main vehicles of encounter between the Seattle people and RC" and in the past had "stimulated the birth of and worked within student collectives, occupied spaces and social forums" (*Liberazione,* December 22, 2001).

In Spain, a youth counterculture has created its own autonomous spaces thanks to the practice of occupation, giving rise to the *movimiento de las okupas.* As in Italy, the phenomenon is marked by heterogeneity of action repertoires, relations with the institutions, and cultural references (Martínez López 2002). In Spain the squatter movement, which is modeled on Italian, Dutch, and German experience, is still extremely fragmented and is focused chiefly on the local level. It has developed conflictual relations with the Movimiento de Resistencia Global, the Spanish version of the antineoliberal movement, perceived as too moderate and bureaucratized (Bonet i Martí 2003).

In Britain, anticapitalist organizations such as Globalise Resistance (GR), People's Global Action (PGA), and the Socialist Worker's Party (SWP) are the most visible components of the movement (Farnsworth 2004). For instance, GR spokesperson Gay Taylor maintains, "I am keen to stick with the name of 'anti-capitalism' as it points the finger at where the problem lies, in the system rather than with particularly nasty individuals or corporations" (*Observer,* July 21, 2002). In Britain, protests against neoliberalism contain groups with strong youth representation, like Reclaim the Streets, which organizes spectacular "street parties" against polluting private transport and the privatization of public transport. It is well known for its "guerrilla gardening" action during the London May Day protest in May 2000.[8]

Elements belonging to the anticapitalist area of the movement took part in the ESF, even if only a few of them formally joined it: the English, Irish, and Greek sections of GR openly supported the initiative; the Italian Disobedients opted for a more autonomous presence, taking part in the official forum events but also organizing parallel discussion groups that took place separately and distinct from the forum.

In the anticapitalist area, it may be concluded, internal competition has led some groups to join the movement's coordination structures, like the GSF and ESF, while others have chosen to remain autonomous, severely criticizing the institutionalization of the movement. Others, like the Disobedients in Italy, have chosen an intermediate position, sometimes joining common platforms, sometimes (afraid of losing their autonomous profile) mobilizing autonomously.

Activists and Networks: From Bloc Recruitment to the Transnational Movement

As we stressed in the introduction to this chapter, organizational networks in the movement play a fundamental part in the mobilization of activists and sympathizers. Looking at the ways they got to know about the movement, 26 percent of those interviewed in Genoa mentioned the organization they belong to; 36 percent stated that the same organization had a significant role in informing them about the anti-G8 demonstrations.

Not only the organizations as such but also the cooperation among them, the networks they form, and the dialogue they initiate encourage participation. In the movement against neoliberalism, participation by individuals not belonging to the organizations that call for the mobilization is particularly marked: among participants, only 44.6 percent at Genoa and 49.3 percent at Florence reported belonging to any of the organizations that had mobilized in those two events. The spread of individual participation indicates the movement's capacity to attract sympathizers from outside the bloc recruitment, which also reflects a new type of militancy that seeks to combine the need for individual expression, typical of postmodern societies, with the development of collective identity. In the movement against globalization, this form of activism appears particularly significant.

Considering only those demonstrators belonging to organizations formally part of the movement and focusing on the most visible and important networks, based on our interviews, antineoliberalist demonstrators affiliated with the area closest to the traditional left represented 39.5 percent of participants at Genoa and 36.4 percent at Florence; 29.9 percent of participants in the Genoa demonstrations and 23.0 in the ESF were members of eco-pacifist organizations; 24.5 percent of participants at Genoa and 34.0 percent at Florence belonged to the more radical area of the anticapitalist left. Other activists stated they took part in the activities not of one organization in particular but of a local social forum, i.e., a network of organizations and individuals active on the issue of globalization (3.8 percent at Genoa and 6.6 percent at Florence).

Focusing attention on the ESF data, and limiting analysis to a few countries, we note some country-specific characteristics. While in Italy and Spain organized activists are members of various sectors of the movement, in France and Germany they are part especially of the antineoliberalist sector, and in the United Kingdom the activists belong mainly to the anticapitalist sector (Table 1). The distribution of affiliation to the various sectors shows greater balance, and hence greater heterogeneity of the bloc recruitment, in Spain and Italy, and to a lesser extent in France and Germany, whereas in Britain the organized component is much more homogeneous. Considering that the number of nonorganized people is higher in Italy and Spain than in Germany, France, or (especially) Britain, we may deduce that heterogeneous bloc recruitment encourages more participation by nonaffiliated individuals: difference attracts.

Though many participants do not belong to organizations formally part of the movement, many of them are or have in the past been members of some sort of political or social group. The ESF data show that even those who are not actual members in any movement organization have past organizational experience similar to that of the organized militants. Out of 13

Table 1. Sector affiliation of ESF participants by country of origin (reduced sample)

Sector affiliation	Country of origin (%)					Total (%)
	Italy	France	Germany	Spain	United Kingdom	
Ecopacifist	24.6	14.0	20.5	17.1	15.0	17.2
Antineoliberalist	37.5	57.0	69.2	28.6	3.4	33.0
Anticapitalist	26.5	26.7	10.3	34.3	80.8	45.0
Local social forums	11.4	2.3	0.0	20.0	0.8	4.8
(Number of organized participants)[a]	(53)	(86)	(39)	(35)	(120)	(333)
Nonorganized participants (%)	61.6	36.8	50.0	65.2	18.2	45.1
(Total number of participants)[b]	(143)	(139)	(81)	(110)	(147)	(620)

[a] Only for organized participants, Cramer's V is 0.32, significant at the 0.001 level.

[b] The Cramer's V of organized/nonorganized participants by country of origin is 0.36, significant at the 0.001 level.

types of political/social/religious groups listed, the nonorganized declared they were or had been members, on average, of 4.8 types of organizations, and the organized of 5.3.

What is in any case striking is the variety of groups that the participants to the GSF and ESF declare they were part of. Participants of the ESF stated they were in or had been in the following types of organizations (Table 2): political parties (42.4 percent), trade unions (44.3 percent), political movements (63.4 percent), NGOs (52.9 percent), feminist groups (29.6 percent), ecological groups (41.5 percent), social voluntary associations (51 percent), pro-migrant organizations (46.1 percent), recreational and sports associations (50.5 percent), student collectives (58.5 percent), social centers (26.8 percent), religious groups (16 percent), and neighborhood committees (27.8 percent). There are national differences: while the British show the highest level of organizational involvement in almost all groups, in all countries there is a prevalence of belonging to movements (even more in Germany), NGOs (slightly more in Germany), voluntary associations, student collectives, and even recreational associations. For other organizational experiences the national differences in membership are more apparent, especially in environmentalist organizations (in France only 12.5 percent), trade unions (more in France, 48.2 percent; and in the United Kingdom, 77.2 percent), in feminist groups (more in Spain, 38.6 percent; United Kingdom, 36.2 percent; and France, 30.5 percent), in associations defending migrants (more in the United Kingdom, 67.1 percent; Spain, 48.6 percent; and France, 46.5 percent), and in social centers (something chiefly found in Italy, 45.5 percent).

The past experiences of individuals in various organizations are fundamental to an understanding of the network dynamics, and individuals can play a fundamental role in interorganizational processes. Studies of social movements using network analysis (Diani 1995) show that participation in multiple organizations favors interorganizational exchanges, facilitating relations among the different groups. It is interesting to note that militants participating in the activities of various groups form networks similar to those making up the sectors we have analyzed, as can be seen from the clusters showing up in a multiscaling analysis (Figure 5). To understand how the clusters are produced, it should be borne in mind that when two groups are close, it means that many activists stated they had participated in both; when two groups are distant, the number of activists sharing experience of participation in both is very limited.

At the top right of the diagram we find a cluster made up of religious groups, NGOs, environmentalist organizations, and voluntary associations constituting the linked archipelago we have called the ecopacifist sector. Overlapping the two left-hand squares we find political parties, trade unions, and political movements forming the sector of the antineoliberal left. Finally, at the center bottom we find the social centers, sometimes overlapping with the student collectives that represent the anticapitalist sector of the movement. The multiscaling analysis enables us to identify two latent dimensions distinguishing the clusters. While the vertical dimension seems to define generational distance (younger members in social centers and student organizations; older ones in more structured organizations), the horizontal one clearly distinguishes between politics-oriented organizations (parties, unions, and political movements) and society-oriented ones (especially ecosolidarity organizations), with social centers and students' associations in between.[9]

While we have noted that the movement networks take shape on the basis of ideological, or political, affinities, this progressive integration of individual networks is the outcome not just of organizational decisions but also of an integration from below brought about by men and women who have participated in the activities of various groups, contributing to the

Table 2. Past and present organizational affiliation of ESF participants by country of origin

Organization type	Country of origin					Total (%)	(N)	Cramer's V	Cramer's V (no United Kingdom)
	Italy	France	Germany	Spain	United Kingdom				
Political party	35.2	32.2	27.5	27.2	78.5	42.4	(266)	0.41***	n.s.
Trade union	28.3	48.2	28.8	28.1	77.2	44.3	(278)	0.40***	0.19**
Political movement and/or network	57.6	56.8	68.6	40.7	89.3	63.4	(396)	0.34***	0.18**
NGO	38.0	46.8	65.8	56.1	63.5	52.9	(329)	0.21***	0.20***
Women's association	21.9	30.5	17.3	38.6	36.2	29.6	(187)	0.17**	0.17**
Environmental association	47.3	12.9	48.1	46.9	55.0	41.5	(261)	0.32***	0.32***
Voluntary group (charity)	46.6	53.6	40.7	52.6	57.1	51.0	(319)	n.s.	n.s.
Migrants' association	29.2	48.2	32.9	46.5	67.1	46.1	(287)	0.28***	0.18**
Recreational and sports association	49.3	48.6	56.8	44.2	54.7	50.5	(316)	n.s.	n.s.
Student group	58.6	45.7	46.3	51.3	82.6	58.5	(367)	0.29***	n.s.
Social centers	45.5	27.5	22.4	20.5	14.8	26.3	(166)	0.25***	0.22***
Religious group	17.9	12.2	20.0	12.4	18.1	16.0	(100)	n.s.	n.s.
Citizen committee	18.8	42.3	22.8	31.6	22.4	27.8	(174)	0.20***	0.21***
(Number of participants)	(142–46)	(137–42)	(76–81)	(112–14)	(147–49)	(623–31)			

Note: Table entries are the distribution of responses to the question of which types of organization ESF participants belong or have belonged to, by country of origin. The percentages add to more than 100 percent because multiple responses were possible.

***significant at the 0.001 level; **significant at the 0.01 level; n.s. = nonsignificant.

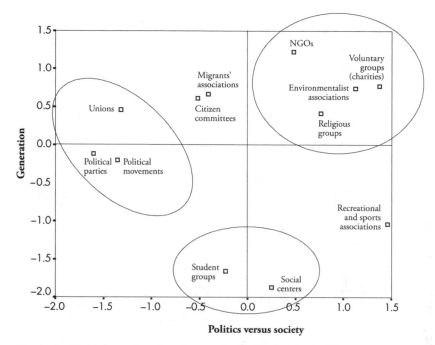

Figure 5. Multidimensional scaling analysis of individual affiliation to organization types (Euclidean distance model).

creation of channels of interorganizational communication and facilitating linkage among different sectors.

If we stopped here, the impression would be that of individual networks integrated only within movement sectors that are more or less homogeneous from the ideological and political viewpoint. In reality, if we aggregate individuals on the basis of the clusters that we found using multi-scaling, distinguishing among those who participated in activities of eco-pacifist, traditional, and anticapitalist left organizations (as shown in Figure 5),[10] and check the overlap among these three aggregates, we note that individuals join not only different organizations in the same sector of the movement, but also organizations in movement sectors with evident cultural differences. In fact, 52.7 percent of the activists have shared experience in both antineoliberalist left and anticapitalist organizations, while 59.6 percent have been in both antineoliberalist left and ecopacifist organizations, and 58.9 percent have been associated with both anticapitalist organizations and ecopacifist organizations. In practice, while 15.4 percent of activists have been or are in organizations of a single movement sector,

35.0 percent participate or have participated in the activities of organizations of two movement areas, and no less than 45.3 percent have been or are members of groups belonging to all three sectors.[11]

The widespread experience of multiple affiliation points to the prevalence of a type of militant typified by a complex identity and open to diversity, which fits the identity of the movement. At the same time, the existence of a network of activists who have participated in organizations of various sectors has certainly facilitated interorganizational relations. We can accordingly conclude that the movement of movements is not a mere coalition among organizations, but a social movement in the strict sense, in which identities are interwoven at both meso- (intergroup) and micro- (interparticipant) levels.

How Democracy (Net)Works

The question of internal democracy is of highest importance for a movement having among its objectives democratic participation and the democratization of the institutions of globalization (see chapter 3 in this volume). How are decisions made in such a movement? How does the structure of the main organizational networks influence processes aimed at guaranteeing participation and internal democracy?

Considering the movement's main organizational sectors, we can see how internal democracy is the object of debate and which solutions are developed and with which effects. We shall look at the cases of ATTAC–Italy, the Lilliput network, and the Disobedients, and then extend the focus to the GSF, ESF, and WSF. To investigate *how* internal democracy is understood, we shall go on to examine the organizational structure (in particular the degree of formalization and specialization, the decision-making body, and the type of leadership) and the ways of making decisions, focusing on the content of constitutions and on the internal debate within the various networks (often structured around a center-periphery dialectic).

In the cases of ATTAC, Lilliput, and the Disobedients, a body exists that has a privileged role in making strategic decisions, though it is not the official top of the organization. Especially in the first two cases, the problems tackled in the search for a participatory model of decision making are similar, and no network has managed to find a fully satisfactory mechanism. The dilemma of how to reconcile efficacy in decision making with participation has been tackled in various ways. As Finelli notes, this search produces "a veritable multiplication of places for 'discussion without decision,' with the risk that 'participatory democracy' may be transformed into 'consultative democracy,' in which members are left only with the possibility of expressing their own needs and desires, while the power of decision remains firmly in the hands of those who set the political agenda and then have the job of summarizing the positions expressed by the militants" (2003, 55).

The three organizational networks we deal with here differ regarding their organizational structure and the models of decision making they adopt. ATTAC–Italy is the organizational network that appears most formalized; the association has a constitution conferring legal personality on it, defining a set of rules and procedures, and clarifying the organizational structure. Membership is tied to payment of a fee and provision of a membership card. The association is marked by a high degree of specialization; the various organizational elements are assigned a precise series of functions with a clear division of labor.

In the case of the Lilliput network, there is no constitution or formal membership cards, but rules and procedures have been defined with great precision. Membership does not entail payment of a fee, but implies full acceptance of the principles and values contained in the manifesto, later supplemented by various declarations of shared principles. The division of tasks has been continually discussed, with the development of considerable specialization attributing specific functions to particular bodies.

The Disobedients have an extremely low degree of formalization. The organization has not adopted a manifesto, still less a constitution; there is no official document defining its structure and functioning. It is loosely constructed, and the level of specialization is very limited. In fact, the functions of the various organizational structures are not clear.

In all three cases explicit reference is made to the theme of participatory democracy. The vocabulary these groups use is innovative. The typical definitions of representative democracy are shunned: there is never any talk of leaders, representatives, or delegates, but only of spokespersons, facilitators, coordinators, and so on. The feeling is that a new model of democracy needs a new grammar and a new vocabulary.

The organizational structure as such is fairly complex in ATTAC and Lilliput, simpler in the case of the Disobedients. In all three cases it is possible to identify a body that makes the strategic decisions for the organization: the national council in ATTAC, the subnode in the Lilliput network, and the council in the Disobedients. These bodies are de facto at the top of those organizations and have aroused criticism from other levels of the organization (especially local ones).

In ATTAC–Italy the bodies performing functions of decision making are the national assembly of members and the national council (NC). While the national assembly is "the highest deliberative body of the association" (ATTAC Italy 2002, Art. 9), a careful reading of the constitution shows that it primarily ratifies decisions already made by the NC. According to the association's constitution, the NC prepares the agenda for the assembly, the report on the association's activities, as well as the program for the coming year, and decides the regulations for preparing and holding the assembly. NC members are chosen by seeking a unanimous consensus, intended to guarantee the involvement of the local level in the process of selection. While appointment of NC members is by consensus, the NC is operational when an absolute majority of its members is present, and decisions are made by a favorable vote of the majority of those present (Art. 14).[12]

In Lilliput, in the first stage of the network's existence, the body hierarchically above the others was the intercampaign table (composed of the representatives of the associations promoting the network), which placed the local nodes, consisting chiefly of individuals active in the field, at the margins of the decision-making process. The legitimacy of this body, however, was soon criticized from within the organization, and the local groups asked for more influence over the organization's decisions. A process of reorganization began, concluding at the second national assembly in early 2002, with more debate on Lilliput's conception of democracy. A new body (subnode) was given the explicit task of limiting the tasks of the intercampaign table, whose role was cut back, attesting to the organization's effort to find a more participatory model of decision making. The subnode proposes and organizes the national assemblies and handles representation of the network to the outside, choosing the most suitable and competent among the members for the specific occasion. While embodying the network's supralocal level, it is understood as a locus of coordination, linkage, and synthesis among the various organizational elements, not as the top of a pyramidal structure. The subnode consists of eleven members who remain in office for one year: two representatives of the intercampaign table, one spokesperson for each of five thematic working groups (nonviolence and conflicts, rights and participation, international trade and finance, fair trade, and environment), and four spokespersons for the local nodes of the macroregional areas (two for northern, one for central, and one for southern Italy). The members of the subnode are replaced in a partial-rotation mechanism so that its work is not slowed down too much when the members are renewed: the constant presence of people with previous experience enables new arrivals to become accustomed to their roles quickly.

In the case of the social centers clustered round the Disobedients, there are decision-making bodies that meet with a certain continuity. The two bodies at the national level are the assembly and the council. They seek unanimity among participants and do not make their decisions by voting (Becucci 2003). The assembly—which meets every two or three months—establishes the movement's political agenda, sets the timetable, and verifies and discusses the content of the political platform. The assembly is not a restricted body, and apart from the local spokespersons anyone who is interested in the life of the network can participate. The council, explicitly inspired by the organizational formula of the Zapatista movement, limits participation to local spokespersons and delegates of the party and trade-union organizations linked to the Disobedients (89).

While the organizational structure of the Disobedients has not undergone revisions or restructurings, some internal tensions have encouraged the organizational evolution of ATTAC and Lilliput since the local groups soon asked for more influence and for limits on the role of the decision-making body. In order to meet the requests for more internal democracy, ATTAC decided to create a link between the national and local levels by setting up macroregional meetings. The 2003 national assembly decided to institutionalize their role by scheduling their meetings every two months with the objective of offering more room for debate and for internal reflection within the association. The institution of macroregional assemblies does not, however, seem to have enabled ATTAC to find the equilibrium between the leaders' need to decide and the rank and file's demand to participate. The NC is in fact criticized by the association for its concentration of power at the top and for its lack of transparency (regarding both communication to the association and employment of financial resources).

The Lilliput network, like ATTAC–Italy, has devoted much attention to the question of internal democracy and has progressively modified and adapted its organizational structure and methods of decision making so as to offer its members greater possibilities of participation. The creation of the subnode has only partially achieved the objectives the national assembly had set itself. Like the intercampaign table in the past, it has been criticized from within for having acted on some occasions as delegates. The subnode has great autonomy in emergency situations, on condition that it gives precise, timely, and transparent reasons for its decisions.[13] This makes it a body that acts very much at its own discretion at the most critical moments in the life of the organization, but at the expense of involvement of the local level. No effort to improve internal democracy of the Disobedients similar to that of the other networks has been noted. The Disobedients have never made known the way council members are selected or indicated when or where the council meets or what decisions it takes.

The center-periphery relationship has been tackled differently in the three cases under examination: in ATTAC the local level contributes to the selection of members of the decision-making body; in Lilliput and the Disobedients, it is represented directly within the body (in Lilliput more than a third of the members of the subnode are chosen by the local nodes; in the Disobedients the local spokespersons on the council represent the policies of the group of which they are an emanation).

Focusing attention on the type of leadership, interesting differences emerge. In Lilliput, leadership is of a diffuse type: decisions are not a monopoly of the subnode. The thematic groups, with the agreement of the national assembly, are entitled to make binding decisions on issues within their competence. The subnode tries, moreover, to bridge the twofold organizational gap counterposing associations and unorganized individuals at both the national and local levels. In ATTAC and the Disobedients, leadership is more concentrated: a directive must receive assembly approval in ATTAC, while the greater informality of the Disobedients leads to emergence of a very limited number of charismatic personalities with large media visibility.

The three networks greatly stress the importance of participation and of new methods for making decisions. Lilliput's choice of innovative decision-making modes derives from its nonviolent identity; ATTAC–Italy and the Disobedients explicitly lay claim to a Zapatista connection.

The methods of decision making are very different in the three networks analyzed. Even though the selection of members of the NC in ATTAC comes about through unanimity, according to its statute the body decides by voting. Lilliput has formally included the method of consensus among the shared criteria (Rete Lilliput 2002) it has adopted, and the Disobedients seek to reach unanimity. In the Disobedients, where there is disagreement on the council by some members regarding decisions under discussion, these decisions are frozen and set aside, pending resumption at a later date. It is important to stress that the Disobedients' unanimity does not coincide with Lilliput's consensus. The method of consensus provides that in the course of discussion the degree of agreement of the group's various members on a specific question, which must be presented clearly and explicitly, be assessed. Confrontation is continued, working on the possibility of reconciling differing opinions on an incremental model, whereby a decision can be brought back into discussion so as to satisfy the widest possible number of people. The consensus method invites everyone to communicate the reasons for any disagreement, clarifying whether they will be prepared to uphold the decision eventually taken without exiting the group.

The consensus method thus builds "agreement within disagreement," since any particular disagreement is always set within a framework of more general agreement, based on respect and reciprocal trust.

Table 3 summarizes the main findings of the comparison among the three organizational networks. We see that the degree of formalization and specialization is highly differentiated: greatest in the case of ATTAC–Italy and least in that of the Disobedients. In all three the main decisions are made by a body that balances the local against the national levels. Leadership is diffuse in the case of Lilliput and concentrated in ATTAC and the Disobedients. Modes of decision making adopted within these bodies range from applying the majority criterion (ATTAC), to the consensus method (Lilliput), to the search for unanimity (Disobedients).

In both Lilliput and ATTAC, a tension remains between the horizontal (local nodes, territorial committees) and the vertical (subnode, national council) elements, tied up with the trade-off between participation and efficiency: the organizations operating at the local level ask for full sovereignty and criticize the arbitrariness of the bodies operating at the national level and the concentration of power at the top. By contrast, no such tension seems to have emerged in the Disobedients, even though the opacity of the decision-making process and of the organizational structure reduces the visibility of dissent for outsider observers.

The principles of participation and dialogue, low recourse to voting, time-limited delegation on specific questions, control of delegates, and the consensus method are met with again in the functioning of the social forums at various territorial levels, often marked by absence of leadership, presence of thematic groups, horizontality, and so on. Criteria similar to those we have seen in the main organization networks marked the cases of the GSF, ESF, and WSF.

In the social forums, alongside open plenary assemblies and thematic working groups, are the council of spokespersons (GSF), the continuity group (ESF), and the organizing committee (WSF), which guarantee operational continuity of the forums. In the words of Agnoletto, "the council of spokespersons had the role to implement the decisions taken by the GSF general assembly, which continued to meet periodically. . . . The council of spokespersons was never seen as a closed structure, its meetings were open to those who accepted the 'work agreement'" (2003, 52).

After the Genoa mobilization against the G8 summit, the council of spokespersons decided to dissolve without creating a body with similar functions. The movement thus went through a phase of assemblies only, which still allowed the definition of objectives, timetables, and campaigns.

Table 3. Organizational characteristics by networks

Organizational structure	Networks		
	ATTAC–Italy	Rete Lilliput	Disobedients
Formalization	High (defined in constitution)	Medium (defined in a manifesto and a document of values)	Weak (not defined in official documents)
Specialization	High (national working commissions)	High (thematic working groups)	Low (no presence of any commission or group)
Main decisional organism	National council	Subnode	Council
Composition of decisional organism	Defined by common agreement between local and national levels	Expression of thematic groups, intercampaign table, local nodes	Made up of local spokespersons and delegates of associated parties and unions
Center-periphery relationship	Local level contributes to selection of members of national council	Local level represented within decision-making body by macroregional spokespersons	Local level represented within decision-making body by local spokespersons
Model of decision making			
Type of leadership	Concentrated (but not individual)	Diffuse (with rotation according to different issues)	Concentrated (charismatic and individual)
Decisional method	Majority rule	Consensus method	Unanimity

Periodic national assemblies, however, soon proved insufficient, and the need emerged to set up a place for the movement's various components to meet, negotiate, and deliberate consensually between one appointment and the next.

In the run-up to the ESF in Florence, this job was done by the organizing committee, an enlarged, heterogeneous body made up of members of the movement's main organizational sectors. According to the account by Tommaso Fattori, one of the social forum spokespersons in Florence, the body defined the political line and guaranteed continuity between one event and the next but did not perform the function of representing the movement. The organizing committee made use of assembly features: itinerant assemblies organized in other European countries brought countries and networks other than the Italian ones into the process. The organizing committee made proposals and indicated possible solutions, but the decisions were made collectively at the international assemblies (interview, May 25, 2004).

With the ESF over, the organizing committee continued for a few months to operate and carry out linkage functions between the various elements of the Italian movement. In March 2003, the national assembly of local social forums held in Leghorn decided to convert the organizing committee into an informal body, called the continuity group, to act as the place for the movement to make decisions on new mobilizations. The idea of giving the antineoliberal movement a lasting structure at the national level by creating the Italian Social Forum was set aside, while the model developed for the GSF and ESF, consisting of ad hoc coordination for single demonstrations or campaigns, was reaffirmed (Fruci 2003).

The WSF, by contrast, first acted through an organizing committee formed by eight Brazilian organizations very different from each other, which was supposed to reflect the heterogeneity of the various currents in the global movement. The organizing committee was supposed to act as a mere facilitator and service body rather than as an executive organ, but de facto had a more important role. It defined the draft "Charter of Principles of the WSF," established the place where the forum would be held, the thematic lines, and—at least in 2001—the names of the main speakers for the plenary assemblies (Schönleitner 2003, 131). Following the criticisms that accompanied the work of the first WSF, in June 2001 a more inclusive international council (IC) was set up and a number of procedural changes made. Currently, the IC contains the members of the original organizing committee as well as dozens of transnational networks, but excludes national-level organizations. The IC has given itself a fluid, open structure that has nonetheless raised criticisms because in reality only those with the financial resources and time to attend the meetings can actually participate.

The method of decision making that typifies social forums organized at various territorial levels is consensual. The Genoa mobilization against the G8 summit represented an important moment because for the first time the consensus method became the joint stock of the Italian movement. According to Roberto Giudici, of FIOM, "Genoa was a school for many . . . by now this method has been adopted by everyone, in the sense that everyone knows it is not possible to close meetings with a position imposed on the others. . . . This mechanism is costly in terms of time, but in the long term pays off, and in my view there is none better" (interview, May 26, 2004).

To enhance its legitimacy, and not only procedurally, the ESF continuity group progressively expanded, keeping itself constantly operational thanks to the use of a very wide mailing list including members of the main organizations of the movement, to which they have very frequent recourse. Though the consensus method is used, the continuity group nonetheless operates informally and with little transparency: meetings are not publicized, and minutes are circulated for internal use only, without being published and made accessible to sympathizers, activists, or those simply interested.

The IC, too, formally uses the consensus method, although some members point out that some opinions seem to count more than others. One IC member says, "What you represent lends strength to what you say" (codas in Schönleitner 2003, 132). The IC, moreover, remains a body with members not elected by anyone, the representativity of which is continually questioned by different organizations in the movement.

In the various organizational sectors, and with the social forums, criticisms of the body set at the summit of the organization have not been lacking. They have, however, encouraged greater inclusiveness, openness, and transparency, and a process of revising operating methods is still not finished. The question of internal democracy brings a tension of ideas within the movement's organizational networks. It seems to be an objective that will be hard to achieve, but it is nonetheless true that this tension sets off important mechanisms of self-reform that steadily open up the organizations to their members' contributions and participation. The consensus method, widespread within the movement, seems to be "functional for safeguarding the unitary-plural nature of the movement as well as members' demands for individual protagonism" (Fruci 2003, 169).

Concluding Remarks

In this chapter, we have highlighted the organization's role in collective mobilization. Past movements—consider the labor movement—tended to be organized in a centralized fashion, partly to maximize the dissemination of information and the mobilization of militants and activists. Since the 1960s, a new family of social movements tried out new organizational formulas, based on small groups linked with each other in networks. This feature of the environmentalist, pacifist, student, and feminist movements is seen still more clearly in the movement for globalization from below. A synthesis of old and new movements, it has often been defined as a movement of movements, or network of networks, to emphasize its characteristic organizational structure that connects different political entities, and organizations structured in differentiated ways, through weak links.

The interorganizational dynamics in a context of weak links thus become fundamental for the construction of networks and for the recruitment of activists, supporters, and sympathizers. We have seen how various mechanisms (social appropriation, competition, cooperation in networks) have mobilized many organizations against neoliberal globalization. Trade unions, religious groups, NGOs, and so on, are increasingly confronted with rank-and-file organizations and have begun to reconsider more radical forms of activism. The integration of networks around common platforms and their mobilization have persuaded many men and women to participate in the various protests.

The emergence of a new international organization like ATTAC has encouraged many actors of the traditional left (unions and parties) to oppose neoliberal globalization and participate in the mobilization. The principles of democratic control of the economy and defense of welfare have acted as a cement of the antineoliberalist left, bringing people's positions closer, as happened with the institutional unions, which during the 1990s negotiated on reform of the welfare state, and the rank-and-file unions, always critical of such reforms.

In any case, the movement against neoliberal globalization has networked together families of movements very different from each other. Their aggregation is often fluid and comes about on the basis of political affinities. Thus, the emphasis on nonviolence and the ethical transformation of relations among men (and women) and between man and nature has brought together religious movements, environmentalist movements, and feminist movements, forming an ecopacifist sector. In Italy this has led to the formation of the Lilliput network, which unites ecologist, solidarity, and religious organizations and constitutes an important component of the movement at the national level.

Moreover, the movement against neoliberalism has reconsolidated the variegated radical organizations pushing for an anticapitalist interpretation of the critique of globalization. The social centers and other radical groupings, marked particularly by the presence of young people and students, represent the most radical sector of the movement. In Italy new networks have arisen, like the Disobedients and the Network for Global Rights, which are with varying results seeking to coordinate the fragmented, unstructured anticapitalist sector.

Cooperation among organizations structured in different ways (parties, rank-and-file groups, institutionalized and rank-and-file unions, religious associations and institutions, environmentalist lobbies, and more radical ecologist groups, etc.) is often the outcome of a number of mechanisms that reinforce each other, especially in a period of very intense mobilization. Even before Seattle, in the 1990s, radical trade union organizations challenged the confederated and institutional unions on the ground of representation of the workers' interests; ecologist groups, often active at the local level around urban issues, challenged the legitimacy of the increasingly institutional- ized environmentalist lobbies and their moderate practices; rank-and-file groups of religious inspiration put pressure on the confessional institutions to get them to face social problems; and among anticapitalist rank-and-file groups, polemics increased between those who were accused of reformism or else of sectarianism. In different ways and at different times, according to the country or the sector of the movement, the groups that started the antineoliberal protest won the sympathies of the members (or the reference base) of the more structured organizations, which, partly because of this pressure, began to join the protest for global justice and in this way began to cooperate with the groups that had previously competed with them for the representation of a common reference base (workers, environmentalists, the religious). The resulting cooperation has not overcome the competition, but has strengthened, or created *ex novo*, interorganizational connections on the basis of which the movement's network of networks is structured.

The activists, moreover, not only encouraged the rapprochement of a few organizations with the antineoliberal mobilization, but also anticipat- ed formal network dynamics through their participation in the activities of groups very different from each other. The widespread, multiple affilia- tions of participants in the ESF points to the existence of dense individual networks.

To cope with this heterogeneity, the movement has turned to innovative practices of internal democracy. In each sector there has been a debate on the forms of democracy needed in order to legitimize decisions on strategic choices and, as we shall see better in chapter 3, negotiate identities. While social movements of the past had already tried out alternative forms of deci- sion making, appealing to such concepts as direct democracy, participation, self-organization, autonomy, and so on, the movement against neoliberal globalization makes increasing reference to the concept of consensus democ- racy. In the past, the main organizational form that was experimented with was the assembly—a mode of decision making that, though based on the direct participation of members, provided for forms of aggregation of opin- ions using the technique of voting by the raising of hands or de facto dele- gation to charismatic leaders. By contrast, the movement today applies the method of consensus, which provides for discussion aimed at overcoming points of division and seeking the solution that can get the highest possible consensus, though not necessarily unanimity on everything.

Each of the networks is seeking to resolve the problem of internal democracy by using partly different practices, sometimes by formalizing procedures (ATTAC and Lilliput), sometimes by trusting to informal rules (Disobedients); by emphasizing the role of bodies set up at a national level (ATTAC) or seeking to give more voice to local groups (Lilliput); in some cases by recourse to decisions based on a majority (ATTAC), in others always seeking the broadest possible consensus (Lilliput), and in yet others still preferring decisions by unanimity (Disobedients). When the networks coordinate with each other in the social forums or in coordination structures to prepare campaigns, the method of consensus, if not of unanimity, becomes necessary for mobilization, the success of which, especially if transnational, depends on effective support from all sectors.

In the movement of movements, the consensual practices applied at various organizational levels, the network, the social forums (local, macroregional, world), the countersummits, the campaigns, and so on, represent not merely a model of decision making conforming with the principles and values that ideally inspire the decision-making centers of institutions (from local government to world governance), but also a *practical* way of solving internal conflicts, setting aside divisions, uniting around points of convergence, and building, through continual negotiation, a new, though always plural, collective identity. From this viewpoint, the network and its various nodes represent spaces for experimenting with new forms of democratic participation in which there is a search for dialogue for the attainment of the common good.

This does not mean that applying the consensus method is always effective or that the movements manage to solve the problem of representation in a satisfying way. On the contrary, the functioning of democracy is still the object of critique within the various networks. Nonetheless, if the movements do not fully succeed in tackling the classical dilemmas of democratic participation (especially representation versus participation, discussion versus timeliness, flexibility versus procedural correctness, trust versus delegation, etc.), they do make them the object of continuous and often self-critical discussion.

3

Master Frame, Activists' Ideas, and Collective Identity

The Meaning Work of Transnational Social Movements: An Introduction

Although forms of contentious transnational actions against international institutions existed prior to the movement against neoliberal globalization (Gerhards and Rucht 1992; Rucht 1999), they often took the shape of transnational protest campaigns—"campaign" meaning "a thematically, socially and temporarily interconnected series of interactions that, from the viewpoint of the carriers of the campaign, are geared to a specific goal" (della Porta and Rucht 2002, 3). Today, by contrast, the movement against neoliberal globalization links different transnational protest campaigns and provides a shared master frame and a series of organizational structures (SMOs, NGOs, national associations) that interact periodically in transnational events (countersummits, world and macroregional forums).

In this chapter, we will argue that the common identity of the movement against neoliberal globalization has been built by way of what Snow and Benford have called "meaning work" (1992, 136), which actors use to convince people to engage in collective action. If "every regime has a legitimating frame that provides the citizenry with a reason to be quiescent" (Gamson 1988, 219), social movements must produce "counter frames," which legitimize unconventional collective action. According to Gamson, "people act on the basis of some meaning system, and the definition of issues, actors, and events is a matter of constant contention. A central part of the symbolic struggle, then, is about the process of constructing specific meanings" (ibid.). This is the reason why "promoting public definitions of problems and their solutions is not just one of many components of protest

61

campaigns and social movements that have to be considered in an analysis; instead, to the extent that movements can exert influence only through mobilizing the public, *it is the key factor*" (Gerhards and Rucht 1992, 572; emphasis added).

Although the meaning work is important in every social movement, be it old or new, it has a particular importance for the global movement of movements because

- both the social constituency addressed by the movement (individual mobilization potential) and the constituency that actually mobilizes are heterogeneous (Andretta et al. 2002, ch. 3; Andretta and Mosca 2003);
- the set of potential mobilizing structures (NGOs, SMOs, political parties, trade unions, voluntary associations) is very heterogeneous, coming from different political traditions, holding different ideologies (see chapter 2 of this volume);
- both the structural and the individual mobilization potentials are geographically dispersed. (Glasius and Kaldor 2002; Pianta 2002)

Thus, a frame analysis approach is useful for investigating the building of a transnational social movement through the symbolic construction of the collective identity.[1] Through meaning work, social movements symbolically construct a collective subject (the working class, the people, the nation, environmentalists, women, etc.),[2] integrate the structural mobilization potential,[3] convince sympathizers to become involved in a collective action, and convince broader public opinion that the movement's claims are "fair" and that the status quo is "unjust."[4]

Consider the mechanisms that, in Sidney Tarrow's view, make the formation of a transnational social movement possible: *diffusion,* "the transfer of information along established lines of interaction"; and *brokerage,* "the linking of two or more currently unconnected social sites" (Tarrow 2002). Our argument is that brokerage is also due to the process of master framing, the building of a more general frame that bridges different sectorial frames (Snow and Benford 1992). Using Tarrow's terminology, we believe that "cognitive mechanisms" are able to influence "relational mechanisms" (the "connections among people, groups, and interpersonal networks") by altering the perception of people and organizations and thus fostering the identification of both organizations and individuals with a social movement.

This can be seen in the movement against neoliberal globalization. In Genoa, 75 percent of the participants of the mobilization against the G8 responded that they identified (somewhat or much) with the movement as a whole, a finding reflected by the ESF participants, 77.2 percent of whom share high identification with the movement as a whole. Such an identification, concurrently with a multiple and layered identity, does not exclude identifying with both a specific sector (about 57 percent in Genoa and as much as 75 percent in Florence) and a specific organization (44 percent and 67 percent respectively).

In this chapter we argue that such an intense and multiple identification has been reached through the symbolic construction of a master frame. In other words, while social movement literature traditionally stresses the role of social conditions, participation in collective action, and the organization itself in order to explain the construction of a collective identity and identification with a movement (but see Rochon 1998 and Jasper 1997), we shall attempt to ascertain the role that ideas play.

By conducting an empirical analysis of the relation between the master framing process and its resonance with individual frames, we also hope to investigate the understudied "relationship between ideological factors—values, beliefs, meanings—and identification with social movements and participation in their activities" (Snow and Benford 1988, 197). It is true that frame analysis has gained a lot of attention at the theoretical level (Klandermans 1992; Snow et al. 1986; Snow and Benford 1988, 1992, 2000; Benford 1997; Hunt, Benford, and Snow 1994; Gamson 1988; Oliver and Johnston 2000; Johnston 1995, 2002), which in turn has stimulated empirical research (among others, Benford 1993; Gerhards and Rucht 1992; Marullo, Pagnucco, and Smith 1996; McCarthy 1994; Nepstad 1997; Weed 1997; Johnson 1997; Johnston and Aarelaid-Tart 2000). Nonetheless, "the question of how participation precipitates the enlargement of personal identity, or the correspondence between individual and collective identities, has not been satisfactorily answered by scholars investigating this linkage" (Benford and Snow 2000, 631; but see Hunt, Benford, and Snow 1994; Hunt and Benford 1994).

The relevance of meaning work can be ascertained by answering the following empirical questions:

- What is the connection between the spread of the movement against neoliberal globalization and the way in which the master frame has been elaborated and negotiated? The answer will be that such a framing process is able to link very different actors from different social, political, organizational, and geographical sites.
- What is the connection between the master frame and activist identification? As we shall see, the master frame "resonates" (Snow and

Benford 1988) with the schemas of activists who belong to different sectors of the movement, as well as of those who mobilize individually.[5]

In order to reconstruct the master frame, we will look at the original call for action against the WTO meeting in Seattle in 1999, the conclusive documents of the WSF held in Porto Alegre, Brazil, in 2001 and 2002; the call for protest against the G8 in Genoa in 2001 and the call elaborated during the ESF held in Florence in 2002. In order to test the resonance of the master frame with activists' schemas, we will analyze the data coming from the questionnaires collected in Genoa in 2001, and at the ESF in Florence in 2002 for the latter case, focusing in particular on participants from Italy, Spain, Britain, Germany, and France.

In order to answer the question whether we are dealing with a mere coalition or with a "real" social movement, we shall analyze the master frame building process and the individual schemas and will contrast individual schemas with the content of the master frame, both cross-country and cross-sector. Finally, we will summarize the empirical results of the chapter and highlight the theoretical relevance of our findings for social movement studies.

The Symbolic Construction of the Global Movement

Sites and Phases of the Master Framing Process

Since Seattle, the contrast between protectionists and neoliberalists was undercut by another cleavage that sets a neoliberal vision in opposition against a neoredistributionist approach (Kaldor 2000). If a social movement expresses a conflict (della Porta and Diani 1999), then the conflict raised by the movement against neoliberal globalization is one between two ways of being cosmopolitan: neoliberal versus egalitarian. This new conflict would not have emerged, however, had social actors not expressed their alternative views of the world.

The countersummit in Seattle shed more light on the process in which NGOs, trade unions, social movement organizations, and other mobilizing structures were building an interpretative schemata capable of lending cohesiveness to various kinds of struggles, campaigns, and mobilizations on different issues while giving them unifying and coherent meaning. From Seattle to Porto Alegre, the movement against neoliberalism tried to make sense of the demand for globalization of rights that had emerged during the collective mobilization of the previous twenty years (Marcon and Pianta, 2002, 6).

The first WSF made it possible to construct alternatives, proposals, and projects that could transform the organizations and movements, which up to then had been acting in uncoordinated opposition against the same international institutions or intergovernmental organizations, into one subject mobilizing on the basis of a shared core of values, beliefs, and goals.

Thus, the master frame was developed through Porto Alegre I (January 2001), Genoa (July 2001), Porto Alegre II (2002), and Florence (November 2002), and continued its development in Europe with the second ESF and all around the world through the organization of macroregional social forums.

One feature of collective frames is that they are "inherently malleable" (Oliver and Johnston 2000, 40), and this enables them to fit into current political contingencies, satisfying the need for continuously negotiating and renegotiating collective identities (Melucci 1996). Collective frames are "adaptive developing structures" negotiated in interactions among subjects: new elements redefining the master frame are added to the original structure as new circumstances emerge (Barlett 1932). Each time the movement mobilizes, there is a new collective negotiation on the basis of a new environment and new joiners. For instance, new conditions emerged from the 9/11 terrorist attack and when the number of the involved individuals and organizations grew from the first WSF (17,000 participants from 27 countries, including 10,000 delegates from organizations, unions, and movements, and 436 MPs) to the second (68,330 participants from 131 countries, including 15,230 delegates representing 4,909 organizations, and 800 MPs). Seattle, Genoa, and the world social forums were cited in the call for the first ESF (Florence, November 2002).

In order to analyze the process of master framing that evolved from Seattle to Florence, we selected five documents jointly created by organizational actors belonging to different sectors of the movement (see chapter 2 in this volume): the calls for protest against the WTO in Seattle 1999 and against the G8 in Genoa 2001, the call of the first ESF, and the two final documents prepared during the world social forums (2001 and 2002). We consider these five documents highly representative since they are the results of a broad exchange of ideas and worldviews by a vast number of organizations.

We will keep in mind the differences between the five documents. We need to distinguish simple, short leaflets from longer, more detailed documents, because the latter provide the actors involved with more scope for explaining their ideas and because the long documents are written after a collective reflection, while the "calls for action" are only meant to mobilize people by means of immediate slogans (see Table 4). The episodes for/in

Table 4. Features of the main events (and related documents) of the movement for global justice

Features	Events					
	Seattle	Genoa	Florence	Porto Alegre I	Porto Alegre II
Date of the event	November 30– December 4, 1999	July 18–22, 2001	November 6–9, 2002	January 25–30, 2001	January 31– February 5, 2002
Type of event	Countersummit	Countersummit	Social forum	Social forum	Social forum
Type of document	Call for action	Call for action and work agreement	Call of the European social movements	Concluding document	Concluding document
Length of document	9 paragraphs	5 paragraphs	4 paragraphs	20 paragraphs	17 paragraphs

which the documents were written are of two types: the Seattle and Genoa leaflets are calls for action for countersummits; the Florence leaflet and the two Porto Alegre documents were elaborated during a social forum. Given the structure of the documents, the cross-temporal analysis will take into account the two long WSF documents on the one hand, and the three short calls on the other.

The Master Frame Structure

Our analysis of the master frame negotiated by different organizations will focus on the dimensions underlined by Snow and Benford (1988, 199–200): the diagnostic dimension—"diagnostic framing involves identification of a problem and the attribution of blame and causality"; the prognostic dimension—"a proposed solution to the diagnosed problem that specifies what needs to be done"; the motivational dimension—"a call to arms for engaging in ameliorative or corrective action."

Beyond these dimensions, we aim to show how part of the framing activities are devoted to the construction of a collective identity. While frames have a "strategic" purpose of mobilizing individuals and collective actors, they are also the "outcome of negotiating shared meaning" (Gamson 1992a, 111). Negotiating shared meanings is a way to build a collective identity (Melucci 1996, 67). As Hunt, Benford, and Snow pointed out, "identity constructions, whether intended or not, are inherent in all social movement framing activities," and frames perform this difficult task by "situating or placing relevant sets of actors in time and space by attributing characteristics to them that suggest specifiable relationships and lines of action" (1994, 185). Therefore, a part of the framing activity is devoted to the specification of an "identity field" that defines the "protagonists," the "antagonists," and the "audience" of the collective action.

We will analyze the dimensions and the relations between the several components of the master frame by showing the "argumentative structure of frames" with the help of tables. As suggested by Johnston (2002), in order to better verify the structure of the argument, we will cite the paragraph numbers of the elements singled out in the text.

"We Are Global"

The march of 300,000 against the G8 in Genoa was opened by a big banner proclaiming "You G8, We six billion." Politics is the sphere within which the friend/foe conflict emerges most clearly, and it is through the framing process that actors define who is the friend, the self, and who is the foe, the other (Hunt, Benford, and Snow 1994).

Table 5 shows the structure of the definition of the self within the five selected documents. The Seattle leaflet refers to "international civil society" (Members of International Civil Society 1999, par. 1), while three years later mesomobilization actors involved in the first ESF claim to be "social and citizenry movements" (European Social Movements 2002, par. 1). From Seattle, through Genoa, to Florence, the less radical definition of "international civil society" became "social movements" from different regions of Europe (ibid.); in both WSFs the actors were defined as "social movements" (World Social Movements 2001, 2002, par. 1). As regards heterogeneity, the leaflets only refer to a geographical difference between subjects, while the first WSF document names different dimensions, claiming that "we are . . . social forces from around the world [that] have gathered here at the WSF in Porto Alegre. Unions and NGOs, movements and organizations, intellectuals and artists" (World Social Movements 2001, par. 1), and again, "women and men, farmers, workers, unemployed, professionals, students, blacks and indigenous peoples, coming from the South and from the North" (ibid., par. 3). The heterogeneousness of the movement became a factor that was attributed symbolic and positive worth at the second WSF, where it was said not only that "We are diverse—women and men, adults and youth, indigenous peoples, rural and urban, workers and unemployed, homeless, the elderly, students, migrants, professionals, peoples of every creed, color and sexual orientation," but also that "the expression of this diversity is our strength and the basis of our unity" (World Social Movements 2002, par. 2).

If we compare definitions of the "self," we see that the first WSF document cites the differences along social, ethnic, gender, political, organizational, and geographic dimensions, while the second WSF document gives fewer dimensions but at the same time underlines how positive these differences are. Against the stigmatizing label "no global" used by the mainstream media, the actors of the movement openly and publicly declare, "We are global" (World Social Movements 2002).

In short, differences in points of views and cultural and political traditions are not only explicit in the documents but are also stated as being a "point of strength" and considered the main feature of the collective subject in mobilization. In other words, as the movement against neoliberal globalization spreads around the world, its internal diversity becomes clear to everyone: public opinion, political institutions, mobilization potential, and so on. In this process multifacetedness becomes an intrinsic element of the movement's collective identity, so intrinsic that it becomes implicit, as it is in the ESF call.

Table 5. Collective identity building in the documents

Collective identity	Event and year					
	Seattle 1999	Genoa 2001	Florence 2002	Porto Alegre I 2001	Porto Alegre II 2002
Self-definition	International civil society	Organizations of the civil society	Social and citizen movements	Organizations and social movements	Organizations and social movements
Dimensions of diversity	Geographical	Geographical	Geographical	Geographical, cultural, political, organizational, social, gender, and ethnic	Geographical, cultural, social, gender, and ethnic
Memory building	Absent	Absent	Present (Seattle, Prague, Nice, Genoa, etc.)	Present (Seattle)	Present (WSF and Genoa)

That we are dealing with the construction of a collective identity is evident in each of the selected documents, but it is even more so in the ESF call, where actors reveal a long "memory": a "narrative identity"[6] of the "Self." In the first WSF document, actors state, "We are part of a movement which has grown since Seattle" (World Social Movements 2001, par. 2). The second WSF document underlines, "We come together again to continue our struggles against neoliberalism and war, to confirm the agreements of the last Forum and to reaffirm that another world is possible" (World Social Movements 2002, par. 2). The ESF leaflet affirms:

> We have come together through a long process: the demonstrations of Amsterdam, Seattle, Prague, Nice, Genoa, Brussels, Barcelona, the big mobilisations against neoliberalism as well as the general strikes for the defense of social rights and all the mobilisations against war, show the will to build another Europe. At global level we recognise the Charter of Principles of the WSF and the call of social movements of Porto Alegre. (European Social Movements 2002, par. 1)

Thus, although the documents of Seattle, Genoa, and Florence are comparable in terms of length, the latter devotes a relevant part to the representation of a collective identity. A collective actor needs a memory in order to perceive the continuity of its existence: "The memory is history in action" (Bauman 1982).

Neoliberalism as the Cause of the Problems

The frame is fleshed out when actors provide a logical connection between themes so that the causes of problems (grievances) are explicitly defined. Different problems can be perceived as having different causes, but if different actors want to mobilize together they must negotiate the logical chain of events that imputes causes to problems. This happens "by identifying culpable agents, be they individuals or collective processes or structures" (Snow and Benford 1992, 137). In the case of the movement against neoliberal globalization, this imputation of common causality has been socially built through what Tarrow (2002) defined as "frame condensation," through which different targets, perceived as causes of the problems, are "condensed" in one "super target."

The process of frame condensation developed especially after the first WSF. In Seattle the target was only the WTO, against which social movement organizations were called to act: "We, the undersigned members of international civil society, oppose any effort to expand the powers of the WTO through a new comprehensive round of trade liberalisation" (Members of

International Civil Society 1999, par. 1). The WTO is quoted twelve times in nine paragraphs. According to social movements, the WTO policies, reinforcing trade liberalization (ibid.), have "contributed to the concentration of wealth in the hands of the rich few; increasing poverty for the majority of the world's population; and unsustainable patterns of production and consumption" (par. 2). The WTO is also opposed because of undemocratic internal procedures (par. 3). In the Seattle leaflet the process of globalization is quoted only twice (par. 4 and 5), as "increasing global economic instability [which brings about] the collapse of national economies, increasing inequity both between and within nations and environmental and social degradation" (par. 4).

Transnational corporations are stigmatized since the WTO and the "Uruguay Round agreements have functioned principally to prise markets open for the benefit of *transnational corporations* at the expense of national economies; workers, farmers and other people, and the environment" (ibid., par. 3; emphasis added). Those agreements (and the liberalization of the market promoted by the WTO in particular) are deemed to provoke social and environmental problems (Table 6).

While in the shorter leaflets explicit reference to neoliberalism is found only in the call of the ESF, in both WSF documents responsibility is attributed to neoliberal globalization that is promoted, reinforced, and defended by a combination of IGOs (WTO, WB, IMF, NATO), a hegemonic superpower (United States), and dominant social actors (multinational corporations) (Table 6). According to the first WSF document, the grievances imputed to the process of neoliberal globalization range from exploitation of workers to poverty; from gender, racial, and ethnic discrimination to environmental problems and the lack of migrant rights. War, too, is logically connected to the process of globalization, represented as an inefficient means for solving the problems triggered by the same process: "Militarism and corporate globalisation reinforce each other to undermine democracy and peace. We totally refuse war as a way to solve conflicts and we oppose the arms race and the arms trade" (World Social Movements 2001, par. 16).

After September 11 and the war in Afghanistan, most of the demonstrations enclose specific calls against terrorism and the war. Since the second meeting of the WSF was held in a climate that had undergone radical change, the diagnostic dimension is again renegotiated and reelaborated. Among the agents of globalization, the United States becomes much more visible and is held responsible for the war, which, in turn, brings about more conflict and discrimination against the Islamic world:

Table 6. The diagnostic dimension of the documents

Causes	Event and year				
	Seattle 1999	Genoa 2001	Florence 2002	Porto Alegre I 2001	Porto Alegre II 2002
Process of globalization	–	–	–	++ (par. 1, 6, 13)	–
Neoliberal model	–	–	++ (par. 1, 2, 4)	++ (par. 2, 4, 6, 8, 14, 16)	++ (title, par. 1, 4, 10, 12)
Capitalism	–	+ (par. 1)	–	–	+ (par. 2)
Dominant cultural model	–	+ (par. 2)	–	+ (par. 1)	+ (par. 4, 8)
IGOs	WTO ++ (par. 1, 2, 3, 5, 6, 7)	G8 + (par. 1)	–	IMF, WB, WTO, G8, NATO + (par. 14, 18)	IMF, WTO, G8 + (par. 6, 9, 15)
USA	–	–	–	+ (par. 16)	+ (par. 4, 8)
Corporations	++ (par. 2, 5, 7)	–	++ (par. 1, 2)	++ (par. 3, 12, 13, 14)	+ (par. 7, 10, 15)
Caused problems					
War	–	–	++ (par. 2, 4)	+ (par. 17)	++ (par. 3, 4, 5, 11)
Social inequality	++ (par. 2, 3, 4)	++ (par. 1, 3)	++ (par. 2, 4)	++ (par. 1, 6, 9, 11, 12)	++ (par. 2, 3, 6, 10, 12, 13 15)
Environmental problems	++ (par. 2, 3, 4)	–	+ (par. 2)	++ (par. 1, 3, 8, 9, 14)	+ (par. 2, 8)
Lack of democratic accountability	+ (par. 3)	–	–	+ (par. 2, 3, 17)	–
Human rights violation	–	–	–	+ (par. 6, 9)	+ (par. 14)
Gender inequality	–	–	++ (par. 2, 4)	+ (par. 5)	+ (par. 2, 3, 13)
Racism	–	–	++ (par. 2, 4)	+ (par. 6)	+ (par. 2, 4, 8)

− not mentioned; + mentioned; ++ central

September 11 marked a dramatic change. After the terrorist attacks, which we absolutely condemn, as we condemn all other attacks on civilians in other parts of the world, the government of the United States and its allies have launched a massive military operation. In the name of the "war against terrorism," civil and political rights are being attacked all over the world. The war against Afghanistan, in which terrorist methods are being used, is now being extended to other fronts. Thus there is the beginning of a permanent global war to cement the domination of the US government and its allies. This war reveals another face of neoliberalism, a face which is brutal and unacceptable. Islam is being demonized, while racism and xenophobia are deliberately propagated. The mass media are actively taking part in this belligerent campaign which divides the world into "good" and "evil." The opposition to the war is at the heart of our movement. (World Social Movements 2002, par. 4)

The U.S. government is also accused of having boycotted multilateral agreements in different domains: human rights, environment, resolution of conflict, and others. The finger is pointed at the United States because it did not sign the Kyoto protocol on environmental problems, and it withdrew from the UN conference against racism (ibid., par. 8).

At the diagnostic level, comparison between the documents of the first and second WSF highlights a more explicit linking of antincoliberalism and anticapitalism–anti-imperialism, with references to the "interests of capital" and the hegemonic power of the United States, which also "protect the interests of big corporations" (ibid., par. 8). It is true that the United States disappears from the ESF leaflet, but we need to recall that during the preparation of the ESF document, in Florence, debate was lively, with the movement being accused of harboring a pathological anti-Americanism. The organizers might have decided not to cite the United States by name in order to avoid such an accusation. The ESF leaflet states that the war, along with other problems, is a direct consequence of the neoliberal model:

We have gathered in Florence to express our opposition to a European order based on corporate power and neoliberalism. This market model leads to constant attacks on the conditions and rights of workers, social inequalities and oppression of women and ethnic minorities, and social exclusion of the unemployed and migrants. It leads to environmental degradation, privatisation and job insecurity. It drives powerful countries to try and dominate the economies of weaker countries, often to deny them real self determination. Once more it is leading to war. (European Social Movements 2002, par. 2)

Condensing the target on neoliberalism (and in other documents neo-liberalism-capitalism-imperialism) allowed a logical connection between the different problems imputed to the same causes. While imputation of common causality bridges different problems such as social inequality, lack of democracy, war, environmental degradation, and so on (see Table 6), social problems are given special emphasis:

> The world in which we are preparing the G8 summit in Genoa is one full of deep injustice; 20 percent of the world population—in countries with advanced capitalism—wastes 83 percent of the resources of our planet; 11 million children die every year of malnutrition and 1.3 billion live on less than one dollar per day. (GSF 2001a)

> The neoliberal economic model is destroying the rights, living conditions and livelihoods of people. Using every means to protect their "share value," multinational companies lay off workers, slash wages and close factories, squeezing the last dollar from the workers. Governments faced with this economic crisis respond by privatising, cutting social sector expenditures and permanently reducing workers rights. This recession exposes the fact that the neoliberal promise of growth and prosperity is a lie. (World Social Movements 2002, par. 10)

Social and Environmental Justice for Another World

Another essential function of the master frame is to find shared solutions for the problems represented. For a mobilization process to be possible in this perspective, not only the causes for the perceived problems but also alternatives to the ongoing situation have to be singled out (see Table 7).

The movement against neoliberal globalization stresses that "another world is possible": a slogan that was not yet present in the Seattle leaflet, but was elaborated during the first WSF (Table 7). In Seattle, the global movement organizations underlined that there are alternatives to the WTO policy regime: a moratorium on trips is "an opportunity for society to change course and develop an alternative, humane and sustainable international system of trade and investment relations" (Members of International Civil Society 1999, par. 9). Although in Seattle it was no more central than other values such as democracy and environmental justice, the most relevant principle on which the mesomobilization leaders based their view of the world was social justice (Andretta et al. 2002, 2003; Andretta and Mosca 2003). The Seattle leaflet contained all the value-based solutions in the seventh paragraph, where the document refers to "development, democracy, environment, health, human rights, workers' rights and the rights of women and children" as well as to "civil society's full participation." Most of these issues are central to both WSF documents (Table 7) and the leaflets of Genoa and Florence.

The prognostic level of the master frame is more detailed in the long WSF documents, where there is room for more specific claims (Table 7). The WSF I document calls for an alternative globalization based on principles different from economic growth and free market, and the dimension of the prognosis focuses especially on social justice while the other dimensions/principles are linked to it. The macroprognosis proposes the "globalization of (especially social) rights" as the solution to poverty, unemployment, and the unequal distribution of resources. In the WSF II document, "social justice" is directly mentioned in the title of the document together with peace and resistance to neoliberalism. Reading the text of the documents, it becomes increasingly clear that "everything" has to do with social justice. Thus, the first WSF document says that "we . . . work for equity, social justice, democracy and security for everyone, without distinction" (World Social Movements 2001, par. 4); the Genoa leaflet refers to the "principles of social justice, solidarity and just and sustainable development" (GSF 2001a); and the title of the second WSF document is *Call of Social Movements: Resistance to Neoliberalism, War, and Militarism for Peace and Social Justice* (World Social Movements 2002).

After Seattle, social justice is always linked to the principle of solidarity. In the Genoa leaflet this link is general, while in other documents the principle of solidarity is referred to for specific situations or populations. The solidarity with the African people is underlined "in defense of their rights to land, citizenship, freedom, peace, and equality, through the reparation of historical and social debts" (World Social Movements 2001, par. 6); the second WSF document calls for mobilizing "solidarity for the Palestinian people and their struggle for self-determination as they face brutal occupation by the Israeli state" (World Social Movements 2002, par. 5).

Social justice is also linked to environmental justice. Not only are global rights extended to nature or the ecosystem, but, as Donatella della Porta (2003a) points out, "new global" movements "underline that most of the victims of the environmental exploitation are the poorest of the planet, forced to live in the most polluted places." In this way postmaterialist demands are embedded in materialist concerns, since environmental problems also affect the material conditions of life:

Table 7. The prognostic dimension of the documents

			Event and year			
Prognostic dimension	Seattle 1999	Genoa 2001	Florence 2002	Porto Alegre I 2001	Porto Alegre II 2002	
"Another world is possible"	–	+ (par. 3)	Another Europe for another world (par. 1, 4, 5); Another world is urgent (par. 3)	+ (par. 1)	+ (par. 2, 5)	
Specific claim 1	Moratorium on TRIPS (par. 6)			Union rights (par. 10, 11, 12)	Debt cancellation (par. 9)	
Specific claim 2	Fair trade (par. 9)			New international rights for employees (par. 12)	Taxation of financial transactions (par. 9)	
Specific claim 3				Rights of free movement (par. 13)	Welfare protection and reinforcement (par. 11)	
Specific claim 4				Debt cancellation (par. 14)	Union rights (par. 12)	
Specific claim 5				Agrarian reform (par. 15)	Multilateral environmental agreements (par. 13)	
Specific claim 6				Multilateral solutions for conflicts (par. 16)	Reinforcement of national policy vs. IGOs (par. 14)	

Principles	Specific claim 7	Specific claim 8		Agrarian reform and abolition of transgenics (par. 15)	Prohibition of military interventions (par. 16)
Social justice	++ (par. 7)	++ (par. 2, 3, 4)	++ (par. 1, 3)	++ (title, 11, 16, 17)	++ (par. 3, 4, 5, 6, 9, 11, 13, 16)
Environmental justice	++ (par. 7)	++ (par. 2, 3, 4)	–	+ par. (11, 16)	+ (par. 3, 8, 9, 14)
Solidarity	–	+ (par. 2, 3)	–	++ (1, 2, 3, 5, 11)	+ (par. 2, 6, 7, 16)
Peace	–	+ (par. 3)	++ (par. 3)	++ (title, 4, 8, 11)	+ (par. 6, 15, 16)
Democracy	++ (par. 7)	+ (par. 4)	–	+ (par. 16)	+ (par. 4, 13)
Human rights	++ (par. 7)	–	–	+ (par. 14, 15)	+ (par. 3, 12, 21)
Women's rights	++ (par. 7)	–	++ (par. 3)	+ (par. 16)	+ (par. 5)
Antiracism	–	–	++ (par. 3)	+ (par. 13)	+ (par. 6, 12)
Fair trade	+ (par. 9)	–	–	–	+ (par. 13)

– not mentioned; + mentioned; ++ central

Neoliberal globalization has led to the concentration of land ownership and favored corporate agricultural systems which are environmentally and socially destructive. It is based on export oriented growth backed by large scale infrastructure development, such as dams, which displaces people from their land and destroys their livelihoods. Their loss must be restored. We call for a democratic agrarian reform. Land, water and seeds must be in the hands of the peasants. We promote sustainable agricultural processes. Seeds and genetic stocks are the heritage of humanity. We demand that the use of transgenics and the patenting of life be abolished. (World Social Movements 2001, par. 5)

Families are forced to leave their homes because of wars, the impact of "big development," landlessness and environmental disasters, unemployment, attacks on public services and the destruction of social solidarity. (World Social Movements 2002, par. 3)

Together with social and environmental justice the antineoliberal movement also proposes peaceful tools for resolving conflicts. The importance of peace is emphasized in the second WSF document after the war in Afghanistan; against U.S. unilateralism, social movements call for multilateral negotiations.

Other values mentioned in the documents are democracy, human rights, women's rights, antiracism, and also fair trade. While the first documents refer especially to democracy from below (Members of International Civil Society 1999; World Social Movements 2001; see also chapter 7 in this volume), or generically demand a more democratic world, democracy becomes a political claim especially within the second WSF document, which states:

people have the right to know about and criticize the decisions of their own governments, especially with respect to dealings with international institutions. Governments are ultimately accountable to their people. While we support the establishment of electoral and participative democracy across the world, we emphasize the need for the democratisation of states and societies and the struggles against dictatorship. (World Social Movements 2002, par. 17)

The Florence document underlines the need for a "social Europe," urged to cut its links with multinational corporations and to concern itself more with social justice and peace (Table 7). While the slogan "another world is possible" became "another world is urgent," the need for "another

Europe for another world" is underlined, stressing that a more social Europe would also ease the spread of alternative models in the world. Social rights are at the core of the prognostic dimension of the ESF call, too. The lack of an explicit reference to the democratization of the EU can be explained by the discord among European social movements about whether or not a macroregional institutional structure such as the EU is needed. As Marcon and Pianta write, "from one side there are those (grassroots movements, and radical groups) that see in a prejudicially hostile way the process of Europe-building, as a pure strategy for building a 'Fortress-Europe.' Others (European Federalist Movement, NGOs, the network for the 'Europe from below', etc.) accept the challenge of Europe-building as an opportunity" (2002, 28–29).

Finally, while a vocabulary of principles exists in each of the selected documents, only the longer WSF documents articulate policy preferences related to those principles (Table 7). The most important specific claims are the protection and the reinforcement of the welfare state, the extension of union rights, a democratic agrarian reform, the taxation of financial transactions, and multilateral agreements for environment and peace.

... From Below

Having defined causes and effects, and having stated that "another world is possible," people are called to mobilize in collective action. Thus, as part of the prognosis, actors utilize "mobilizing" words that call for action. The documents selected often use words such as "struggle," "mobilization," and "resistance" (Table 8):

> We commit ourselves to support all the struggles of our common agenda to mobilise opposition to neoliberalism. (World Social Movements 2001, par. 12)

> We are building a large alliance from our struggles and resistance against a system based on sexism, racism and violence, which privileges the interests of capital and patriarchy over the needs and aspirations of people. (World Social Movements 2002, par. 2)

> We have come together to discuss alternatives but we must continue to enlarge our networks and to plan the campaigns and struggles that together can make this different future possible. Great movements and struggles have begun across Europe: the European social movements are representing a new and concrete possibility to build up another Europe

Table 8. Vocabulary of actions

Vocabulary	Seattle 1999	Genoa 2001	Florence 2002	Porto Alegre I 2001	Porto Alegre II 2002
			Event and year		
Struggle, mobilization, demonstration	−	+ (par. 5)	++ (par. 1, 4)	++ (par. 2, 4, 7, 12, 13, 16, 17, 18, 19, 20, 22)	++ (par. 2, 3, 4, 6, 9, 11, 16)
Civil society meetings	+ (par. 7)	−	+ (par. 4)	+ (par. 3, 4)	+ (par. 2)
Building and strengthening alliances	−	+ (par. 5)	++ (par. 3, 4)	++ (par. 1, 4, 17)	+ (par. 2)
Making aware	−	++ (par. 3, 4, 5)	−	−	−

− not mentioned; + mentioned; ++ central

for another world. We commit ourselves to enlarge our networks for the next year in the following mobilisations and campaigns. (European Social Movements 2002, par. 4)

Also very often stressed is the need to strengthen the network of movements, to widen the network, by building new alliances and broadening the collective identity, once again for more mobilization and more protest campaigns.

Struggle and mobilization are at the core of the call for action, and the question of which kind of protests social movements should perform is explicitly treated in the charter of principles, approved by the WSF International Council in June 2001 and then voted on and passed at the second WSF. This charter of principles, explicitly quoted in the ESF call (European Social Movements 2002, par. 1), states that the movement is against violent practices.

Struggle, mobilization, meetings, and communication both inside and outside the movement are certainly de facto demands for democracy. Since mobilization is becoming more and more constrained by government-implemented public security policies, and participation in them inhibited by violence between some activists and police, the metaquestion of the right to protest becomes central (see also chapter 6 in this volume).

On examining the results of the analysis of the selected documents, we note that the master frame built and negotiated during different counter-summits and social forums provided a bridge between different frames, linking social justice with solidarity and environmental concerns in particular, but also referring to women's rights, peace and democracy, as well as human rights and antiracism. In this framework the problems are attributed to the neoliberal globalization process as well as to capitalism and imperialism. Social justice, solidarity, and environmental justice operate as broker frames, mediating the cognitive connections between different frames. The cognitive connections reinforce the relations between different organizations and sectors: social justice is directly linked with the frames of old social movements (unions, left-wing parties, and radical anticapitalist movements); environmental justice links all the frames that emerged with new social movements; the solidarity frame is widespread among religion-based movements. The frame bridging is provided by a "logical" connection between causes, problems, and solutions.[7] The different frames are bridged by attributing the sectorial problems they evoke to the same macrocause: neoliberal globalization. Finally, democracy, especially democracy from below (direct participation and protest), is to be considered a sort of metaframe, since it constitutes the *conditio sine que non* for the other principles/values to be established.

The master frame provided the symbolic basis for unifying old with new social movements, religious with secular movements, workers with peasant movements, antiauthoritarian women and student movements with more established and bureaucratic unions and leftist parties, "polite" and professionalized NGOs with "impolite" and very loosely connected radical grass-roots movements. The construction of a collective identity that implies such cognitive and organizational connections is especially clear in the documents that, besides giving good reasons for people and groups to network and mobilize, shape an "identity field," a "we" with a "memory" against the construction of a "they," the agents of neoliberal globalization.

Although the "moral basis" of the calls for action is the set of problems that actors impute to neoliberal globalization, it is interesting to note that the motivational dimension of the master frame is built on a cosmopolitan view in which human beings and their ecosystem, on behalf of whom movements claim to act, must be defended. However, when social movements move from the global level to the macroregional one, they tend to culturally specify their struggle, especially by adapting the diagnosis and the prognosis to local situations, without deemphasizing the global dimension of the frame.

Activist Schemas and Master Frame Resonance

If a collective identity process were really at work, the meaning work of meso-mobilization actors should be expected to resonate with that of activists and supporters. In order to analyze individual schemas of the mobilization, we asked ESF participants an open question about what, in their view, was the main goal of the movement. The answers were then classified according to the dimensions stated by respondents. Prior to the quantitative analysis that follows, therefore, an important part of this work was to perform a qualitative interpretation of individual texts.[8] ESF participants mostly referred to the diagnostic and prognostic elements of the master frame structure: only 2.0 percent of respondents referred to a mere antiglobalization schema.

Social justice. As many as 40.9 percent of respondents pointed to the social dimension of the problem and interpreted the movement as a struggle for social rights, workers' rights, and social justice. They emphasized, for instance, that the goal of the movement is "to give the rights back to people of third world countries who have been exploited by the powerful countries of the world." Particular stress was laid on the problem of unequal distribution of resources between north and south, suggesting the possible solutions of cancelling the foreign debt of poor countries and of diffusing and strengthening social rights globally.

Democratization from below. As many as 39.5 percent of participants express the need for a democratization of both IGOs and authoritarian (and democratic) regimes. They also underline that such democratization should be achieved from below, through mobilization and civil society meetings: the call is "to democratize the process of globalization, changing its emphasis toward rights, active citizenship, and participation."

Ethics, values, solidarity. Participants often (34.5 percent) expressed the need for a moral change, of values that are consistent with human relations based on solidarity. In the words used by one of them, the movement should "stimulate a large number of consciences, and above all get people involved in the transformation of minds and life style."

Anticapitalism. Other respondents referred to a classic anticapitalist schema—they wanted "to change the world in a socialist way, to destroy capitalism." In fact, they interpreted the movement's mobilization as against capital, which in this phase is "globalized," or by defining the movement's goal as revolutionary (23.7 percent).

Antineoliberalism. The antineoliberal schema as such was mentioned by 21.1 percent of participants who wanted "to suggest an alternative to the neoliberal model." They referred either to the diagnostic structure of the master frame (mentioning WB, IMF, WTO, or multinational corporations as "agents of neoliberalism") or the prognostic side of the frame, demanding political control of the market at the global level, taxation of financial transactions, and so on.

Ecopacifism. The ecopacifist schema resonates with 16.3 percent of participants. In this case participants stress the need for nature or animal protection and for sustainable development, or they underline the need for peace—e.g., "to preserve cultural identities and biodiversity"; "to reach a world of peace."

Despite the plausible hypothesis that the mobilization of the first ESF, organized especially against the U.S. government threat of war against Iraq, might have stressed a much more pacifist schema, the schemas of the activists in Florence are very similar to those of Genoa in 2001, before September 11: while only 4.1 percent referred to an antiglobal schema, 16.2 percent expressed the antineoliberal frame, 11.1 percent referred to anticapitalism, 37.2 percent to social justice, and 29.8 percent either underlined an ecopacifist frame or stressed ethics and solidarity as the main goals of the movement. Finally, as many as 40.8 percent referred to democracy from below (Andretta et al. 2002, 99). According to the activists of both Genoa and Florence, the war is an effect of neoliberalism.

The relative continuity of the way in which activists frame the world from Genoa to Florence shows that a collective identity with shared ideas is really at work. This is confirmed also by the fact that the activists adopted frames that are relevant in the structure of the master frame: the cause is either neoliberal or capitalist globalization, and the diagnosis is more social justice, more solidarity, more environmental justice, and more democracy.

A first glance at the individual schemas therefore seems to support the hypothesis that the frame bridging operating within the organizational master frame successfully resonates with activists' perception of the political reality they want to change by mobilization.

A Transnational Movement or a Transnational Coalition?

If the meaning work of the mesomobilization actors resonates with individual activists, this does not necessarily mean that we are dealing with a real transnational social movement. On the contrary, one can easily argue that this may be the result of the coalition of different sectors, and that participants mobilize following their own sector, on the basis of their own sectorial frames. This may be interpreted as a successful case of a coalition, with individual sectors recruiting their own micromobilization potential and connecting them with each other in "block recruitment" (Obershall 1973, 117; Jenkins 1983, 62). If what we observe is, instead, a real social movement, then the diffusion of new and similar ideas, values, and frames should be found cross-nation and cross-sector. Three situations can thus be postulated:

1. Ideas shared by activists are influenced by the nationality; the specific political culture, the political cleavages, the types of social movements typical of each country shape activist schemas.
2. Activists adopt above all collective frames that belong to their organizational sectors; thus, activists affiliated with an environmental movement organization adopt an environmentalist frame, and so on.
3. The master frame is widespread; therefore, we observe the minimal condition for a social movement to exist: shared ideas and values.

Table 9 shows the percentage of people from different nations who adopt different schemas. The most relevant differences are the far higher percentage of anticapitalists among UK participants, and the higher percentage of antineoliberals among French and German participants. Social justice, which is at the core of the master frame, is everywhere dominant (particularly in Spain) except in Britain. While ecopacifism is somewhat more concentrated in Britain and Germany, nationality does not affect the distribution of this or of the remaining schemas (see Cramer's V).

Table 9. Schemas of ESF participants by country (reduced sample)

Type of Schema[a]	Country of origin (%)					Total (%)	Cramer's V
	Italy	France	Germany	Spain	United Kingdom		
Antineoliberalism	17.5	31.4	30.1	15.6	13.6	21.1	0.19**
Social justice	43.0	43.0	43.8	54.2	25.8	40.9	0.19***
Anticapitalism	13.2	10.7	15.1	22.9	50.0	23.7	0.37***
Ethics	27.4	43.3	32.4	37.6	31.5	34.5	n.s.
Ecopacifism	16.1	9.2	23.0	14.1	20.8	16.3	n.s.
Democracy from below	43.8	38.3	33.8	42.1	38.5	39.5	n.s.
(Number of interviewees)	(114)	(121)	(73)	(96)	(132)	(536)	(536)

[a] Dummy variables (percentages of yes)

***significant at the 0.001 level; **significant at the 0.01 level; n.s. = not significant

The distribution of schemas reflects the characteristics of the national social movement sector that, in each country, mobilizes against neoliberal globalization—or at least of those who adhere to the ESF. The prevalence of the radical antagonist Globalise Resistance (a network led by the Trotskyite Socialist Workers Party) in the United Kingdom and of the antineoliberal ATTAC in France (where it was founded)[9] and in Germany (where it is particularly strong)[10] seems to confirm this hypothesis.

However, if we check more generally the relationship between sector affiliation and individual schemas (Table 10), we can see that participants do not adopt only sectorial frames. Anticapitalists stress an anticapitalist frame much more than others, and those belonging to the institutional left (unions and leftist parties) adopt the antineoliberal frame a little more than the others. Yet, all frames are present in each sector, and social justice and democratic participation are the most central frames in each sector, except the anticapitalist one. What is more, the structure of the individual schemas of the unorganized (participants with no organizational affiliation) is similar to that of the organized, except for the scanty presence of the anticapitalist schema.

In short, we observe the minimal condition for a social movement to exist: shared ideas and frames. According to the definition of the self, these ideas are plural and intertwined, diverse but not mutually exclusive. This means that participants as well as organizations maintain their own identity, but they contaminate it with other meanings, symbols, and frames.

The Network of the Meanings: Reconstructing the Chaos

So far, we have discussed the ideas of activists by focusing on the dimensions, often more than one, that they referred to in their answers. It is interesting to see what kind of schema participants have bridged when their answer mentions two or more dimensions. While the "ecology of the mind" has been deconstructed for analytical purposes, it is useful to reconstruct individual meanings to single out which schemas participants connect in their "view of the unjust world."

First, we tried to see which are the most common bridging schemas; that is, if somebody refers to one frame, what is the likelihood that she or he bridges it with at least one other? Table 11 shows the correlations between each schema and schema bridging (whether an activist referred to only one schema, or bridged two or more schemas). Most of the schemas appear to be bridged with others, especially those on social justice, ecopacifism, and ethics solidarity. Second, we set out to see which frames are more connected

Table 10. Schemas of ESF participants by sector affiliation (dummy variables)

Types of Schemas	Sector Affiliation (%)					Cramer's V[a]	Unorganized	Cramer's V[b]
	Ecopacifist	Anti-neoliberalist	Anti-capitalist	Local social forums	Total (%)			
Antineoliberalism	16.9	26.0	14.7	20.8	19.7	0.13*	16.1	n.s.
Social justice	31.9	40.5	27.7	27.1	33.2	0.12*	42.6	0.09**
Anticapitalism	6.3	16.1	43.7	18.8	23.3	0.36***	10.6	0.17***
Ethics	39.6	28.7	28.8	20.8	30.7	0.12*	33.9	n.s.
Ecopacifism	22.2	17.6	17.8	18.8	18.8	n.s.	18.0	n.s.
Democracy from below	49.4	42.6	38.1	50.0	43.2	n.s.	42.1	n.s.
(N)	(160)	(242)	(231)	(48)	(681)	–	(672)	–

***significant at the 0.001 level; **significant at the 0.01 level; n.s. = not significant

[a] Cramer's V of cross-tabulation between organized participants only

[b] Cramer's V of cross-tabulation between organized and unorganized participants

with each other (not counting respondents who referred to only one, since we are interested in what kind of connection activists perform when they bridge schemas). Through the results of these correlations we can reconstruct activists' schema bridging. The most striking aspect is that the two most connected schemas are ethics and ecopacifism. It should be noted that this link is the basis of the alliance between new social movements and religious associations (see chapter 2 in this volume). Social justice is especially linked with ecopacifism, while both anticapitalism and antineoliberalism are connected with the idea that global problems can be solved through democratic participation. This is not only a left-wing view, since those interested in ethical issues also believe that democracy is important.

All schemas appear connected with each other. Moreover, ecopacifism emerges as a broker schema that mediates the connection between other important schemas (see Figure 6), while the centrality of democracy shows its metafunction. These networks of meanings, along with the importance of values such as social justice, resonate with the master frame. The activists have given a logical order to the multiple definitions of the reality through their patient negotiation of symbols.

Table 11. Individual schema bridging

Schema bridging[a]	Pearson correlations
Ecopacifism	0.43**
Ethics	0.35**
Social justice	0.31**
Antineoliberalism	0.22**
Democracy from below	0.18**
Anticapitalism	0.10*
Most bridged schemas	
Ethics/ecopacifism	0.24**
Social justice/ecopacifism	0.19**
Anticapitalism/democracy	0.13**
Antineoliberalism/democracy	0.11**
Ethics/democracy	0.10**
(Number of interviewees)	(1,030–1,384)

[a] dummy variable (0 = one frame; 1 = two or more frames)

**significant at the 0.01 level; *significant at the 0.05 level

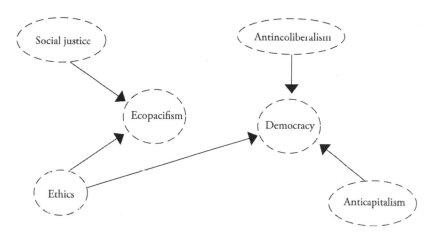

Figure 6. The network of activists' schemas. The arrows reflect existing significant correlations.

Framing Processes and Transnational Movements: Toward a Conclusion

This chapter focused on the symbolic construction of the collective identity on which the movement against neoliberal globalization is based. The hypothesis we suggest is that movements built by interconnecting organizations that differ in their logic of action, type of identity, and country of origin, if they want to succeed in mobilizing and creating a new collective identity, must engage in an intense activity of negotiation with the purpose of building collective frames to be shared by the individual and structural potential mobilizations. Our results confirm, as Gerhards and Rucht (1992) suggested, in addition to temporary and ad hoc alliances for protest campaigns, that framing is central not only for keeping together heterogeneous groups, but also for the construction of a social movement. The master framing enables different themes to be interconnected, convincing groups from different countries and/or active on different issues to join a common struggle: "The larger the range of the problems covered by a frame, the larger the range of societal groups who can be addressed with the frame and the greater the mobilization capacity of the frame" (580).

The master frame also connects the themes and the problems in a logical way, specifying how one is conducive to the others: "the better the various defined problems can be argumentatively connected with each other through a master frame, the more plausible the master frame appears, and the greater the mobilization capacity of the master frame" (ibid., 581).

Finally, the master frame condenses the causes of the various problems into a macrocause, the process of neoliberal globalization: "the more individual problem definitions can be embedded in a generalized world view, the more plausible the problem definitions, and the higher the mobilization capacity of the frame" (ibid., 581). Our analysis confirms that the master frame symbolically integrated the mesomobilization actors of the transnational movement. What is more, the master frame resonates with the system of meanings shared by most of the activists and supporters, as the schema analysis of participants at the Genoa protest and at the ESF of Florence demonstrated. Our findings suggest that the master frame, by bridging social justice, ethics, and environmental justice and by emphasizing democracy from below as a metavalue, provided the symbolic umbrella under which old and new social movements, issues, and organizations have been linked.

Crucially important is the phase of negotiation (and integration) of meaning. The negotiation was successful because it addressed not only interests but mostly identities. The process of meaning negotiation acquires legitimacy from its development in "deliberative settings," such as the social forums and the countersummits.

The result is not a uniform collective identity, which is in any case something the movement opposes, but a strong identification with a collective *process* (as opposed to a collective *subject*). As we saw, activists identify more with the movement than with the single, well-structured organizational bodies that take part in it. Nonconflicting schemas of interpretation, widespread trust, identities, and strong identification are crucial dimensions of the identity of the movement for a globalization from below.

Heterogeneity triggers an ongoing *process* of identity building, open to continual renegotiation. The ensuing collective identity is necessarily plural and open so that dialogue continues during the various protest campaigns against a state of affairs perceived as *unjust*. The discourse is prevalently (both old and new) left-wing and focuses on those values of social justice and democracy, solidarity and the environment. Nowadays, the global movement seems to reflect a search for a redefinition of a (plural) left-wing culture.

As we are going to see in what follows, various conditions facilitate the meaning work and the symbolic integration, or rather the creation, of a collective identity. The development of new technologies, such as the Internet, helps explain how the actors can reach such a high level of networking and of identity negotiation at the global level (Bennett 2003; see also chapter 4 in this volume). Common protest campaigns provide arena and motivation for frame bridging (see chapter 5 in this volume). Especially since one of the most important features of postmodern individuals is their multiple identities, the negotiation of symbols and identities is particularly relevant for today's social movements (Bateson 1990; Epstein 2000; see also chapter 8 in this volume).

4

Global-Net for Global Movements? A Network of Networks for a Movement of Movements

Social Movements and the Internet: An Introduction

The Internet is often considered a symbol of globalization and a means for disseminating ideas and moving capital at the global level. The Internet is both an opportunity and a challenge for social movements. Similar to earlier technological innovations (Tarrow 1998, ch. 3), it has broadened political communication and made it easier and faster. It gives the new movements what printing, the postal system, the telephone, and fax represented for movements in the (far and more recent) past. At the same time, however, it contains risks typical of new technology, namely, generating alienation by eliminating face-to-face contact and increasing hierarchical power structures by centralizing control of complex technology. Both scholars and social movement activists are aware of this complex blend of advantages and risks.

The dimension of communication has always been a strategic dilemma for social movements. The mass media are a significant (often ephemeral) source for attesting a movement's existence: a movement lacking media coverage is, in the public eye, nonexistent (Rucht 2004). Media-spawned communication affects different people in different ways, and this has obliged social movements to seek communication strategies capable of satisfying their own constituencies while increasing support and sympathy within the public opinion. In a comment still relevant today, Michael Lipsky (1965) pointed to the role of the media as selector of information about protest, with violent protest often getting more attention but being stigmatized. Furthermore, the media are not a mere projector (with a greater or lesser degree of accuracy) of the protesters' identity but also a fundamental partner for their interactions (Neveau 2000).

Computer-mediated communication (CMC)—in particular, the Internet—gives social movements the ability to spread uncensored messages and to influence mass media. While social movements have traditionally created their own communication media (including publishing houses, journals, and self-managed radio stations), which were, however, predominantly inward-oriented, the Internet has enormously increased the potential for developing alternatives and making the border between inward- and outward-oriented communication much more permeable. Indeed, CMC differs from the traditional media in that it favors "disinter-mediation," especially facilitating resource-poor actors: movements present themselves directly to the general public with low costs. Some observers optimistically stress the capability of CMC to create a new comprehensive, pluralistic arena for political communication open to social actors whose access to the traditional media is not extensive or unfettered. The "individualized identities" typical of a networked society discover creative forms of organization in the Internet (Castells 1997). Besides making communication easier, the Internet also seems to have some effect on how movements structure themselves by fostering loose ties and ideologically heterogeneous campaigns (Bennett 2003). In fact, the Internet theoretically favors movements with polycentric (and nonhierarchical) forms of organization (Gerlach 2001).

Nevertheless, even within the movement, there is growing concern on the specific problems CMC raises: from commercialization and problems of reliability (Rucht 2003, 26–28) to censorship and control. Many believe that Internet campaigns have "inherently weak mechanisms of information quality control," and the "Internet is a better medium for disseminating information and opinions than for building trust, developing coherence and resolving controversies" (Clark and Themundo 2003, 114).

Scholars also disagree about the effects of CMC in terms of empowerment of the poorer: while some stress a potential equalization (e.g., Myers 2001), others suggest instead either a neutral impact (Margolis and Resnick 2000) or even further concentration of power (McChesney 1996). Not only does CMC seem easier for the elite to use than for the masses, but it also tends to reproduce hierarchy, developing vertical relations instead of interactive, horizontal relationships (Rucht 2003, 28). Online activism could became a low-cost (but low-effect) substitute for offline protest (31).

In social movements, and in other fields too, only recently has empirical research begun to produce more nuanced interpretations of the effects of the Internet as a challenge and an opportunity. In particular, empirical studies on social movements have singled out some specific contributions that the Internet makes to the activities of these collective actors. First, its purely instrumental use is helpful in the organization and logistics of demonstrations and as a means for different groups to keep networked. Second, the Internet can also be a specific means for the direct expression of dissent and protest. Third, it has a cognitive function, enabling information to be disseminated and public opinion to be sensitized on issues scantily covered by mainstream media, and also reinforcing collective identities.

In this chapter we will focus on these uses of CMC by the movement for global justice, with special attention given to the organizations involved in the movement and their activists. The movement for global justice has been particularly interested in the Internet as a means for transnational communication. The emphasis the movement places on its global identity and transnational aims (see chapter 3 in this volume), as well as on a networked organizational structure (see chapter 2), and its attention to the development of alternative knowledge are all factors in the high relevance the Internet has for the movement.

As in the other chapters, we shall present data collected during two supranational protest events: the anti-G8 protest in Genoa in July 2001 and the ESF in Florence in November 2002. In both cases, we analyzed the Web sites of the main organizations involved and interviewed activists using structured questionnaires.[1]

An analysis of the GSF and ESF Web sites and of how activists use the Internet allows us to develop some hypotheses about how certain Internet functions are put to use. We shall discuss the purely instrumental function (stressed by Diani 2001, among others), seeing the Internet as an additional logistical resource for resource-poor actors. We shall analyze the use of the Web as an instrument of protest (della Porta 2003b), the Internet being not only a tool to organize protest but also a means for performing "a new repertoire of collective action" (Cardon and Granjon 2003). We shall study the capability of the Internet to develop a symbolic function (Freschi 2002), favoring identification processes. Finally, we shall consider the cognitive function of the Internet, in particular its potential for informing and sensitizing public opinion on issues given scant coverage by the mass media (Warkentin 2001).

Organizing via the Internet

The Internet provides social movements with a cheap and fast means of international communication that lowers mobilization's cost and favors highly flexible, loose organizational structures. The Internet "becomes an organization force shaping both the relation among organizations and, in some cases, the organizations themselves" (Bennett 2003, 156). CMC facilitates internal and external communication, enabling the same message to be sent simultaneously to hundreds of addresses, overcoming barriers in space and time. Being horizontal, bidirectional, and interactive (Bentivegna 1999), the Internet favors participatory organizational processes (Warkentin 2001). Whenever the networked organizational structure of contemporary social movements reaches across international borders, CMC makes it easier to transform groups of geographically dispersed individuals into a densely connected population, resolving one fundamental problem of mobilization (Diani 2001). Organizational structures can be shaped by CMC since, as Smith writes, "the advancement of communication and transportation technologies has made more decentralized organizational structures viable" (1997, 58). According to Castells, the Internet "fits with the basic features of the kind of social movements emerging in the Information Age. . . . To build an historical analogy, the constitution of the labour movement in the industrial era cannot be separated from the industrial factory as its organizational setting . . . the Internet is not simply a technology: it is a communication media, and it is the material infrastructure of a given organizational form: the network" (2001, 135–36). As Naomi Klein observed, the use of the Internet is "shaping the movement on its own web-like image," with hubs at the center of activities, and spokes "that link to other centers, which are autonomous but interconnected" (2002, 16).

Most scholars agree that, at least in the short run, CMC's impact on organizational structures would be highly varied: organizations with a longer history would be reluctant to adopt CMC and, even when they do, they would continue to use it similarly to the old media of communication without exploiting many of its more innovative aspects such as interactivity. In fact, while "newer, resource-poor organizations that tend to reject conventional politics may be defined in important ways by their Internet presence" (Bennett 2003, 145), established organizations seem to have a conservative approach toward CMC (Smith 1997). As Tarrow argues, "the Internet as a form of movement communication has had a more transformative effect on new movement organizations than on established ones, which continue to rely more on face-to-face communication and on conventional organizational channels of communication" (2003, 31). But we should also consider that some resources available to an organization facilitate more effective use of the Internet—as some findings on political parties (Margolis and Resnick 2000) and NGOs (Warkentin 2001) seem to point out.

Research on nonconventional (and conventional) political participation has stressed that the organization of supranational protest has very high transaction costs—which may go some way toward explaining why protest remains at a national if not at a local level despite the fact that higher competencies are devolved at the international level. However, the Internet has substantially reduced the cost of communicating with a large number of individuals spread all around the globe. Already during the campaign against land mines, it was observed that "the global web of electronic media, including telecommunications, fax machines, and especially the Internet and the World Wide Web, have played an unprecedented role in facilitating a global network of concerned supporters around the issue" (Price 1998, 625). In the last few years, the use of CMC has been crucial in the organizational phases of very large, transnational demonstrations that have been staged with a frequency and number of participants previously unheard of. CMC makes organizing transnational mobilization easier, whether in the form of a series of demonstrations all going on at the same time in different countries (as happened in the hundreds of demonstrations against the war against Iraq on February 15, 2003) or in the form of protest events in one place with the participation of activists from different states and continents—as was the case of the WSF. Connected rapidly and cheaply over the Internet, networks of activists and an increasing number of global organizations have worked together in Seattle, Genoa, Porto Alegre, Florence, Paris, and elsewhere.

For the transnational meetings held in Genoa and Florence, the Internet had an important logistic function. The site of the GSF, which coordinated the protest in Genoa, contained a map of the city with meeting points, a calendar of the activities during the days of the protest, some documents, press releases, informational material, and links to the various organizations that signed the "working agreement" (the document containing the main rules and guidelines of the Genoa protest that the organizations of the GSF committed themselves to respect). Just how international the event was appeared manifest by its multilanguage Web site: the most important documents were available in English, French, German, Italian, Portuguese, and Spanish.

Similarly, CMC made it possible for the organizers of the ESF to considerably lower the costs of mobilization by providing virtual visitors with information on the genesis and objectives of the social forum, its official program, and its preparatory and conclusive documents. Visitors to the Web site could register for the forum online and book a place to stay during the ESF (many of which were offered free of charge by Florentines). An online forum was created to discuss and make decisions on the official program: everyone could propose (and organize, once accepted) a specific workshop. The ESF Web site was used to recruit voluntary work and volunteers for fund-raising and appeared in English, French, German, Italian, and Spanish.[2] The ESF Web site was particularly attentive to communicating the content of the forum and made a press area available with news, press releases, press clippings, and a press kit with the basics on the ESF. Here, activists and professional journalists created an open space for exchanging information in which every type of material (documents, texts, audio and video products) produced at and about the ESF could be uploaded, downloaded, and freely used and distributed, bypassing copyright rules. Constant and frequent access to a nonpublic mailing list allowed the spokesmen of the main organizational sectors to organize social forums and other forms of mobilization.

The main networks of organizations involved in the Genoa and Florence protests also had their own Web sites. The international platform of ATTAC facilitates diffusion throughout the intercontinental network because the global mailing list assures rapid communication and a notable saving of money. It also guarantees democratic transparency in communications (ATTAC 1998). According to Christophe Ventura, the person entrusted with international relations in the French branch of the association, the creation of the ATTAC associations outside of France is a spontaneous phenomenon in which the Web site has played an important role (in Ancelovici 2002).

During the organization of the Genoa events, the Web site of Rete Lilliput (the Italian ecopacifist network) was frequently updated with documents, information, bibliographical references, and articles written on particularly successful initiatives held by local branches. It also contained links to the associations who promote the network and its friends. Online petitions and campaigns are frequently promoted and supported from this Web site.

The network of anticapitalist organizations (mainly social centers) also uses the Internet extensively. During the anti-G8 protest, the European Counter Network Web site was particularly rich and interactive, publicizing and coordinating protests and campaigns. Furthermore, the perception of the usefulness of the Internet can be seen in the number of Italian social centers that, in addition to having pages on this Web site, have created their own specific domains.

Genoa and Florence were nothing new in this respect. Even before Seattle, organizing supranational protest was made easier by Web sites devoted to specific events, the majority of which disappeared after the event, leaving behind a valuable archive for us to study. These Web sites contained information on the various initiatives leading up to the demonstrations and on the logistics of the protest events themselves.

As our data confirm, CMC is a fundamental means of communication among activists of the global justice movement: in Genoa, 64.9 percent of interviewees declared that they used the Internet regularly; in Florence 94.1 percent stated that they used it at least once a month, and almost 50 percent daily (Table 12). The difference in how activists of different nationalities use the Internet does not reflect the general differences in Internet rates of access among selected European countries (northern Europe is more connected than southern). In general, as other research had already indicated (Bédoyan, Van Aelst, and Walgrave 2004), activists from abroad tended to make more frequent use of the Internet than did locals.

While the Internet provides social movements with the means for managing logistics, the extent to which it has an equalizing effect is still an open question. Reflecting on this, McChesney (1996) talks of a "partial" public sphere in cyberspace, access to the Internet being limited to an elite with high levels of education and income, while female and older cohorts are less present. Indeed, the Internet is the cause of a new form of inequality that has been described as the digital divide. Differences emerge in Internet access between different territorial levels (not only rich regions versus poor ones but also between rich and poor people in the wealthy nations), different social classes in the same nation (penalizing those lacking economic and cultural resources), and between social sectors with different degrees of interest in politics (favoring groups of citizens already active and interested in politics) (Norris 2001). If the digital divide seems to decline in some geographical areas, however, this trend is not homogeneous (Castells 2001, ch. 9). It is significant that institutions of global governance have recently inserted the issue of digital divide in their agenda.

Our data on ESF participants confirm that movements suffer a certain degree of digital divide, but also point to the role played by the movement organizations in socializing their members in the use of the Internet. In order to explain the differential use of the Internet by our activists, we tested five hypotheses that we considered plausible:

1. *Socio-demographic hypothesis.* Since all surveys indicate that the selectivity of Internet access is linked to gender, age, education, and income, sociodemographic features could explain Internet use.
2. *Media consumption hypothesis.* People desirous to obtain information and who have the means to access it tend to use a variety of different sources, and previous trends in communication media consumption could explain the use of the Internet.

Table 12. Use of the Internet by ESF participants' countries (reduced sample)

Internet use	Italy	France	Germany	Spain	United Kingdom	Total (%)	Retrocumulative (%)
			Country of origin (%)				
Never	9.5	7.2	0.0	6.2	4.1	5.9	100.0
Once a month	6.8	8.0	4.8	2.7	6.8	6.0	94.1
Once a week	10.9	8.7	6.0	9.7	10.1	9.4	88.1
Several times a week	32.7	25.4	37.3	25.7	37.2	31.5	78.7
Daily	40.1	50.7	51.8	55.8	41.9	47.2	47.2
(Number of participants)	(147)	(138)	(83)	(113)	(148)	(629)	(629)

Note: Cramer's V = .099 (nonsignificant).

3. *Organizational belonging hypothesis.* Since social movement organizations (SMOs) can motivate marginal and disadvantaged subjects to participate, present or past membership in SMOs that use the Internet can play an important role in extending Internet access and literacy.

4. *Participation hypothesis.* Since CMC influences the possibility of participation in politics (Hill and Hughes 1998), those who are more politically committed will be more motivated to use this new media in order to enhance their participation; taking part in an election or a similarly wide repertoire of action would suggest also making use of the Internet.

5. *Cosmopolitan identity hypothesis.* Seeing oneself as belonging to large-scale territories (Europe or the world) is generally linked to a cosmopolitan mentality; here the use of the Internet would be particularly developed since it enables information to be obtained on different countries and fosters contacts with people in other countries.

The effect of these sets of variables on CMC has been checked empirically using a model of binary logistic regression (Table 13). We transformed the "use of the Internet" variable in a dummy variable excluding the three intermediate categories of the original (five-point scale) variable. This decision stems from previous analyses of the same database that indicated clearly that the main differences in Internet use were between two groups: nonusers and daily users (Mosca 2003). The backward stepwise method confirmed the influence of sociodemographic variables (among them education, with a regression coefficient[3] of 4.36, significant at the 0.001 level; age, with 2.84, significant at the 0.01 level; and gender, with −2.24, significant at the 0.05 level), but also highlighted the positive influence of listening to news on the radio (regression coefficient 2.07, significant at the 0.05 level) and the negative impact of disruptive forms of participation (−2.30, significant at the 0.05 level). The most important variable in the model, however, is familiarization with new technologies (in particular, past/present use of CMC in organizations to which the interviewee belonged/belongs to) (regression coefficient 6.66, significant at the 0.001 level).

This suggests that if an individual has used the Internet inside an organization, the probability of frequent use of it afterward increases. We can thus suggest a general hypothesis: if CMC is used by the organization an individual belongs to, accessing the Internet tends to become an important activity for previously "unwired" individuals. This hypothesis stresses the role of the organization in making its members familiar with new technologies and suggests that the model of (socioeconomic) centrality is

Table 13. Determinants of Internet use by ESF participants (binary logistic regression model)

Use of the Internet (dummy)	T statistics
Sociodemographic variables:	
Gender (woman = 0)	−2.24*
Age (four categories)	+2.84**
Level of education (three categories)	+4.36***
Media consumption:	
Listen to radio news (four degrees of frequency)	+2.07*
Organizational variables:	
Familiarization with CMC in organizations to which the interviewee belonged/belongs (dummy)	+6.66***
Participation variables:	
Disruptive forms of participation (additive)	−2.30*
Constant	−0.11
Cox & Snell R square	0.15
Nagelkerke R square	0.34

Note: The variables were entered in the order presented in the table; a backward stepwise method was applied.

Note: The variable "age" had the categories 18 or older, 19 to 25, 26 to 35, 36 and older; the variable "level of education" had the categories primary school completed, secondary school completed, higher level of education.

***significant at the 0.001 level; **significant at the 0.01 level; *significant at the 0.05 level.

not a satisfactory explanation, either for political participation in general (Pizzorno 1993) or for participation in the information society. This hypothesis is furthermore supported by other studies that have already indicated that, in the south of the world especially, NGOs have made marginal social groups familiar with political use of the Internet. Information on Chiapas spread thanks to the technological support provided by a Mexican group of NGOs (Cleaver 1995, 1998; Castells 1997). An analysis of Web site links points to the brokerage role played by the Zapatistas Global Support: "Zapatista-related sites are crucial to global NGO networks, and contribute to binding them" (Garrido and Halavis 2003, 181). NGOs also performed an important role in the creation of the first electronic networks, which allowed social movements to become independent of government support in their use of CMC (Stubbs 1998).

There is, however, no technology-driven homogeneity in the use of CMC. As we shall see in more detail, different organizational sectors of the movement as well as their activists make different uses of CMC. As shown in Figure 7, if we cross-check ESF participants' use of the Internet with their sectorial affiliation (ecopacifist, antineoliberalist, anticapitalist), we find that CMC is more used by organized activists than by nonorganized ones. This is particularly true for ecopacifists and antineoliberalists, while the pattern of Internet use by anticapitalists is more similar to that of non-organized participants.

The Internet is especially used as a way to access circuits of alternative information (90.7 percent), to obtain information on what protest events a movement is organizing (84.5 percent), and to get immediate data on the contents, program, and logistics of the forum (79.7 percent) (see Figure 8). Activists use CMC not only to gather information but also to exchange opinions and to participate in online surveys and petitions. The online petition seems to be the best-known and most-used protest tool (used by 66.1 percent of the sample), while the Net strike—which will be examined in the next section—is less present, although still a significant tool (19.2 percent have used it). While those who use the traditional media of press and television are more numerous, the role of the Internet in political communication and mobilization is evident when one considers that 62.2 percent of Internet users state that CMC influenced, at least "a little," their decision to participate in the Genoa demonstration (Andretta et al. 2002). It is interesting to note that political use of the Internet is more frequent among activists who belong to the principal networks of the movement.

Organizational sectors, moreover, have certain peculiarities in the way

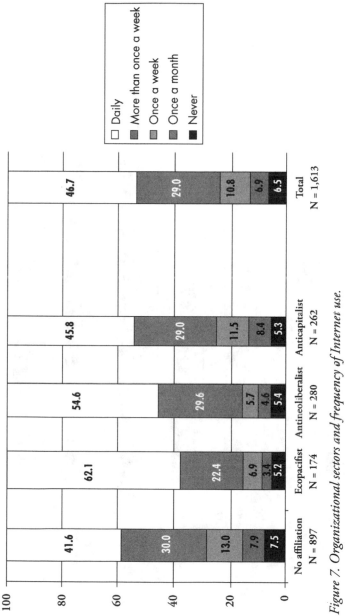

Figure 7. Organizational sectors and frequency of Internet use.

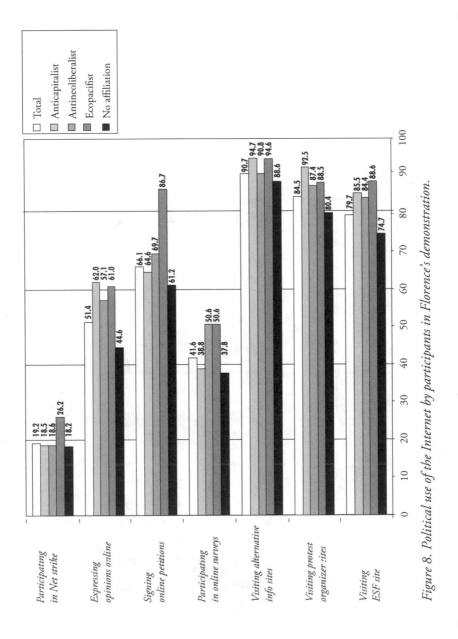

Figure 8. Political use of the Internet by participants in Florence's demonstration.

they use the Internet. Anticapitalists make less use of online surveys and petitions (they are apparently aware that this can lead to violation of privacy, an important factor for them since they tend toward more disruptive forms of protest) and use the Internet mainly to find out about alternative Web sites (94.7 percent) and to gather information on protest organizations (92.5 percent). Ecopacifists log on to the Internet for many reasons, particularly to take part in online surveys and petitions and to express political opinions online (a characteristic they share with anticapitalists). More than a quarter of ecopacifists take part in Net strikes. The use of CMC by antineoliberalists is very similar to the average, with a preference for online surveys and petitions.

Protesting over the Internet

As mentioned earlier, the Internet is also a means for *protest* and is exploited for online mobilization and the performance of acts of dissent. This is the case for online petitions, Web site defacement or cloning, Net strikes, and mail bombings. The term "electronic advocacy" refers to "the use of high technology to influence the decision-making process, or to the use of technology in an effort to support policy-change efforts" (Hick and McNutt 2002, 8). Most hackers who log on to the Internet to participate in online protest belong to the global justice movement and raise specific issues such as free access to information (in particular, against copyright and for free software) and right to privacy (Castells 2001, ch. 2; Freschi 2003; Jordan 2002).

CMC has made it possible to conduct campaigns beyond borders against transnational corporations such as De Beers, Microsoft, Monsanto, Nike, and others, especially via *online petitions* (some students even talk of "dot-causes," see Clark and Themundo 2003). International mobilization through online petitions also denounced certain human rights violations and the death penalty, putting pressure on governments. These campaigns grew to be less centrally controlled, more difficult to turn on and off, and always changing in terms of networks and goals (Bennett 2003, 150).

One tactic used by online activists is to create *Web sites* (with domain names such as http://www.worldbunk.org or http://www.whirledbank.org) that mock international organizations and their activities. Similarly, fake Web sites are built using the names of international organizations (e.g., http://www.gatt.org or http://www.seattlewto.org or http://www.genoa-g8 .org) in order to attract users looking for the official Web sites (Vegh 2003).

Another form of online protest, the *Net strike,* proliferated in recent years among radical organizations as a "virtual practice for real conflicts" (according to the association StranoNetwork; see Freschi 2000, 104). Net striking consists of a large number of people connecting simultaneously to the same domain at a prearranged time in order to jam a site considered a symbolic target, which makes it impossible for other users to reach it. The mobilization and its motivation is normally communicated in advance to the owner of the site against which the Net strike will be made. A Net strike is comparable to a physical procession that occupies a road to make it inaccessible. When a Net strike is in progress, online protesters activate a channel of communication (generally a chat line or a mailing list) in order to coordinate their action of protest. A Net strike was promoted against the WTO Web site during the protests in Seattle, ideally linking offline and on-line environments (Jordan 2002). Some groups prefer Net striking to online petitions because a petition allows the construction of a database containing personal information, and that is considered a threat to privacy.[4]

Similar to the Net strike, but less used, *mail bombing* consists of sending e-mails to a Web site or a server until it overloads and gets jammed. This online form of action was criticized because "its eventual success does not depend on the force of the arguments but on the mere power of computers and bandwidth available to the aggressor as compared with that of the victim" (Carlos 1997). Both Net strikers (how to distinguish between users and protesters among people connecting to a Web site?) and mail bombers are not easily identifiable since they normally use encryption software to safeguard their privacy and to keep their identity hidden.

Cyberprotest is promoted by one of the most important Web sites of the Italian social centers (http://www.ecn.org). The European Counter Network (ECN) represents the virtual place for cohabitation and meeting of most Italian social centers. In fact, it "has favoured a great external visibility, but above all a great mutual knowledge between the different local experiences of the movement" (Freschi 2000, 98). It represents a sort of platform to coordinate mobilization, support protests and campaigns, and allow people to exchange opinions.

During the Neapolitan protests against the UN Global Forum (in March 2001), prior to the Genoa protest, some organizations promoted Net strikes to challenge the forum. After some initial success, the Web site that offered technical information for protesting online (http://www.netstrike .it) was closed by the judiciary. However, the information immediately spread within cyberspace, and the Web site involved was cloned and reproduced on about ten servers in different countries that were not subject to Italian magistracy (Jordan 2002).

Our data on ESF participants show that the more an individual is connected to the Internet, the more she or he uses all the participatory possibilities offered by CMC: from consultation of sites related to organization of protest events and alternative information to participation in online surveys and petitions, to expression of opinions and participation in Net strikes (Kendall's Tau ß varies from 0.21 for participation in Net strikes to 0.30 for participation in online petitions, all significant at the 0.01 level).[5]

While online petitions, campaigns, and Net strikes are often ignored by those they are directed against (Rucht 2003), their impact on observers depends on how much they capture the attention of the mass media (Gurak and Logie 2003, 26) and leads more to loss of face than loss of money (Vegh 2003). Beyond the concrete effects, however, it has been repeatedly observed that the use of online activism can replace offline activism—thus becoming a simulacrum of real protest.

In order to test this hypothesis, we analyzed to what extent online and offline forms of protest exclude each other. As our data show (Table 14), there is no negative correlation between online and offline activism: offline and online protests are strongly related and tend to reinforce each other.

Table 14. Correlations between online and offline forms of action (Pearson correlations)

	Online forms of action	
Offline forms of action (dummy variables)	Petition	Net strike
Convincing someone to vote for a party	n.s.	n.s.
Party activism	n.s.	n.s.
Petitions, referendums	0.18**	n.s.
Leafleting	0.07**	0.11**
Public meetings	0.06*	0.06*
Strikes	0.02	0.09**
Sit-ins	0.06*	0.14**
Boycotts	0.15**	0.12**
Occupation of schools or universities	n.s.	0.06*
Occupation of abandoned buildings	n.s.	0.16**
Violence against property	n.s.	0.14**
Voting	0.07**	−0.14**
Demonstrating	0.06*	n.s.
(Number of participants)	(1,261–1,533)	(1,253–1,524)

**significant at the 0.01 level; *significant at the 0.05 level; n.s. = nonsignificant.

Sometimes they are resorted to simultaneously to heighten protest visibility. In particular, some online forms of action are correlated with specific forms of offline protest: online petitioners are more likely to be also offline petitioners and boycotters, while Net strikers have a more varied (mainly unconventional and radical) offline repertoire of action.

Internet and Nonvirtual Identities

Cyberspace has been singled out as a promising setting for deliberative forms of democracy.[6] Scholars of social movement have underlined its capacity to generate new identities. For example, Park observed that "not only the formation of collective identity is easier due to the Internet's ability to put [together] people of similar grievances in disparate geographical areas, but also the diffusion of collective identity is faster and easier" (2002, 19). If Diani (2001) claims CMC's contribution to the collective identities of social movements is mainly in reinforcing existing ones, Freschi (2002) studied how virtual communities can develop an identifying function, creating social networks with internal solidarity and common beliefs, acting online and offline. In fact, "real communities can and do take root in Internet-based space" (Gurak and Logie 2003, 43).

Our research indicates that CMC is conducive to making people think. Online forums and mailing lists favor discussion on specific topics (such as logistics, forms of actions, agreements among organizations, and slogans) before a protest begins and, later on, collective reflection on demonstrations among distant activists. Before the countersummit in Genoa, the Internet provided occasions for dialogue within the movement. Discussion forums and mailing lists facilitated the emergence of common interpretative schemas among activists and organizations. In particular, the activists of Lilliput (http://www.retelilliput.org) made extensive use of the Internet, not only to spread information but also to discuss internally themes of interest (for instance, with a list focusing on the G8 countersummit), through a national, regional, and local system of newsletters and mailing lists.

Local groups use mailing lists to communicate between one (physical) meeting and another. The Web site of Lilliput periodically activates lists of discussion on issues that the organization puts on its agenda, allowing interaction between geographically distant subjects in discussion and in the preparation of events such as regional and national meetings. Some weeks before the G8 summit in Genoa, the Lilliput site had a chat line that enabled synchronous discussions between visitors. After Genoa, the Web site promoted online surveys among its users to express their opinions about the GSF and to canvass opinions on various forms of mobilization in particularly delicate protest events.

Before the Genoa protest, the Web site of the Tute Bianche (White Overalls) (http://www.tutebianche.org) hosted a lively discussion forum on which forms of action should be adopted in Genoa. Recalling the Zapatistas' experience of *consulta* (Cleaver 1998), they promoted a referendum asking cybervoters: "(a) Will you support disobedience to the ban on demonstrations and the enclosure of forbidden areas? (b) Do you think that mass invasion of a forbidden area is a viable common purpose? (c) Do you agree that people need collective self-defense in order to keep the police off, avoid man-to-man fights, degeneration, beatings, and mass arrests?"[7] The consultation was published in four languages and received significant mass media attention and coverage.

Their presence on the Web enabled organizations of the GSF and the ESF, even the more radical ones, to base their protest activity against the G8 on transparency and publicity. From the analysis of mailing lists (Cristante 2003) that were accessible on their Web sites, it can be seen that the debate has been opened also to very different actors.

This leads us to another question: the type of identity fostered by the Internet. A broad range of empirical studies seems to indicate that Internet users have richer social relationships (Hampton and Wellman 2001; Haythornthwaite 2001a; Howard, Rainie, and Jones 2001; Katz, Rice, and Aspden 2001; Nie 2001; Müller 2002). According to one of these studies, online networks often have their roots in offline ones, with a strong overlap between the two environments, and furthermore, "online communication services broaden the network of social relations, providing access to people and information, not only on a *global* level, but also in a geographically smaller *regional* or *local* context" (Müller 2002, 8). According to other empirical research, "The Internet favors glocalization: it increases the local contacts as the global ones [increase]" (Hampton and Wellman 2001, 492). Caroline Haythornthwaite (2001b) suggests that a medium such as e-mail can be established to act as a diffuse, background contact mechanism, connecting the very weakest of ties, and requiring little work by the individual to access the social network. CMC can create connections between distant, isolated networks, favoring collective action toward a common goal.

In theory, the Internet fosters pluralist, open identities. If the Internet multiplies the stock of social ties for individuals, allowing them to activate a wide and variegated net of latent ties,[8] transforming them into weak ties (Granovetter 1973), we might expect a greater opening toward the external environment from people using CMC and, accordingly, a greater availability to identify with a broad range of collective actors. Indeed, Internet enables contact to be made between individuals completely unknown to each other (when the knowledge is mediated by the common affiliation to shared spaces for communication such as newsgroups or mailing lists) or to maintain very weak ties through irregular, occasional exchanges of messages. This process is enhanced since "in sharp contrast to telephoning, online messages are extremely non-intrusive because receivers can retrieve, read, store (or delete) and answer them at any chosen time" (Geser 2001). Therefore, CMC enables the establishment and maintenance of a broader stock of latent ties that can then be activated very quickly and used selectively according to each situation and specific necessity (Geser 2001). As a research study on peace activists in eight nations indicated, the more that individuals participate in multiple types of organizations, the more frequently they use the Internet (Bennett, Givens, and Willnat 2004). However, other researchers stressed a sort of balkanization of the Web, with a tendency for Web users to contact only groups with an ideology similar to their own. For instance, Sunstein (2001, 59) applied a link analysis to a random sample of sixty political Web sites and found that only 15 percent provided links to Web sites with different opinions, while almost 60 percent linked with Web sites of the same ideological orientation as themselves. Furthermore, when a site publishes a link to a site that holds an opposing view, it normally does so to criticize it.

We assessed the impact of CMC on identification processes at a micro-level with the ESF survey data. In our model, we considered a broad set of variables in order to point out the main causes for people identifying with the movement, an organizational sector, or a specific group.[9] While sociodemographic variables are not relevant, such processes are particularly influenced by organizational belonging (although there is a high percentage of nonorganized individuals who have a high level of identification with the movement in general and with an organizational sector), by previous participation in demonstration (which increases identification with a movement sector), and by a cosmopolitan vision (which means identification with the whole world). Media consumption can also play a role in identifying with a social movement or an organizational sector. It is interesting to note that the Internet has an influence in the identification process with a specific organization (regression coefficient 2.65, significant at the 0.01 level) and an organizational sector (regression coefficient 2.09, significant at the 0.05 level), but not in the identification process with the movement in general. Hence, if the Internet strengthens identification, this is especially true under conditions of ideal or ideological proximity such as in the case of areas of the movement or specific organization characterized by internal homogeneity (in regard to frames and forms of action). We also considered that if the Internet tends to produce a higher trust in the movement, it should also be positively correlated with multiple membership—which, in general, has an important role to play in integrating different areas of a movement (della Porta and Diani 1999; see also chapter 2 in this volume), encouraging participation and favoring mobilization of resources, and stimulating information exchange and the adoption of convergent interpretative schemas. The processes of exchange established on an interpersonal and inter-organizational level have positive effects because they promote cooperation and diffusion of trust. In fact, in our data, we found a significant correlation between multiple membership and use of the Internet (Kendall's Tau ß is 0.15, significant at the 0.05 level).[10]

Trust is often considered as easily spreading from one object to another. In order to evaluate if the use of the Internet accounts for trust in institutions and political actors, the data set was tested for the difference in trust between the group of interviewees not using the Internet at all and the group of interviewees who use it daily.[11] Our data indicate, however, that if controlled by other variables (particularly education), the use of the Internet does not explain trust in different institutions.

Spreading Information via the Internet

The Internet also has a *cognitive function* through information dissemination and gathering. A case often quoted is the *Ejército Zapatista de Liberación Nacional*, which attracted attention via the Internet on a region of the globe that was until then virtually unknown and on a mobilization that the traditional mass media had neglected. Online resource networks facilitate organization: they function as a common Internet getaway to hundreds of NGOs; they offer them and individual activists Internet-based services; they provide established means for the affiliates to communicate; they serve as information resource sites for whoever is interested (Warkentin 2001, 143). Also, new media like the Internet can influence the traditional mass media (among others, Bennett 2003).

Epistemic communities and advocacy networks (Keck and Sikkink 1998) communicate information on global issues; they highlight the negative consequences of economic globalization and point to possible alternatives to neoliberalism. They encourage the creation of the movement for global justice by providing alternative knowledge on specific issues, as well as access and visibility on the Web, and link organizations acting in different parts of the globe. Beyond supranational protest events, long-lasting campaigns make use of the Internet: "weblogs, lists, and networked campaign sites create an epistemic community that makes the campaign a source of knowledge about credible problems, while making the target an example of both problems and solutions" (Bennett 2003, 153). Within the global justice movement, some organizations specialize in the diffusion of information via the Internet. The Institute for Global Communication (IGC), the Association for Progressive Communication (APC), and OneWorld are online resource networks that operate as Internet portals for a large number of NGOs. The IGC (http://www.igc.org) is a network of networks, incorporating PeaceNet (pacifist portal promoting the constructive resolution of conflicts), EcoNet (the world's first computer network dedicated to environmental preservation and sustainability), WomensNet (portal advancing the interests of women worldwide), and AntiRacismNet (platform providing information and technical support for those interested in issues of civil rights, racism, and diversity-related issues). LaborNet—also originally part of the IGC, and now with an autonomous network (http://www.labornet.org)—connects labor protest on the Internet. Another anti-neoliberal portal focusing on the issue of labor and unemployment is the Web site of Euromarches (http://www.euromarches.org), created in 1997 to mobilize against unemployment, insecure jobs, and poverty in Europe. As the site specifies, "within this network, these organizations regularly exchange information, experiences and reflections, defining what they have in common; they elaborate common claims at the EU level and organize together some actions at this level."

In 1990, the IGC cofounded the APC (http://www.apc.org) in partnership with six international organizations, creating an international coalition operating in more than 130 countries that includes twenty-five affiliated (wholly autonomous) members and forty partners. Since 1995, the APC has had consultative status to the UN Economic and Social Council (ECOSOC). Its mission consists of empowering and supporting organizations, social movements, and individuals in and through the Internet in order to contribute to equitable human development, social justice, participatory political processes, and environmental sustainability.

OneWorld (http://www.oneworld.net) claims to be the online media gateway that most effectively informs a global audience about human rights and sustainable development. It created themed portals on AIDS (http://www.aidschannel.org), the knowledge divide (http://www.learningchannel.org), the digital divide (http://www.digitalopportunity.org), and for counterinformation in general (http://www.mediachannel.org). Besides OneWorld, there are lots of networks that promote alternative and critical information, such as the French Samizdat (http://www.samizdat.net), the German Nadir (http://www.nadir.org), the Spanish Nodo50 (http://www.nodo50.org), and the Italian ECN. For instance, Nodo50, similar to other networks located in Europe, is a server hosting alternative and anticapitalist groups (over 750); it was created in 1994 to provide virtual support to the "¡50 años bastan!" (Fifty years is enough) campaign challenging the commemoration of the fiftieth anniversary of the WB and the IMF (Bonet i Martí 2003; Pastor 2002). Since then, it continues a campaign of counterinformation "to spread the real struggles starting from cyberspace."

The better-known alternative media is Indymedia (http://www.indymedia.org), which on its home page defines itself as "a collective of independent media organizations and hundreds of journalists offering grassroots, non-corporate coverage. Indymedia is a democratic media outlet for the creation of radical, accurate, and passionate tellings of truth." Indymedia is formed by more than fifty nodes all around the world. The raison d'être of the network is critique of the established media (Rucht 2003) and promotion of the "democratization of information" and "citizen's media" (Cardon and Granjon 2003). Open publishing is an essential element of the Indymedia project, which allows everybody (from independent journalists to unknown activists) to publish the news they gather instantaneously on a globally accessible Web site since there is no editorial board filtering information (Cristante 2003; Freschi 2003). Anyone who respects a few ground rules can create a local knot of Indymedia. Indeed, besides global issues and counterinformation on the main network, local knots of Indymedia have dedicated themselves to the coverage of specific mobilizations against neoliberal globalization. For instance, in June 2001 a demonstration against a meeting of the WB in Barcelona (later cancelled) was the occasion for the formation of a local knot of Indymedia. In the days of the Seattle protest, Indymedia claimed to have received 1.5 million hits.

Due to its multimedia nature, CMC offers important tools to organizations active on human rights violations, police repression, and environmental pollution. "Anyone interested in knowing about any harmful, unethical, or wasteful activities of companies or governments can now locate Web sites that contain a constantly updated historical record of transgressions against public interest" (O'Brien 1999). Webcams enabled activists to shame enterprises who contaminated the environment by discharging toxic liquid into rivers (Warkentin 2001, 78). Police violence in Genoa was documented by video activists using their cameras and spreading photos, images, and films through the Internet. In Florence, activists organized a group of people "armed" with cameras against the police.

In short, CMC creates easily accessible spaces in which any organization can, at a low cost, communicate interpretative schemas and definitions of the situation that are alternative to the official ones spread by the mass media.

CMC provides movements with the opportunity to create unmediated and unfiltered flows of information, addressing public opinion and diversifying the message in accordance with their specific target. Nevertheless, cyberspace also seems to possess, at least partially, hierarchies and gatekeepers of different types (Koopmans and Zimmerman 2003): the visibility of Web sites is submitted to a series of criteria, and actors who are more gifted with resources can enhance their presence in cyberspace through professionals who have more knowledge of the rules that favor prominence on the Internet.

The fact that the Internet makes an enormous quantity of information available does not automatically increase interest in politics per se (Margolis and Reisnick 2000). In this sense, there is a risk that the Internet will merely turn out to be a new, additional resource for those already involved in public life (Bimber 1998, 30). CMC would then simply be a new resource for old activists and would not be a means of involving new social sectors in politics (Bentivegna 2002).

The development of the Web had a major effect on the political functioning of the Internet because it heightened the problem of news verification (Gurak and Logie 2003, 26; see also Lebert 2003, on Amnesty International). Rucht (2003) rightly observes that information in cyberspace is unreliable because there are no obligatory checking procedures and also because of the highly temporary nature of the Internet itself (online information tends to disappear, whereas information in traditional media is usually archived and accessible).

Although CMC increasingly is becoming a source of information for journalists of more traditional media (Cardon and Granjon 2003), the capability of information to spread from cyberspace to more traditional media is unclear. As Bennett notes, "since Seattle, it seems that a more familiar press pattern has emerged in both US and European media coverage of demonstrations: protesters have generically been cast as violent and anarchists, and even equated with soccer hooligans in some European accounts" (2003, 162). According to a research study on media representation of the Genoa G8 summit (Vindrola 2002), during the days of the meeting the three most important Italian television news broadcasts dedicated only 1.7 percent of the time spent on the summit to the countersummit agenda, and 20.8 percent on the agenda of the official meeting; most television coverage focused on security and public order (33.3 percent) and the organizations of protest (21.7 percent); the police (27.7 percent) and the Black Bloc (13 percent) had the highest level of visibility, while the GSF got scant mention (9.6 percent). Similarly, research on the press coverage by four of the most important Italian newspapers before, during, and after the summit indicated low attention was given to the content of the summit and of the protest (9.4 percent, mainly devoted to the official agenda of the protest). Another research study on the coverage of the G8 in Genoa (looking at eleven Italian newspapers in the period between July 20 and 23, 2001) confirmed this result: 41.6 percent of articles on the summit focused on violence, 17.9 percent on the official summit, and 14.4 percent on the countersummit, with only 4.7 percent on the issue of globalization (Cristante 2003, 83). Also, in the coverage of the ESF (Cosi 2004) in the period analyzed (from October 23 to November 23, 2002), only 21.3 percent of the articles selected from the three most important Italian newspapers gave coverage to the contents of the social forum; almost 50 percent in the period leading up to the ESF (alarm phase) were devoted to violence and public order. Studies on media coverage of the movement for global justice in other European countries show similar results: newspaper coverage of the Spanish European union presidency was centered mainly on security and public order (37 percent), while 17.2 percent of articles covered alternative globalization (Jiménez 2002); only 6.6 percent of German press coverage of five protest events in Seattle, Prague, Genoa, Gothenburg, and Berlin reported on the substantive arguments of the institutional organizers, and 3 percent on those of demonstrators, while violence, police, and security scored 26.8 percent (Rucht 2003). The passage "from desktop to television screen" (Bennett 2003) seems quite difficult.

Opinion polls indicate, however, that the movement on globalization had indeed a high capacity of agenda setting, turning attention to globalization processes and global issues. In countries like Italy, it was able to attract support from a very wide base. Moreover, in various countries, on some of the issues it addressed—such as genetically modified (GM) food, third world debt, and more recently the war—movement concerns have been widely shared by public opinion. Our data (see Figure 8) confirms that the Internet is a source of information for activists and works as a message amplifier.

The Internet as a New Resource for Social Movements: Some Conclusions

CMC has increasingly become a vitally important resource for those social movements that have acquired heightened visibility in the public sphere during recent years: the Internet has had and will continue to have a meaningful effect on collective action. As we have pointed out, the Internet empowers SMOs performing a series of fundamental functions: it modifies the organizational structure of social movements (more and more rhyzomatic, flexible, and polycentric) and makes organizing demonstrations easier; it increases the possibilities for a direct intervention in politics through different forms of cyberprotest; it influences identity processes and helps to spread alternative information.

As for the *organizational function,* our data indicated that SMOs made wide use of the Internet for the preparation of the transnational protest against the G8 in Genoa and the ESF in Florence, and that the activists who took part in these demonstrations were also frequent cyberspace navigators. Different sectors of the movement made different uses of the Internet. Our empirical analysis confirmed that, despite the diffusion of CMC, the digital access is still selective—sociodemographic variables like gender, age, and education still affect access to and regularity and frequency of use of the Internet; however, SMOs tend to "socialize" their activists to the Internet. Familiarization with the new technologies through participation in organizations has an equalizing effect, reducing the digital divide. In addition, activists belonging to the main organizational sectors of the movement are more likely to make further use of it as a tool for political participation.

A lot of *protest* takes place online—the most frequent are petitions, but more disruptive forms such as Net strikes are also spread. Our data disprove pessimistic claims of a progressive substitution of offline activism with online protest: activists perform their actions both offline and online, using cyberspace as a new resource to increase their chances of success. There is no reason to see offline and online environments as alternative to each other. Since they are more and more integrated and overlapping, human activities (such as protest) take place in both environments.

The Internet facilitates the construction of new, flexible *identities;* it operates as an intervening variable extending individual social relationships by demolishing space-time barriers. Indeed, the very characteristics of cheapness and rapidity of the Internet enable people to accumulate a stock of latent ties that can be rapidly transformed into qualitatively superior relationships producing growth of the weak ties and social networks in which an individual is embedded. CMC multiplies the probabilities to maintain this kind of tie and, above all, to reactivate it with extreme facility and rapidity. The extension of individual social relations via the Internet favors identification processes (but not trust in institutions); the analysis of the empirical data seems to point out a positive relationship between the use of the Internet and such variables in organizational sectors and single groups.

As for its *cognitive* function, we noticed the movement for global justice made wide use of the opportunities offered by the new media to create unmediated flows of communication with their constituency and with public opinion. Portals, Web sites, and Indymedia devote themselves to the production of alternative information, which is communicated over the Web.

Although the Internet helps to spread information with important agenda-setting effects, the passage from micro to mass media is problematic, and social movement initiatives risk being lost in cyberspace. Media coverage of protest events in particular tend to focus more on law-and-order problems than on substantive proposals.

Notwithstanding the "bad" coverage in the mass media, however, a series of surveys (see della Porta 2003b, ch. 5) indicates that the movement for global justice is successful in sensitizing public opinion on important issues related to the process of globalization. Even if the movement Web sites rarely get direct media coverage, it seems the Internet plays a fundamental cognitive function in circumventing the mass media.

5

Media-Conscious and Nonviolent? Protest Repertoires

Repertoires of Action: An Introduction

Studies on social movements have often emphasized the importance of protest as a form of action, which if not unique is at least more typical of the "powerless" (Lipsky 1965). Starting from the idea of a repertoire of protest, studies went on to examine how the forms of action developed and how they were adapted to environmental circumstances. Research pointed, in particular, to the tension between the limitedness of known, legitimate repertoires and the need on the part of the movements to invent new (and newsworthy) models in their interactions with the state, its police forces, and the mass media (Tarrow 1994; della Porta 1995; Tilly 1978). Emphasis has often been placed on the strategic dilemmas the movements have to address, hemmed in between the need for visibility and the danger of being stigmatized, between the power of numbers and the bolstering of identities, between bearing witness and being effective. Furthermore, researchers explain the choice of a repertoire of action sometimes as the strategic outcome of a learning process and sometimes as the result of imitation and perverse effects. In particular, the radicalization of forms of action has often been accounted for as the result of having to adapt to closed political opportunities, which weakens the potential effects of more moderate forms of action and is the (undesired) cause of progressive isolation (della Porta 1995; DeNardo 1985).

Research into social movements in democracies in the north of the world has singled out a trend toward the normalization of protest. On the one hand, unconventional forms of action have gained greater acceptance within a variety of social and political groups; our societies are thus defined as

118

being movement societies (Tarrow and Meyer 1998; Neidhardt and Rucht 1993), with a growing number of groups increasingly resorting to complex and heterogeneous repertoires of action (Dalton 1994). On the other, as we have said, protest became normalized in that more extreme forms tended to give way to moderation. Paradoxically, as more protest actions became legitimized, many social movement organizations (SMOs) shifted toward more conventional forms of action (such as lobbying), commercialization, and getting involved in voluntary work (della Porta 2003c). Finally, it has been noted that protest has become ever more media-conscious in the sense of it being organized as a media event.

How does the movement against neoliberal globalization fit into this framework? As we shall see, the movement has a consolidated repertoire of action. In particular, its activists have used conventional and nonconventional forms of action in the past, achieving varying degrees of disruptiveness. Traditional demonstrations were flanked with occupations, petitions, and boycotts. The movement is also capable of innovation; countersummits and campaigns are new forms and have rapidly become widespread. Many SMOs seem to have halted their march toward more conventional forms of action and more and more perceive the street as the main forum for airing their grievances. Opinions in the movement diverge, however, on the very issue of how to demonstrate. While strategies tend to be predominantly nonviolent, ideas differ on which forms of action are legitimate, and more radical forms of action survive at the fringes of large demonstrations.

The activists against neoliberal globalization make use of a heterogeneous repertoire, transforming and adapting the forms of action developed by earlier movements that merged into them: from the institutional pressure by NGOs to pilgrimages by religious groups, from direct action by environmentalists to the ritualization of clashes in civil disobedience implemented by the Tute Bianche (White Overalls), from the occupation of public buildings by the student movement to the large marches of the labor movement. While the actions adopted in the eighties and nineties seemed so "civilized" that observers started to speak of lobbies (even if of a public interest character), since Seattle the emergence of new repertoires and the resurgence of street demonstrations signaled a new cycle of protest. This shared participation in campaigns and countersummits has fostered links of solidarity among different actors, although lively debates surround the strategies for large-scale demonstrations, as well for more everyday action, in terms of legitimacy and effectiveness. Even though diversity in strategy is accepted to a certain extent—theme-based squares, for example, or different parts of demonstrations protesting in different ways—the legitimacy of a number of forms of radical action (such as using passive means of defense against police aggression) or the usefulness of some moderate ones (in particular lobbying) have been questioned by both outside observers and the activists themselves.

Protests against neoliberal globalization have often succeeded in exploiting the growing importance of the media, especially television, offering news with high media value. The more or less indulgent press coverage of the WTO protests in Seattle highlighted the spectacular impact of the demonstrations. We have noted that in Seattle there were environmentalists dressed up as turtles, theater groups, human chains, religious services, and windows smashed by the Black Bloc (BB). An activist noted: "The action included art, dance, celebration, song, ritual and magic. It was more than protest; it was an uprising of a vision of true abundance, a celebration of life and creativity and connection, that remained joyful in the face of brutality and brought alive the creative forces that can truly counter those of injustice and control" (Starhawk 1999). High-visibility initiatives and a multiplicity of tactics continued after Seattle; the social and political heterogeneity of the movement has led to cross-fertilization among various repertoires with the accent placed on staging "festivals of resistance." Puppets made in ad hoc workshops, musical bands, and theatrical performances have been increasingly seen in demonstrations and sit-ins. In Prague, to counter the military symbols of the anarchists, there was the "pink march" with women of the Tactical Frivolity group who defended their choice of active nonviolence, affirming: "We are a colourful party in the street, a carnival with theatre, pink fairies and radical cheerleaders, clowns and music, a creative, magical and confrontational dance that take decisions in a horizontal manner through affinity groups. We want to reduce aggressivity to a minimum with imagination, samba, art, playing with space (and the police), to create a relaxed atmosphere with good vibes" (Pink Silver March 2001). From the Reclaim the Street festivals to the theatrics and provocation of ACT-UP, protesters are seeking visible, innovative forms of action.

While the great majority of protesters far prefer nonviolent strategies to violent ones, the logic of the media has inevitably highlighted the more radical forms of protest within mass demonstrations (which totaled fifty thousand participants in Seattle, sixty thousand in Nice, two hundred thousand in Genoa, three hundred thousand in Barcelona, and one million in Florence), in particular stones thrown at windows, but also clashes between demonstrators and the police. Initially tolerated in the name of pluralism, though not implemented by the majority of demonstrators, violent repertoires have become increasingly stigmatized both in principle (seen as a form of accepting the violence of the system and even more as behavior akin to war) and for their practical effects in isolating protest. Relations with those who use violent forms of action have, thus, become progressively difficult, and a number of measures have been adopted to protect peaceful demonstrations from the risk of escalation. These range from the creation of green areas (areas free from tear gas) within the march (such as in Quebec City), to dividing marchers over different areas depending on the practiced action strategy (such as in Prague), and finally, to signing agreements that ban violent tactics (such as in Genoa).

Using our interviews with the GSF and ESF activists, as well as the focus groups and content analysis of organizational documents, we shall observe that the movement for a globalization from below can count on support from activists possessing broad skills in protesting that were honed in part in previous waves of mobilization. To the existing protest repertoire, the movement has added other forms of protest, such as campaigns, boycotts, and countersummits, as well as revamping strategies of nonviolence and civil disobedience. Although mainly peaceful, protesters on global issues have also included exponents of the BB, with their tactics of causing material damage to symbolic targets. Although at the Genoa countersummit a multiplicity of forms of action were tolerated, activist criticism of violence has increased.

Activists and Protests: A Plural Repertoire

The movement's repertoire of action on globalization is highly varied; it features a certain amount of continuity with the past tradition as well as some innovative aspects. Interviews with demonstrators confirm that the various protest networks can count on activists who have over time gained extensive skills in nonconventional political activism developing a rich and varied repertoire of action. The activists interviewed in Genoa seek to influence politics by using both conventional and innovative forms of action: convincing someone to vote for a party (52.3 percent); signing petitions (88.6 percent); leafleting (78.5 percent); participating in public meetings (96.2 percent), sit-ins (68.8 percent), boycotts (67.8 percent), strikes (82.7 percent); occupying public buildings (72.3 percent) or abandoned buildings (32.9 percent). Some interviewees also include violence against property in their action repertoire (10.6 percent). The degree of similarity of the protest experience acquired by activists among the various organizations and networks seems to be high—from public meetings to boycotts, from sit-ins to occupying public buildings such as schools and universities—while at the same time not ruling out the classical form of political party activism. However, some types of experience are more widespread in some sectors than in others. For example, more activists from the social centers have occupied public buildings (schools and universities) and squatted in private ones (especially unoccupied premises such as disused factory buildings), as well as resorting to forms of violent action against property. On the other hand, there is less availability by Rete Lilliput activists to use violence against property and an overall preference for more conventional forms of action, albeit not political party–based forms. ATTAC activists, even those not belonging to a political party within the network, are the most active in both conventional and party-based initiatives. In short, it seems that movement activists are used to many ways of protesting and being politically active, combining conventional and nonconventional actions. It is interesting to note that a widespread usage of diversified ways of activist protest (including occupying schools and squatting) also characterized protesters who stated that they did not belong to any organization.

Also, the ESF activists (Table 15) declared experience in diversified forms of activism, confirming the differences among movement sectors. Alongside less conventional forms there appear more institutionalized forms of political participation, such as party activism or attempting to convince someone to vote for a certain party. These, however, are more common within the antineoliberalist and anticapitalist sectors than among activists closer to ecopacifism (such as Rete Lilliput in Italy) and the local social forums, or to those not belonging to an area of the movement. Petitions, referendums, leafleting, public meetings, and strikes are, with few exceptions, all part of the repertoire common to activists of the various areas and are only slightly less present among those who stated they did not belong to any organization. In addition, forms of action that are more disruptive (such as sit-ins) and innovative (such as boycotts) are implemented to a similar extent by activists of the various areas, while occupying schools and universities is more common to activists of the antineoliberalist and anticapitalist sectors. Greater differences emerge in the form of occupation of abandoned buildings, obviously practiced to a greater extent by activists of the anticapitalist sector that are normally set up within them, and by those who state their belonging to the local social forums. Finally, repertoires that include violence to property are present, albeit to a limited extent, in the anticapitalist sector (17.7 percent) and social forums, and almost completely absent among ecopacifists and antineoliberalists. The data on the ESF point to activists practicing a largely homogeneous and decidedly nonviolent repertoire, with a somewhat greater reliance on traditional forms of action on the part of ATTAC and the Rifondazione Comunista (RC) party, and a greater use of radical repertoires by the social centers.

Table 15. Forms of action used in the past by ESF participants, by sector affiliation (% of affirmative answers per column)

Form of action	Sector affiliation (%)					Total (%)	Cramer's V
	Ecopacifist	Anti-neoliberalist	Anti-capitalist	Local social forums	Unorganized		
Convincing someone to vote for a party	52.3	68.9	70.8	45.1	45.1	54.5	0.22***
Party activism	31.0	55.6	70.6	35.3	23.3	37.4	0.38***
Petition, referendum	88.5	94.9	96.6	94.1	88.5	91.7	0.13***
Leafleting	83.9	89.9	97.0	88.2	67.6	78.4	0.29***
Public meeting	88.1	94.6	90.5	98.0	88.0	89.8	0.09**
Strike	76.0	82.1	82.8	88.5	82.3	81.9	n.s.
Sit-in	72.7	73.0	83.7	84.3	70.9	73.9	0.11***
Boycott	82.2	73.2	85.1	80.8	65.4	72.1	0.18***
Occupation of schools or universities	56.0	52.9	73.9	62.7	62.9	63.9	0.10**
Occupation of abandoned buildings	17.4	27.3	34.2	36.0	26.1	27.0	0.10**
Violence against property	5.7	6.5	17.7	14.3	9.2	9.9	0.13***
(Number of interviewees)	(172–77)	(275–80)	(264)	(49–52)	(887–95)	(1,647–65)	

***significant at the 0.001 level; **significant at the 0.01 level; n.s. = nonsignificant.

In cross-national comparison (Table 16), it emerges that more moderate forms of protest (from petitioning to leafleting, from participating in public meetings to striking) were used by almost all the interviewees with no significant differences between one country and another (except for a lower participation in strikes in Germany and Great Britain). More disruptive forms of political participation, such as sit-ins, boycotts, and occupying buildings, have been extensively resorted to, however, with some differences among the countries: for example, more squatting (long-term occupation of buildings) in Italy, France, and Germany; very widespread occupation of schools and universities in Italy; more boycotting in Great Britain, France, and Germany, and more sit-ins in Spain and Great Britain. Confirming the result of the survey on the Genoa Social Forum, only a very small minority of activists in every country resorted to forms of violence against property. Besides, there seems to have been a fall in the number of Italian activists with prior experience in violence against property following the debate on the dangers of escalation after the G8 clashes in Genoa (6.1 percent against 10.6 percent at Genoa).

Finally, the difference between generations is small (Table 17). Obviously, the young, in general, have less prior experience with forms of protest (indeed, many of them had their first political socialization in the new global movement) and even less in party activism. The activists of the upcoming generation have, instead, greater experience in occupying schools and universities. Awareness of globalization issues among the twenty-year-old age group seems to have emerged especially in the course of protests within the education system—especially against reforms aimed at introducing privatization, which are perceived as a neoliberal attempt at commodifying an acquired right. In Italy, for example, waves of protest targeted first the reform proposals put forward by the center-left government and then—in the name of "another school is possible"—a later project elaborated by the center-right government.

Activists, therefore, combine forms of protest typical of many earlier movements. Some are more conventional, while others have been integrated modularly in the mobilization resorted to by other actors. More typical of the movement are forms of action such as boycotts and countersummits that combine specific strategies.

Campaigns and Boycotts

Campaigns—combinations of protest actions on specific issues—are a mobilization strategy that has encouraged the emergence of transnational links and links among groups active on various issues. Numerous groupings have

Table 16. Forms of action used in the past by ESF participants by nationality (% of affirmative answers per column)

Form of action	Country of participants (%)						Total (%)	Cramer's V
	Italy	France	Germany	Spain	United Kingdom			
Convincing someone to vote for a party	54.4	67.2	58.5	39.8	81.6		61.5	0.29***
Party activism	35.1	36.0	26.8	31.9	73.5		42.7	0.35***
Petition, referendum	91.2	95.0	92.7	83.2	97.3		92.2	0.18***
Leafleting	73.2	83.7	83.5	69.9	96.0		81.6	0.25***
Public meeting	97.3	92.0	91.5	88.5	75.7		88.7	0.25***
Strike	95.3	82.4	59.8	94.7	65.1		80.6	0.36***
Sit-in	82.9	64.0	63.4	80.5	72.5		73.3	0.18***
Boycott	69.9	77.4	71.6	52.2	86.5		72.5	0.25***
Occupation of schools or universities	74.8	59.7	45.1	54.9	65.5		61.8	0.19***
Occupation of abandoned buildings	26.9	33.8	24.7	21.6	16.3		24.7	0.14*
Violence against property	6.1	13.0	11.0	13.4	11.5		10.8	n.s.
(Number of interviewees)	(145–49)	(135–39)	(79–82)	(111–13)	(147–49)		(620–30)	

***significant at the 0.001 level; *significant at the 0.05 level; n.s. = nonsignificant.

Table 17. Forms of action used in the past by ESF participants by age cohort (% of affirmative answers per column)

Form of action	Up to 1956	Year of birth (%) From 1957 to 1966	From 1967 to 1976	From 1977 onward	Total (%)	Cramer's V
Convincing someone to vote for a party	69.7	61.1	53.4	50.4	54.9	0.13***
Party activism	56.0	48.6	36.2	31.1	37.6	0.18***
Petition, referendum	93.4	95.2	93.9	89.7	91.9	0.08*
Leafleting	87.6	88.7	79.6	73.2	78.6	0.15***
Public meeting	93.9	90.9	90.5	88.2	89.8	n.s.
Strike	86.7	82.3	83.4	79.8	82.0	n.s.
Sit-in	74.3	75.8	77.1	71.9	74.1	n.s.
Boycott	72.0	81.6	77.1	67.5	72.3	0.12***
Occupation of schools or universities	59.4	63.4	64.2	64.9	63.8	n.s.
Occupation of abandoned buildings	28.6	30.1	29.8	24.2	26.9	n.s.
Violence against property	10.5	14.8	9.8	9.0	10.1	n.s.
(Number of interviewees)	(206–12)	(183–86)	(455–62)	(798–804)	(1,645–63)	

***significant at the 0.001 level; *significant at the 0.05 level; n.s. = nonsignificant.

formed around campaigns for canceling the foreign debt owed by poor countries (Donnelly 2002; Grenier 2003), against NAFTA and the Multilateral Agreement on Investments (Kidder 2002), or to increase access to HIV/AIDS drugs (Mowjee 2003). Less visible, but significant nonetheless in the construction of resources for the global movement, have been campaigns conducted by NGOs active on environmental issues as well as on questions of peace, employment, women's rights, and the rights of indigenous peoples. These and other campaigns—against land mines, large-scale dam construction (such as the Narmada Dam in India), the destruction of the Amazon forest, child soldiers, and for the establishment of a tribunal to examine allegations of war crimes, genocide, and crimes against humanity (Glasius 2002)—achieved some degree of success because of the capability of international coordination (through Global Exchange, Transnational Resources and Action Centre, Coalition for an International Criminal Court) to galvanize the public opinion of different countries, sometimes even by means of direct action.

The underlying logic of these campaigns is the *naming and shaming* that, especially when conducted against transnational corporations, aims at making public opinion aware of especially glaring cases of denied human rights by spreading detailed information about them and often by asking people to punish the companies involved by boycotting their products. The Clean Clothes Campaign—launched in 1993 by a coalition of student associations, religious groups, human rights organizations, and trade unions—aimed its protest against department stores like C&A, Peek & Cloppenburg, and M&S Mode who, it was alleged, were selling products manufactured in conditions of extreme worker exploitation, with low salaries and safety, in countries like South Korea, Bangladesh, Hong Kong, Mexico, Guatemala, and Honduras (Mies 2002). Other, later examples of boycotts aimed at corporations were to involve Shell, for polluting the North Sea and the Niger River (and indirectly for the brutal repression of protests staged by the Ogoni people); Nike, for subcontracting production to small enterprises in Indonesia and Vietnam that use child labor as well as highly polluting products; Nestlé, for contributing to the spread of children's diseases by lowering their immune response by promoting the use of powdered milk in developing countries; Monsanto, for producing sterile seeds; Unilever, for introducing GM soybeans on the market; Del Monte, after the broadcast of a videotape showing the slaughter of dolphins during tuna fishing; McDonald's, for allegedly using the meat of animals raised extensively on antibiotics (which allegedly produces an addiction effect on consumers); Bridgestone/Firestone, which was obliged to rehire workers it had fired; and the Pfizer pharmaceutical company, which had to abandon its claim on the patent for life-saving anti-AIDS drugs in poor countries in Africa and in Brazil.

Many of these campaigns made use of a form of action that, although inherited from the past, gained new support and meaning: the boycott. In a situation in which transnational corporations have increasing power (according to the activists, even more power than many nation-states), protest strategies have to adapt by finding means that can directly damage the targeted economic enterprises. The boycott of specific companies follows this logic, exploiting the corporation's particular need for a clean image that relies more on its logo than on the quality of specific products. Since, according to a popular slogan, "The world is not for sale," the use of alternative forms of "fair" consumption is a way of denouncing commodification, at the same time practicing alternative forms of exchanges.

Providing an alternative consumerism (and investment) are the microcredit programs operated by ethical banks (in Italy, the Banca Popolare Etica; at the European level, the International Association of Investors in Social Economy). Certificates awarded for environmental respect and for workers' rights, as well as for adopting "best practice," encourage responsible investment in sustainable products and impede manufacturers of "bad" products (such as arms and GM organisms), especially via the stock markets.[1] Action against mass consumerism was also developed at local levels in the eighties and nineties with initiatives against the privatization of public spaces in major shopping centers and with the creation of consumer cooperatives (Sklair 1995).

On the issue of development in general, a number of research groups have arisen whose aim is to spotlight the still unused economic capacity of national governments. These groups include the International Budget Project in budget analysis and, in Italy, Sbilanciamoci, which has developed projects (presented by left-wing parties) for alternative national budgets, in which expenditures are shifted from arms purchases to demining, from incentives for road transport to pollutant reduction, from maintaining death duties to introducing the Tobin tax.

Campaigns also make use of testimonials from religious backgrounds; vigils and fasts are organized as a way of expressing sharing in the suffering of the poor. In autumn of 2001, for instance, the Catholic Pax Christi and the Beati i Costruttori di Pace (Blessed Builders of Peace) organized a "human chain of fasting together with our sisters and brothers in Islamic communities who are celebrating Ramadan." The fast was accompanied by prayers and ecumenical ceremonies, and was presented as a form of introspection and spirituality that expressed "profound solidarity with the victims of every armed conflict being fought at this very moment in many parts of the world" (Beati i Costruttori di Pace and Pax Christi 2001).

Besides achieving some of their aims, especially that of engaging public opinion, campaigns had the effect of drawing people together and linking different claims. In Italy, for example, a number of organizations that had worked together in campaigns to highlight the inequalities produced by globalization (such as Sdebitarsi, the Campaign to Reform the WB, the Stop Millennium Round Campaign) joined forces in an intercampaign table in late 1997 and agreed on a common platform. As we have noted (see chapter 2 in this volume), these bodies emerged in 1999 as Rete Lilliput, structured in a network of local knots, and in early 2000 reached a common agenda and completed a manifesto. The campaign against the Narmada Valley dam brought together the local population and global activists and linked concern for the human rights of the indigenous people who were going to be displaced with the defense of nature (Khagram 2002).

The Countersummits: From Lobbying to the Red Areas

An equally efficient networking resulted from the countersummits, the meetings promoted by organizations within civil society to be held alongside and to counter the official summits held by major international organizations. Present since the eighties in the repertoire of protest, these have changed over time, and now greater emphasis is placed on street demonstrations while lobbying has come under increased criticism. NGOs critical of neoliberal globalization have in particular resorted to pressures at both national and international levels. From human rights groups to environmentalists, advocacy networks—composed of activists, bureaucrats belonging to international organizations, and politicians from many countries—have won significant gains in a number of areas such as a ban on land mines, decontamination of radioactive waste, and the establishment of an international tribunal for violations of human rights (Khagram, Riker, and Sikkink 2002; Klotz 1995; Risse and Sikkink 1999; Thomas 2001).

Some NGOs have not only increased in number but also strengthened their influence in various stages of international policy making (Sikkink and Smith 2002; Boli 1999). Their assets include an increasing credibility in public opinion[2] and a consequent availability of private funding.[3] Their widespread presence throughout the territory enables NGOs to collect information at local levels providing a sort of grassroots implementation of supranational decisions. Specific knowledge, combined with useful contacts with the press, makes many NGOs seem reliable sources and, by turning the spotlight on new issues, makes the governance process more transparent (Schmidt and Take 1997). With a professional staff on hand, they are also able to maintain a fair level of activity even when protest mobilization is low. Their independence from governments, combined with the good reputation that has often been built by solid work at local levels, enables them to perform an important role in mediating interethnic conflict (Friberg and Hettne 1998). Finally, they enhance pluralism within international institutions by representing groups who would otherwise be excluded (Riddel-Dixon 1995).

Informal negotiations have enabled some IGOs to co-opt social movement associations that agree to work through discreet channels. In particular, the United Nations has shown itself open vis-à-vis NGOs. As early as 1948, the Nongovernmental Conference of NGOs with consultative status (CONGOS) was set up, and by the nineties it had reached the respectable membership of 1,500 (Rucht 1996, 33). In the EU, the Parliament in particular but other bodies as well have held informal exchanges of information with various types of associations (see, for example, Marks and McAdam 1999; Mazey and Richardson 1993; della Porta 2004). Some measure of success, albeit partial, has been registered even with governmental organizations not generally open to the outside, such as the WB's willingness to adopt criteria of environmental sustainability and fairness and some (minimal) degree of transparency in the IMF. As has been noted, "International public institutions are modifying in response to pressure from social movements, NGOs and business actors, but this varies across institutions depending upon institutional culture, structure, role of the executive head and vulnerability to civil society pressure" (O'Brien et al. 2000, 6).

Nongovernmental organizations have thus been accorded the status of actors, and on occasion important ones, of world governance, and have been acknowledged as participants in the development of international norms (such as those on human rights) and on their implementation (Pagnucco 1996, 14). Besides a certain degree of institutional recognition, NGOs specialized in development assistance have received funding for the development programs they have presented or for joining projects already presented by national or international governments (O'Brien et al. 2000, 120). Many are also involved in managing funds earmarked for emergencies and humanitarian aid that now make up more than half the projects of the WB (in the offices of which many NGO specialists work) (Brecher, Costello, and Smith 2000, 114).

A risk of co-optation and, especially, ineffectiveness in attempts to sway intergovernmental organizations by lobbying has been noticed, however.

MEDIA-CONSCIOUS AND NONVIOLENT?   131

First of all, not all NGOs are independent of governments or major corporations. Mistrust is indicated from the use of such acronyms as GONGOs (government-organized NGOs), BONGOS (business-organized NGOs) and GRINGOs (government-run/initiated NGOs). NGOs are, furthermore, prevalently based in the north of the world (two-thirds of UN-registered NGOs have their headquarters in Europe and North America), and this reproduces, at this level too, the inequalities of power between rich and poor countries (Sikkink 2002). Major associations, in particular, are organized hierarchically and have limited transparency in the way they work (Schmidt and Take 1997; Sikkink 2002). In a time of cutbacks in public spending, they run the risk of being exploited to supplant an increasingly failing public service (Chandhoke 2002, 43). Intergovernmental organizations have, furthermore, preferred dealing with larger, more top-heavy NGOs that are less monitored by their base of support (ibid.).[4]

While NGOs doing lobbying were the first to mobilize against international financial institutions (in particular the WB, IMF, and WTO), protests developed as skepticism grew as to the efficacy of lobbying, and perception spread of the failure of this approach to reform large NGOs (Brand and Wissen 2002). In fact, in January 2002 at the UN Conference on Development, a split grew between the UN and NGOs, the latter blaming the former for failing to keep to the commitments it had made at the Millennium Summit (in particular to cancel the foreign debt of poor countries and to increase aid by developed countries to at least 0.7 percent of their GDP). The final communiqué of the Monterrey Global Forum, which was signed by three hundred NGO representatives admitted to the sessions, states that the agreement provides no resources for implementing the development aims of the Millenium Summit and criticizes the economic model prescribed by the international financial institutions. Similarly, major environmentalist organizations had been complaining for some time about the lack of implementation of the commitments taken on at the Rio de Janeiro summit on the environment. Therefore, while lobbying continues to be practiced by new global organizations, as a strategy it is seen as definitely insufficient.

This lower confidence in lobbying is reflected in the evolution of the so-called countersummits. Countersummits have been defined as arenas of "international-level initiatives during official summits and on the same issues but from a critical standpoint, heightening awareness through protest and information with or without contacts with the official version" (Pianta 2002, 35). In this perspective, international organizations have acted as a coral reef aiding the forging of links between activists from different countries (Tarrow 2001, 15).

After some preliminary experiences in the eighties, countersummits multiplied over the succeeding decade, along with large-scale UN conferences, supported by frenetic NGO activity. These dealt with the environment and development in 1992 in Rio de Janeiro, human rights in 1993 in Vienna, world population in 1994 in Cairo, social development in 1995 in Copenhagen, and women's rights in 1975, 1980, 1985, and 1995. After the protest meetings during UN conferences, a more visible series of countersummits took place against intergovernmental organizations—between 2000 and early 2001, 60 percent of the eighty-nine countersummits registered in a recent survey. As far back as 1984, countersummits were held to contest G7 meetings (of the world's seven most highly industrialized nations), putting forward proposals on alternative development (Pianta 2001, 90). Opposition to the policies of financial institutions gained visibility in 1988 when eighty thousand demonstrators in West Berlin protested against the summits of the WB and the IMF. Prepared through extensive networking among hundreds of groups active in different fields, the demonstration criticized the policies of those institutions considered responsible for the underdevelopment of the south of the world, demanding, even then, that poor countries' foreign debt be wiped out (Gerhards and Rucht 1992). The Berlin protests served especially to identify the movement's principal adversaries, the international financial institutions and upholders of an unfair world economic order. In 1990, in New York, NGOs from the north and the south of the world protested against the WB and the IMF summit; that same year, in Brussels, thousands of European, Japanese, North American, Korean, African, and Latin American farmers contested the negotiations on the constitution of the WTO (Brecher, Costello, and Smith 2000, 37). In 1994 in Madrid, a demonstration challenged the fiftieth anniversary of the IMF and the WB; countersummits were held during the meetings of the two organizations in Hong Kong and at the World Economic Forum in Davos, Switzerland, both in 1997. Demonstrations were held against the G7 at Lyon in 1996, Denver in 1997, Birmingham in 1998, and Cologne in 1999. After Seattle, demonstrations were held in Prague against the WB and the IMF summits. In December 2000, protests were organized against the EU summit in Nice—especially against the expected decisions regarding the status (merely declarations of intent for the future constitution of the EU) to be attributed to the "charter of fundamental rights." In Italy in 2000, the MobiliTebio platform organized protests against the biotechnology exhibition in Genoa; Maggio2000 coordinated mobilization against the European Conference for Development and Security of the Adriatic and the Ionic area in Ancona; similar protests were staged against a NATO meeting in Florence and the summit of the Organization for Economic Cooperation and Development (OECD) in Bologna. In one week of protests against the G8 summit in Genoa in July 2001, there were public forums, marches, symbolic performances, sit-ins, and actions of civil disobedience.

The countersummits were organized along two main themes that were initially dealt with separately but became increasingly interwoven: civil rights (peace, human rights, the environment, democracy) and, with growing emphasis later, social rights (policies on economics, development, and safety in the workplace) (Pianta 2002). Mobilization initiatives were variously composed (Ceri 2001): in Seattle there were more labor union supporters concerned about WTO policies; in Naples, at the international conference on e-government, hackers claimed the right to privacy and to free software; in Genoa, activists more concerned with development in the south of the world demonstrated against the G8; at the Food and Agriculture Organization (FAO) meeting in Rome, many farmworker organizations were present.

All these meetings had the effect of reinforcing transnational and, increasingly, transissue links. Countersummits have extended mobilization to new geographical areas and social issues forming transnational networks that, in turn, have facilitated mobilization beyond the boundaries of single states. It is precisely this construction of supranational connections that NGO representatives emphasize as one of the main positive spin-offs of countersummits (Pianta and Silva 2003). Participation in these events grew notably between 2001 and 2002; in one-third of countersummits there were marches with over ten thousand demonstrators, and in seven over eighty thousand (ibid.).

Direct Action between Nonviolence and Civil Disobedience

The movement prefers nonviolence as both an option of value and a strategic choice. In Genoa the work agreement of the GSF bound the signatories to "respect all forms of direct, peaceful, nonviolent expression and action declared publicly and transparently" (GSF 2001, 39). About 90 percent (95.7 percent for the Rete Lilliput, 92.7 percent for the area of ATTAC, and a lower 78.9 percent for the social centers) of the demonstrators interviewed in Genoa declared never having resorted to violent tactics. References to Gandhi and Martin Luther King are frequently made by the groups especially concerned with the development of nonviolent techniques, which often require specific training.

For the pacifist movement, nonviolence was the unavoidable choice in rejecting an aggressive system. In Seattle, the Direct Action Network had organized preparation courses in nonviolent resistance, especially for staying passive even when charged down by the police and arrested. The Italian Rete Lilliput activists define their strategy as nonviolent; it "encompasses information and denunciation in order to heighten awareness and weaken centers of power, critical consumerism and boycotting as a way of applying pressure on companies, and experimentation with alternative economic initiatives and sober lifestyles to prove that fair-based economics are possible" (Rete Lilliput 1999).

While nonviolence does not exclude direct action, the latter—conducted in a way so as not to harm people—is still at the heart of the repertoire of civil disobedience. Typical actions have been the destruction of fields of GM maize by the Confédération Paysanne, Greenpeace raids against whaling boats, blockages of nuclear sites, and episodes of passive resistance to police intervention. It was no coincidence that before Genoa, demonstrators in Italy and abroad were perfecting what in Great Britain is called "pushing and shoving," the shoulder-to-shoulder pressing that police and strikers do in picket lines. Crucial in the revival of civil disobedience in demonstrations against globalization is symbolic provocation: "Confrontations are staged at the fence—but not only the ones involving sticks and bricks: teargas canisters have been flicked back with hockey sticks, water cannon have been irreverently challenged with toy water pistols, and buzzing helicopters mocked with swarms of paper airplanes" (Klein 2002, xxv).

Civil disobedience is the particular cornerstone of Ya Basta, an organization born in 1996 at the first intercontinental meeting against neoliberalism held in Selva Lacandona, headquarters of the Zapatistas in Mexico. Despite the warlike symbols used by the Zapatistas and the massacre of *indios* perpetrated by paramilitaries close to the regular army, the Chiapas revolution will be remembered as having been oriented to using the Internet more than machine guns. The Zapatistas are described as warriors who do not shoot (Benenati 2002, 111). In the "yellow" march in Prague, Ya Basta was defined by the *Guardian* as "the most disciplined, stylish and effective of all Europe's direct action groups" (September 27, 2000, 18). Its activists intended to "liquidate" the IMF with water pistols and water bombs: "We are criminals, delinquents, outlaws: using our weapon we should take what is ours . . . and if we want to liquidate them, what better weapons than water filled weapons" (in Chester and Welsh 2004).

In Italy, the White Overalls, who are close to Ya Basta, define their civil disobedience as nonviolent but "protected, collective and self-organized" (White Overalls n.d., "What White Overalls Are"): protected in the sense that demonstrators wear materials for their physical safety when clashes with the police occur, but they do not carry any object of aggression; they define themselves as "a nonviolent movement, which does not, however, mean Ghandi-type pacifism." The White Overalls state that they belong to the border area between violence and nonviolence, affirming that these two concepts for them are no longer "ideological decision or a fetish to defend in every place and at all times." Their civil disobedience is based on staging conflict by simulating street clashes "in order that the real, planet-wide conflict gets talked about." The action consists in reaching police lines and proceeding to move into the out-of-bounds red areas: "we attempt both symbolically and in reality to push forward during demonstrations towards places where civil society is barred." The White Overalls cover their bodies with protective materials (foam rubber padding, shin pads, helmets, and often underwater swimming masks or gas masks for protection against tear gas). They use car-tire inner tubes to keep the police away from the head of the march, and plastic shields held overhead like a turtle shell to protect them against police batons. They proceed with their hands up as a sign of nonaggression and are prepared to hold up against being charged down by the police without hitting back and while protecting themselves using "only instruments of collective and personal defence, never offence."[5]

The dress and turtle-shell array are mainly symbolic, staging violence instead of perpetrating it. According to the White Overalls, symbolically breaking through police lines is good for media coverage, showing at the same time the violent face of the system, the violence of its structure: "our action aims to show how in point of fact institutional violence is often used between imperial power and the multitudes" ("White Overalls and Violence"). In recent years, many social centers that had previously supported open clashes with the police have been won over to the strategy of civil disobedience, transforming physical clashes into prevalently peaceful rituals. In the White Overalls' document "From the Multitudes of Europe, Rising Up against the Empire and Marching on Genoa" (White Overalls 2001c), they mention a "mytho-poietic initiative straddling the whole of the twentieth century reclaiming the most long-standing methods of revolt. To turn all these allegories into something concrete and tangible, we thought of the idea of street demonstrating inspired by certain old paintings and prints where carts armed with ram horns would be used to break down the Wall of Shame." And in the pact with the city of Genoa, they describe "a war . . . fought with bodies, words, gadgets and mechanical instruments thought up in the peaceful workshops of our imagination" (White Overalls 2001a). Similarly, the language of the White Overalls and that of the Disobedients is sprinkled with metaphors like "empire," "fortress," "siege," and "lords' castle."

This ritualization of the conflict has been highly successful because it offered a viable alternative both to clashes and to the traditional, ritual peaceful marches spreading rapidly throughout Europe and the United States. It has been pointed out, however, that while rejection of violent action has grown within the movements, the concept of civil disobedience has broadened to include nonviolent resistance. This, in turn, includes tactics that heighten the danger activists run of being physically hurt should the police step in (for example, chaining themselves together during sit-ins and blocks) or, instead, reduce the level of physical injury during passive resistance to arrest (such as the foam-rubber padding worn by the Disobedients). Direct, nonviolent action, therefore, does not rule out passive resistance and accepts that a minimum of lawlessness is involved; what the minimum should be is the subject of debate both inside and outside the movement.

The Black Bloc and Mediatized Violence

At the fringes of many demonstrations on globalization are the small splinter groups of the BB that practice forms of urban warfare using offensive weapons to attack property and, less frequently, in clashes with the police. Consisting mostly of young and very young people grouped around radical forms of conflict (from the *Autonomen* in Germany to the young Basque *borrokas*), BB members generally preach the legitimacy of destroying property as a symbolic act. In the words of one of them, "As a protest tactic, the usefulness of property destruction is limited but important. It brings the media to the scene and it sends a message that seemingly impervious corporations are not impervious. People at the protest, and those at home watching on TV, can see that a little brick, in the hands of a motivated individual, can break down a symbolic wall. A broken window at Nike Town is not threatening to people's safety" (BB 2001a).

Although the various BB nuclei find their common ground in the acceptance of, or even exaltation of, the destruction of the symbols of globalization, variously justified as a response to the violence of the system, they remain distinct from each other in the forms of action they consider acceptable. The violence in Gothenburg was defined on BB Web sites as "brainless militancy, militancy as an end in itself." Two Berlin *Autonomen*, interviewed by *Tageszeitung* (August 1, 2001), were critical of the fact that, during the anti-G8 protest in Genoa, three banks with apartments located in the same buildings had been set on fire, thus endangering the inhabitants. BB Web sites also debated the fact that, contrary to what happened earlier, in Genoa direct BB action was not restricted to targeting the symbols of capitalism (banks and transnational corporations) but also vented its fury against small shops and private (and, in some cases, small) cars.

This absence of a clearly defined organizational structure makes the BB a volatile subject. The various nuclei act mainly independently from each other with no leader or spokesperson. In their definition of themselves, "there is no standing Black Bloc organization between protests . . . the Black Bloc is a tactic, similar to civil disobedience" (BB 2004). A very loose network links small "affinity groups" and groupings of anarchist inspiration composed of small nuclei of a dozen people or so, who all know and trust each other. The BB may, therefore, be considered as uncoordinated small groupings that, when participating in marches and demonstrations, resort to the same forms of action based on throwing stones and sometimes Molotov cocktails against the headquarters of companies held to be symbols of neoliberal globalization.

From Seattle to Genoa, these small groups appeared to increase their number, but they also seemed more and more isolated from the movement—which, in Genoa, built barriers to keep them out of the march besides unequivocally branding them as "extraneous" to it. The relationship between the BB and other sectors of the movement has always been strained and, one mobilization after another, has deteriorated. As early as Seattle, a number of activists of the nonviolent area of the movement tried to stop the "blocers" from destroying property. In Genoa, the BB, together with a number of anarchist (and anti-imperialist) groupings, stayed out of the GSF, refusing to sign the work agreement to practice nonviolent tactics. In the appeal they made, they stated: "we don't want to feel restricted by the GSF guidelines . . . we have set up the *International Genova Offensive* so that we can organize ourselves how we want" (BB 2001a). Isolating the BB, however, has meant that the nonviolent demonstrators were left with less negotiating power over the more radical groups. Characterized by a very loose coordination and increasingly hostile to the movement, the BB have often spurned even minimal nonbelligerent pacts (and in Genoa sometimes attacked demonstrators as well as trying to invade the headquarters of the GSF).

After Genoa, however, most large-scale demonstrations against globalization, at least in Europe (such as the ESF in Florence and the pacifist marches of February 15, 2003), went off completely peacefully. The self-critical debate held by radical groups, greater vigilance, and policing service organized by the various coordinators of the protest (though armed with cameras instead of blunt instruments) seem to have broken the spiral of violence that in Prague, Gothenburg, and Genoa sometimes gave the impression of spinning out of control. The growing public consensus for the movement's concerns has curtailed the tendency of governments and police forces to implement harsh forms of repression, which had characterized many early new global demonstrations.

Countersummits and a Multiplicity of Repertoires

In part because of the presence of the BB, in part because of the failure of the police to protect the public right to demonstrate peacefully, one feature common to many countersummits has been frequent clashes with the police: at Davos, Washington, Prague, the Hague, Nice, Davos again, Naples, Quebec City, Gothenburg, and then Genoa. While demonstrators managed to delay the opening session of the WTO by surrounding the summit headquarters at Seattle, later, in Washington, Quebec City, Prague, Nice, Gothenburg, and Genoa, there was an increasingly stringent isolation of the areas where heads of state and high-echelon bureaucrats were meeting. In general, important international summits are extremely delicate events in terms of managing law and order since this is combined with protecting the security of foreign personalities.

The risk of real threats to the lives of foreign governors is combined with the symbolic need for the host government to appear, in the eyes of international public opinion, to be able to assert the monopoly of force in its own territory as a corollary to its sovereignty. The authorities of various countries reacted to transnational protest involving peaceful and nonpeaceful resistance by creating no-go areas around the summit and limiting the freedom of movement from one country to another (see chapter 6 in this volume).

The activists consider that the very fact that these summits cannot be held without some law-and-order problem is success of at least a symbolic nature. As Naomi Klein has written, "The fences that surround the summits become metaphors for an economic model that exiles billions to poverty and exclusion" (2002, xxv). Since the creation of red zones as no-go areas to the demonstration, the aim of the mobilization has shifted—for some demonstrators at least—from attempting to halt the summit's agenda to breaching the prohibitions and barriers that prevent demonstrating in areas declared out-of-bounds. From Seattle to Genoa, the conflict surrounding violation of the red area has become radicalized with, on the one hand, an escalation of the strategies adopted by police in defense of the summit meeting places, and on the other, a multiplication of the tactics tried out by demonstrators in order to penetrate them. While blocking access to delegates in Seattle by joining hands in a human chain was a relatively peaceful event, the objective of breaching the red areas and breaking down the "walls of shame" involves a somewhat more direct interaction with the police. This has led to a radicalization of the conflict that spiraled out of control in Gothenburg with the police opening fire and wounding three demonstrators. The escalation continued in Genoa with a demonstrator being killed by a carabiniere.

How clashes occur during demonstrations depends on the techniques adopted by the police as well as on the conduct of demonstrators. We shall look at the former in the next chapter; as for the latter, during summits escalation also depended on the complexity of the forms of action adopted by the various groups involved in the protest.

Many countersummits combined various forms of action. If we take the Genoa demonstrations as an example, the groups adhering to the GSF signed a work agreement recognizing a plurality of forms of action (GSF 2001c, 39). In a press conference on June 2001, the spokesperson of the GSF stated: "we emphatically repeat that the demonstrations and actions which we shall promote during the G8 summit shall be peaceful . . . we solemnly declare that we have chosen to act in a wholehearted respect for the city and we have chosen not to carry out attacks on any person whether or not he or she is wearing a uniform" (GSF 2001b).

The organizations of the GSF used, however, many different repertoires of action (Figure 9) with the capability of generating high media impact. The main initiatives of the countersummit included an international forum (July 15–22), a march in support of the rights of migrants (July 19), initiatives to penetrate the red area (July 20), and a mass demonstration (July 21). The attack on the red area was planned as a collective action "by means of multiple, diversified actions, through protesting and disobeying, by surrounding with bodies and words and by disobeying the prohibition of access" (GSF 2001c). Bearing in mind the experience gained in the mobilization in Prague, the GSF planned to divide up the streets and squares of the city in accordance with the particular form of action each network planned on implementing on the basis of a "pact of mutual respect."

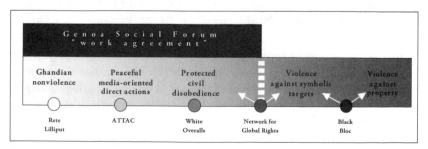

Figure 9. Genoa protest networks' forms of action.

For example, for July 20, the day for laying siege to the red area, the GSF planned a combination of diversified repertoires. While Lilliput, ATTAC, and the Network for Global Rights organized theme-based city squares, the White Overalls planned a march from the Carlini Stadium to Piazza Verdi and then an attempt to penetrate the "wall of shame" and symbolically invade the red area.

The nonviolent activists, organized by both lay and religious associations, gathered in Piazza Manin. In order to emphasize the nonviolent nature of their protest, the Rete Lilliput members painted their hands white, holding them high in front of the police. When the BB broke into the Lilliput theme-based square, a number of nonviolent protesters attempted to act as a buffer with their hands on high between the forces of law and order and the radical groups.

ATTAC, together with left-wing political parties and trade unions, had gathered in Piazza Dante, proclaiming their intention of penetrating the red zone with music, noise, balloons, banners, eggs, and garlic. In its repertoire, ATTAC followed the example of Greenpeace by organizing spectacular initiatives with high media impact; two activists from the ATTAC square managed to get past the net and were immediately arrested by the police (ATTAC–Italy 2001).

On the same day, the White Overalls organized an authorized march during which they aimed to get close to the red area. Prior to the summit, they had promoted public training sessions to prepare their activists in civil disobedience (Velena 2001, 133–39). During a press conference in Palazzo Ducale, where the summit was going to be held, their spokesperson, Luca Casarini, read out the much-debated "Declaration of War against the Powers of Injustice and Poverty," which stated that the White Overalls would not tolerate police repression: "if we must make a choice between clashing with your troops of occupation and buckling under, then we are in no doubt— we'll clash. We're on the warpath too. We'll be in Genoa and our army will disobey your impositions. We're army, born to split up but not before defeating you" (White Overalls 2001b). Criticized from within the GSF, the White Overalls called another press conference declaring "peace to the city of Genoa and its people," promising not to smash windows or commit acts of aggression, and inviting other areas of the movement "to respect the city and its inhabitants" (White Overalls 2001a). The decision not to wear the usual white overalls came from the idea that civil disobedience "was so widespread it could no longer be considered a White Overall tactic but a universal tactic" (*Il Manifesto,* August 3, 2001).

On July 20, the Network for Global Rights, which had been accepted by the GSF provided it toned down its actions, met in Piazza Paolo da Novi, focusing its claims on employment issues. Despite the resistance the Network put up, the square was rapidly overrun by the BB. The Network had stated that its relationship was "critical and constructive with the GSF" (Piedmont Regional Branch of the Network for Global Rights 2001). It promised to adopt forms of action that would be "absolutely respectful of Genoa and its inhabitants although . . . not supine but ready to protect ourselves " (ibid.). The COBAS, a grassroots trade union that belonged to the Network, shared those ideas, affirming, "we go to Genoa with anger and determination but with absolute pacifism provided we are given the guarantee to demonstrate freely. We shall accept no prohibitions . . . we shall bear the means for defence in order to guarantee a 'security service' which will allow everyone to demonstrate safely" (COBAS Confederation 2001).

While rejecting many of the characteristic features of the White Overalls and their context, the Network had attempted to win media coverage in the months leading up to the G8 summit in Genoa with some spectacular initiatives. For instance, on the eve of the meeting between representatives of the Italian government and the leaders of the GSF, they sent a letter to the minister of the interior that contained a spent pistol-bullet casing. This act, highly criticized by other GSF leaders and repeated immediately after the European summit held in Gothenburg, was aimed at convincing the minister not to arm the police during the anti-G8 demonstrations in Genoa.

On July 20, anarchists against the G8, anti-imperialists, and the radical grassroots union representatives joined together in a western suburb of Genoa (far away from the red area) in a march of workers on strike. In one interview, an anarchist activist stated that "not only was there never any indication that the red area had to be broken into, but from the very first coordination meetings of anarchists against the G8, the idea of making a show out of the clashes was rejected because there was obviously a lot at stake and the danger of harsh repression was high. We wanted to keep clear of the clash-repression mechanism the national and international institutions were trying to push the movement into."[6] Although keeping their distance from the BB, the anarchists affirmed that "the destruction of property is in no way comparable to the violence perpetrated by those who bombard defenceless peoples and who decree their death through hunger, disease and torture. Or who cuts short the life of a young demonstrator by killing him with a pistol" (*Umanità Nova,* no. 28, 2001).

As mentioned, unlike what had happened before in Genoa, BB direct action did not target just the symbols of capitalism.[7] Furthermore, some BB demonstrators attacked GSF marchers (for instance, those belonging to the Network in Piazza Paolo da Novi). Very similar to the BB forms of action are those followed by the anarchist-insurrectionalists whose aim is to "contribute to developing incipient revolts in mass insurrections and thereafter in real revolutions . . . we are in favor of immediate, destructive attack against single capitalist and state structures, individuals and organizations" (Bonanno 1999, 29).

Activists and Violence: The Learning Process and Strategic Dilemmas

While the majority of demonstrators reject strategies involving violence, there is still a small but significant percentage that thinks it necessary to react when charged down by the police (see chapter 6 in this volume). While this stance on reacting to police intervention seems less widespread throughout movements than in the past (della Porta and Reiter 2003), it does heighten the probability of violent reaction when the police step in with measures that are considered aggressive. Interviews held in Genoa show that while only 6.7 percent believed resorting to violence was necessary (a mere 1.1 percent for Rete Lilliput and 4.2 percent for ATTAC, with a high of 20 percent for the social centers), it was held to be "unpleasant but understandable," especially in self-defense during police charges, by more than half of the activists in ATTAC (52.1 percent) and the social centers (60 percent). At the ESF, too, the stance of activists vis-à-vis violence was varied. In general, sympathy for violence falls from the use of violence against property in nondemocratic regimes through that in democracies, to the "defensive" use of violence when being charged down by the police.

Setting up focus groups enabled the use of violence to be analyzed in depth. In the opinion of the activists who took part in our focus groups, violence is not a problem (any longer): "It seems like no one mentions it any more, also because in the end only the Black Bloc are violent, but they're not even part of the movement" (FG 3i, 84).[8] The movement's practices are judged to be "highly proper" since, as one activist emphasized, "Honestly, I have never seen violence perpetrated in reality" (FG 5c, 133). The success of the ESF, despite the virulent media campaign carried out on the alleged risks of vandalism, is attributed to a fundamental agreement within the movement:

> FG 4d: It amazed me: we got to the demonstration day with practi-
> cally no apprehensions, as though something had happened in these
> three days, as though we had taken its pulse and realized that nothing
> serious could happen . . . I don't know . . . the feeling I had, and that
> speaking to a lot of people they had too, was one of self-control.
> FG 4g: Of reciprocal trust . . .

FG 4d: Yes, trust, and then the degree of individual civic sense of each person in those three days seemed so high to me that nothing could happen. (105)

This does not mean, however, that there is a uniform opinion in the movement as to what constitutes legitimate forms of protest. There is a split among militants as well as among the different organizations on the option of nonviolence, which some define as a tactical option and others an ethical belief. While nonviolence "is a tactic everyone agrees on" (FG 4f, 107), "it can only be beneficial" (FG 4d, 107), debate is still open on "how to apply this to street marches."

On the one hand, violence is rejected because "it plays into their hands." Violence is spotlighted by the media and generates stigmatization. As one activist put it, "You need very little violence, [only] capsizing a refuse container, and when you do that, you've given them the right to do everything because . . . a violent movement is obviously easier to stamp on, to show up in a bad light" (FG 1c, 17). In particular, for a movement capable of mobilizing big numbers, violence is perceived as bad strategy: "I think one of the reasons the movement has staked a lot, at least up to now, on grow ing in strength and not in aggressiveness is also to make people aware . . . that if you break a small pane of glass, that's how the media will label the movement: the broken window . . . not what's behind it, the aspirations and the plans within the movement" (FG 6a, 158). In this perspective, there is a widespread belief that nonviolence is necessary. The absence of violence in the Florence demonstrations is seen not only as positive, but also as a sign of the movement having become more mature and being able to learn from past mistakes. While "in Florence coming out to march was the right choice, coming out to march peacefully with as many people as possible," in Genoa, instead, "there wasn't enough information and talk among all the groups and their practices" (FG 2d, 55–56).

On the other hand, a more fundamental opposition to violence is gain ing ground, branding it as "ethically wrong," "nonviolence as an ideal" (FG 1b, 18).[9] Nonviolence emerges as "the only way to respond if we want to be different, we have to be coherent. The means must be the same as the end . . . that is, if we start saying the end justifies the means we won't get anywhere, it's old and it's been proved that it's not true and, in the end, the means becomes the end and you fall into the trap" (FG 4a, 107). Violence is thus seen as something the adversary uses: "In my opinion, it's us who are struggling against a violent world and we don't want it to be, so we mustn't use the same weapons as them which might be easier, it would be a shortcut to fight violence with violence. . . . If we're fighting against a certain kind of power because it's violent, we can't turn violent too, because, if we do, we look like that too and so, in the end, the difference isn't so big, that is, there's no difference in the end" (FG 1h, 18).

Violence is also wrong because it leads to a "prevarication—minorities who take over the action of a majority . . . prevarication through the mechanisms of power or even physical violence, but all those mechanisms of power based on prevarication" (FG 4g, 106), and "the minority that imposes itself on the will of the majority . . . it gave you the feeling of those ideas of the '70s and proletarian avant-gardism, the great unwashed masses who, although agreeing on the objectives, didn't have the strength, the energy, and all that sort of thing" (FG 5d, 107). Indeed, the view that one "who thinks in terms of avant-gardism is obviously thinking in military terms" (FG 5c, 136) seems to be fairly common. More than in the movements of the past, rather in direct contrast with them, militarism is criticized as being tied to a wrong-headed concept of an "armed" conquest of power: "The workers' socialist communist revolutionary movement of the twentieth century certainly had a militaristic aspect. Something military in its makeup. It was seen in its language, that, and putting the conquest of power at the top of the list of how to change society from inside. This, too, was a way of accepting militarism in politics and this I think has now to be let go of and rejected" (FG 6e, 160).

Another debate is on the semantic content of the word "violence," which can be limited to verbal aggressiveness or can concentrate on actions of physical violence. As one activist points out, "We all agree not to kill anyone, but we don't agree on where violence starts" (FG 2g, 58). On the one hand, marches, with the potential counterpoint of the police, are looked on askance—seeing as how "Countering the police is useless and . . . every act of violence that aims at, I dunno . . . I get up there facing them and set fire to a soccer ball and give them a pleased look . . . things like that . . . or other useless things that set them off . . . or I go there and chant murderer in their face . . . all this is violence . . . it's certainly violence" (FG 1g, 18). On the other hand, the disobedience practiced by the White Overalls is considered legitimate: "this movement cuts violence out and isn't violent but certainly does allow disobedience, in my opinion, as a means of social intervention that expresses alternative social values . . . well, occupying houses to give shelter to evicted folk . . . is that violence?" (FG 6c, 161).

More important, forms of action that can be both effective in attracting attention and nonstigmatizing are still to be developed. While the activists agree that violence is counterproductive, there is a perceived risk in rejecting more disruptive, and thus somehow more visible and effective, forms of action outright: "In my opinion this is a mistake on the part of the movement, precisely because there are fundamental differences between so-called violence and civil disobedience, and there is the tendency, thought out or spontaneous, I don't know, to leave it a bit to one side" (FG 3f, 58). While by using violence "it's too easy for you to play into their hands, and you also run the risk of undermining the issue you're trying to further," there is the fear for "the tendency to indiscriminately define as violence any kind of action that creeps just over the borderline of demonstrating and shouting peace," or the fact that "civil disobedience which is now seen the same as those who set fire to Esso when there are a great many shades of struggle that, in my opinion are fundamental, and on the contrary, from the movement's point of view, civil disobedience has become discredited, I think . . . it's not used enough" (FG 3d, 57).

The quest for consensus seems to have led to a focus on nonconflictual forms of action: "Other forms of struggle that don't mean violence are often kept at arms-length by the movement, perhaps so it'll be able to line up behind the term of pacifism that means everything but means nothing" (FG 2c, 58). Thus, for a time at least, what had once been considered fully legitimate forms of action, such as occupying, were looked on askance. Note two activists, "if by violence you mean anything that violates the constituted order and all the laws that exist, well then I'm violent . . . we're all violent" (FG 2a and 2c, 58).

After Genoa it seemed as though the issue of modes of acting had had a disrupting effect on the movement, but the differences seem to be on the decrease. In particular, while the social centers have given up using protective materials in post-Genoa demonstrations, the ethical nonviolents have declared that even some disruptive forms of disobedience are legitimate. The focus groups noted this growing consensus: "One thing I heard a lot in the past from the Rete Lilliput, but not now, was the critique of the aggressiveness of their language, you know, Casarini [a spokesperson of the Disobedients] says, we want to break into the red area, . . . breaking into the red area doesn't mean killing somebody . . . also because . . . the nonviolent movement has always flown the flag of disobedience, hasn't it?" (FG 4c, 103). "The nonviolent movement has been very radical, that is, breaking into the red area. . . . The Disobedients, at least as far as I know, are the perfect nonviolents here, because they deal well with the media, they plan out their action toward an objective, they say what it is, and they do it without using weapons, banking, as Casarini says, on their bodies, don't they? And that's the idea perfectly" (FG 4g, 103).

Consensus also emerges through a learning process in which the mistakes made in Genoa are recognized, in particular a certain naïveté on the part of the movement:

> FG 4g: We've taken on board the idea of not answering back when provoked, that our objective, our enemy, isn't the policeman; the aim is something else, which seems obvious but it's not 100 percent understood.
>
> FG 4e: In Florence, anyway, it was the exact opposite; if some ass had tried to kick up a fuss there would have been fifty people there to stop him . . .
>
> FG 4g: Maybe that didn't happen in Genoa . . .
>
> FG 4b: There wasn't that in Genoa . . .
>
> FG 4a: No, not at all . . .
>
> FG 4f: At Genoa it was one big mess-up . . .
>
> FG 4a: A mess-up and a half . . .
>
> FG 4d: Yes, but not so much a messed-up organization as messed-up minds . . .
>
> FG 4e: Yes, but we were all pretty scared . . .
>
> FG 4b: It's also because we weren't prepared because, for example, when these so-called Black Blocs started chucking cobblestones everybody just stood there . . . in disbelief. It wasn't as though anybody stepped in to stop them. (102–5)

Giving up more disruptive forms of action is seen as the price to pay, temporarily at least, in order that the movement not be widely tagged as radical. In one activist's opinion, "After what happened in Genoa, it became clear that we had to wake up and get wise on how to deal with provocation" (FG 4g, 103). It is therefore perceived that "strong . . . ways of conflict, but disobedience, too, we had to leave behind because they leave the door open to clashes and to us getting this violent label; so lately we've had to march an awful lot, and this is fine considering the state we're in, it's OK because by now we've taken . . . we've got dignity . . . but then again it's limiting . . . it's harder to go and occupy nowadays. . . . I wouldn't like us to take this too far . . . it's that when we're faced with the tactics of our adversary, we've got to retreat to positions that are a bit weaker . . . we've got to think about this a bit. . . . I wouldn't like this to go too far and for us to take it on board too much." (FG 4f, 108)

The Repertoire of the Protest: A Conclusion

One characteristic of the social movement is, as we have seen, its use of complex protest repertoires with, in addition, the capability of innovating with respect to previously adopted forms of action. In particular, since Seattle, activists critical of globalization have used nonconventional and mostly nonviolent forms of action. Many of these are inherited from past movements, but many have been renewed and adapted, emphasizing their media slant and their capability of cross-national dissemination. Particularly innovative are the forms of action oriented toward consumerism—especially boycotts—able to address the growing power of major corporations not directly responsible to the electing public, and highly sensitive to the attitudes of the buying public. Another form of innovative action, particularly suitable for gaining international visibility and for highlighting the shift of decision making toward international organisms, is the countersummit, which exploits the window of visibility offered by summits. Both forms of action can strengthen the supranational links among groups.

Despite this ability to adapt, the movement for globalization from below is faced with the eternal strategic dilemma between disruptive action, which is good for grabbing media attention but risks stigmatization by public opinion, and more conventional forms of action, which enhance legitimization but lower visibility and the capability of mobilizing activists (Lipsky 1965). As has been noted for many movements in the past, while a certain degree of nonconventionality is intrinsic to protest, an action seen as overly radical risks alienating public opinion. The research shows that movement organizations and their activists are aware of the risk that radical actions involve and also of the need to seek disruptive forms of action. Projecting the protest into the media is perceived as a resource and a hazard in this sense: media resonance is considered an important result but certainly not the sole aim of the protest, which is also a relevant tool for building collective solidarity. While the repertoire of potential actions seems effectively limited, there is a continual quest for forms of action that can help generate recognition as well as identity "in action." Having a plurality of actors involved in the movement means special challenges, but the protest repertoire does not seem prisoner to any process of radicalization; activists show a great willingness to reflect and self-criticize on past mistakes.

Especially after Genoa, debate within the movement on the dangers of using radical forms of action, violence in particular, has intensified. Criticism within the movement has often focused on the negative effect that clashing with the police, setting fire to cars, and smashing windows has on the public image of protesting.[10] Furthermore, there is growing criticism in the movement against violence because it is a form of action considered typical of the enemy. In particular, with mobilization expanding against the second war in Iraq, the option for nonviolent repertoires have been defended with increasing vigor as being necessary and coherent with the aims of a movement that repudiates the use of force as a means of resolving conflicts. Besides, in Italy in particular, after the violence of the seventies, a drastic swing in the relationship between social movements and violence emerged with the demonstrations against the NATO installations of Cruise and Pershing II nuclear missiles in the early eighties. While violence in the seventies was legitimated first as a means of defense in clashes with the extreme right and the police and then later increasingly as an expression of the combativeness of some of the organizations within the movement, the peace movement has always held violence to be both counterproductive tactically and, especially, ethically wrongheaded. After the first episodes of civil disobedience in the nonviolent obstruction at the Comiso military base where the missiles were to be installed, nonviolence has always been brandished as a necessary expression of a rejection of the militarism, machismo, and violence of the opponent.

After Genoa, and even more after September 11, the greater attention demonstrators have paid to the self-control of the marches and the renewal of negotiations with the police have reduced the chances of escalation: the ESF in Florence, among others, went off without a trace of violence despite real fears and exaggerated scaremongering beforehand. While conviction toward nonviolence on the part of the vast majority of the activists is something new—and hence a radical discontinuity—vis-à-vis the seventies, it must be added that the Genoa demonstrations set off a cycle of protest that, in the years 2001, 2002, and 2003, saw many marches with a much higher number of participants than the organizers' most optimistic hopes. Despite the G8 clashes in Genoa and the escalation of protests at Seattle, Prague, and Gothenburg beforehand, the big marches of later months and years (including the closing march of the ESF, around which so much alarm had been created by the mass media) went off in a peaceful manner.

It should be added that the activists in this cycle of protest, although nonviolent, have a lot of experience in repertoires of civil disobedience, which had begun to spread in the early eighties. As is typical of protest, not only is this form of action fairly unconventional, but it is also somewhat ambiguous in terms of its legality. Just as striking and marches were on the fringe of legality in the early days, so are blocking roads and railways and occupying schools and public buildings (which constitute a large part of the background of a great number of activists). Indeed, civil disobedience is a strategy based on the limited breach of rules and aimed at rendering protest as visible as possible, grabbing media attention to highlight the relevance of the activists' cause through the intensity of their commitment. While symbolic provocation and limited lawbreaking are typical components of protest—as unconventional acts—managing them is an extremely delicate matter, as witness the railway blockages against the second war in Iraq, and often involve a difficult balance between acknowledging the right to nonviolent protest and repression of unlawfulness. The harsh behavior of the police in Seattle and Genoa was attributed to the growing tendency on the part of the police to lump civil disobedience and violence together (see Klein 2002, 123). Besides, squatting and blocking roads have been defined as violent forms of action not only by parties of the center-right but also by many politicians of the center-left coalition. Furthermore, a split emerged after Genoa in the form of criticism to the forms of direct action implemented by the Disobedients. It does, however, look like consensus has been reached recently between the various actors of the movement on the use of nonviolent resistance—such as blocking trains that transport war material or dismantling the centers where immigrants are detained who are awaiting extradition because of illegally entering the country.

6

Transnational Protest and Public Order

A New Escalation

Social movements direct their demands to institutions chiefly by using forms of protest. Their very use of unconventional forms of action involves the state not just as a counterpart in negotiation on the movement's objectives, but also as the guarantor of public order. One important aspect of the institutional response to the protest is the strategies for controlling it. An important theme is the relationship between police and movements.

In authoritarian regimes the sole criterion for evaluating internal security forces is their efficacy; in democratic systems the chief pointer to the democratic success not just of the police as an institution but of the state as a whole is the capacity to reconcile respect for freedoms and individual rights with protection of public security and public order. For the police in modern democratic societies, *protest policing,* the control of protest, is one of the most delicate tasks: at stake are not only personal freedoms but also citizens' rights to political participation, and thus the very essence of the democratic system. The public order strategies employed by the police reflect the respect the state shows for the rights and freedoms of citizens. In this sense, a policeman acting to control protest demonstrations is perceived not just as a representative of political power but also as an indicator of the quality of democracy in the political system.

The police forces often constitute the state's most immediate face in the eyes of demonstrators, influencing their strategic choices: traditionally, demonstrators respond to very repressive police strategies with a radicalization of forms of protest. At the same time, *protest policing* is a key feature for the development and the self-definition of the police as an institution and as a profession.[1] The gradual affirmation of the police as the main agency specializing in this task was of fundamental importance for the process of modernization and professionalizing of the police forces in Europe in the nineteenth century. Moreover, waves of protest have had important effects on both the public-order strategies and the organization of the police—observed, for instance, by Jane Morgan (1987) in her research on the police in Britain. In contemporary democratic societies, the way the police forces tackle protest seems to be a significant, if not a dominant, aspect of their self-image (Winter 1998a).

According to many studies, since the 1970s modes of controlling protest in Western democracies have became more tolerant (della Porta and Reiter 1998a). The police forces have developed new public-order strategies based on the search for dialogue with the new social movements, and are characterized by less frequent recourse to force and a growing tolerance toward new forms of protest, even formally unlawful ones such as civil disobedience. Over the same period, studies on social movements wondered if they were becoming institutionalized, or at least "civilized," with a reduction in more radical forms of action.

After decades of apparent normalization of the confrontation between police and protest, recently more attention has been given to the dangers of radicalizing political and social conflicts. In the history of the movement for globalization from below, clashes between police and demonstrators have been frequent. The authorities attributed responsibility for those clashes mostly to the extreme fringes of the movement allegedly using urban guerrilla tactics, but also to the movement as a whole, accusing it of ambiguous positions on the question of violence. On the other hand, the police have been criticized by the movement and a sizable part of public opinion for disproportionate actions infringing on the civil rights of the majority of peaceful demonstrators. The EU Network of Independent Experts in Fundamental Rights (CFR-CDF), set up by the European Commission in September 2002, emphasized: "Police conduct at demonstrations organized on the occasion of big international summit meetings constitutes a source of particular concern" (EU Network of Independent Experts in Fundamental Rights 2003, 58). Even the movement's more moderate sections have seen the clashes on the street as part of a broader strategy of repression against the movement: uncoincidentally, Naomi Klein titled a section of her book "Fencing in the Movement: Criminalizing Dissent" (2002). Soon after Seattle Jackie Smith warned, "The repression faced by protesters should raise warning flags for scholars of social movements about how globalization affects democracy" (2001, 16).

Criticism of the police is in fact not limited to their intervention in the streets but extends to operations during the preparatory phase of demonstrations. They have been accused of trying to impede demonstrations by an outright ban (e.g., in Davos in 2001 or in Munich in February 2002, and on other occasions, as in Prague in September 2000 when an initial ban was lifted by court order) or by obstructing access to the demonstration site (in the case of the WEF in Davos in January 2003). They were further criticized for suspending the free movement of people inside the EU by re-introducing border controls, for dubious intelligence activities and intrusive Internet surveillance, for indiscriminate searches of private homes and organizations' offices on a feeble legal basis, and for various acts of intimidation, either directly (e.g., in Munich in February 2002, associations involved in the preparation of the demonstration against the NATO security meeting were threatened with a cutoff of public funding), or indirectly, by making protest seem so scary that nobody wants to go (Klein 2002, 133ff.).

Media images focused the attention of world public opinion on the clashes between the police and demonstrators. In Seattle, on the occasion of the protests against the WTO meeting in November 1999, and at numerous subsequent demonstrations, the police were accused of excessive use of force against peaceful demonstrators and innocent bystanders. The indiscriminate use of tear gas and nonlethal weapons on protesters not involved in violent behavior or posing any threat to property or the police was specifically criticized. The use of firearms at Gothenburg (EU summit, June 2001)—which only a month later was to repeat itself with more tragic consequences at Genoa—led to the recommendation by the UN Human Rights Committee (in its concluding observations on the fifth periodic report of Sweden) that during demonstrations the state party should ensure that no equipment that could endanger human life was used (Human Rights Committee 2002, 2).

Reports of unjustified arrests and, above all, disrespect for the rights of people in police custody, from verbal abuse to physical maltreatment, accompanied numerous demonstrations in Seattle, Prague, Gothenburg, Genoa, and Barcelona (in June 2001 and March 2002), among others. Criticism was also raised with regard to the judicial proceedings: for the trials of demonstrators some have talked of "judicial repression," and various human rights organizations and institutions have warned of a climate of impunity in connection with judicial proceedings against members of the police forces. It was alleged that police faked evidence against demonstrators in Gothenburg, in Genoa, and in Saloniki, Greece at the EU summit in June 2003.

How is this regression to be explained? What special challenges does the movement improperly termed "no global" present to police forces and governments? What internal features of police forces and which external factors have facilitated the escalation? We shall endeavor to think about these points from more than a merely Italian perspective. We shall briefly illustrate two different protest policing styles, setting Italy in this context and picking out the specific features of police action at Genoa. We shall explain the features of protest control at Genoa by discussing three different approaches: on a first interpretation, the public-order problem must be tackled, namely, the certain features of the movement that determine the police response; a second stresses the importance of internal features of the police, such as their professional culture and organizational structure, both filtered through police knowledge, i.e., the way the police perceive their role and outside society; a third focuses on such external factors as the role of government or the size of the civil rights coalition, counterpoised as defending the right to express dissent to the law-and-order coalition. After Genoa, a supranational level of public order to explain Italian police conduct has also been evoked (IPIC 2001c, 161, 165).[2] A concluding section will seek to understand, by considering the ESF in Florence in November 2002, what lessons have been drawn from the Genoa experience by the political authorities, the police, and the movement.

De-escalation or Escalation? Public Order and International Summits

Escalated Force and Negotiated Management: Two Protest Policing Styles

Research has picked out three main strategic areas for protest control that are favored differently by the police in various historical periods (della Porta and Reiter 1997): *coercive strategies,* use of weapons and physical force to control or disperse demonstrations; *persuasive strategies,* attempts to control protest through prior contacts with activists and organizers; *information strategies,* consisting of widespread information gathering as a preventive feature in protest control, and the collection of targeted information, including the use of modern audiovisual technologies, to identify lawbreakers without having to intervene directly.

Police actions can vary in terms of force used (brutal or soft), extent of conduct regarded as illegitimate (ranging between repression and tolerance), strategies for controlling various actors (generalized or selective), police respect for the law (illegal or legal), the moment when police act (preemptive or reactive), the degree of communication with demonstrators (confrontation or consensus), the capacity to adjust to emerging situations (rigid or flexible), the degree of formalization of the rules of the game (formal or informal), the degree of training (professional or improvised) (della Porta and Reiter 1998b, 4).

It has been noted that the combination of these dimensions tends to define two different internally consistent protest policing styles (see Table 18). The first, *escalated force*, gives low priority to the right to demonstrate, innovative forms of protest are poorly tolerated, communication between police and demonstrators is reduced to essentials, and there is frequent use of coercive means or even illegal methods (such as agents provocateurs); the second, *negotiated management*, by contrast, sees the right to demonstrate peacefully as a priority, even disruptive forms of protest are tolerated, communication between demonstrators and police is considered basic to peaceful conduct of protest, and coercive means are avoided as far as possible, emphasizing selectivity of operations (McPhail, Schweingruber, and McCarthy 1998, 51–54; della Porta and Fillieule 2004). To these dimensions one might add the type of information strategy police forces employ in controlling protest, with a distinction between generalized control and control focused on those possibly guilty of an offense.

In Western democracies, there was a radical transformation in strategies for controlling public order and associated operational practices and techniques from the escalated force model to negotiated management, particularly following the great protest wave that culminated in the late 1960s. While the widespread conception of rights to demonstrate one's dissent has tended to become more inclusive, intervention strategies have moved away from the coercive model predominant until then. During the 1970s and 1980s, though with pauses and temporary reversals, we may note a growing trend to tolerate minor breaches of the law. Among changes apparent in strategies for controlling public order is a reduction in the use of force, greater emphasis on dialogue, and the large investment of resources in gathering information (della Porta and Reiter 1998a). These strategies, called de-escalation (or, in the Italian case, prevention), are based on a number of specific pathways and assumptions. Before demonstrations, demonstrator representatives and the police have to meet and negotiate in detail on routes and conduct to be observed during demonstrations (including the more or less symbolic violations permitted demonstrators), charges are never to be aimed at peaceful groups, agreements reached with demonstration leaders are never to be broken, and lines of communication between them and the police must be kept open throughout the demonstration. The police must first and foremost guarantee the right to demonstrate peacefully; violent groups must be separated from the rest of the march and stopped without

Table 18. Styles of protest policing

Type of strategy	Protest policing styles		Italian case		
	Escalated force	Negotiated management	Italy in the 1980s and 1990s	Genoa anti-G8 demonstrations	Florence ESF
Coercive strategies	Massive use of force to deter even minor violations	Tolerance of minor breaches	Selective tolerance	Massive use of force even against peaceful demonstrators	Low visibility of public order units
Persuasive strategies	Intimidating use of relations with organizers	Partnership aimed at ensuring the right to demonstrate	Informal negotiations	Low trust in negotiation	Informal negotiations
Information strategies	Generalized and indiscriminate information gathering	Information gathering focused on punishing offenses	Generalized information gathering	Generalized information gathering and alarmist use of information	Generalized information gathering

endangering the security of the peaceful demonstrators (Fillieule and Jobard 1998; McPhail, Schweingruber, and McCarthy 1998; Waddington 1994; Winter 1998b; della Porta 1998).

Though these are developments common to Western democracies, the differences among the various national models in state responses to the new challengers have not disappeared. In postwar Italy, in the special climate of "Cold Civil War," a particularly marked form of the escalated force model developed.[3] The early 1960s, with center-left governments, were typified by détente, but elements of traditional strategies reemerged with the wave of protest in 1968, which in Italy was particularly long and conflict ridden. During the 1980s and 1990s, there was a shift from the escalated force model to negotiated management, albeit with some peculiarities. The change was promoted not so much by political institutions as by the movement to democratize the police that developed within the police forces themselves, basic to the 1981 reform that led to the demilitarization and unionization of the state police (della Porta and Reiter 2003).

As regards coercive strategies, there was increasingly less recourse to force, though the harder control repertoire survived and was used in particular against the social centers and in controlling hooliganism of sports fans. In persuasive strategies, there was an evolution from the use of various forms of intimidation to negotiation toward the common end of guaranteeing the holding of peaceful demonstrations. By contrast with other countries, however, negotiating practices were not formalized, nor did specialized police units emerge for dialogue with organizers. This opened the door for an opportunistic use of negotiation. Smaller changes came in the use of information strategies, where the traditional conception of the police as the chief intelligence gatherer for the state continued to prevail (della Porta 1998).

It should be stressed that even "policing by consent" (Waddington 1998) is a police strategy to control protest, albeit respecting demonstrators' rights and freedoms as far as possible. What was seen by many as the consolidated post-'68 standard, no longer in debate, proved fragile when faced with the new challenge of a transnational protest movement. The Genoa G8 reignited an almost forgotten debate on the fundamental rights of citizens and the question of how much power the state is allowed in protecting the rule of law (*Der Spiegel,* no. 31, 2001, 22ff.). Police forces that had, in a period of demand for greater security by citizens, seen themselves legitimized—in the Italian case by the fight against terrorism and later against organized crime—were again being associated with the image of the brutal truncheon wielder. While the change to us seemed sudden, it should be borne in mind that at the time of the "end of history" thesis various warning signs were noted only with difficulty. Amnesty International (AI), for instance, in recent years has expressed concern with police conduct in the great majority of current EU member states. The EU Network of Independent Experts in Fundamental Rights affirmed: "Violence committed by the police remains a source of concern in all the member States of the EU" (EU Network of Independent Experts in Fundamental Rights 2003, 57).

As we have emphasized, strong criticisms of police conduct in various countries, in Europe and in North America, were made because of their actions in the preparatory stage of movement demonstrations, their actions on the streets, and their treatment of persons detained, regarding their preventive and information strategies as well as their coercive strategies. The negotiated management model in fact seems to have been applied inconsistently in many demonstrations organized by the movement for globalization from below, especially those against the international summits, in the course of which a long escalation has come about. In particular, the administration of public order at the summits often seems not to have been able to defend the right to demonstrate peacefully.

Preventive Strategies

Genoa confirmed the strategy of physically isolating the locations for the summit by partly closing access roads to the city and setting up a buffer zone (the yellow zone), with restrictions on freedom to demonstrate, and a fortified red zone, where the summit was to be held, which was barred to demonstrators. In mid-July, while tall barriers were being set up to protect the red zone, closure of the railway stations, airport, and motorway tollbooths was announced. The red zone, with thirteen access portals and a five-mile perimeter (at Prague it had been a little more than one mile, and at Quebec less than four miles), closed not just the areas for the summit, but also several city streets, like Via XX Settembre, the location of major commercial centers.

In the preparations for the G8, the governments' attention was concentrated on keeping violent foreign activists out of Italy through massive frontier controls. On July 11 the Schengen agreement on free movement of people within the EU was suspended until midnight on July 21. Border checks were carried out on 140,000 people, and 2,093 were rejected, 298 of them alleged members of the Black Bloc (BB) and 1,795 for other reasons (IPIC 2001f, 139). Among these were cases like the translator for the

Council of the EU, who reached Milan by air but was rejected at the frontier "because he arrogantly declared he was going to Genoa to demonstrate" (in *Diario*, Genoa special issue, supplement to no. 31, 2001, 13).

Particularly in the endeavors to keep violent activists, or those so presumed, far from the city hosting the summit, even before the Genoa G8 a European level of protest policing was manifest, part of the cooperation among European Community police forces started in the mid-1970s and which with the Maastricht Treaty (1993) became the EU's "third pillar"; even after the Amsterdam Treaty (1999), however, this cooperation retained its intergovernmental characteristics. At a meeting of the European Council for Justice and Home Affairs on July 13, 2001, held after the Gothenburg incidents in order to increase collaboration among the various national police forces to ensure peaceful holding of the summits, the German minister Schily proposed to "Europeanize" and apply to the "no globals" a German practice developed to oppose soccer hooligans and later neo-Nazis. It consisted of the *Ausreiseverbot,* a ban on leaving the country.[4] Schily's proposal—providing for the creation of a European database of the "violent" and the introduction to all EU countries of the instrument of the *Ausreiseverbot*—met resistance from other member states. Referring to a joint action decided (without debate) in May 1997, the Council ultimately recommended increased information exchange, the deployment of liaison officers, the national implementation of an *Ausreiseverbot,* and, if it proved essential, the temporary reintroduction of internal border controls on the basis of article 2.2 of the Schengen convention.[5]

Previous experience with movement demonstrations in other countries and their own influenced the strategies of the police forces. In Sweden, after criticisms for excessive use of force by the police during the ECOFIN summit in Malmö on April 21, 2001, the social-democratic government announced that for the Gothenburg summit it wished to pursue a policy of dialogue with the movement.[6] For the first time in their history the Swedish police set up a contact group with the protest organizers, and numbered helmets were introduced to facilitate identification of individual police officers (a measure that was withdrawn directly after the events in Gothenburg). In Italy, with the center-left government still in office, the demonstrations against the Global Forum on e-government in Naples on March 17 ended in violent clashes. After some attempts to force the police cordons by the more radical fringes of the demonstrators, charges caught the peaceful groups while the procession was breaking up.

By contrast with Sweden, it does not seem that the Naples precedent led to efforts to strengthen the search for dialogue with the movement or bring in measures to enhance the accountability of police personnel in Italy. The preventive strategies pursued by the Italian police in the preparatory stage of the Genoa G8, to the contrary, did not favor negotiation, even though police leaders repeatedly claimed they had sought to set up a relationship and open lines of communication with protest movements. In contacts with protest organizers, the authorities, with the center-left government still in office, long sought to persuade the movement to drop any demonstration around the summit, an attitude that in itself provoked protest actions.[7] The impression of low trust in negotiations seems confirmed by the fact that the *questore* of Genoa, the person in charge of arranging the public-order services, claims to have seen Margherita Paolini—mandated by the center-left government to communicate with the GSF and much admired by a part of the movement for her great experience in seeking to smooth relations between institutions and civil society (IPIC 2001j, 83ff.)—only once, and did not regard her as a valid interlocutor (2001f, 43).

The Gothenburg events led the new center-right government to prioritize dialogue. The negotiations with the movement, until then conducted at a local level, were entrusted to the national coordination of police forces.[8] As at Gothenburg, where the contact group started operating only five weeks before the summit, specific negotiations on hosting demonstrators and on the carrying out of protest actions began only after much delay: the first meeting between the GSF and the national police chief was on June 24.

Communication between police and the movement has often fallen short, not just at the preparative stage of protest events but also on the street. As the report by the commission of inquiry into police actions at Gothenburg points out, the contact group during the operational stage was hampered by an uncertain definition of its powers.[9] At Genoa, on more than one occasion the organizers could not contact the police: the Lilliput pacifists assembled in Piazza Manin, for instance, were informed by telephone by a GSF spokesperson three-quarters of an hour ahead that a BB group was probably moving toward the square. All efforts to contact the police failed. The nonviolent activists managed to defend the square from the BB people, but then fell to a police charge (IPIC 2001j, 34ff., 59, 125ff.). On their part, police figures complained that various GSF spokespersons had, even with the demonstrations still going on, given contradictory indications and requests.

Other messages sent out by the police to the movement as preventive measures confirm the impression of deviation from the negotiated management strategy, or at least of inconsistent application of it. The instrument of the internal expulsion notice was used to keep away some Italian social-center militants from Genoa, with a ban on returning to Genoa for three years (Pepino 2001, 895). Searches of private houses and social centers were carried out, often problematically based on Article 41 of the Penal Code, which allows searches without authorization by a magistrate but only for weapons and in exceptional cases of necessity and urgency.[10]

Information Strategies

The information strategies employed at Genoa, as later in Florence, seem to be characterized chiefly by the indiscriminate and generalized collection of information. We shall return later to the effect that the alarmist use of this information—which recalls the case of the 1968 Democratic Party convention in Chicago (Donner 1990, 116–17)—seems to have had on police preparations and the officers' emotional states.

The collection of information aimed at rejecting presumed violent activists at borders, partly through collaboration with other European police forces, has proved of little use. Two hundred ninety-eight people were rejected as BB members, while the number of arrivals was estimated at 2,000, and the Italian police had compiled a list of 1,439 names (ICIP 2001f, 134ff.). There also seems to have been a lack of use of specific information by the police: for instance, SISDE (civil secret service) had informed police headquarters that on July 20 a BB group would assemble in Piazza da Novi, allocated to the Network for Global Rights as its theme square. The police did not act, and the Network felt compelled to abandon the square (Gubitosa 2003, 170ff.). At both Genoa and Gothenburg, information strategies instead had an important part in subsequent identification of activists responsible for episodes of violence.[11]

Coercive Strategies

The toughness and nonselectivity of many police operations at Genoa and the elements of downright illegality that are emerging from inquiries by the magistrates led to the assertion from inside the police that "we 'saw' ourselves and found we were different from what we thought we were, what we believed we were."[12] The police made massive use of tear gas and irritants (with over 6,200 grenades launched on Friday and Saturday), ignoring a February 2001 circular from the police chief recommending maximum caution and care in using truncheons or tear gas.[13] Members of the police forces fired at least twenty pistol rounds, one with a fatal outcome (IPIC 2001c, 145). Repeated violent charges on both Friday and Saturday massively involved the great bulk of peaceful demonstrators, too. On the initiative of some of the most senior police officers present, armed vehicles were driven at high speed into the crowd (Gubitosa 2003, 219ff.). There was no provision to protect demonstrators with a police cordon opening the procession (IPIC 2001c, 164; Gubitosa 2003, 505), and as at Gothenburg, operations against BB provocations (all far away from the red zone) were failures.

Genoa seems to mark the culmination of the escalation of coercive strategies employed against the movement. At Gothenburg individual officers had recourse to firearms, wounding three demonstrators, one seriously, but the Swedish police did not use tear gas, and public demonstrations organized by the movement were able to take place peacefully. At Prague there were 600 wounded, including 150 police; for Genoa estimates reach over 1,000 wounded (Gubitosa 2003, 177f.). As at Prague and Gothenburg, the large number of detentions was reflected only minimally in arrest warrants, mostly against foreigners.[14] If nothing else, this seems to point to police inability to detain violent individuals, who on figures supplied by the police themselves were much more numerous, or to supply the magistracy with sufficient proof to validate detentions.

A clear move away from negotiated management strategy, providing for clear agreements on permitted initiatives and forms of protest, can be seen in the key event at Genoa, when a carabinieri contingent charged the Disobedients parade, on an authorized route and, according to various evidence, still peaceful up to that point.[15] The official version from the police, that the attack was started by the demonstrators, was watered down in the majority report by the parliamentary commission, given the quantity of evidence and video material that refuted it.[16] As far as is known, no effort was made by the police forces to communicate with the contact group, which (as always) was at the head of the Disobedients' march. There are worrying implications in the version supplied in an interview with the police officer leading the carabinieri squad. He said the attack was necessary because with the red zone at their backs they could not let the march advance as far as Piazza Verdi, that is, the point up to which police headquarters had itself given authorization.[17] While the Disobedients claim it was a premeditated trap, it seems no less serious if the order to charge was the outcome of incompetence, confusion, or a collapse in lines of communication and command.[18]

Until the charge, there had been no incidents, except for pieces of vandalism by BB people not on the march, but "disorder was," according to *La Stampa* newspaper correspondent Giulietto Chiesa (2001, 44), "from that moment the direct, unambiguous outcome of a choice by the carabinieri." In fact, self-defense and solidarity reactions, including violent ones, were triggered: "The carabinieri advance accordingly met with resistance which, apart from being active, was inevitable: either you wait for the truncheon to hit you, or you defend yourself. Thus, before my very eyes, the two or three thousand young people heading the march were converted into active, angry combatants" (45). During these clashes a carabinieri Land Rover was trapped, and its occupants were attacked by the demonstrators: one of the carabinieri inside fired, killing a twenty-three-year-old Genoese demonstrator, Carlo Giuliani.

Some episodes that occurred after the demonstration was over, or at any rate happened off the streets, clearly bring out conduct by members of the police forces that even spokesmen for the center-right majority have termed particularly serious and seems to display a punitive imprint.[19] The break-in at the Diaz-Pertini school, which the GSF was being allowed to use as a dormitory, was based on Article 41 of the Penal Code. However, the search was aimed at finding material useful for reconstructing the facts, not just weapons. The police found the time for planning meetings at police headquarters and communicating with the national police chief, but not for applying to the magistrates for authorization, though they were informed of the impending action (Pepino 2001, 895). Sixty-two of the ninety-three demonstrators detained inside the school were hospitalized, with prognoses ranging from five days to indeterminate. Out of ninety-three arrests, there were seventy-eight applications for confirmation; no fewer than sixty-six arrests were not confirmed, with only one remand in custody and one residence ban. The police report of an attempt to stab an officer inside the school was denied by a subsequent carabinieri investigation. The list of objects confiscated includes ten Swiss knives, various gas masks and swimming goggles, one wig, various greaves and other physical protections, six films and three audiotapes, two Walkmans, three cell phones, seventeen cameras, sixty black t-shirts and other clothes the same color, and one red flag (Gubitosa 2003, 386ff.). It now seems established that the two Molotov cocktails presented as the most serious evidence of the dangerousness of the people inside Diaz-Pertini had been brought and deposited in the school by the police themselves (Gubitosa 2003, 389ff.). In another part of the school complex, the police broke into the headquarters of the Genoa Legal Forum and Indymedia, destroying the lawyers' computers and taking away video and paper materials, including denunciations collected against the police.

Hundreds of men and women detained by the police at the Bolzaneto barracks also complained of brutalities; they stated they had been repeatedly beaten, forced to sing songs against communists, Jews, and gays, and threatened with sexual abuse. Talks with lawyers were delayed on the basis of a previous agreement with the prosecution service postponing exercise of the arrestee's right to confer with a defender (Pepino 2001, 902). Foreign detainees (mostly EU citizens) were given expulsion orders without going before a magistrate. Many expulsions, always accompanied by a ban on return to Italy without special authorization from the Ministry of the Interior, were based on police detentions that the magistracy had already, by not confirming them, pronounced illegitimate. There was an attempt to expel an Italian citizen with dual nationality (Swiss and Italian), and to expel to her homeland a Turkish woman who was a political refugee in Switzerland under the 1951 Geneva Conventions. Subsequently, the magistracy accepted all the appeals against expulsion orders by EU citizens (and ten of the twelve from non-EU citizens) (Genoa Legal Forum 2002, 157ff.).

The Movement as a Public-Order Problem?

Violence and the Movement

What, then, were the causes of the escalation? What impelled the move away from détente strategies to control public order? A first answer—suggested by, for instance, the majority report of the parliamentary investigative commission—puts the blame on demonstrator conduct (see Figure 10). We read there, for instance, that "on both 20 and 21 July the intention for soft control of public order clashed with the mass provocations brought by the intermingling—unopposed by the organizers—of a crowd of some 10,000 violent individuals in the peaceful demonstration; this intermingling made it impossible to separate the violent from the nonviolent" (IPIC 2001a, 221). The parliamentary majority, accusing the GSF of playing a double game, claims that "throughout the G8, the violent, subversive sector of demonstrators took advantage of tolerance by the peaceful demonstrators. These took no specific actions aimed at identifying, isolating or excluding violent and subversive individuals" (243). The day after the searches at the Diaz-Pertini school, Prime Minister Berlusconi declared that it was impossible to distinguish between the GSF and the BB.

As we have seen in chapter 5, our research to the contrary points to a very widespread rejection of violence, whether from support for the ideology of nonviolence or as a politically opportune strategic choice. Ninety percent of demonstrators interviewed by us at Genoa stated they had never used violent tactics. For 40 percent of those interviewed, recourse to violence was always to be condemned, 53 percent regarded it as undesirable even if justifiable, and only 6.7 percent as necessary. Still clearer is the nonviolent option emerging from the data collected at the Florence ESF: for 51.7 percent of the participants interviewed, even violence against symbols

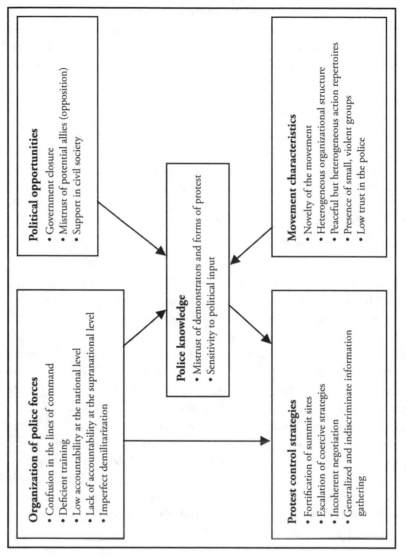

Figure 10. Explanations of protest control strategies in Genoa.

of neoliberalism is always to be condemned; only 5.5 percent considered it necessary.

The Movement's Novelty and Network Structure

While the movement is mainly peaceful, some features certainly do not facilitate control of public order. The movement's novelty—even in the most ordinary sense of its apparently improvised origins—tests police capacity to properly assess its numerical strength, cohesion, and the objectives of protest actions. Already after Seattle, and later after Gothenburg and Genoa, the police claimed they had to face absolutely unheard-of phenomena. While these assertions, particularly in the Italian case, seem exaggerated, the fact remains that in the new globals we are once again, after a long period of social and political peace, seeing a widespread street movement that challenges not so much a particular political decision as a model of development for society.

The movement's networked, heterogeneous structure, more marked than in the past, the emphasis on the absence of leadership in the name of the capacity for self-administration from below as a positive value, and the renunciation of unity in the name of contamination may make dialogue with police forces more complicated. Traditionally, organizational fluidity and inability to self-administer order on the marches is interpreted by those in control of public order as risky, potentially multiplying the number of groups to negotiate with and reducing capacity for control over their rank and file.[20] Police spokesmen heard by the parliamentary investigative commission in fact repeatedly stress the difficulties of dialogue with an entity like the GSF, made up of eight hundred components and unable to guarantee any real representativity in relation to the totality of demonstrators. However, negotiated management strategies are a police tool for establishing, through actively pursued dialogue taking account of demonstrators' interests and objectives, clear rules for carrying out a given demonstration and for reaching the objective of reducing violence on both sides, even when (if not especially when) confronted by heterogeneous groups.

The Movement's Repertoires of Actions

Also heterogeneous, as we have seen, are the new globals' range of actions, another feature of the movement that, according to police spokesmen heard by the parliamentary commission, made control of the streets more complicated. We have said that, compared with other movements, the movement against neoliberal globalization has more awareness of the risks associated with the use of violence, leading a good part of the participants to practice nonviolence—that is, to reject violence even in defensive form—and another part to regard violence as at least tactically risky. While the movement presents itself as nonviolent, an option that at Genoa was formalized by the signature of a "work agreement," there is nonetheless an acceptance in it of the diversity of the repertoires of action adopted by the various groups in the name of tolerance for different lines taken and also, perhaps, of the tactical advantages that might arise from complementarity between symbolic provocations and nonviolence, play and civil disobedience. For the police it became necessary to prepare flexible responses adapted to the various action strategies coexisting within one and the same demonstration.

From journalistic reports of preparations for the civil-disobedience actions, one may further deduce a certain unawareness or underestimation of the possible risks by movement activists: while the actions planned for Genoa were apparently intended to be confined to ritualized, symbolic confrontation with the police at the entrance to the red zone, civil-disobedience strategies bring along the danger of misunderstanding and disproportionate response, especially if, partly because of lack of dialogue between movement and authorities, there is uncertainty or lack of understanding of the objectives being pursued. Hence, there is a need for prior clarification of the objectives of disobedience actions and of the limits beyond which coercive intervention will be triggered.[21]

While at Genoa there was no lack of individual episodes following the model of tolerance for formally illicit forms of protest, before the parliamentary investigative commission the ex-questore of Genoa Colucci pronounced the ranges of actions not only of the Disobedients but also of the "pacifists" to be illegitimate. In connection with the Disobedients' announcement that they wished to prevent the summit by peacefully blocking entry, he stated, "You have to tell me if an intention like that can be called peaceful; at that point what was being rather clearly stated was a no longer verbal but also physical challenge" (IPIC 2001f, 52). Citing the pacifists' attempt to create a human buffer between the violent demonstrators and the police, Colucci declared, "I ask: does 'creating a human buffer between the Black Bloc and the police' not perhaps mean putting oneself in between in order to prevent the police from acting?" (15).

On the sidelines of the demonstrations, for instance, at Gothenburg and Genoa, there were the little groups of so-called BB people practicing forms of "urban guerrilla warfare," using improper weapons to attack things and, more rarely, in clashes with the police. The BBs, with extremely poor levels of coordination, are, as we have seen, increasingly isolated from the movement and increasingly hostile to it (at Genoa they repeatedly attacked demonstrators as well as seeking to invade GSF headquarters). The difficulty in controlling BB violence is, however, seen as a limit to the movement, both by the social-center wing—"I think the path the Black Blocs have taken is a blind alley, bound to lose, but we cannot ignore it. . . . We have sinned by presumption: we thought the GSF could represent the whole protest" (Casarini, in *La Repubblica,* July 3, 2001)—and by the more moderate groups—"The GSF's responsibility is to have ignored their presence to the last, and underestimated their destructive violence. This unconsciously prepared the 'playing field' for the Black Blocs" (in *Altreconomia,* no. 20, 2001, 5). When small violent groups are present, the police have the certainly not easy task of separating the *casseurs* from the other demonstrators to protect the latter physically as well as their right to demonstrate peacefully.

Fortification of Summit Sites

The heterogeneity of the action repertoires and the presence of small groups practicing violence against things played a significant role in a situation of special tension. The strategy of movement mobilizations in conjunction with major international summits poses special problems for the police. International summit meetings are traditionally delicate situations for police maintenance of public order as they also involve the protection of foreign dignitaries. Defense of the right to demonstrate comes into tension with the objective of guaranteeing the safety of guest heads of state or government.[22] Symbolically, the host nation-state has a need to assert itself before international public opinion as able to display its monopoly of force in its own territory, an indispensable corollary of its sovereignty in international interactions. But the fortification of the summit sites produces effects that tend to be dangerous; concentrating police efforts on defending it greatly restricts the kinds of protest that can be peaceful but visible and increases the distance between the rulers and the population. The perceived risks of invasion reduce the room for dialogue and encounter between demonstrators and the institutions, as well as between demonstrators and the press.

From Seattle to Genoa, conflict around breaches of the red zone became characterized by an escalation of police strategies to defend summit sites, and a multiplication of tactics tried out by demonstrators aiming to penetrate them: some threw paint balls (or garlic, in Genoa); the nonviolent lay down in front of the entries; the civilly disobedient people attempted physical pressure on the gates. In some cases (though not in Genoa), anarchist groups sought to force the blockades. As happened to the workers' movement with pickets, the student movement with occupations, the peace movement with sit-ins around Cruise and Pershing II missile installation sites, and the antinuclear movement with blockades on nuclear power stations or radioactive waste transports, so the summit sites became the terrain of direct interaction between police forces and the movement for globalization from below.

The Movement's Image of the Police

While attempts at more or less symbolically penetrating the red zone necessarily lead to physical contact with the police, probabilities of such interaction becoming violent are also influenced by the attitudes prevailing in the movement. We have said that, by comparison with other movements, the movement against neoliberal globalization shows greater awareness of the risks associated with the use of violence. However, trust in the police is very low as shown by our data: only 10.3 percent of the Genoa demonstrators, though mostly interviewed before Carlo Giuliani's death, trusted the Italian police greatly or somewhat, and the figure remains extremely low even for the most moderate groups (barely 9.3 percent of the nonviolent activists of Lilliput, for instance). These results were confirmed at the Florence ESF (see Table 19): only 6.0 percent of those interviewed (9.2 percent in the ecopacifist area) stated they had some or much trust in the police, while 66.5 percent (93.3 percent of the anticapitalist area, 59.3 percent of anti-neoliberalist, and 53.2 percent of ecopacifists) had none. Trust in the police is still lower among activists who were present at the Genoa protests against the G8 and those who have taken part in movement demonstrations in their own countries.[23]

Activists' opinions on police presence on the streets, even if marked by some diffidence, nonetheless indicate that the police role as guarantor of a good outcome to the demonstration is broadly accepted (see Table 20):[24] while only 3.6 percent of those interviewed at the ESF thought that a police presence is necessary to oppose the actions of violent groups, the majority find it either useful for ensuring the regular holding of the demonstration (30.5 percent) or tolerable if police do not have firearms (27.4 percent).[25] For over one-third of those interviewed, however, police presence is unnecessary (19 percent) or even harmful (19.6 percent).[26] An experience like the G8 days at Genoa increases mistrust even among nonviolent activists: 29.3 percent of interviewees who had taken part in the July 2001 demonstrations found police presence at demonstrations harmful, as against 15.3 percent of those who had not taken part. This trend typifies not just the social centers, where 52.8 percent of participants (33.6 percent of nonparticipants) agree with this attitude, but also the ecopacifist area (14.8 percent as against 8.8 percent).[27]

Table 19. Trust in the police by ESF participants, by sector affiliation

	Sector affiliation (%)					
Trust in the police	Ecopacifist	Antineoliberalist	Anticapitalist	Local social forums	Unorganized	Total (%)
None	53.2	59.3	93.3	82.4	62.8	66.5
Little	37.6	35.3	5.9	17.6	29.9	27.5
Some	9.2	5.1	0.4	–	6.4	5.4
Much	–	0.4	0.4	–	0.9	0.6
(Number of interviewees)	(173)	(275)	(253)	(51)	(873)	(1,625)

Note: The Cramer's V of ESF participants by organizational sector is 0.16, significant at the 0.001 level.

Table 20. Opinions on police presence by ESF participants, by sector affiliation

	Sector affiliation (%)					
Opinion on police presence	Ecopacifist	Antineoliberalist	Anticapitalist	Local social forums	Unorganized	Total (%)
Necessary	4.1	3.2	0.4	–	4.7	3.6
Useful	36.0	36.9	8.9	28.8	33.5	30.5
Tolerable	34.3	30.1	16.2	21.2	28.8	27.4
Unnecessary	15.1	18.3	30.8	21.2	16.5	19.0
Always Harmful	10.5	11.5	43.7	28.8	16.6	19.6
(Number of interviewees)	(172)	(279)	(247)	(52)	(869)	(1,619)

Note: The Cramer's V of ESF participants by organizational sector is 0.17, significant at the 0.001 level.

Activists' attitudes toward types of police action again stress the potentialities but above all the need for dialogue: a little more than half (51.9 percent) of Genoa interviewees accept the police detaining demonstrators responsible for disorder and violence, but reject (82.8 percent) restrictions by the police on the possibility of demonstrating and police using water cannons (75.2 percent opposed) or charging demonstrators (84.9 percent opposed). Even among the most moderate activists, there is marked rejection of general actions against demonstrations as a whole, with greater favor for selective measures aimed at the individuals committing acts of violence. Therefore, de-escalation tactics may meet with collaboration by the nonviolent and strengthen the option for nonviolence as politically opportune by the intermediate component.

It should be stressed that for a high percentage of activists interviewed on the occasion of the Florence ESF, violence as self-defense in the event of violent repression of a protest demonstration is necessary, and for over one-third justifiable in all cases (see Table 21). Personal experience of the Genoa events strengthens this position: 23.6 percent of those who did not take part in the demonstrations against the G8 find violence necessary as self-defense; 41.9 percent of those who did take part do. This trend is particularly marked among activists with no organizational affiliation (21.6 percent as against 42.9 percent) and in the anticapitalist sector (46.3 percent as against 66.4 percent), though also strong in the antineoliberalists (19.0 percent as against 25.0 percent) where, moreover, condemnation of this form of violence goes down from 17.4 percent to 8.3 percent. The sole exception is the ecopacifist area, where ideological nonviolence is most widespread: condemnation of violence as self-defense increases (from 20.9 percent to 30.8 percent).

Factors Internal to the Police Forces

The potential dangers for the security of international summits, the presence of small groups attacking the police using urban guerrilla tactics, the inability (or refusal) to set up a stewardship service, the manifold types of attitude involved, the novelty of the movement and its transnationality, the widespread mistrust of the police—all are features that made the administration of public order more complex. This does not, however, explain the abandonment of strategies of de-escalation, which in any case were developed not for peaceful marches but specifically to contain violent minorities, while at the same time guaranteeing and defending the right of the nonviolent majorities to demonstrate. Specifically, the antiglobalization demonstrations feature the typical condition for employing de-escalation strategies:

Table 21. Opinion on violence as self-defense by ESF participants, by sector affiliation

Use of violence as self-defense	Sector affiliation (%)					
	Ecopacifist	Antineoliberalist	Anticapitalist	Local social forums	Unorganized	Total (%)
To be condemned	25.0	14.4	2.1	10.0	12.7	12.6
To be condemned/justifiable	14.9	15.1	6.2	6.0	13.6	12.6
Justifiable	34.5	37.6	23.9	44.0	36.4	34.7
Justifiable/necessary	11.9	11.8	11.9	2.0	10.5	10.8
Necessary	13.7	21.0	56.0	38.0	26.8	29.2
(Number of interviewees)	(168)	(271)	(243)	(50)	(863)	(1,595)

Note: the Cramer's V of ESF participants by organizational sector is .016, significant at the 0.001 level.

the presence of a majority of peaceful demonstrators, whose right to political expression is a higher value, to be defended even against the violent attitude of a minority. After so many years, which internal features of the Italian police may have contributed to the reappearance of many elements of an escalated force strategy on the occasion of the G8 in Genoa?

The Image the Police Have of the Movement

The literature, in order to explain police conduct, has stressed the importance of their professional culture, particularly the aspect that many police actions are provoked by situations of the moment rather than by well-defined rules or orders. The need to decide on the spot whether or not to intervene leads policemen to develop stereotypes of people and situations perceived as possible sources of difficulty or danger. These stereotypes, filtered through police knowledge, become a sort of guideline for the actions of individual policemen and the force as a whole, with distinctions, for instance, between "good" demonstrators (peaceful, pragmatic, with a direct interest in the conflict and a clear aim) and "bad" demonstrators (predominantly young, misinformed, destructive, professional troublemakers with no direct interest in the conflict) (della Porta 1998; della Porta and Reiter 1998b).

The information strategies used for the Genoa G8, with indiscriminate, widespread collection of information, led the police to an undifferentiated image of the "no globals" as bad demonstrators. Ex-head of UCIGOS La Barbera said, in connection with the documentation of the secret services on the G8 (364 documents), that there was a

> multitude of information, in the bulk of cases without any basis. . . . For instance, the SISDE [civil secret service] note of 20 March 2001 foresaw the use of bladders full of blood, at least in part human, collected with the complicity of doctors, veterinarians and nurses, to be thrown during the demonstrations. SISDE note of 5 April: the antagonists had gathered a sizable number of old tires to set on fire and roll down the descending streets leading to the sea, where the police forces were to be stationed. SISDE note of 30 March: the antagonists were allegedly intending to rent a satellite channel in order to disseminate protest worldwide. . . . SISDE note of 19 July: the 'white overalls,' to break into the red zone, were alleged to have planned two human 'testudos' of 80 militants each. (ICIP 2001f, 66)

Another SISDE note even says that Casarini's "right-hand man" had the task of training young people from the Rivolta social center militarily "with the strategic aim of teaching the most sophisticated techniques of the most modern urban guerrilla warfare. . . . At Genoa, all have been ordered to carry slings for launching ball bearings so as to pierce the security shields" (*La Repubblica,* June 23, 2001). Information from the secret services filtered through the press alleged that the demonstrators planned to take policemen hostage to use as human shields. There was also talk of Forza Nuova neofascists armed with knives and of extreme self-injuring gestures by PKK Kurds (*La Repubblica,* September 3, 2001).

The negative image of the "no globals" as troublemakers also dominates the analysis of the organizational sectors of the movement that was prepared before the G8: the "pink" block of pacifists, who would, however, seek visibility in actions pursuing the goal of obstructing, boycotting, and delaying the work of the summit; the "yellows" of the social centers and the White Overalls (the so-called Disobedients), ready for civil disobedience and direct action not excluding recourse to violence; the "blues" of the autonomous groups and anarchists, willing to use direct, violent action against the police, even by way of provocation; and the Black Bloc, the element of greatest risk to public order (ICIP 2001f, 60). This assessment of the blue and yellow blocks seems to take little account of their evolution; many in recent times had abandoned more direct, violent types of action in favor of "protected civil disobedience." Recognizing the development of their strategies would have facilitated opening a constructive dialogue that could eventually lead to mutual trust. Still clearer were assessments of the movement given after Genoa: in retrospect, the whole GSF was portrayed as untrustworthy, with a large proportion of the demonstrators sharing responsibility for the violence.

The dominant image of the "no-global" demonstrator seems based not so much on analysis of the new movement as on a reprocessing of experience and images from the foregoing decade (della Porta and Reiter 2003, 287ff.), which had become part of the police knowledge. While during the 1990s the public-order discourse in Italy had become depolarized and de-ideologized, accompanied by a clear dominance of "soft policing," at the same time hard approaches toward small antagonistic groups survived. Foremost among these were the social centers, which were perceived as detached from a larger movement, or "political family," and hence as isolated and with no cover. Furthermore, in the absence of mass demonstrations, soccer hooliganism emerged as the biggest public-order problem. Indeed, the image of the "no globals" as "summit hooligans" is what most insistently emerges in the Italian and the European media, especially after the Gothenburg clashes.[28] The experience of hooliganism is emphasized by Alessandro Pilotto of the police Sixth Liguria flying squad: "It seems incredible, but did anybody ask if someone, accustomed on an everyday basis for years now to hold at bay thousands of enraged fans from the most diverse sporting backgrounds, can manage to recognize, understand, and peacefully confront those parading in front of them with shields and helmets? After months of a publicity barrage will there not be a conditioned reflex that will trigger every self-defense mechanism in your possession?" (Zinola 2003, 135).

The alarmist notions underlying the image of the "no globals" as bad demonstrators—even though subsequently regarded as "absolutely at the limit of the ridiculous" (according to Forza Italia member of Parliament Cicchito, in ICIP 2001f, 69)—had noteworthy effects on police forces' attitudes in Genoa. As one policeman said: "The tension among us was sky high: for the whole foregoing week we had been told that the demonstrators would have pistols and would be throwing infected blood and ball bearings covered in acid at us. On the Friday evening after that lad's death they told us that a carabiniere had died too" (quoted in *Diario*, no. 32–33, 2001, 18). More important still, the alarming information influenced police tactics and personnel deployment, confirmed by ex-questore Colucci in relation to the indication that police personnel might be attacked and kidnapped. Accordingly, "the initial option to use few men so as to fight and move more easily over the territory (groups of 40, 50 or 60 people) was perforce overcome by the idea of setting up bigger squads" (ICIP 2001f, 23).

The Italian Police Organizational Model

While the prevailing image of the demonstrators among police forces did not favor de-escalation strategies, organizational features may have enhanced aspects of greater toughness in control of public order. In general, certain features of police organizational structures, particularly their degree of militarization, their accountability, and their politicization (as against professionalism), are central for the quality of a democracy. A high degree of police militarization may, through the type of weaponry and training, predetermine certain types of action and preclude others, as well as creating a climate of separateness and mistrust in relations between the police and citizens. Especially important is the extent to which the police, both as an institution and as individuals, are responsible for their decisions in action, such as through the identifiability of the individual police officer (through visible identification numbers or badges), the possibility of independent review of police decisions, and the presence of procedures facilitating submission of formal complaints by citizens.

From the organizational viewpoint, the traditional model of the Italian police forces seems remote from the democratic ideal. Both the state police and the carabinieri have been highly militarized bodies with particularly marked centralization reflected in close political dependence on the government. The national police reform law of 1981 reached the objective of demilitarization only to a limited extent, even though within European police forces themselves this is regarded as an essential condition for a democratic police. Only the state police took on nonmilitary features, while the carabinieri and the financial police, also employed in public order, remain military. Law 78/2000, on the reordering and coordination of police forces, aggravated the difficulties traditionally bound up with the presence of a large number of police forces: unclear definition of the division of competencies, in particular between state police and the carabinieri, limitations on the civilian public security authorities, and wide margins of autonomy for the carabinieri and the financial police. Moreover, the problems of limited accountability of the Italian police and low professionalism, also in the sphere of public order, already noted by the movement for police democratization in the 1970s, continue to exist. The failure of the control of public order in Genoa brings out the still obvious shortcomings in the organizational structure of the Italian police forces.

Lines of Command in the "Country of Five Police Forces"

The breakdown of the police communication system and command and coordination structure has been identified as one of the causes that in Gothenburg led to situations defined as "police riots" (Peterson 2003, 7ff.), that is, police officers disobeying the orders of their own hierarchical superiors, which seem also to have marked the Genoa days. In Italy, the joint presence of various national police forces, with a historical rivalry and imperfect coordination, renders the organization of police operations particularly complicated—difficult as it already is for major events, often involving big problems for the policemen—and at Genoa seems to have severely effected the lines of communication.[29]

During the Genoa days, communication between the interforce operations room at police headquarters and carabinieri units came about not directly but through the provincial carabinieri operations room or in the field in the form of direct communication between state police officers and commanders of the individual carabinieri groups. Direction of public-order services always goes to state police officers *(funzionari)*, who, however, when they have to lead carabinieri units, cannot give orders directly to the men under them but must go through carabinieri officers. At Genoa the carabinieri were all in direct contact among themselves and with their provincial operations room through throat microphones. Neither the state police officers directing the services nor the operations room at state police headquarters were inserted into this network; they were linked through a separate radio network. These coordination and communications difficulties seem to have had an impact on specific episodes, including the events leading to the death of Carlo Giuliani. Vice questore Adriano Lauro, in charge of around a hundred carabinieri, explains the dynamics of his group's retreat that left the jeep isolated in Piazza Alimonda: "I was in charge of public order, but had to give orders to the captain materially in command of the men. At that moment, in that situation, it was impossible to find the captain among a hundred carabinieri all dressed the same! Moreover, they were linked by throat mikes, but I wasn't linked with them. Consequently I was unable to give the captain orders. A disordered withdrawal is not controllable at moments like that" (IPIC 2001i, 72). It should be added that, according to the police officers' association, in Genoa the two radio links between police headquarters and the carabinieri had already failed on Friday, July 20 (*La Repubblica*, August 17, 2001).

The lack of coordination seems greatest during the break-in to the Diaz-Pertini school by the Reparto mobile (public-order unit), which was supposed to secure the building; the Squadra mobile (local crime squad) and the DIGOS (local political police), which were to do the search; and the Nucleo preventivo anticrimine (preventive crime squad) and the carabinieri (a total of 275 men), who were to guard the building from outside. The contrasting versions of the break-in to the school show a situation of great confusion in lines of command, emphasized also by the center-right coalition (IPIC 2001a, 233). The break-in to the Diaz-Pertini school, furthermore, brought out a problem that seems to typify the whole police operation in Genoa: the police chief of Genoa, the top leader for deployment of public-order services, and the other local officers were flanked by leading national officers present in the city with no clear identification of specific competencies. Not surprisingly, further confusion in lines of command and responsibility were the outcome.

Training and Professionalism

The police forces that tackled the anti-G8 demonstrations in Genoa were going through a period of restructuring: on June 16, 1999, a working group had been set up to bring the mobile squads into line with the changed requirements of public-order duties. At the hearing before the parliamentary investigative commission (IPIC 2001i, 29ff.), Valerio Donnini (in charge of this reorganization) explained how over the course of several years the mobile units had had their uses steadily diversified, being used as reservoirs of personnel and increasingly less typified as public-order units. The incidence of wounds and injuries among personnel had increased, both at soccer events and at large street demonstrations, indicating a lack of training in the units (31). It was intended to set up specialized multitask units among the mobile divisions for deployment on more challenging public-order duties, to update the equipment of the mobile divisions, to emphasize training, to develop operational methodologies appropriate to the various types of demonstration, to identify a specific training ground for nationwide use, and to create unitary control and guidance structures for the units from different police forces.

The imminence of the G8 summit made available the financial resources to achieve the almost complete modernization of equipment for the public-order divisions (not just of the state police but also of the carabinieri and the financial police), regarded as necessary for the new requirements. For weapons, all components of the mobile divisions used at Genoa had been authorized to use spray cans with irritant CS gas to immobilize possible "antagonists" at close quarters (IPIC 2001i, 75), and use of the "tonfa" truncheon, already allotted to carabinieri mobile battalions, had been limited to a single specialized unit of the first Rome mobile division.[30] As a first step toward setting up special units among the mobile divisions for deployment on the most challenging public-order duties, a volunteer-based experimental squad had been formed within the first Rome mobile division, a decision that after Genoa—where the squad was one of the units who searched the Diaz-Pertini school—was criticized even within the police. Gigi Notari, from the secretariat of the police union SIULP, stated: "I think the NOA [the experimental squad] should be dissolved, since we have seen the results. The union opposes the trend to creeping militarization of the police" (*Gente,* August 14, 2001, 22).[31]

An assessment of the dangers the movement would present, based on the reports of the secret services, seems to have strongly influenced the specific training of the police divisions for the G8. Giuseppe Bocuzzi, an officer of the seventh Bologna mobile division, describes the training at Ponte Galeria as follows: "The course began in the run-up to the G8 emergency, and I felt that it was improvised. . . . They taught us only to repress, not to prevent; the no-global movement was presented to us as the enemy; there was no training about the various components of the movement, no distinction between violent and peaceful groups. We were prepared for much throwing of Molotovs, for walking through flames, for hitting the deck running" (*Diario,* no. 18, 2002). For vice questore Angela Burlando, the courses did not construct a serene atmosphere: "When they did the course at Ponte Galeria the officers were bludgeoned about these risks. When we desk officers went there for a day, I saw that risks were being presented, with specific, proper forms of defense. But the emphases were perhaps unnecessary" (Zinola 2003, 81). Among things allegedly underestimated were the physical and mental state of the personnel and possible responses in a situation of tension and physical stress (124). The main instrument of coercive action by the police—the baton charge—in fact sparks off a cocktail of psychological conditions that reduce self-control.[32]

The biggest emphasis in the training done in the run-up to the Genoa G8, in addition to personnel safety, was on challenging direct, violent attacks against police forces, which had been identified as a new feature in street incidents (IPIC 2001i, 31; IPIC 2001d, 67), and the problem of separating small violent groups from the great bulk of peaceful demonstrators was neglected. Indeed, Carabinieri commanding general Siracusa asserted: "We shall certainly have to reconsider a number of aspects, especially as regards isolating the troublemakers from those who are by contrast peaceful" (IPIC 2001d, 94).

For the G8, all police personnel had received a manual instructing police officers to keep to cautious, measured rules of conduct and not to regard the demonstrators as enemies (see the citations in Gubitosa 2003, 70). However, as Filippo Saltamartini, SAP (police union) general secretary, states, the pamphlet would ultimately be an attempt to offload responsibilities: "The booklet did not go to any teaching institutions or the police stations, no discussion meetings were organized; that is, its contents did not become part of the common stock" (*Micromega*, no. 4, 2001, 83). Even had such discussion meetings been held, it should be stressed that convinced application of a negotiating, dialogue strategy requires intense, specific information and education work within the police. Experience teaches that strong mistrust of the strategy among policemen must be overcome, and margins for action existing in specific situations must be brought out (Driller 2001, 36ff., 46ff.).

A direct connection between the survival of militarized features in the organization of the mobile divisions, more than in other sections of the Italian police, and the insufficient attention to professionalism further emerge from the utilization for public order of auxiliary personnel on military national service or substitute service for national service. Carabinieri mobile squads, normally earmarked for public-order deployment, are mostly made up of draftees on voluntary service (70 percent) (IPIC 2001d, 67). According to the carabinieri commanding general, at Genoa out of 6,300 carabinieri, 1,700 were auxiliaries, i.e., young draftees (*La Repubblica,* July 27, 2001), as was the carabiniere who killed Carlo Giuliani. The state police mobile divisions until 2000 were primarily made up of auxiliary draftees or retained draftees (70 to 80 percent), with an extremely high turnover (almost total every two years), and it was only after 2001, when the proportion of auxiliaries was reduced, that the percentage of full-time officers rose at all significantly (Colomba 2003, 194). The Unione sindacale di polizia complained that over 50 percent of personnel in the thirteen mobile divisions deployed in Genoa consisted of auxiliaries on draft service (*Liberazione,* August 21, 2001). The recruitment mechanisms brought in for the period after abolition of the draft, scheduled for January 1, 2005, will reserve 60 percent of places in the competitions for those coming from the armed forces. In all probability, this will enhance the militarized features of the personnel.

Not having recent relevant experience of maintaining public order during political demonstrations, police in Genoa borrowed tactics from those tried out in other emergencies. We have already mentioned the repercussions that the absolute predominance of hooligan control in the work experience of the mobile divisions may have had on operations. Strategies used at soccer grounds for isolating and protecting some areas seem to have been applied in concentrating control in the red zone, and in parts of the yellow zone. Many detainees testified that the penitentiary officers in the special units (GOM) applied the same techniques to demonstrators—stand up and face the wall—as those used in order not to be recognized by Mafia members; the same seems to be true of the operative units of the carabinieri (NOCS), who acted with covered faces.[33] The presence in Genoa of special units set up chiefly to fight organized crime—like the GOM and the NOCS—indicates how the very personnel deployed make control strategies developed to fight the Mafia or control soccer violence spill over into control of political demonstrations.

Accountability

Terrorism, Mafia, and soccer hooliganism emergencies have given the Italian police ambiguous powers—considerable powers were already guaranteed by the consolidated text of the public security laws adopted during the Fascist period, which have not been completely reformed. A broad conception of public order as being a higher order than civil and political rights, the capability of carrying out searches even without warrant when looking for weapons, and conspiracy offenses with generic definitions—at Genoa many arrestees were initially accused of being part of an association for committing crimes of devastation and plunder—are all features enhancing the possibility of arbitrary actions by the police authorities.[34]

In addition is the problem, not solved by the 1981 reform, of the limited transparency of the police forces in interactions with citizens: identification numbers are concealed, complaint procedures are tortuous, and powers of review exclusively internal. The uncertain definition of the powers of the DIGOS, the political police units—authorized to collect information on all political and social actors with no checks by the judicial authorities or constitutional limits—is one of the most glaring examples of severe limits on democratic accountability of the police forces. These limits are still more marked for the carabinieri (who have always been closed to any outside eyes, as shown, for example, by the absence of academic research on them) and for the special divisions.

The EU Network of Independent Experts in Fundamental Rights recently underlined that, in general, the complaints procedures in most member states are not satisfactory because they do not provide for an independent investigative structure (EU Network of Independent Experts in Fundamental Rights 2003, 57ff.).[35] In specific cases connected with the movement, the problem of internal police investigative procedures has been raised in connection with Sweden and the Czech Republic.[36] Already after the Naples incidents, AI had asked, in a letter to the Italian Ministry of the Interior, for an independent commission to analyze police tactics and conduct and to examine the accusations of violence and mistreatment, both on the street and in police barracks (AI 2001).[37] After Genoa, the government and the parliamentary majority displayed little desire to favor an independent review of police operations. In Parliament, the majority rejected the setting up of a commission of inquiry (which would have had the powers of a court of justice), conceding to an investigative commission only after intervention by the president of the republic, with the consequence that the contrasting versions given by various police officials about individual episodes could not be cleared up. Various center-right figures attacked the magistracy when it opened inquiries into police conduct for the Naples and Genoa events. The three senior officials removed from their posts after Genoa were reappointed to new prestigious posts inside the police forces (Gubitosa 2003, 419ff.). No other disciplinary measures following the inspections ordered by the Ministry of the Interior have been made public. The commission of inspection on Bolzaneto appointed by the Ministry of Justice included the very person in charge of coordinating the activities of the Genoa penitentiary administration (IPIC 2001a, 246).

The climate within the police forces is, moreover, unfavorable to independent review, as demonstrated by the stances of the police unions; at least initially all or almost all were concerned with fiercely defending the actions of the police forces. Already on July 22, 2001, the SIULP (the most representative police union, and a protagonist in past years of the political fight to demilitarize the force) expressed "sincere, heartfelt thanks to the government representatives" for having indicated their own solidarity with the policemen deployed at Genoa (Pepino 2001, 894). On August 22, SAP, the second-largest trade union, protested against the decision by the magistracy to investigate the 140 policemen present at the Diaz-Pertini school, accusing them of "shooting at sitting ducks," while a picket was organized at the prosecution offices by the Coordination for Trade Union Independence of the Police Forces (COISP) on the day when some officers were being interrogated. The small right-wing union LISIPO talked of the "steady rain of warrants raising demotivation almost to the point of psychological disarmament" (*La Repubblica*, August 23, 2001). In a communiqué in Naples, SIULP dictated the "sole, necessary" conditions for guaranteeing public order at the NATO summit scheduled for September 2001: "The police will guarantee security only on definite conditions: single command, adequate deployment of men, the essential logistics, but above all an end to the campaign of hatred, delegitimation and criminalization of the police forces."[38] Scoppa of the COCER (the carabinieri trade-union-type organization) called for "a climate of serenity. Continuation of the attacks is causing severe loss of motivation among people who do not feel at all guilty. . . . We have to see the protection of our personnel guaranteed, who should not be risking, in addition to their personal safety, criminal and administrative proceedings or even only suffering condemnation from a part of public opinion" (*Micromega*, no. 4, 2001, 70, 72). The police unions and many police circles reject the proposal for a code of ethics for conduct, as recently introduced in Portugal, calling it insulting (Zinola 2003, 187).

From within the police, however, there has also come a move to return to a path of reform, with the call to embark on a confrontation with the movement specifically to avoid the risk of a delegitimization of the police among at least a part of the population. The SIULP stated it is necessary to open up dialogue with the antiglobals (SIULP 2001). The further left SILP-CGIL criticized the "purely military conditions of the public order seen at Genoa," warning against "favoring the break between police and civil society, who must instead attain a dialectical relation of mutual control and vigilance" (*Il Manifesto*, August 21, 2001). The capacity of the police unions to play an innovative and educational role seems, however, limited by a corporatism enhanced by the two decades of delays in implementing the police reform of 1981, particularly as regards careers, with a consequent explosion in the number of unions, accused in several quarters of becoming clientele-based. In a situation of polarization around public-order issues, although some trade unionists reaffirm the need to repair the break with part of the citizenry, the threatening tones against those who "delegitimize" the police forces have grown within the police, making further escalation to be feared.

External Factors: Politics and Protest Policing

Another historically consolidated feature of the Italian police is that they continue the model of the king's police, or police of the monarch, traditionally present on the European continent, by contrast with the citizens' police of the English-speaking world. The Italian police were built up and legitimized as a primarily political instrument, formed and utilized chiefly for public-order tasks, with close links to the central government. This tradition, criticized by the police-reform movement, nonetheless seems to have kept its heritage, both in the still-militarized elements of the police organization structures and in a police knowledge extremely sensitive to the political attitudes of the majority. In these circumstances the public-order response is heavily influenced by the political response made to the movement, at both supranational and national levels. Particularly in evolved democracies, it is not just the government position that is important: a first sign of an opening toward new challengers has often been the formation, following street incidents, of a *civil rights coalition* defending the right of dissent and protest and opposing a *law-and-order coalition* ranked in defense of the police and of order.

The Law-and-Order Coalition

It has often been stressed that police actions are sensitive to behavior and attitudes toward specific movements present in political institutions. The conduct and attitudes of institutional political actors before, during, and after Genoa indicate a closure toward not just the issues presented by the various currents in the movement but to the very identity of the movement, finding difficulty in recognizing it as a political subject. The movement called into question the legitimacy of the "Big 8" to decide for everyone—"You G8, we six billion"—and the government responded with a refusal to recognize the movement as an interlocutor, interpreting and presenting it instead as a primarily public-order problem.

We have already emphasized that, for the center-right government and parliamentary majority, the Genoa violence was a direct result of behavior and features of the movement. Even several months after the Genoa demonstrations, Minister of the Interior Scajola claimed, and at other times denied, to have given, after Giuliani's death, an order to fire on anyone seeking to enter the red zone, justifying himself by the presence in Genoa of "200 thousand hotheads whose ranks may have been infiltrated, and pointers to terrorist attacks from all the intelligence services" (*La Repubblica*, February 16, 2002). The majority has also tirelessly defended the police operations in Genoa. The G8 summit is claimed to have "secured all the preset objectives in terms of both content and the administrative/logistical aspect, as well as the aspects of security and protection of public order" (IPIC 2001a, 242). Only the connivance of a large part of the demonstrators with the violent sectors had "made it impossible for the forces of order to have recourse to established techniques for controlling marches, preventing disorder, isolating the violent and protecting peaceful demonstrators" (243). Criticism of police operations is confined to a reference to "a few excesses by individual members of the police forces" with a refusal to discuss them in order not to interfere with the judicial authorities (245). The recommendations for the future do not go further than a call for greater coordination among the police forces and more effective cooperation in the sphere of information and prevention among individual European countries.

The "line of dialogue" carried out by the new Berlusconi government after the Gothenburg events thus seems to be chiefly instrumental, dictated by the "need to avoid the worst by providing an outlet for nonviolent challenge, offering room for dialogue and promoting visibility for the peaceful sector of the movement."[39] Neither the specific public-order problem nor the "strong appeal to the inviolability of the constitutional principles of freedom to display one's opinion and respect for the person," with which the majority of the investigative commission concludes its report, are linked with the demands for democratic participation coming from the movement.[40]

The Civil Rights Coalition

The center-left opposition has explained the Genoa events as a political option of at least a part of the government, if not the whole—in particular, the most right-wing part of the coalition, Alleanza Nazionale (AN). Main responsibility for the errors in controlling public order is assigned to instrumentalization of the police forces by the right, most visibly expressed in the presence of Deputy Prime Minister Gianfranco Fini and three MPs from his party in the carabinieri operational command room at Genoa.[41]

According to the center-left coalition proposal for a concluding document to the work of the investigative commission, the presence of the AN MPs was not just a specific attempt to exercise an illegitimate influence but also a pointer to the general attempts by the more extreme wing of the majority coalition to force the issue on public order. The center-left coalition denounced "the attempt by the most extremist component of the majority to open up a laceration between the forces of order and civil society" (IPIC 2001c, 95). Declarations by AN speakers, including Deputy Prime Minister Fini, even before the summit are said to have dwelt on the confrontational atmosphere, proclaiming that every street demonstration was by violent and subversive groups, and guaranteeing that in the event of clashes no responsibility would on any account be allotted by the government to the forces of order (103ff.).

As a matter of fact, center-left parties insisted that the ambiguous conduct of part of the movement supplied the pretext for giving a violent image of the whole of it. The perception of the movement as a public order problem was, however, not only a concern of the center-right parties; it was, in fact, shared also by part of the center-left coalition. This position reflects the uncertain recognition of the movement as a legitimate political actor by the center-left coalition. As we are going to see in the next chapter, already the Amato center-left government had taken an ambivalent position toward the movement organizers, starting negotiations with them but not pursuing these negotiations in a coherent way. Perceptible before the elections in May 2001, the skepticism and uncertainty as to the attitude to adopt toward the emerging movement continued when the center-left coalition went into opposition. Not only did the center-left coalition in opposition keep supporting the G8 summit they had organized when in government, but they also kept an ambivalent position toward the countersummit. On Thursday, July 19, the center-left coalition was still divided on whether or not to take part in the Saturday demonstration; after Carlo Giuliani's death on Friday, the Democrats of the Left (DS) withdrew their support.

Subsequently, too, the center-left coalition did not line up as decisively in defending dissent as Italian left parties had traditionally done, and many DS figures criticized the GSF. In part these criticisms concerned the movement's strategies—in the motion concluding the work of the parliamentary investigation proposed by the center-left coalition, criticisms of the demonstrators were, significantly, directed not just at those who engaged in violence but also at those who proposed civil disobedience: "certain groups of demonstrators have neither isolated nor condemned violence, have employed aggressive language, have not clearly marked the boundary that exists between civil disobedience and violence, have engaged in ambiguous conduct such as replaying for television cameras the techniques for breaking into the red zone" (ICIP 2001b, 96). While on the one hand the minority emphasized in the concluding section of its report that dissent cannot be regarded as a pathology and that the possibility of displaying and organizing it is the very essence of democracy, on the other it warned that dissent must not only never take violent forms but not even indulge in ambiguous or violence-tolerant conduct: "democracy is in fact not just the exercise of pluralism; it is first and foremost the exercise of responsibility" (111). Over and above an inability to control the violent individual, the movement was held to be not legitimate, having no election mandate or institutional power to deal with the world's problems, and was accused of representing an antipolitical reaction (see chapter 7 in this volume).

In its criticisms of the police operations in Genoa—insufficient psychological preparation of officers, unselective information activity, lack of coordination among the various police forces—the center-left minority report made no reference to problems or gaps in the Italian police system, and attributed the blame to the government's nonexistent or mistaken input. It is important to bear in mind that the political responsibility of the center-left, in government until a few weeks before the Genoa summit, was not confined to the preparatory stage of the summit but extended to those reforms of the public-order system that some saw as not done or wrongly done: it was in fact a center-left coalition legislative measure that had further strengthened the traditional autonomy of the carabinieri. According to the minority report, by contrast, the lack of coordination among the various police forces in Genoa was not to be regarded as a structural problem (ICIP 2001b, 85ff.). Moreover, its list of previous clashes between the movement and police significantly did not refer to Naples (98). Perhaps in an attempt not to alienate the police forces, the head of the DS parliamentary group Luciano Violante, interviewed in La Repubblica (July 30, 2001), attributed the beating and harassment of demonstrators to "small groups of violent individuals," upholding the same "rotten apple" theory as the center-right. In the investigative commission, the center-left did not call in question the exclusively internal nature of the review power (ICIP 2001b, 68), and only Rifondazione Comunista (RC) asked for measures aimed at allowing personal recognition of individual police officers (IPIC 2001c, 166). Finally, while on the one hand the center-left called dialogue an "essential factor in the success of a public-order activity" (ICIP 2001b, 88), on the other it ruled it out for public-order ends, specifically for the new globals, a heterogeneous movement without "a recognized capacity to control the street" (98). So conceived, dialogue was a reward for groups able to guarantee public order. The movement seems to have significant consensus in society, specifically confirmed in the debate on the violence at Genoa. While Genoa divided public opinion in its verdict on the movement, the police conduct was denounced by a broad range of associations forming a strong, if fluid, coalition supporting civil rights. Some surveys, moreover, indicate a certain concern on the part of public opinion.[42] These concerns reflect the stances of professional and volunteer associations, which even if not directly supporting movement demands nonetheless criticized breaches by the police of the right to demonstrate. Protests at the handling of public order in Genoa were expressed by the Union of Criminal Lawyers, objecting to obstacles to exercising the right of defense (*La Repubblica*, August 1, 2001). The deputy secretary of the National Magistrates' Association, Salvi, complained of pressure on judges by those wanting a stronger police and faster proceedings (*La Repubblica*, July 25, 2001). Criticisms came also from the National Association of Parents of Young Recruits: "How can the leadership command [of the police] take the liberty of putting boys in such difficult positions?" Among others, 530 university teachers asked for a commitment by president Ciampi to clarify the causes and dynamics of the repression in Genoa (*L'Unità*, July 27, 2002). The Web site of the Mani Tese organization, like other associations sensitive to the issues raised by the demonstrators, put black borders on its pages in mourning for the Genoa events. A committee of inquiry was promised by the Reporters sans Frontières association. AI protested at the breach of rights of the accused, and also called for an international commission. The National Press Federation expressed "severe protest at the police action at the Social Forum press center."[43]

On July 24 there were demonstrations throughout Italy: the slogans were "Black overalls, blue uniforms, none of us want any more provocation" (rhymes in Italian); "Dying at twenty is madness, let us disarm the police" (*La Repubblica*, July 25, 2001). Demonstrations protesting the conduct of the Italian police were held not just in Italy but also abroad: on July 21 in Paris, Vienna, Berlin, Madrid, Ankara, Buenos Aires, and São Paulo; and later in Paris, Dublin, Pamplona, Zurich, Bern, Lugano, Manchester, Barcelona, and Amsterdam, among others. The anniversary of Carlo Giuliani's death were marked by protests in various cities, and at many movement demonstrations after Genoa slogans and banners continued to call for clarification of the responsibilities in the handling of public order in the days of the July demonstrations. Significantly, the Second Social Forum's international camp site at Porto Alegre was dedicated to

Carlo Giuliani, confirming the emergence of a sort of transnational coalition for civil rights. At least initially, the international press was, if not always sympathetic to the globalization themes, critical of the way the police acted in Genoa.[44] Under the pressure of national public opinion, European governments too put some pressure on Italy.

A Supranational Level of Protest Policing?

The post-Genoa debate in the public sphere thus indicated that police inability to control the violence of the BB, their toughness in challenging and de facto preventing any act of civil disobedience whatsoever, and above all the impression of widespread violent and brutal behavior by police forces themselves shook not just Italian but also European, if not worldwide, public opinion. Moreover, post-Genoa highlighted the transnational nature of the movement and of the response to it, in terms of both politics and public order. There were protest demonstrations in all or almost all European states at Italian embassies and consulates, directed primarily against the repression in Genoa, but also against their own country's police—even including, according to the press, incendiary attacks against police vehicles and buildings in Hamburg and Berlin. Debate was focused on the strategies applied against the movement before the summit and the response of the politicians in their own countries to movement demands. The movement challenge to the police and to politics is global, or at least European. After Genoa, president Freiberg of the German police union stressed the shortcomings in the European integration process, with the exception of economic affairs. Also internal security has to be taken seriously as a common European concern. "If in an increasingly united Europe citizens' demands are no longer being handled by the politicians of their own countries, these citizens also have the right to demonstrate peacefully in Paris, Genoa or anywhere else and to have their exercise of the right to demonstrate protected by the police forces of the various countries. . . . Faced with disorders, no Minister of the Interior can seek justification in the fact that it happened in another country. The citizens too take Europe seriously" (GdP 2001).[45] The shift of decisions to the supranational level, in other words, brings out the need to extend rights to demonstrate supranationally instead of to restrict them.

The supranational level of protest policing was stressed by RC in their report to the parliamentary investigative committee: what had happened might be "the fruit of a new public-order system to be called globalization or, if you like, international policing."[46] In identifying this supranational level, the RC report points to a feature that, as mentioned above, emerged in the EU particularly after the Gothenburg and Genoa summits. According to the depositions before the Italian investigative commission, the closer collaboration among various national police forces after Gothenburg was not a full success in Genoa (ICIP 2001f, 135ff.). Subsequently, a Belgian report on the actions of European police forces at the EU summit in Laeken stressed the difficulties of cooperation (Busch 2002, 54ff.).

Apart from its efficiency, the "international police" came under attack after Genoa especially for its lack of respect for civil liberties and individual rights. In its recommendations passed after Gothenburg (Council of the EU 2001) the EU Council for Justice and Home Affairs did mention the need for a constructive dialogue with the organizers of demonstrations, but it elaborated exclusively on measures focused on keeping activists presumed to be a danger to public order and security away from the summit if not from the country hosting it. In these efforts it showed scant respect for data protection and the individual quality of the right of free movement within the EU. Above all, the purely intergovernmental character of police cooperation between member states greatly enhances the difficulty for the citizen to individuate those politically and juridically responsible for restrictive measures and to find redress. Before movement activists, soccer hooligans had encountered the same problem. In November 1992 two Welsh fans, brothers Gwilym and Rhys Boore, were detained and then deported by the Belgian police, their names having been supplied by the British police on the basis of erroneous information received from the Luxemburg authorities. It took the brothers six years to get their names removed from Belgian, British, and Schengen records (Peers 2000, 188). The single measures of police cooperation have to be seen against the general background of developments in the justice and home affairs field within the EU, characterized by deficiencies in accountability and scarce involvement of national parliaments and the EU Parliament, largely confined to a purely consultative role.[47]

The European Parliament recommendation to the European Council, voted by the plenum on December 12, 2001, and based on the Watson report (Committee on Citizens' Freedoms and Rights, Justice, and Home Affairs 2001), on the one hand strengthened the civil rights coalition, but on the other hand lays bare this very dilemma. It brings out "not a few shortcomings" in member states' responses to the Nice, Gothenburg, and Genoa demonstrations, recommending *against:* blocking frontiers or denying the right to cross them to individuals or groups seeking to take part peacefully in legitimate demonstrations; any new type of blacklist; the use of firearms and disproportionate use of force, with national police forces instead instructed to keep violence under control and safeguard individual rights even in the mass confusion, where violent criminals mingle with peaceful, law-abiding citizens. Other recommendations—to adopt a joint definition of a "dangerous individual" and dangerous conduct that might justify preventive measures (which particularly in Genoa struck at people even for legitimate behavior) and to avoid any sort of discrimination between nationals and EU citizens in the event of arrest or legal proceedings, guaranteeing defense by an advocate of one's choice even in the event of summary proceedings—bring out the fact that the existence of comparable internal standards is not regarded as sufficient to guarantee the new quality of exercise of the citizens' right to demonstrate and protest Europe-wide.

The European Parliament's recommendations do not seem to have been given any great consideration by European institutions themselves. The security handbook (Council of the EU 2002)—called for by the Council (Justice and Home Affairs) conclusions of July 13, 2001—was produced by the Police Co-operation Working Party without reference to the European Parliament recommendations, though the Parliament too had called for it. The handbook, approved by the Council at its meeting on November 28–29, 2002, suggests discussing future revisions only in committees of experts (Police Chiefs Task Force and Article 36 Committee). While the importance of dialogue is emphasized ("dialogue and cooperation with demonstrators and activists should be actively pursued by the police authorities"), Article 2.2 of the Schengen convention is specifically singled out as a useful preventive measure, ignoring the observations on this point made by the Parliament.[48]

As far as the European Council is concerned, an Italian initiative led to the passage of a resolution (on April 29, 2004) on security at European Council meetings and other comparable events. In order to limit inconveniences in the application of Article 2.2, it calls on member states, among others, to give precedence to intelligence-led checks on individuals when there are substantial grounds for believing that they intend to enter the member state with the aim of disrupting public order and security at the event or committing offenses relating to it (Council of the EU 2003). If this resolution seems to indicate a growing respect for the individual right of free movement within the EU, it remains to be seen whether it will suffice to eliminate the kind of violations stigmatized in connection with the policing of the Genoa G8, where demonstrators were turned back at the Italian border not only on the basis of faulty information on their person but also because they happened to be traveling on the same bus with activists considered "dangerous." The resolution certainly doesn't solve one basic problem inherent in similar measures: the lack of a definition accepted by all EU member states of "public order and security" or of an agreement on what are "substantial grounds."

Particular emphasis should go to the lack of competence of the European institutions and the problem of noninterference in the domestic affairs of a member state, with whom in fact the responsibility for the maintenance of public order lies. The European Parliament's annual reports on civil rights in the EU have also criticized police operations in Genoa. The 2001 report deplores "the violations of fundamental rights such as freedom of expression and movement, the right of due process and the right to physical integrity that have occurred during public demonstrations, particularly at the time of the G8 meeting in Genoa" (Committee on Citizens' Freedoms and Rights 2002, 12). The opinion of the committee on petitions for this report, with direct reference to the case of the "aggressive and violent policing of the anti-WTO [sic] demonstrations in Genoa," stressed that "the European Parliament largely lacks the means to do something immediately and effectively when such violations occur, beyond the political condemnation that a resolution allows" (92). In fact, the committee on petitions, on October 6, 2003, when replying to a petition from a citizens' group on Genoa, confined itself to asserting that no further action was possible (Meyer-Falk 2003).

The emergence of terrorism with the dramatic attack on the Twin Towers limited the support for the civil rights coalition, as well as giving rise to attempts at both the national and supranational levels to link the new global movement with subversion.[49] For the inauguration of the training school's academic year 2001–2, SISDE director Mario Mori stated, "It is a movement not in itself of a subversive nature, which yet like all dissent movements that have emerged into the limelight of European politics in the twentieth century seems extremely permeable to extremist infiltration which does have rebellious, destabilizing potential."[50] Even if the movement is not linked directly with Islamic terrorism, a presumed common anti-Western line is emphasized. In reference to the Genoa G8, we read in the report on information and security policy (second half of 2001) presented by the Italian government to the senate: "The symbolic scope of the event as a potential catalyst for many vehicles of threat was confirmed, on the information level, by indications of possible convergence of activation of Islamic fundamentalism, ideological terrorism and the autonomous and anarchic area, and on the factual level by the violence employed by the squads of the so-called Black Bloc."[51] Attempts to link the movement with terrorism were noted also at the European Council.[52]

The Lessons of Genoa and Protest Policing at the Florence ESF

At Genoa, as on other previous occasions, the security of the summit was the chief objective; the right to demonstrate peacefully was subordinate. The novelty of the movement severely tries police capacity to assess its objective and strategy properly. While it is largely peaceful, widespread mistrust of the police, the conflict around the red zones, the simultaneous presence of socially and politically heterogeneous groups and sometimes tiny but vigorous violent fringes enhanced public-order maintenance problems. Above all, these features make it easy for the police to categorize demonstrators as dangerous by attributing credibility to the most dramatic information on their intentions. Police knowledge that is suspicious of emergent, variegated collective actors, moreover, was interwoven with an organizational structure of the police forces still marked by incomplete democratic reform—partly militarized, poor accountability, uncertain professionalism, and bad coordination. The hypothesis that the brutality of police action at Genoa derives from a political order requires as a corollary police forces endowed with an organizational structure and a professional culture that predispose them to follow indications for actions that are not just "tough" but go beyond the limits of legality.

This does not alter the fact that the hardening of the police response to the movement for globalization from below finds its main explanation in the (lack of) political response to the protest. The government and the center-right majority have refused to recognize the movement as an interlocutor, instead interpreting and presenting it as a public-order problem. Recognition of the movement as a legitimate political actor seems, however, uncertain, even by the center-left opposition, which in the case of the protest against the Genoa G8 did not line up so decisively in defense of dissent as the parties of the Italian left had traditionally done. The movement's apparent isolation from institutional political forces and its prevalent presentation as a public-order problem were combined with the historically consolidated feature that the Italian police forces follow a "king's police" model, with a police "knowledge" extremely sensitive to the political orientations of the majority.

While the Gothenburg and Genoa events bring out the transnational nature not just of the movement but also of the response to it, in both political and public-order terms, the national models of policing nonetheless remain identifiable.[53] Many of the elements that emerged at Genoa can be explained as partial reaffirmation of the traditional response to new challengers in Italy: an overall strategy tending to exclusion instead of inclusion;

a mistrust of more direct forms of political participation and a tendency to see in public demonstrations an attempt to overthrow the parliamentary majority; and organizational gaps in the police, such as the lack of coordination among the various forces, low accountability, inadequate public-order professionalism, and a public-order culture that does not favor the right to demonstrate (della Porta and Reiter 2003). These national characteristics, however, seem to be reinforced rather than checked by the EU's approach to protest policing.

It must be stressed that one cannot talk of a return to the period of the "Cold Civil War" of the 1950s, as shown by the many peaceful demonstrations held since autumn 2001. A decisive factor in this context was the civil rights coalition in general (not only in Italy), and its staying power, which was not due to support by parties of the institutional left, but to the rootedness of the civil rights coalition in Italian and international civil society. Other factors also contributed to a correction of the Genoa line: criticisms by other states as well as by European and international institutions, the manifest lack of success of the police operations, and the clear illegalities that emerged from inquiries by the magistracy.[54]

Reflection in institutional terms on the Genoa errors is expressed, for example, in the conclusions of an Interior Ministry committee on reorganization of the mobile divisions, made public in October 2002. The committee stresses the need for training and practice courses for all police forces (not just for special squads) and especially for the mobile divisions, with the aim of training officers in relationships and contact with demonstrators in emergency situations. There are also calls for institutionalization of contact groups to guarantee the right of assembly and to isolate and challenge the violent. Finally, there are recommendations to strengthen lines of command and abolish the tonfa truncheon. CS tear gas could be used as an extreme resort in tackling particularly serious situations that cannot be handled otherwise (*La Repubblica*, October 10, 2002).[55]

The committee's conclusions seem to officialize a return to the negotiated management strategies that had been abandoned in Genoa. Considering specifically the protest policing on the occasion of the Florence ESF in November 2002—where a huge demonstration against the war in Iraq (500,000 participants) remained absolutely peaceful, refuting the highly alarmist rumors coming particularly from the center-right on the eve of the event—we shall seek to understand what has changed in street tactics and what lessons have been drawn from the Genoa experience by the political authorities, the police, and the movement.

A first feature to stress is that the negotiations between the authorities and the organizers, as at Copenhagen on the occasion of the EU summit in December 2002, started months ahead and were conducted with the prefect as constant interlocutor, thus permitting a reduction in mutual mistrust. Despite the movement's heterogeneity and a climate of high tension fed by many center-right figures and sections of the press virulently campaigning against the event, authorities and movement participants were positive on the dialogue. To counterbalance the effect of the alarmist reports coming from the secret services, widely disseminated in the press, a one-month course by sociologists and psychologists for policemen deployed in Florence was organized (*Il Manifesto*, November 1, 2002).

The results of focus groups that we conducted (see chapter 5) show that processes of self-critical reflection are at work inside the movement. The self-critical reflection brought about a commitment to contribute to the peaceful holding of the demonstration with a stewardship service of their own.[56] Apart from the different nature of the occasion, one should also bear in mind that the organizers for the ESF included part of the institutional left and major European and Italian trade union organizations.

The self-critical reflection after Genoa seems to bring out the point that the movement, while seeking to moderate its forms of action (for example, in Florence—and other demonstrations immediately after Genoa—the Disobedients did not wear their usual protections), feared a tendency to label as violent certain effective, high-profile forms of direct action it internally accepts as legitimate. Police attempts, for instance, on the occasion of the European summit in Copenhagen in December 2002, to exclude these forms of action in principle and block them even by questionable preventive measures may bring about radicalization of clashes, especially if combined with a trend, noted in challenges to President Bush's policies in the United States, to confine protest to peripheral, isolated areas, giving it low visibility.[57]

As for the G8 Day in July 2002 in Genoa commemorating the events of the previous year, in Florence state police and the carabinieri operations were run from a single operations room directed by the local police chief. At the Genoa G8 operations were run from two separate operations rooms, one directed by national vice chief of police Andreassi (Zinola 2003, 139). The police—who indicated to lawyers on the demonstrators' legal team their intention to wipe out the image of Genoa (*Il Manifesto*, November 6, 2002)—accompanied the march but remained "invisible" as far as possible, a strategy recalling the one often used in the 1980s and 1990s with the social centers (della Porta 1998).[58] A special telephone number was activated for communication between prefect and organizers.[59] While border checks remained and people were turned back on the basis of the questionable expulsion measures taken at Genoa (*Il Manifesto,* November 7, 2004)—the Schengen agreement was once again suspended from November 1 to 11—no restrictions were imposed on the places for ESF initiatives, many of which took place in the city center.

If these features seem to confirm a return to negotiated control strategies by the Italian police, that does not mean that Genoa can be classed as just an incident along the way. The chosen tactic of remaining invisible as far as possible, as well as the specific training concentrated on prevention, also met with criticism from within the police, with the SIULP in favor and the SAP opposing. It was claimed from within the police that the peaceful holding of the Florence ESF depended—apart from the police preventive services—not on dialogue but on the fact that by contrast with Genoa there was neither an opposing party to challenge nor a red zone. Only the presence of a stewardship service organized by the CGIL alongside the movement's stewardship service had given the necessary security guarantees (Colomba 2003, 204ff., 212; Zinola 2003, 173ff.). There seems, therefore, a persisting mistrust of the movement as a credible interlocutor for dialogue on the carrying out of demonstrations. The Genoa events did not lead to a full debate on structural problems in police organizations but to specific adjustments on the occasion of individual events.

The center-right temptation to portray the movement as a public-order problem, especially after September 11, even ranking it alongside terrorism, and to denounce public demonstrations as attempts to overthrow the democratically elected majority seems to remain high. For its part the institutional left continues to be divided in its attitude toward the movement, some of them seeing it as a disturbing, dangerous element. Above all, political forces have not proved interested or ready, at national or European levels, for open discussion on public-order strategies and on democratic control over the nascent EU internal security apparatus.

It thus becomes clear that the development of strategies for keeping public order is not following an unambiguous trend toward de-escalation but taking on an at least partly cyclical dynamic. It should be recalled that these strategies are not technical questions but reflect the quality of democratic systems. The Swedish Commission on the Gothenburg events stated, "The events that took place in Gothenburg cannot merely be regarded as public-order issues to be dealt with by the police but also as political issues relating to democracy, influence, exclusion, etc." The commission stresses "the importance of political dialogue in the form of discussion and through other channels of influence and participation in democratic decision-making processes—at the international, national and local levels. It is crucial to find forms for such discussion between decision-makers and today's opinion movements" (Justitiedepartmentet Betänkdande 2001, 7f.).

7

Politics, Antipolitics, and Other Politics: Democracy and the Movement for Globalization from Below

Political Opportunities for the Movement: An Introduction

"Democracy of the moderns"—that is, contemporary democracy as a system that governs territories of large dimensions—is fundamentally representative democracy: decisions are made by representatives, through standardized procedures, that are supposed to guarantee equality among citizen-voters and (electoral) accountability of those who represent them. The model of direct democracy runs against this one; it is based on unmediated participation by the public in decision making and is defined as "the democracy of the ancients." Participation not restricted merely to elections is also essential for modern democracies that gain legitimacy through the principle of majority decision making and through their ability to submit decisions to the "test of the discussion" (Manin 1993). In the past, most participation developed within political parties, where the reference to common values permitted the formation of collective identities—or at least the subordination of individual egos to a common program (Pizzorno 1977, 1981). Due to the subsequent weakening of the identity-building functions of political parties (della Porta 2001), in contemporary European democracies the role of social movements as arenas of public debate on political issues and of construction of collective identities has increased. Today, the seemingly increasing gap between representative and participatory forms of democracy, which political parties had somehow bridged, has increased the interest for other forms of democracy variously defined as participatory, deliberative, discursive, negotiated, cooperative, and consensual.[1]

196

The search for alternative models of democracy is particularly central for social movements in their theoretical elaboration and in their practice. Past research has indicated that social movements have criticized representative institutions and proposed alternative models of democracy. More or less raising fundamental criticism of conventional ways of political participation, their influence moved from politics to metapolitics (Offe 1985). In this sense, "the stakes and the struggle of the left and libertarian social movements thus invoke an ancient element of democratic theory that calls for an organization of collective decision-making referred to in varying ways as classical, populist, communitarian, strong, grassroots or direct democracy against democratic practices in contemporary democracies labelled as realist, liberal, elite, republican or representative democracy" (Kitschelt 1993, 15). Movements experiment with these models of democracy, both in their internal structure and in their interactions with the political institutions. Internally, as we saw in chapter 2, social movements have—with a greater or lesser degree of success—attempted to develop an organizational structure based on participation (rather than delegation), consensus building (rather than majority vote), and horizontal networks (rather than centralized hierarchies). As challengers, social movements interact, in their external environment, with polity members (Tilly 1978)—with representative institutions and public administrations—especially within the new arenas of direct democracy. They have demanded, and sometimes secured, decentralization of political power, consultations of citizens involved in particular policies, and appeal procedures against administrative decisions.

The relevance of the debate surrounding internal democracy is heightened by the transnational nature of the movement for global justice. The external challenges facing this movement are about the very meaning of politics and democracy, especially when specific decisions and, more generally, norm making shift to multilevel governance with great relevance to the political opportunities available for challengers. Studies on social movements have often highlighted the role of political opportunities in promoting collective action, the underlying concept being that participation increases with more channels of access to public decision making. For political institutions, access is generally considered to be more open as the administrative unit becomes more decentralized and the legislative, executive, and judiciary powers become more distinct. Furthermore, it has been noted that protest cycles coincide with an opening of the political system: the availability of allies, divisions within the government, or institutional reforms make bottom-up access easier (Tarrow 1994; della Porta and

Diani 1999). An important role in the development of social movements has been played by potential institutional allies, left-wing political parties in particular.

The movement for globalization from below seems to contradict these hypotheses since it grew quickly at a time when political opportunities were diminishing. In fact, by subtracting decision making from the nation-state, globalization jeopardizes the principles and institutions of representative democracy that have been built up around the nation-state (Dahl 1999; Pizzorno 2001). Internal and external factors challenge the traditional forms of legitimization of democracies, among them the following:

- a shift in the axis of power from politics to the market, with neoliberal economic policies increasing the power of multinational corporations and reducing the capacity of traditional state structures to control them (Pizzorno 2001)
- a shift in power from parliament to the executive and, within the executive, to the bureaucracy and to semi-independent agencies/authorities (Moravcsik 1999)
- a shift in the locus of power from national to supranational levels, with increased power wielded by a number of international organizations, especially economic ones (WB, IMF, WTO), and a number of macroregional organizations (first and foremost the EU) (Haas 1964; Scharpf 1997; Held and McGrew 1999)

There is another challenge facing contemporary movements. Social movement theory stresses the role of political allies—especially that of left-wing political parties—in favoring mobilization. During the protest cycle of the late sixties and early seventies, the emerging New Left criticized the institutional left for the alleged betrayal of their original "revolutionary" values (Pizzorno 1996), but the traditional left-wing party channeled many of the emerging demands to the representative institutions. Since the eighties, a de facto division of tasks developed: social movements retreated to the social sphere and political parties represented them in political institutions. As we shall see in this chapter, the recent acceleration of the evolution from mass parties to professionalized parties without a geographic base has reduced the potential for contacts and alliance between left-libertarian movements and left-wing parties (Katz and Mair 1992; della Porta 2001). Moreover, with the crisis of Keynesian economic policies and the hegemony of neoliberal ideology, the potential for forging alliances in the party system also declined, at least in the Western democracies (della Porta 2003a).

Transformation in political parties reduced the potential for alliances for the movement for global justice.

In terms of national opportunities, at the turn of the millennium the Italian center-right government can count on a rock-solid parliamentary majority, and this curtails legislative-executive dialectic. In addition, since high-profile personalities are the subject of judicial inquiries, the executive seems intent on extending its control over the judiciary. Furthermore, a center-right government whose main coalition partner has strong neoliberal leanings and whose next-strongest partner has a long-standing law-and-order electoral platform is faced with an opposition composed of a center-left alliance that is weak in both electoral and organizational terms and has the two largest groupings in it—DS and Margherita—competing for the centrist electorate. At the European level, too, the institutional left seemed, at least initially, hostile to the issues behind mobilization against global neoliberalism and its forms. At the Genoa G8 demonstrations in particular, protest was aimed at the leaders of the eight countries, which included politicians from the European left.

While the political conditions seemed unfavorable to protest on issues of globalization, the movement, as we shall see, has made major inroads toward redrawing the boundaries of politics, broadening them to include a public opinion that is increasingly receptive to criticism of globalization. At the same time, the movement has nudged the left toward some self-criticism and has exploited existing resources and channels already opened by previous waves of mobilization.

In this chapter, we shall look at some of the main aspects of the interaction between movements and politics. First of all, what is the substance of the movement's criticism concerning the existing practices of democracy at transnational and national levels, in the institutions and the parties? And what alternative concept of democracy does the movement propose? Viewing political parties as potential allies, we shall focus on the shifting opportunities for the movement in the multilevel structure of governance, sliding from mistrust to some timid attempts at dialogue.

The Movement's Critique of Representative Democracy

The self-definition as "a movement for a globalization from below" emphasizes the stigmatization of a top-down representative democracy. Together with free-market politics, the forms of representative democracy are also widely criticized. The movement is critical of national institutions, thought to be powerless or at best inadequate to guide globalization, as well as supranational ones, because of the specific policies they adopt and because of their deficit of democratic accountability. The traditional model of democracy for national states is challenged not only by the actual influence of economic corporations and intergovernmental organizations, but also by internal developments, such as the greater power of the executive vis-à-vis parliament and the personalization of politics through manipulative use of mass media, all of which make existing models of democracy based on electoral accountability insufficient.

Activists internalized the criticism of representative democracy. Among the demonstrators in Genoa, trust in representative institutions tended to be low and with significant differences regarding single institutions (Table 22). In general, some international organizations (especially the EU and the United Nations) are seen by activists as more worthy of respect than their national government but less so than local bodies. On this point there are also differences in the degree of trust expressed by demonstrators who identify with one of the three organizational networks. For local bodies, the trust score is a relatively high 55 percent for the ecopacifist sector activists, but it declines among activists belonging to the antineoliberalist one (40.2 percent) and is lower still for anticapitalists (20.3 percent). Trust is very low for Parliament (26.4 percent), probably also because of its identification with the center-right majority, and here, too, registers higher for the ecopacifists (32.4 percent) than for antineoliberalists (31 percent) or anticapitalists (9.9 percent). These differences are also seen in the rating of the EU and the United Nations, which approximately a quarter of the interviewees overall have trust in, rising to one-third of those belonging to the Lilliput network, but dropping to one-fifth of the demonstrators who identify with the other two networks.

Diffidence by activists in the institutions of representative democracy is cross-national (Table 23). Trust for national government is particularly low—especially among Italian and Spanish activists (facing right-wing governments),[2] but also among British activists (whose national government is Labour). Not even parliaments, supposedly the main instrument of representative democracy, are trusted (with an even lower rating among Italian interviewees than at Genoa). There is instead markedly greater trust in local bodies (especially in Italy and France) and, albeit somewhat lower, in the United Nations, especially among Germans, whereas the EU scores a level of trust among activists barely higher than for their national government. Italians, by contrast, show a lower level of trust in Parliament, but a relatively higher trust in local governments, the United Nations, and the EU.

When these figures are compared with Eurobarometer data for the

Table 22. Trust in political actors and in representative institutions, by sector affiliation (Genoa 2001)

Bodies trusted a lot or quite a lot	Sector affiliation (%)				
	Ecopacifist	Antineoliberalist	Anticapitalist	Total (%)	Cramer's V
Local bodies	55.0	40.2	20.3	41.0	0.27***
Parliament	32.4	31.0	9.9	26.4	0.21***
European Union	35.8	30.1	11.6	27.8	0.21**
United Nations	33.3	37.9	14.3	30.6	0.20**
Parties	26.9	50.9	30.0	37.0	0.23***
Trade unions	43.0	67.0	38.0	51.2	0.26***
Social movements	91.8	96.5	90.0	93.2	n.s.
(Number of interviewees)	(107–10)	(113–17)	(69–71)	(291–95)	

***significant at the 0.001 level; **significant at the 0.01 level; n.s. = nonsignificant.

Table 23. Trust in political actors and institutions by country of ESF participants (data in italics refer to entire population)

Bodies trusted a lot or quite a lot	Country of Origin (%)					Total (%)	Cramer's V
	Italy	France	Germany	Spain	United Kingdom		
Parties	18.9	22.7	6.0	14.4	22.1	17.9	0.15*
Parties[a]	*15*	*13*	*17*	*24*	*15*	–	
Unions (excluding Italians)	–	67.4	37.7	45.3	71.9	58.5	0.28***
CISL/UIL	8.7						
CGIL	58.2						
Grassroots trade unions	62.6						
Unions[a]	*34*	*36*	*34*	*37*	*39*	–	
Movements	86.1	95.6	85.2	92.7	84.4	88.9	0.15*
NGOs[a]	*39*	*42*	*30*	*69*	*30*	–	
Voluntary associations[a]	*57*	*63*	*48*	*68*	*63*	–	
Local governments	50.0	46.0	28.9	34.5	18.4	35.0	0.25***
National parliaments	11.8	20.2	14.6	18.2	2.8	13.0	0.19***
National government[a]	*33*	*30*	*37*	*48*	*33*	–	
National government	3.4	9.3	8.5	1.8	2.7	4.9	0.14*
European Union	22.3	12.5	10.0	10.2	3.4	11.8	0.20***
United Nations	17.7	27.7	37.0	17.4	8.2	20.1	0.23***
United Nations[a]	*57*	*44*	*48*	*58*	*55*	–	
(Number of ESF interviewees)	(138–45)	(126–36)	(76–83)	(106–11)	(136–47)	(589–614)	

***significant at the 0.001 level; *significant at the 0.05 level

[a] *Source: Eurobarometer 57* (Spring 2002)

whole EU population, a number of interesting features emerge on activists in the various countries. While trust in parties among the populations as a whole has a low level of swing, trust in parties by activists seems to vary more widely, a little above the population average in Italy, France, and Britain, but much lower in Spain and Germany. Great variation is also seen in attitudes toward trade unions: while data for the population as a whole are cross-nationally similar, activists have higher trust not only in Italy (where the difference depends on the trade unions) but also in France, Spain, and Britain, although less so in Germany. Activists everywhere have much less trust in governments and parliaments than do the overall population of their respective countries, with the lowest figures for the Spanish (conservative) government and Britain's New Labour government. Activists are also strongly critical of left-wing majorities (which one participant in the focus groups, significantly, defined not as "favorable" but as "less bad"). Similarly, there is greater variation among activists than in the population as a whole for trust in the United Nations.

Difference in judgment on the various supranational governmental institutions is also seen in the difference in willingness to negotiate with them. For the GSF, no fewer than 75 percent of interviewees responded that in general they would be willing to negotiate, the percentage falling dramatically when the question referred to specific institutions. Almost half the interviewees, however, believed that negotiating with the UN and the EU would be useful (50.2 and 47.8 percent respectively), much higher than those who thought it worthwhile to negotiate with the Italian government (35.3 percent) or with international financial organizations involved in furthering liberalist policies (14 percent), the G8 (8.2 percent), or NATO (6.6 percent).

What reasons are given for the general lack of trust? There is widespread belief that national institutions are ineffective in combating neoliberal globalization. One activist says, "For better or worse, many of us who believed we were living in a democracy have woken up. We've realized we were not even valued properly, we were not even really electors, we were no use to anything or anyone, since these agreements did without government bodies or especially parliaments" (FG 5b, 127). On the other hand, local institutions are perceived as being closer or at least more approachable, if for no other reason than their physical proximity to the public. The forums held by representatives of local institutions, often alongside the WSF, testify to this greater trust.

At the supranational level, the greater delegation of power to institutions with no democratic accountability is considered particularly dangerous for democracy. In November 1999, the declaration of international civil society against the Millennium Round at Seattle proclaimed, "We, the undersigned members of international civil society, oppose any effort to expand the powers of the WTO through a new comprehensive round of trade liberalisation" (Members of International Civil Society 1999). The movement, in particular, targets international organizations that, like the WTO, the WB, and the IMF, are accused of imposing their will on national governments by wielding the carrot of funds and the stick of conditionalities. By blocking funds or imposing sanctions against protectionist policies, they are seen as the main culprits in forcing neoliberal policies on developing and developed countries and even for overturning decisions taken democratically by the individual states. On the occasion of the fiftieth anniversary of Bretton Woods, the "Fifty years is enough" campaign denounced the failure of the IMF and the WB, demanding a radical reform of their policies and a democratization of their structure. In May 2000, the INGO Millennium Forum urged the United Nations "to reform and democratize all levels of decision-making in the Bretton Woods institutions and WTO and integrate them fully into the United Nations system, making these institutions accountable to the Economic and Social Council" as well as "to ensure greater transparency and democracy and to support the establishment of a consultative mechanism with civil society" (UN General Assembly 2000). Rete Lilliput and others have emphasized with regard to the G8 that "the non-legitimacy . . . of exclusive political summits (G8—European Commission) deciding unilaterally and behind closed doors has emerged as an evident political problem even though no real change has as yet come about" (Rete Lilliput 2001).

The UN is also being called on to democratize. The appeal of the first UN Assembly of Peoples reads:

> We, women and men, peoples of the United Nations, want a more humane, just, fair, solidary and democratic international order. . . . We pledge ourselves to act in order that inside the system of the United Nations conditions appropriate for the exercise of international democracy are created via the institution of a parliamentary assembly of the United Nations, the formation of a congress of local powers of the United Nations, the strengthening of the status of the NGOs and the tripartite composition (government, parliament, non-governmental associations) of the national delegations to the various organs of the United Nations, the strengthening of the systems of guarantees, starting with the international court of justice, as well as the reform of the security council

in order to make it really democratic and representative. (UN General Assembly 2000, 141)

Similar criticism is leveled at the EU, whose broadest authority is in the area of free market competition and which is accused of using it to impose neoliberal economic policies. The emphasis on free market and privatization as well as the restrictive budgetary policies set by the Maastricht parameters are stigmatized as jeopardizing welfare policies. Activists also criticize the European stance in foreign policies and ecological issues, denouncing a subordination to U.S. leadership. Also under scrutiny is the democratic deficit of the EU that stems both from the weakness of the parliament vis-à-vis the commission and the council, and the lack of transparency in the modus operandi of the so-called Eurocracies. During the ESFs of Florence and Paris, proposals were tabled for democratizing community institutions that went beyond the legislative-controlled executive that national models propose. The European Convention was seen, in particular by the groups most open to dialogue with the institutions, as an opportunity for applying pressure in order to strengthen the civil and social rights of European citizens. Not only was criticism aimed specifically at the drafted European Constitution, but interest was also stirred for participation from below in the definition of its contents.

In addition to greater democracy within European institutions, the ESF proposed a charter emphasizing social rights, an area in which the Treaty of Nice is perceived to be lacking. Indeed, EU policies are criticized for being essentially neoliberal with privatization of public services and flexibility of labor worsening job security. Under the slogan "another Europe is possible," various proposals were tabled including "taxation of capital" and, again, the Tobin tax. Demands were made for cuts in indirect taxation and assistance for weaker social groups, as well as a strengthening of public services such as education and health care.

Activists from the various countries are strongly critical of present EU politics and policies. There is a general consensus that the EU favors neoliberal globalization and widespread doubt as to its capability of mitigating the negative effects of globalization and safeguarding a different social model of welfare. While Italians have greater trust in the EU, and British activists are confirmedly more Euro-skeptic (followed by French and Spanish activists), altogether the differences are small. The data regarding trust in institutions confirm this strong critical feeling of European institutions, with about half of the sample declaring total mistrust in the EU and a tiny minority expressing high trust.

The denunciation of a "democratic deficit" in supranational governmental structures does not just boil down to demanding a strengthening of nation-state sovereignty. Activists have put forward many different proposals that not only question the neoliberalist forms of global economic development but also raise the issue of democratic participation in globalization processes. While the issue of whether a global structure of governance is preferable to a macroregional one is still being debated, consensus seems to be emerging around the idea that governing globalization cannot be left to national states. Together with demands for the curtailment in the scope of international financial organizations ("shrink or sink") and the increased weighting within them of developing countries, there is a call for new global institutions (such as an International Court of Debt Insolvency). At the supranational level, a proposal emerged to subordinate international organizations involved in economic policy to the United Nations and to make the latter more democratic. For example, the third assembly of the United Nations of Peoples held at Perugia in 1999 proposed "democratizing the economy," reclaiming "political control over companies, finance and international institutions," and entrusting "to a reformed United Nations—instead of to groupings of wealthy countries like the G7—the task of administering interdependence with an eye to the 'common good' so that it may intervene in economic decisions that are at the root of world problems" (in Pianta 2001, 152). Setting up a permanent forum of global civil society, monitoring the legitimacy of acts of the Security Council by the International Court of Justice, broadening the Security Council itself, doing away with permanent membership for the major powers, and the gradual phasing out of the veto power of some countries are other proposals for reforming the United Nations often put forward in manifestos and appeals during countersummits. In order for a supranational equivalent of "state of law" to be established, it is proposed that a permanent international criminal court be established to investigate war crimes and crimes against humanity. Although still being debated by the various organizations, the very existence of these proposals proves that, despite criticism of existing intergovernmental organizations, there is awareness of the need for some standard of international governance.

The activists of the ESF express strong interest in the building of new institutions of world governance: about 70 percent of the respondents are quite or very much in favor of this, including strengthening the United Nations, an option supported by about half our sample (Table 24). Furthermore, about one-third of activists agree that in order to achieve the goals of the movement, a stronger EU and/or other regional institutions are necessary (with much lower support among the British activists). There is also a high affective identification with Europe: about half the activists feel quite or strongly attached to Europe as a territorial unit.

Table 24. What would be necessary to achieve the goals of the movement (ESF, reduced sample)?

Degree of agreement	Country (%)					Total (%)	Cramer's V
	Italy	France	Germany	Spain	United Kingdom		
Strengthen national governments?							
Not at all	57.3	49.6	56.3	48.5	87.9	61.4	0.21***
A little	26.6	18.7	27.5	25.2	4.3	19.5	
Enough	14.0	20.3	11.3	15.5	5.7	13.2	
Very much	2.1	11.4	5.0	10.7	2.1	5.9	
Strengthen the European Union and/or other regional institutions (Mercosur, Arab League, etc.)?							
Not at all	33.8	32.8	44.4	34.6	85.2	47.5	0.27***
A little	28.1	18.0	22.2	28.0	5.6	19.8	
Enough	27.3	25.4	14.8	25.2	4.9	19.5	
Very much	10.8	23.8	18.5	12.1	4.2	13.2	
Strengthen the United Nations (giving them power to make binding decisions)?							
Not at all	27.7	29.4	27.4	27.4	76.9	39.1	0.26***
A little	18.4	12.7	14.2	14.2	7.0	13.9	
Enough	29.8	26.2	31.1	31.1	6.3	23.2	
Very much	24.1	31.7	27.4	27.4	9.8	23.9	
Build new institutions of world governance?							
Not at all	24.1	15.3	31.3	11.4	21.3	20.3	0.18***
A little	15.6	4.4	13.4	10.5	6.4	9.7	
Enough	24.8	27.7	21.7	23.8	7.1	20.8	
Very much	35.5	52.6	33.7	54.3	65.2	49.3	
(Number of interviewees)	(140–43)	(123–37)	(80–83)	(103–7)	(141–43)	(590–607)	(590–607)

***significant at the 0.001 level

Democracy and Parties

Mistrust spreads from the representative institutions to their main actors: political parties, including the parties of the left. In Genoa, a mere 37 percent of our interviewees trusted political parties a lot or quite a lot—a lack of confidence constant over all three organizational networks (Table 22). Confidence in the movements, on the other hand, is expressed by 93 percent of interviewees with even higher percentages for demonstrators who identify with an organizational network. Confirmation of how cross-nationally spread these results are emerges in Florence (Table 23), where a mere 15 percent of interviewees from the ESF have enough or much trust (even less than in the Genoa survey) in parties, with extreme expression of *Parteiverdrossenheit* (being fed up with parties) among German activists, seen, notably, in the strong criticism of the national red-green government coalition that led to the formation of ATTAC–Germany. Significantly, trust in parties rises with the respondent's age (only 18 percent of ESF participants between nineteen and twenty-five years old trust parties enough or a lot), but it does not correlate with the respondent's level of education.

By contrast, respondents reveal strong, and spatially fairly homogeneous, trust in social movements and voluntary associations as actors of "different" politics (ranging from 84 percent among the Germans and British to 96 percent among the French) (see Table 23). Everywhere, activists show much higher trust in movements than found in the Eurobarometer survey for NGOs and voluntary associations, and to some extent, ESF participation may have had a homogenizing effect. Data from the Eurobarometer survey are more varied, with Spanish and British activists proportionally much more skeptical than their fellow citizens, but French and German ones are relatively more trusting.

Why this criticism? In the past, social movement activists had often presented ideological criticism of traditional left-wing political parties, supporting radical and often revolutionary ideals. The responses to our questionnaires confirm, first of all, that activists are quite homogeneous in seeing themselves on the left of the political spectrum (Table 25). While criticism of market deregulation and cultural homogenization also find expression in religious fundamentalism and conservative protectionism, these forms of antiglobalization stances are not present in the movement, which has a clear left-wing profile. Although not right-wing or centrist, neither is the majority of the interviewees radical. Our data on identification within the left-right continuum of the ESF reveal a constant majority of activists who define themselves as leftist, with only a minority considering themselves "radical leftists" (Table 23). In Italy, from Genoa to Florence, the movement seems to have extended its appeal to the more moderate left—but those who declare themselves as center-right are an exception. Non-Italian ESF activists defined themselves primarily as leftists, with a significant component as extreme leftist and a small number who saw themselves as center-leftist. With the exception of British activists, the great majority of whom were extreme leftists (68 percent, followed at a distance by the French at 37 percent), placement on the left ranges from 44 percent of Germans to 53 percent of Spaniards, and 51 percent of Italians. Significantly, many activists refuse to locate on the left-right axis—with the highest percentage among post-materialist Germans (17.5 percent) and ethnonationalist Spaniards. From this viewpoint, the movement emerges from a critique of the policies followed by national governments in various countries—including those of the left—and by intergovernmental organizations.

The low level of trust in parties can also be seen in the data on respondents' proximity to a political party. In Genoa, among a population of which 37.5 percent identifies with the far left, 54.2 percent with the left, and 7.3 percent with the center left, no less than 12.3 percent declared no feeling of proximity to any party. While Rifondazione Comunista (RC)—as mentioned, supporting the movement since the very beginning—is considered close by 63.5 percent of the interviewees, the parties of the center-left coalition are perceived as distant by almost all activists at Genoa: only 10.2 percent indicated the Democrats of the Left (DS) as the closest party to them, 3.8 percent the Girasole (Sunflower, an electoral list comprising greens and ex-socialists from the SDI), 2.7 percent the Party of Italian Communists, 2.7 percent the Margherita (Daisy, the central wing of the center-left coalition). What is interesting is that the percentage of respondents close to RC is high also among interviewees from the ecopacifist sector (53.6 percent), rising to 72.4 percent for the antineoliberalist area (which, however, also includes RC militants). As far as the left wing of the center-left coalition is concerned, while support for the DS is 11.8 percent within the ecopacifist sector, it is still low, even lower than the average for the other two networks. It is only among anticapitalists and ecopacifists that the Girasole coalition—comprising greens and the SDI—manages to cling to a level of support, in any case low, of about 7 percent (Table 26).

Criticism aimed at the old left political parties—especially those potentially closer—addresses mainly their alleged acceptance of neoliberal ideology. As GSF spokesperson Vittorio Agnoletto observed, "When, in recent years, the European left was in power in almost every country in the EU at the same time, it chose not to espouse alternatives to neoliberal

Table 25. Self-location on the left-right axis by events and nationality (Genoa 2001 and Florence 2002)

Events	Self-location (%)						(Number of participants)
	Extreme left	Left	Center-left	Center	Center-right and right	Refuse to locate[a]	
Genoa	37.5	54.2	7.3	0.6	0.4	–	(683)
ESF interviewees by country (reduced sample)							
Italy	28.9	50.7	4.9	0.7	0.7	14.1	(142)
France	37.3	44.9	4.5	0.7	0.0	12.7	(134)
Germany	25.0	43.8	13.8	0.0	0.0	17.5	(80)
Spain	23.6	52.8	5.7	0.9	0.9	16.0	(106)
United Kingdom	68.1	26.4	2.1	0.7	0.7	2.1	(144)

Note: Cramer's V for ESF is 0.19, significant at the 0.001 level.

[a] This question was not posed to participants in the Genoa protest.

Table 26. Closeness to political parties by sector affiliation of the participants (Genoa 2001)

Political party	Sector affiliation (%)			
	Eco-pacifist	Anti-neoliberalist	Anti-capitalist	Total (%)
Rifondazione Comunista (RC)	53.6	72.4	64.2	63.5
Democrats of the Left (DS)	11.8	12.1	4.5	10.2
Girasole (Sunflower)	6.4	0.9	4.5	3.8
Partito dei Comunisti Italiani	5.5	1.7	–	2.7
Margherita (Daisy)	7.3	–	–	2.7
Others	6.3	2.5	4.5	4.7
None	9.1	9.5	22.4	12.3
(Number of interviewees)	(110)	(116)	(67)	(293)

Note: Cramer's V is 0.27 significant at the 0.001 level.

Note: Three of today's political parties stem from the Italian Communist Party (PCI): the social democratic majority of the Democrats of the Left (DS), Rifondazione Comunista (RC) as the union of those opposing the break with the communist tradition by the social democratic majority of the PCI decided in 1991, and Partito dei Comunisti Italiani, founded in 1998 in opposition to the decision of RC to withdraw its support for the center-left government of Romano Prodi. The Margherita is a federation of moderate parties of the center-left coalition Ulivo. The SDI emerged from the collapse of the Italian Socialist Party.

globalization" (2003, 147). The same idea is expressed by a priest and activist of the movement, Vitaliano della Sala: "Social injustice has at the same time an economic and an ideal root because it is based on the assumption that from the egotism of a few can stem the well-being of everyone. This is what the right believes in—an all-supreme market that produces wealth for all beginning from personal enrichment and, unfortunately, when it is in power, the left puts it into practice" (in Scateni 2003, 68). More generally, the new-global activist and journalist Naomi Klein observed, "All over the world, citizens have worked to elect social democratic and workers' parties, only to watch them plead impotence in the face of market forces and IMF dictates" (2002, 21).

Even more than their specific policy choices, activists contest the parties' conception of politics as an activity for professionals. The gap in ways of conceiving and doing politics is perfectly summed up in this dialogue at a focus group with members of the Florence Social Forum (see chapter 1 in this volume):

FG 4b: I think the parties feel threatened by this type of [movement] participation. . . .

FG 4a: I don't think they understand it at all. . . .

FG 4b: Because they're all going through a crisis of representation too . . . they are not representative of anyone, as things are. . . .

FG 4b: On the one hand there's also a completely different model of self-representation, etc., that doesn't fit, doesn't gel with a party's way of selection from above. . . .

FG 4g: They don't even let themselves be called in question. . . .

FG 4e: I'd at least have expected from the left-wing parties a minimum of attention, whereas instead they looked down on it: now it's clear that the Forum has brought so many people together, so many people that had stopped doing politics because they were sick of the parties on the left, so instead of being looked down on I'd have expected a minimum of attention for a movement that, for better or worse, manages to mobilize a whole lot of people . . . but it didn't happen. (94)

Data from the focus groups show that the demand for politics coincides with a demand for participation, and one criticism of the parties is that by now they have become *bureaucracies* based on delegation. In one activist's words, the movement marks "the passage from representation to participation" (FG 2c, 42). It's the discovery that "I don't have to be represented, but I can represent myself, so that I myself can participate in something and don't have to feel locked out" (FG 4a, 88).

Parties are stigmatized as bearers of a wrong idea of politics as done by *professionals,* interested in exploiting the movement for electoral purposes and denying its political nature. It is particularly experienced activists who perceive, and criticize, the defense by parties and public administrators of a sort of monopoly of political knowledge:

There are two attitudes toward the [ES] Forum, and the parties manage to have them both at the same time: one is seeking to put their hat on the Forum by attempting to identify with it . . .; the other attitude, instead, is more or less cryptically to downgrade what the Forum tries to say: "they're kids; yes, their enthusiasm is important, but the big issues are discussed elsewhere" . . . that's very serious, yes . . . I'm reminded of a great e-mail that came on the mailing list: "I'm fed up with being called a kid." (FG 4d, 94)

Reforging the Polis: An Alternative Conception of Politics

Our data seem to indicate that, instead of choosing radical ideologies or "going back to the private" (or social) sphere, activists addressed political challenges by attempting to redefine politics. The search for the polis, which political parties and institutions are accused of betraying, is expressed as the need for the public (as opposed to professionals) to reclaim political activity, stressing participation (as opposed to bureaucratization) and attempting to construct values and identities (as opposed to administrating the existent). In the nineties, disappointment with "ordinary" politics was expressed in a return, if not to private life, at least to social life (joining the voluntary sector, seen as different from politics), but now the movement is seen as based on the interaction between society and politics. As one activist of the generation that became socialized in the nineties ("the years with no movements") puts it: "I never went in for politics, but before I always did voluntary stuff . . . according to me there's now this merger between voluntary work and politics strictly speaking . . . and this is maybe the novelty that gives the impetus, the fuel that makes the forces of two worlds that were perhaps a bit separate before come together" (FG 3i, 77).

By contrast with the movements of the seventies, the left critique largely avoids ideologism. The New Left was fascinated by a possible revolutionary seizure of power; today's activists instead present their action as *pragmatic, concrete, and gradualist.* The objective of the movement is to "make the world aware": it "does not aim to take power, but to change society in its relationships, its feelings, and how people are treated, to build a different world; and a different world is built from below" (FG 5b, 128). In the words of one participant in the focus group, the movement is a river, and "the broader the river, the slower it flows . . . sometimes it even seems as if it flows underground. Just because it's so broad, every time it has to redefine its way of doing things in relation to what's happening around it, fortunately it does so in the broadest possible way, and perhaps the most democratic and mixed up. . . . The movement is like water permeating and flowing everywhere, so that when it knocks the wall down it already owns the field" (FG 3c, 66).

Activists perceive the role of politics as seeking a common understanding of the common good through discussion and debate. What activists see as party politics, including left-wing party politics, is merely administering what already exists, as against a search "in movement" ("that's why it's called a movement: ideas and consequently practices, too, are in movement").

Participation is seen as an antidote to the "sterility" of politics in the eighties and nineties:

> In recent decades, politics had become dried up. . . . Every so often some-one says politics never makes a jump; but politics almost always moves forward in jumps, a bit like earthquakes: those plates pushing day after day, until all of a sudden the earthquake finally happens. It was a bit like that, then . . . it exploded partly because of the need people felt to ex-press their condition, express it themselves without having to go through somebody else. . . . The purely representative machinery of politics had more or less broken down or gone off the rails so people who had borne the brunt of neoliberalism felt the need to express this condition of theirs themselves, and just by expressing it get over the first hurdle of their own difficulties. (FG 3f, 63–64)

Party politicians are stigmatized for referring to a "*prepolitical move-ment* clamoring to be listened to but which then has to be translated into a project and a political program by those who do politics in the institutional sense of the word. . . . I remember an interview with the Florence mayor after the Social Forum when he said 'you can't ask these young people to express political projects, it's we who have to interpret them'" (FG 6e, 143). Politics is instead experienced as involvement by the public (even individu-als) in developing demands and responses:

> It's no longer the way it was, with the movement on the one hand with its spontaneity, asking questions, and on the other the politicians giv-ing answers or trying to. . . . In this case the answers come along with the questions, and the questions come along with the answers, because the thing is being built: that is, the possible world is being built. Parties, associations, organized groups, were just what had set themselves in the past as those who came up with the answers (ideologically, institution-ally, and existentially). (FG 2a, 42–43)

The pluralism of the base of reference is bound up with an assertion of equality, which rules out delegation in the name of everyone's equal right to speak for themselves. The movement is in fact defined as "a form of rela-tions among forces, political movements, organizations, etc., that have not worked together before; it manages to hold so many approaches together by endeavoring—and I think this is the great effort—not by compelling, basically, and in so doing it broadens the struggle" (FG 2b, 38). As "a net-work linking a whole series of environments, people with a common sense of things they want to change, even if there are profound differences among them," the movement is praised for building up from the "substrate common to all the identities inside it, . . . for a moment setting aside for the common good the more specific objectives each identity has and must certainly keep as its own" and "nonetheless realizing the strength to be found from unity in diversity" (FG 2c, 38). For older activists, the movement reopens a public arena that had been closed off in earlier decades: "I come from the old twentieth-century militancy of the fifties, sixties, and seventies, but then came the yuppie years, the eighties, and then the terrible nineties where there was no room for political action except what was decided by the various kinds of political bureaucracies. . . . So to me it was a reopening of a public space of meetings, debates, and initiative which certainly . . . may well be the beginning of a new politics, no longer delegated or entrusted to the competent, to technicians, but taken on by people as their own primary responsibility" (FG 6e, 143).

The very essence of the movement, its "constant becoming," is also seen as the search for questions and answers that delves into the activist's own wealth of subjectivity: "politics is also a competition among ideas, not just getting something organized, it's also choosing what to organize around, otherwise we risk falling into a logic that I feel is old, according to which politics means organizing—the bureaucratic bit, coordination, you've got one task and him another, it's him being up top and you down below" (FG 2a, 48). The encounter between the old and new generations of activists is perceived as based on "the same desire for something different, but something very instinctive, joyous, celebratory, practical (not just talked about but practiced too) . . . a chance for doing politics that immediately becomes a building of public places, building the polis, not organizing in order to win votes, to become a majority, to govern and change the world, but right now, on the spot, because you manage to build relationships, set up contacts, do concrete things. Doing politics straight away in this sense, making society, *making the polis,* has been the most exhilarating part of it for me" (FG 5e, 123).

Criticizing representative democracy does not, however, mean a brusque abandonment of dialogue or interaction with the institutions. While stating they have no intention of taking power or, as happened in the seventies and eighties, of setting up new parties, activists express their awareness that making "another possible world" cannot be separated from taking part in public debate and decision making. In the south of the world, especially, the electoral successes of parties actively critical of neoliberalism is seen as a way for experimenting with bottom-up policy-making models. This leads to focusing attention on new ways of decision making in which the public is directly involved. The participatory democracy of the Zapatista communities is often cited, in which decisions are made unanimously by an assembly open to all (Benenati 2002, 40). One model in the development of concrete bottom-up democratic proposals has been, especially, the participatory budgeting tried out in the city of Porto Alegre and subsequently extended to other governments, both in Brazil and elsewhere.[3] Having gone through many stages of development, participatory budgeting has become extremely complex in an attempt to get around some of the well-known limits of assemblyism (in particular decision-making impasse) and especially to exploit the advantages of direct democracy in terms of increased citizen participation and empowerment. Following in part the Porto Alegre model, the second WSF sought to formalize principles of participatory democracy, tried in the south of the world, in the New Municipal Charter.

Parties and Movement from Seattle to Genoa: Between Lack of Knowledge and Diffidence

As we have already mentioned, while there has been tension between movements and parties, the success of protest has come from movements forging alliances with institutional actors and so getting access to the decision-making process. Furthermore, waves of protest have often spurred institutional actors into creating new parties and transforming others. While criticism of institutional politics from within the movement for a globalization from below is linked with a focus on participative democracy, it is important to examine how left-wing parties have reacted to this criticism, their original hostile diffidence giving way to timid overtures, with substantial differences between one country and another.

Institutional actors during and immediately after Genoa refused to recognize the movement as a political subject, even more than the issues it was raising. To the activists who disputed the legitimacy of the eight "giants" to decide on behalf of everybody—"You G8, we 6 billion"—the Italian government responded by refusing to acknowledge the movement as a partner to be talked with, seeing and presenting it instead mainly as a problem of public order (see chapter 6 in this volume). Before, during, and after the G8, the government persisted in viewing the movement as mainly a problem of public order. The relationship with the GSF progressively worsened during the days of the protests, and the government put the full blame for the disorders on the organizers. After the searches at the Diaz-Pertini school, Berlusconi declared that it was impossible to tell the difference between the GSF and the BB. The parliamentary majority accusing the GSF of duplicity affirmed that "for the whole duration of the G8, the violent and subversive part of the demonstrators took advantage of the tolerance of the peaceful demonstrators. In no way did the latter ever take any concrete initiative toward making known, isolating, or expelling violent or subversive elements" (IPIC 2001a, 243).

Apart from the specific problems of public order (see chapter 6 in this volume), in general the nonrecognition of the demonstrators and their spokespersons—also in terms of their electoral lack of accountability (in not having been elected by anyone)—is contrasted with the responsibility of elected leaders. Together with the movement, therefore, the very legitimacy of the protest is questioned, considering politics in the street an illegitimate interference with elected representatives who, among other things, are presented as the only ones with any real interest in fighting world poverty.

Despite the almost natural premise for dialogue, if not alliance, with the institutional left on the issues of social justice and sustainable development, the recognition of the movement as a legitimate political actor by the Italian center-left parliamentary opposition remained uncertain. The center-left coalition was fragmented, and during the days of Genoa, its biggest constituent party was going through the difficult phase of reelecting its leader. The debate on the preparatory phases of the G8 demonstrations evolved without any interaction with the main center-left parties who, except for RC and some greens, seemed to turn a blind eye to or be ignorant of the growing mobilization on the issue of globalization. As the philosopher and ex-mayor of Venice, Massimo Cacciari, pointed out, "Thousands of young people have been talking about these issues for a year and nobody has noticed. But more than that, they've been doing it without any politician taking part" (in *Limes*, April 2001, 109). Later, the spokesman for the GSF, Vittorio Agnoletto, noted, "Not only had the great part of the center-left failed to see that the Genoa mobilization would have taken place, but afterward it was obvious they had failed to comprehend the roots of the movement of movements; they were not ready conceptually and therefore unable to analyze it" (2003, 32).

Already before Genoa, the stance of Giuliano Amato's center-left government vis-à-vis the demonstration organizers seemed to waver between being open and being uninterested. To begin with, on the basis of recommendations that had emerged from the earlier Okinawa G8 summit in July 2000 that there should be a greater involvement of civil society in the decision-making processes in which major international issues were at stake, the Amato government seemed willing to single out reliable partners inside the movement, even to the point of organizing a kind of forum parallel to the official one.[4] Indeed, it was not even ruled out that dissenting suggestions and alternative proposals be taken into consideration by the government and included in the Italian agenda for the G8. On the basis of these expectations, the GSF contacted international organizations, envisaging a large-scale countersummit. Afterward, the apparent drop in interest from mid-February onward and the absence of any input from the government inhibited the openness of the moderate wing of the movement to cooperation and strengthened the position of the hard-liners who had always preached the uselessness of dialogue with the institutions.[5] Around the same time, from April 20 until the beginning of June, there was, as we have seen (chapter 6 in this volume), an absence of dialogue at the local level between the prefect and the GSF on the modality and times of the protest demonstrations.

The skepticism and uncertainty on what stance to take toward the emerging movement continued even when the center-left coalition went into opposition. Before the G8 summit, the center-left opposition had tried to reach an agreement with the center-right majority by voting motions with cross-party majority/opposition abstentionism. On July 19, it was still split on whether or not to take part in the Saturday march; the left wing of the DS was in favor of going to Genoa (two theme-based areas of the party and its youth movement were members of the GSF), while some members of the Margherita Party and even some from the DS were against. Umberto Ranieri, former undersecretary at the Foreign Ministry stigmatized the "narrowness of the answers the no-globals are suggesting." The leader of the CGIL trade union, Sergio Cofferati, was critical of the DS's decision to join in and turned down the call that Vittorio Agnoletto, spokesperson of the GSF, had made to the trade unions to participate and, with their reputation as responsible actors, to protect the movement from attempts to criminalize it. After the death of Carlo Giuliani, the DS withdrew from the Saturday march, and in a TV interview broadcast live the candidate for the post of national secretary, Fassino, read a communiqué inviting party members not to go to Genoa: "What has taken place and what is presently taking place in Genoa is very serious. The DS have therefore decided not to go to Genoa, and invites everyone not to participate in the demonstration. . . . In the light of what has happened and in these conditions, it is no longer possible to guarantee either the barest conditions of personal safety or that respect of the nonviolent criteria that are fundamental for us" (*Il Giornale,* July 21, 2001).

The DS were also split over their judgment on the GSF, often accused of being unable to keep the protest peaceful. The forms of action adopted by the movement came under fierce criticism that swung between timidly defending the peaceful demonstrators and stigmatizing the Disobedients. Even long after the Genoa event, a spokesperson of the GSF spoke openly of an attempt staged by the center-left to split the movement into "good guys and bad guys": "some people [in the center-left] . . . have actively worked toward a criminalization of the movement and in so doing show themselves as being very short-sighted and indifferent toward the scenarios that could have opened up, not to mention their undying illusion of being able to build their own fortunes by allowing the right wing to defeat the movement" (Agnoletto 2003, 157).[6]

Even after profound changes in the structure of the party, the traditional tendency of the Italian Communist Party (PCI) of disowning any autonomous opposition movement to its left (della Porta 1996) is reflected in the hostility expressed by the majority of the DS to the global justice movement, which it criticized in both form and content. The movement was stigmatized as being ingenuous, if not Luddite, because it would not accept the unavoidable progress of which globalization is one aspect, as Fassino, the DS secretary, commented in an interview: "We have to ask ourselves what these young people represent, the extraordinary sensitivity that makes them want to struggle on behalf of the world's poor, but also the wishful, indeed ingenuous thinking they have of being able to stop the world" (*Corriere della Sera*, July 22, 2001). The DS party president, D'Alema, was to talk of the movement asking the right questions but coming up with answers that were partially wrong, criticizing especially the delegitimization of the summits (*La Repubblica*, July 18, 2001).

Mistrust of movement activists increased during the center-left governmental experience. When the DS went into government between 1996 and 2001 after a very long, unbroken spell in opposition, focus was shifted away from party life to public administration,[7] and a moderation of party priorities on various issues presented as a sign of responsibility toward the country. Within this type of context, the movement was clearly perceived as a disturbing element. At best, the role of the party is emphasized as being different from the movement's, the party being perceived as an actor of institutional politics, profoundly different from civil society. The center-left candidate for premiership, Rutelli, emphasized that "those with institutional responsibilities can't behave like a kid at Seattle" (*La Repubblica*, July 18, 2001), and the DS party whip in the Senate, Violante, and others hesitated to dialogue with the GSF spokespersons because of the latters' uncertain democratic investiture: "I don't know if they represent anything and if so what. Instead we must talk to individual organizations that are the loyal representatives of real people and ideals" (*La Repubblica,* August 10, 2001).

Bitter criticism of the mobilization against neoliberal globalization is not constrained to the Italian institutional left. In other parties of the European left, interest in the movement arose only very recently. A claim to the primacy of representative politics has been energetically expressed by heads of center-left government—as the British prime minister Tony Blair repeated prior to the Genoa summit: "The way we who govern take decisions is democratic: we present programs, we take part in elections, we are elected by the people. Not only are these street demonstrations not sensible, because we meet to discuss matters and questions that are crucial for the world, but they are also completely antidemocratic when they fall back on violence. And I think that we politicians are far too apologetic toward them" (*La Repubblica,* July 18, 2001).[8]

The very issues raised by the movement, which take up the traditional social-democratic critique of market liberalism as being incapable of guaranteeing economic development and social justice, embarrass center-left governing politicians who have accepted and practiced some of these neoliberalist ideas. As the German chancellor Gerhard Schröder meaningfully declared, "We can attempt to discuss with the more intellectually reachable part of the movement . . . their idea that globalization can even be dangerous, for example, in the relationship between politics and economy, or widen the gap between rich and poor countries are issues we have to face. But let there be no misunderstanding, I think they're wrong. So far globalization has proved to bring bigger markets and these present more opportunities than risks" (*La Repubblica,* July 13, 2001).

Furthermore, all or most of the members of the various European governments, even the center-left, have called the protest useless, since they themselves were attending to the problems of the south of the world, with some even voicing doubts on the legitimacy of the demonstrations by the "self-appointed saviors of the earth" because their protests were against summits held by democratically elected representatives. While it should come as no surprise that the Italian president of the Council of Ministers, Berlusconi, saw the specter of communism behind the protests, it is somewhat odd that a former member of the extraparliamentary left of the seventies, the German foreign minister Fischer, did accuse the movement of "sterile anticapitalism," declaring on the same wavelength as Bush, "But are we really sure that antiglobalization is in the interest of the Third World?" (*La Repubblica,* July 25, 2001).

Parties and Movement from Genoa to Florence: A Difficult Dialogue

Persisting mistrust notwithstanding, especially after Genoa, the institutional European left was beginning to sit up and take notice. The dialogue, however, is rocky. As the movement focused attention on the issue of globalization, and neoliberalism in particular, the social democrat parties were obviously embarrassed by their past support, at local and national government levels, of policies of privatization of public services and flexibilization of the labor market. Concerning the forms of protest, the social democrat parties continued to insist on their political monopoly, leaving the movement, at most, the job of being a marker for the problems, while denying it any role in working out the answers.

In their reflection on globalization, and especially on trade liberalization, European social democratic parties were for a long time advocates of the positive effects it brought in terms of development and equality, although there was no lack of dissent. As early as 1998, the Council of the Socialist International had underlined the risk that globalization would strengthen social inequalities and vulnerability to economic crises, pointing the finger at globalization policies based on principles of deregulation that led to economic recessions and social dumping (Socialist International Council 1998). One year later, the Socialist International redoubled its criticism of the neoliberal policies of the "almighty marketplace" that reduced state interventionism to a minimum and of an "individualism destroying the public sphere" (Socialist International 1999), proclaiming "the primacy of politics for providing answers to the challenge of globalization."

In Germany, self-critical reflection began after the demonstrations in Genoa in the form of a long-distance exchange of views between two old friends and companions of the militant left of the seventies in Frankfurt: Daniel Cohn-Bendit, now a European MP for the French Green Party, and Joschka Fischer, at that time Germany's foreign minister. Cohn-Bendit, referring to comments Fischer had made about the movement, advised him not to talk, as a current representative of government, as stupidly as rulers in the seventies had done (interview with the *Frankfurter Rundschau,* August 1, 2001). He warned his generation against behaving the way the Schmidt government had done when faced with the antinuclear and pacifist movements, incapable of comprehending the dimension of moral indignation behind the protest. This opened a chasm between social democracy and social movements and eventually led to the birth of the Green Party (interview with *Tageszeitung,* August 15, 2001).

Criticism from within the parties of the red-green governing coalition for not having been able to come up with adequate replies to the movement led to a number of members taking a more open stance. In an interview with *Der Spiegel* (no. 34, 2001, 24ff.), then foreign minister Fischer, while repeating the importance of nonviolence, emphasized how reformist policies need pressure from below. Chancellor Schröder, during an SPD economic forum, defined no-global demonstrators as "young, committed people who keep on pointing out to us that large-scale economic development must have a social and environmental sensitivity" and calling for "more policies" for democratic globalization (*Tageszeitung,* September 5, 2001). Resolutions presented at the congress of both the Green Party (Bündnis 90/Die Grünen 2002) and the SPD (SPD 2001) similarly addressed these points. It was no coincidence that the German president, Johannes Rau, echoed many demands made by critics of globalization in his speech "Chance Not Destiny— To Shape Globalization by Political Means."

In the German Parliament, the debate on the presentation of the preliminary report (October 18, 2001) and the concluding one (June 28, 2003) of the Enquete-Kommission on globalization[9] (established in December 1999), on issues such as regulation of international financial markets and the introduction of environmental and social standards, highlighted the different positions of the parties and showed how these differences tied in with the diverging assessments of the protest against neoliberal globalization and the role NGOs and the movement should have within a system of global governance. While the Christian Democrat opposition, who considered the NGOs part and parcel of violent demonstrations, deemed that their role should be restricted to acting in a consultative capacity to Parliament and government, the left-wing majority envisaged worldwide protection of public goods—the environment, social and economic stability, the rule of law, access to education and information and infrastructures—the main objectives of global governance perceived as a form of systematic cooperation between state and nonstate actors that should be developed as the bearing pillar of a worldwide culture of democracy (Deutscher Bundestag 2002, 14/195, 19048ff.; 14/246, 2488ff.). The commission president, Ernst Ulrich von Weizsaecker (SPD), laid particular emphasis on the need to reinvent democracy at the supranational level.

In France, leaders of the left, including then Prime Minister Jospin, showed increasing sensitivity to the issues the movement was furthering, as demonstrated by the large delegation of French politicians who attended the second meeting at Porto Alegre, which included seven cabinet ministers and three candidates for the presidency of the republic. In April 2001, Lionel Jospin underlined the importance of "a form of world public opinion": "Members of associations, trade unionists, university people, men and women are beginning to mobilise planet-wide. . . . In Seattle at the end of 1999 and then alongside the meetings of the IMF, the WB or the Davos Forums, and more recently at Porto Alegre, this movement has borne witness to a raised awareness of what is at stake politically in globalization" (Jospin 2001). After Genoa, the French socialist party in government condemned the "distinguished weakness" of the G8 final decisions "on the great part of the world's problems, in particular on crucial issues of the development of the south and of environmental protection" (PSF 2001).

After the Genoa demonstrations, a richer debate began to emerge on globalization and the movement within the left-wing political parties in Italy. Even before the G8, the movement had enjoyed some support from within the DS—in particular, its youth section (Sinistra Giovanile) and Altrimondi (Otherworlds), the theme area of the DS, were part of the GSF. L'Unità (a daily newspaper linked to the DS), had called the Saturday demonstration in Genoa "one of the biggest demonstrations of political protest of the last ten (or twenty, or thirty or forty) years," describing "the joy of a movement in the realization of being born, being alive and having a future" (July 22, 2001). After the events of Genoa, criticism became more acute in areas nearer the DS (including the L'Unità Web forum), focusing on the party's vacillations and especially its withdrawal from the Saturday demonstration. At the Feste dell'Unità, the party's fund-raising kermis held during the months of July and August, debate on the DS not having taken part in Genoa was intense. In Florence, the president of the Tuscan Regional Council, Martini, who had marched in the Saturday protests in Genoa, pointed out that "major popular democratic forces who are used to handling movements can no longer stay aloof. Many young people told me: if there had been the strength and experience of the trade union, or of some other mass organization, the march would have felt better protected" (La Repubblica, Florence edition, July 25, 2001). The leaders of the left minority within the DS were to appeal both before and after the party congress of November 2001 for dialogue with the social forums, who counted many institutional left-wing party members among their numbers.

It was especially through the organizational process of the ESF that a part of the institutional left got closer to the movements. The Florence meeting enjoyed the support of the Tuscan regional president, Claudio Martini of the DS. The CGIL trade union took part in the forum (and the speech of its general secretary, Gugliemo Epifani, was applauded) as did the left-wing of the DS and a number of politicians from the Margherita party. The former CGIL secretary general, Sergio Cofferati, who did not go to Genoa, was in the march organized as the closing event of the Social Forum and said, "the left and politics look with great attention and sympathy at this movement. I believe that we have an obligation to dialogue with it." He emphasized, "This movement is different from the ones of the 70s. They wanted to be parties but this one is asking the parties for help. Anyone who doesn't see that is mistaken" (*Corriere della Sera*, November 10, 2002). After the ESF, the president of the European Commission, Romano Prodi, observed, "We've got to listen to them. That's not to say you've got to indulge them or agree with everything they say. But exactly in these moments of change the voice of the young is of fundamental importance" (ibid.).

The secretary for the economic affairs of the French Socialist party, Bernard Soulage, referred to the Florence ESF as a public success, emphasizing the need to defend public services (*Le Monde*, November 30, 2002). Again, commenting on the ESF, the French socialist leader François Hollande pointed out, "For democracy to dominate globalization a new pact is needed between the popular movements, social actors and progressive parties" (2002). In 2003, at the second ESF in Paris, Hollande again emphasized the need to govern globalization politically and forge alliances "with the often anonymous militants of the another-world-is-possible movement. These often obstinate organizations have been questioning us for a long time. These movements who challenge an order which ultimately is indeed nothing more than world disorder. We cannot do without them, we need them. Yes, we have to have a close relationship with the movements for a different globalization. Yes, there is need of an international civil society. Yes, we need NGOs. Yes, we need new forms of citizenship" (Hollande 2003). In a comment on the WTO meeting in Cancún, the German SPD parliamentary group dubbed as failed the attempt to "see in trade deregulation alone the answer to the world's problems," highlighting, instead, the need to tackle the problems of developing countries' foreign debt, environmental protection, and social policies with real material support (SPD 2003). A parliamentary motion tabled by the SPD and Greens, again on WTO policies, emphasized the importance of public service and criticized the lack of democracy in international organizations (including "the top echelons of the EU," in particular the lack of transparency and "arrogance" of EU bureaucracy) (SPD and German Greens 2003). At the second ESF, in Paris, the European Socialist Party, their MPs, and the Socialist International held a Global Progressive Forum. Its inaugural document states, "We need global progressive alliances for change. Such alliances have to bring progressive political forces together around shared political aims. They will go beyond the borders of social-democracy and include progressive civil society organizations, NGOs, trade unions, business and academics devoted to building a sustainable world of democracy, peace, security and social justice" (Party of European Socialists 2003).

The relationship between social democratic parties and movements remained, however, a difficult one. First, differences between the social democratic parties in the various countries persisted. After having been criticized for their neoliberal policies and then voted out of the national government, the French socialists tried to improve their image among movement activists, proclaiming their support for the values of global justice. The German social democrats, albeit somewhat more reservedly, revised their stance on globalization, although the red-green government initiated reforms denounced by activists as the dismantling of the welfare state. The DS in Italy seemed divided, with the majority wing looking askance at what was happening at the street level. While the Spanish PSOE dedicated a window in its Web site to globalization, New Labour didn't mention any criticism of globalization on its Web site and fell back on foreign policy to praise British intervention "as a key member of the UN, NATO, the EU, the Commonwealth, WTO, G7 and the International Monetary Fund and WB," defining labor's approach as playing "a leading role to advance an international agenda that promotes the universally shared values of freedom, human rights, the rule of law, democracy and the value of justice" (New Labour 2004). And while Continental European socialist parties lined up against military intervention in Iraq, New Labour's Web site emphasized that "Britain is a force for good in the world and has intervened militarily to defend human rights and the rule of law in Afghanistan, Iraq, Kosovo, East Timor and Sierra Leone" (ibid.). Generally, the growing criticism of neoliberal globalization by the main left-wing parties was often perceived by movement activists as a strategic move to co-opt electoral supports through symbolic declarations that were not supported (especially when the parties were in government) by a sincere belief in the danger of the neoliberal policies of privatization and market deregulation.

Furthermore, there was still strong mistrust of the movement forms by socialist parties. In Italy, with the exception of Claudio Martini, president of the Tuscan Regional Council and the left wing of the DS (in addition to Rifondazione Comunista and the Greens), politicians from the center-left coalition (with the exception of the Greens) did not intervene firmly in the defense of demonstration rights in Florence until a few days before the

ESF, when Fassino made a sort of commitment to watch over it. DS participation in the ESF proceedings was more unofficial than official, with a position defined as "embarrassed and vacillating: between the fear of losing out at the center to the Margherita party that (with few but worthy exceptions) snubbed the forum, and losing out at the left to Sergio Cofferati who quite some time previously had announced his intention to take part in the Forum's closing demonstration" (*Il Manifesto,* November 6, 2002). Nor were the two main parties of the center-left coalition present at the ESF closing demonstration—or either of the two leaders, Fassino and Rutelli. Commenting on this, Tuscan Regional President Martini observed, "They would have done better to have been here" (*Corriere della Sera,* November 10, 2002). The party secretary, Fassino, responded that he had not taken part because his presence "would have signified unreserved alignment with a movement on the part of a party whose confines stretch well beyond the demonstrators" (*Il Manifesto,* November 12, 2002). Rutelli, then leader of the center-left coalition, declared he wanted to do everything possible so that the movement "wouldn't close in on itself in futile anti-Americanism," all the while "warning" against resorting to violence and repeating that movements and parties "must learn to live together, staying separate" (*Corriere della Sera,* November 11, 2002). During the ESF, Luciano Violante underlined, "It's not true that globalization signifies poverty," although he did admit it entailed greater inequality, and emphasized the importance of a globalization of rights. Criticism of the DS decision not to participate also came from the party's left wing, whose spokesperson, Fabio Mussi, stated, "Fassino would have done well to come. This is where politics is, this is where our people are" (ibid.).

The image the institutional left had of the movement, even those who were sympathetic to its aims, remained that of a phenomenon that spurred politics. The document of the European socialists spoke of a network of "political and non-political progressive forces" (Party of European Socialists 2003). While proclaiming the need to forge an alliance with the movement, the secretary of the French Socialist Party Hollande, again claimed a different role for the party, stating, if "it is normal that the movement has its aspirations, forms of organization and ways of intervention in its own sphere," then the Socialist Party must "claim its own role as a political organization," and he went on to define the party as an "extension, armed hand, development and political tool of a movement for a different globalization" (Hollande 2003). That "parties and movements should not get mixed up" was repeated by the DS secretarial coordinator Vannino Chiti, while the small Party of Italian Socialists warned of a split between "maximalist left" and the "governing left" (*Corriere della Sera,* November 11, 2002). Indeed, the movements are still mainly considered as stimulants to politics but incapable themselves of developing answers to the world's problems. Sergio Cofferati, former secretary-general of the CGIL trade union, although he did march in the demonstration that concluded the ESF, said, "The thread that unites so many initiatives is rights to be defended or extended. *It is the duty of politics to attend to the task of strengthening this thread and spinning it.* Also because the movement that has risen over these last few months has two very important positive characteristics, namely, a return to personal commitment based on ideals, combined with the awareness of not being able to take the place of politics" (*Avvenire,* November 9, 2002; our italics). And again, "political parties, as we have known them historically, must change their structure, at least in part, and open up to the movements: *The movements are by definition bearers of partiality and often have radical features.* . . . It is, however, important for traditional political parties to find the will and the way to start a dialogue" (*Il Manifesto,* November 12, 2002; our italics).

The reawakening of interest in the more participative forms of politics is, therefore, viewed by social democratic parties as a danger. As part of the electoral reservoir of the institutional left, movement activists are challenging a new party model, one that is built around elected representatives and privileges a relationship with the electorate managed by mass media communication experts and opinion pollsters (della Porta 2001). In a leading article on the movements after the ESF in the critical left-wing daily *Il Manifesto,* Luigi Pintor repeated that "governments, traditional political forces, the regimented media and those that set themselves up as the left without being left wing haven't understood anything of this growing innovative phenomenon that's cutting through barriers. The democratic upsurge of the days of Florence astonished them because they have forgotten what democracy is all about" (November 12, 2002).

The timid openings on the part of the socialist parties assuredly mirror the more consistent criticism leveled at neoliberal globalization by trade unions (see chapter 2 in this volume) and, on a more general level, by public opinion. Indeed, protests against globalization seem to have been successful in awakening public opinion to some of its challenges. In June 2001, a short time before the G8 summit at Genoa, a CIRM poll revealed that 45 percent of Italians felt sympathetic with the movement's arguments, 28 percent did not, and 27 percent had no opinion (*La Repubblica,* June 17, 2001). A later survey by Simulation Intelligence Research showed that 81 percent of Italians were in favor of canceling third world debt, 63.5 percent were in favor of the Tobin tax, 70.4 percent in favor of doing away with tax havens, 79.7 percent in favor of "equality of economic and working conditions for workers worldwide," 70.4 percent in favor of the battle against GM foods, 55.3 percent in favor of freedom of movement for migrants, and 73.8 percent were unconditionally opposed to war. Overall, 19 percent of those surveyed replied that the no-global movement was very positive and 50.9 percent quite positive (only 16.1 percent felt it was quite or very negative). Again, in Italy, a 2003 survey conducted by the Demos and PI agency showed that 52 percent of the population had taken part in political and protest demonstrations over the previous year, with an especially high percentage among the young. This same survey revealed that 33 percent of Italians had taken part in peace marches during 2003, 15.5 percent had taken part in boycotts against certain brand names, and 65 percent were concerned about the possible effects of globalization. While unemployment was the most serious problem signaled by the interviewees, private institutions (the stock exchange, banks, industrialist associations, and privatized health care) saw public faith in them drop sharply (74 percent of those interviewed replied that "the state should not 'make room' for the private sector in health care and education") (*Venerdì de La Repubblica,* December 19, 2003, 27 ff.). In 2004, the position of rigorous pacifism ("against the war, without if and without but") was supported, according to a Demos survey, by two-thirds of the Italian population, and about one-third of the sample declared they had taken part in protest against the Iraq war (*La Repubblica,* May 23, 2004).

Dissent concerning neoliberal strategies is also emerging within the political and nonpolitical elite. In the mid-nineties, leaders of many Western states were moving away from the pure liberalism of the Thatcher and Reagan years. In the international arena, sometimes from unexpected quarters, opinions were making themselves heard, calling attention to the issues of social services and market reregulation (O'Brian et al. 2000, 9). A "United Nations Conference on Trade and Development" report of 1997 admitted, "Rising inequalities pose a serious threat of a political backlash against globalization, one that is likely to come from the North as well as from the South" (Klein 2001, 262). The *Financial Times* (August 31, 1999) wrote that we went "from the triumph of global capitalism to its crisis in less than a decade." After the Asian crisis, disagreement emerged between the WB and the IMF. At the dawning of the new millennium, greater openness toward economic policies, which if not Keynesian were at least oriented toward toning down free market excesses, was applauded symbolically in awarding the 2001 Nobel prize for economics to George Akerlof, Michael Spence, and Joseph Stiglitz, three American scientists who proved that even within a system of free market competition, an asymmetric distribution of information has negative effects on the markets not contemplated by neoliberal theory. Joseph Stiglitz, former advisor to President Clinton and a leading economist at the WB until 1999, maintained that "capital market liberalization has not only not brought people the prosperity they were promised, but it also has brought these crises, with wages falling 20 or 30 percent, and unemployment going up by a factor or two-, three-, four- or ten" (quoted in Brecher, Costello, and Smith 2000, 8).

The potential competition that social democratic parties faced in electoral terms from the parties of communist and green derivation, which seemed favored and transformed by the movement, can explain the fact that to a certain extent they have taken criticism of globalization on board. Both communists and greens, with different emphasis in different countries, have always been open to initiatives for another globalization, with the green parties interested in denouncing environmental disasters resulting from deregulation, and the communist parties criticizing the social effects of neoliberalism. Although quite a few initiatives launched by the movement explicitly excluded political parties in order not to be used, both greens and communists, especially their youth federations, were present at the GSF and the ESF.

While especially after the fall of the Berlin Wall they were seen as being doomed to a more or less rapid demise, the French (PCF), Spanish (PCE), Italian (RC), and German (PDS) Communist parties saw an opportunity for mobilization in the globalization protests. It is no coincidence that not only do the Web sites of these parties dedicate ample space to globalization-related issues, but they also have areas dedicated to the movement and links to its organizations. In general, communist parties emphasize the anticapitalist dimension of the struggle against deregulation, focusing on social issues and employment. When European parties of the left (including the PCF, the German PDS, the Italian RC, and the Spanish Izquierda Unida) met in Paris on the occasion of the second ESF, they declared that "Europe has to be a factor of progress and promotion of human rights," denouncing the Maastricht agreements as instruments of "inequality, unemployment, precariousness and exploitation" (Left European Parties 2003). On the same occasion, the seventh conference of the European anticapitalist left, including the French Trotskyist party, Ligue Communiste Revolutionnaire, proposed "another Europe, built from below by the revolt of the exploited and oppressed from all member countries" (European Anticapitalist Left 2003). Making reference to the class struggle, RC in Italy promoted an Alternative Forum for a Social Europe (RC 2003). In Spain the PCE declared itself part of the "resistance movement for an alternative to neoliberal globalization, which represents the present-day, world-wide expression of the capital-labour contradiction" (PCE 2002). In France, the PCF aimed at "calling into question the dogma that the market is sacred" and setting up in Europe "alternative economic and social policies with different priorities to benefit employment and training, public services, and a courageous policy of investment in the environment. What is needed is taxation on capital movements. What is needed is a shift in priorities: the human being and not money" (PCF 2003).

The European green parties, too, have forged alliances with the movement for global justice, in many cases since the very first protest demonstrations, emphasizing in particular the need to defend sustainable development against "the sack of the planet's environmental resources" (European Green Parties 2003) and growing awareness on social issues. As early as January 2000, calling for participation in the demonstrations against the World Economic Forum in Davos, the French Verts denounced "those who, for over thirty years, have organized deregulation and laid the greater part of humanity open to precariousness, impoverishment and the destruction of resources and the environment" (Les Verts 2000). In the German Grüenen, in the government since 1998 and often accused of taking up compromise positions on social rights, criticism of globalization as "wrong in principle" began to emerge (Bündnis 90 2003).

Politics, Antipolitics, and Other Politics: A Conclusion

To conclude, the global movement suggests a conception of democracy as a search for a common good, starting from a pluralist confrontation among equals. These features seem linked with some internal and external resources for the movement, yet they also create new challenges. The quest for models of internal democracy is bound together with the search for "another" democracy—and "other politics"—also at local, national, and supranational levels. Criticism of both the form and substance of institutional politics has made it difficult for the movement to interact with the elite on the right but also, and less obviously, on the left, too.

The movement is highly critical of public institutions. The protest is not only developing largely outside political parties, but is also generating strong criticism of representative democracy. The demand for left-wing policies intersects with a rejection of the idea that politics is a specialized activity for a few professionals occupying elective posts in the public administration. Indeed, demands for left-wing content and more participatory politics come together in the criticism aimed at the main political parties of the left.

These are seen as emphasizing their function of managing administration at the expense of the building of collective identities. They tend to approach the potential electorate through the media and to perceive it as predominantly centrist and moderate, thereby discouraging the activist circles who are by definition attached to organizational identities and more sensitive to ideological incentives (della Porta 2001). Mutual mistrust thus grows between the parties who seek to replace activists by surveys and promotion campaigns, emphasizing legitimation of a representative-delegate type, and the activists who instead stress politics as direct participation (see chapter 2 in this volume)—and in particular between center-left parties looking for the floating electorate in the center and the demonstrators who criticize bipartisan agreements on neoliberal policies. While the search for new forms of democracy resonates with the demand for growing participation— partly because it is increasingly less satisfied by the political parties—the question of how the movement's demands get represented in the institutions nonetheless remains unanswered. To accusations of being antipolitical or at best nonpolitical, activists respond with a concept of politics as an activity based on participation by everyone rather than delegation to a few professionals. Moreover, the essence of politics is considered the development of "demands and responses," namely, constructing identities rather than occupying power.

In the face of challenges from multilevel governance to old models of representation, the movement for globalization from below finds itself facing the difficult search for democratic institutions that are not just participatory, but also effective in influencing public policies toward principles of social justice. One older-generation activist asked, "This indispensable networking that constitutes the vitality of this movement . . . is it enough to fully express political projects?" (FG 6e, 161). And the political effectiveness of the movement is regarded as a problem even by the youngest—"the great strength is that there are big issues around on which there is strong convergence. The problem now is where do we go next in the sense of providing answers and doing things" (FG 2e, 39).

The problem of building political alliances within institutions is perceived by activists, but is certainly far from solved. Nevertheless, the movement seems to have reflected, or even accelerated, some shift in public opinion as well as among experts expressing growing concerns with social inequalities and increasing demands for state (and multilevel) steering of economic processes. These emerging concerns have opened up some debates about the dark side of globalization even in a defensive institutional left.

8

The Global Movement and Democracy

The protests in favor of globalization from below have been seen as an example of the emergence of a global public sphere as well as of the re-emergence of a demand for a new politics. The movement for a globalization from below differs from movements that preceded it: it has a variegated identity, a weakly linked organizational structure, a multiform action repertoire. These features are shaped and changed in interactions with a complex, multi-level political system; the movement challenges the meaning of politics and democracy when specific decisions, and rule making more generally, are shifted to a supranational level of government.

While countersummits and transnational campaigns have attracted great interest, many scholars are nonetheless skeptical as to the nature of the phenomenon. Is it really a social movement, or is it composed of more occasional coalitions (Tarrow 2005)? Are the issues truly global, or do they reflect a permanent hegemony of the north over the south of the world (Sikkink 2004)? Are there innovations in the forms of mobilization, or are they mere adaptations of now ossified repertoires? In this chapter, we shall summarize the main results of research into the movement for global justice, comparing them with hypotheses emerging from the literature on social movements, to see how far they can be applied to the emerging new movement.

The protests against the G8 in Genoa and the ESF in Florence were part of the many, increasingly massive transnational protest events that developed in the world's north and south, especially after the WTO protests in Seattle, demanding global justice and democratization from below (Pianta and Silva 2003). Given these unexpected developments, a general question has been asked more and more often by both scholars and activists: is there a new global movement?

We can break down this question into several smaller ones: Is there a global movement? Does it have new features? If so, are the concepts developed in social-movement studies still sufficient to address the new actors?

A New Global Movement?

Some scholars deny that the mobilization around globalization can be defined as part of one movement: the organizational structure is allegedly too weak; supranational protest events are too scattered; the collective identities are too heterogeneous; or the conflict is an old one (for instance, Tarrow 2005; Rucht 2002b). All through this volume (see also della Porta 2004), we have challenged these statements, suggesting that countersummits and campaigns have condensed a network of formal organizations and informal groupings that, although very loose, is nonetheless sustained in time. If transnational protest events are still rare, they are less and less so; moreover, global issues and multilevel governance are increasingly the target also of local and national protest. The development of "tolerant identities" did not eliminate the cultural and political differences between the movement sectors, but allowed transnational activists to elaborate a new, common layer by successful frame bridging. Finally, if the left-right cleavage is reinvigorated in the mobilization for a globalization of rights, the definition of global conflicts takes into account recent changes in the political and social structure. While the term "coalition" has often been used, especially for organizations for specific campaigns, the frequent overlapping memberships (of both organizations and individuals) in several campaigns, as well as the intensification of the interactions over time, displays, in our opinion, a network nature typical of social movements. Recognizing that the degree of "netness," identification, mobilization, and cleavage homogeneity of a movement has always varied (and is difficult to assess empirically), the results of our research seem to indicate that a movement on global justice is truly in the making.

Other questions that remain open, which we will try to address in this final chapter, refer to the global nature of the movement as well as its newness—in terms not so much of the definition of the new class actor of postindustrial society (Touraine 1978), but more of the presence of emerging characteristics in organizational structures, action repertoires, and identity discourses.

A Global Movement?

Social movements have been defined as movements composed of networks of groups and activists, with an emerging identity, involved in conflictual issues, using mainly unconventional forms of participation (della Porta and Diani 1999, ch. 1). As we suggested in the introduction, *global* social movements can therefore be understood as transnational networks of actors that define their causes as global and organize protest campaigns that involve more than one state.

Looking at *movement identities,* our research indicates that a large majority of the activists taking part in recent demonstrations against international summits identify themselves with a movement critical of globalization. The presence of such a movement is moreover acknowledged by opponents and sympathizers as well as by the press. The semantic conflicts over the definition of the movement as "no global," and the plurality of names proposed for it (from the Seattle people to the movement for globalization from below, for global justice, or for a globalization of rights), testify to a still uncertain specification of the movement's core goals, a fate that has been shared by several movements in the past (for example, the '68 movement). Our research confirms, however, that the protesters we have interviewed (both in the surveys and in the focus groups) as well as the organizations some of them belong to define themselves as part of a global movement. Not only do they know about other parts of the world and express solidarity toward the poorest people in the south, but they define themselves as global citizens.

If we look at the dimension of unconventional *action,* the activities of transnational social movement organizations (TSMOs) have expanded from lobbying to protest: since Seattle, and in Europe with even more intensity since Genoa, global politics have gone onto the streets. As research indicates, protests addressing supranational institutions and organized transnationally are only a small percentage of all protest events, but they seem to have increased dramatically in number and salience since 1999. Our research confirms that participation in these supranational protests is still dominated by local activists—as was true in Seattle and in other demonstrations in Europe[1]—but there is a very significant involvement of activists from abroad. What is more, these protests target supranational institutions, at the same time raising concerns about the extension of demonstration rights transnationally.

The complex interaction between local and supranational activism is reflected in terms of *organizational structures:* in the emergence of more

TSMOs and, especially, transnational coalitions of social movement organizations, but also in the growing presence of locally active networks structured around global issues (Diani 2005). These groups occasionally participate in transnational protest events, but their activities remain strongly rooted at the local level. As our research indicates, the organizational networking of various groupings goes beyond the large countersummits, developing informally in transnational communication and greatly facilitated by the Internet.

Finally, looking at the *definition of the conflict*, local, national, and transnational organizations agree in defining their scope as global, addressing corporations as well as IGOs as main enemies. Transnational aims are articulated at the national and subnational levels, too, and this is why national political opportunities continue to have a relevant influence on global movements that are also active nationally (see Rootes 2005). Our research shows that individual activists and movement organizations alike are far from advocating a return to the nation-state. To the contrary, there is a widespread belief that the problems produced by neoliberal globalization can be solved only through global politics.

What are the consequences of going global? Does it produce additional new features? In all dimensions, the emerging movement seems to present a blend of path dependency and learning processes. Empirical research indicates that this movement, like other movements, developed under a situation of constrained learning: the repertoire of organizational models is limited and builds on the experiences of previous movements; however, past experiences are critically reflected on, and new solutions are adopted from previous waves of contention with elaboration, rediscussion, change, and adaptation. The organizational dilemmas the activists have to face are largely the same as other movements have had to suffer, but new dilemmas are coming from new challenges and opportunities.

As in the past, the movement is formed by networks of networks, but the new definition as a "movement of movements" stresses the preference for even more flexible organizational formats. The definition of the conflict is a blend of Old Left attention to issues of social justice with new social movements' focus on differential rights and positive freedoms, which are more and more integrated in common visions. Tolerant identities develop through intense processes of frame bridging. Protest combines the traditional repertoires built up during previous cycles of protest (especially in the consolidation of nonviolent forms of action) with some innovations (in particular, consumerist forms of protest, as well as new tactics of civil disobedience). Let us look at these emerging features in more detail.

A Movement of Movements: Networking Heterogeneous Actors

The literature on social movements has asked what conditions favor the aggregation of the weakest interests. Charles Tilly (1978) maintained that the mobilization of groups is influenced by their level of *catnet,* a combination of features associated with social *category* and density of social *networks.* In fact, the move from an aggregate of individuals sharing particular characteristics to a social group as a community capable of collective action is facilitated by the simultaneous presence of specific category features and of networks of relationships binding together the individuals sharing those features (della Porta and Diani 1999, ch. 2). That participation opportunities increase for social groups typified by structural similarities and intensity of social relationships has been pointed out by numerous studies on the trade-union movement. The labor movement was in particular associated with the presence of great masses of workers doing similar jobs and tending to spend not just their working time but also their leisure time together, living in neighborhoods located near the factories. The presence of socially homogeneous networks marked by intense social relationships is held to have favored the option to cooperate. Collective action is then supposed to have enhanced an awareness of having interests in common—increasing what Karl Marx called class consciousness.

The movement of movements is typified in this connection by a situation very different from that of the labor movement and from many social movements that succeeded it and tended to refer to a homogeneous basis in terms of generation (the student movement), gender (the women's or gay liberation movements), or social position (chiefly involving the middle classes). The movement about globalization is instead heterogeneous not just socially but also from the generation viewpoint, as well as seeking to communicate with diverse, distant national cultures. More than in recent movements, the lack of homogeneity in terms of category is compensated for by the presence of high associational density. Membership in a movement is favored by incorporation into informal networks of individuals sharing an interest in particular causes: it is through these links that potential activists develop their worldview and acquire mobilization skills (della Porta and Diani 1999, ch. 5). It is also promoted by membership in formal organizations that often act as recruitment channels: the greater the number of organization memberships, especially of a more explicitly political nature, the greater the likelihood of individuals participating, given both greater contacts with people engaged in a specific cause and a set of experiences useful for new mobilization.

Research in the eighties and nineties has described a progressive institutionalization of social movements, at least in Western democracies (della Porta 2001). Some movement organizations had become better structured, at national or even supranational levels, had acquired substantial material resources and a certain public recognition, had set up paid staffs thanks to mass membership drives, and were replacing protest by lobbying or concertation actions. They had, that is, become interest groups, albeit for a common good. Other groups, involved in the process of contracting out social services, had entered the so-called nonprofit sector, acquiring professionalism and often administering public resources, also with little recourse to unconventional political action. Protest in the meantime had become the heritage of citizen committees, often fragmented down to street or neighborhood level, with pragmatic objectives of protecting limited territories. Even the social centers seemed caught between commercialization in administering spaces for alternative culture and radicalization of forms of action.

Notwithstanding their apparent institutionalization, many of these associations and groupings converged in the protests for global justice. Mobilization of these associational networks is suited by a particularly flexible, multicentric organizational structure. As we have seen, both the GSF and the ESF involved hundreds of groups that continue to have a life of their own, coming together with variable geometries according to the circumstances. The structure already typical of other movements (especially the women's and peace movements) turns up in the movement for globalization from below in a more highly networked version. The function of the coordination bodies, and of spokespeople, is continually being debated, with constant attention to the autonomy of the various submovements, while seeking (although not always successfully) to avoid competition among them. The new communication technologies—primarily the Internet—have steadily reduced the costs of mobilization, allowing slender, flexible structures, and facilitated transversal interaction between different areas and movements. Transissue as well as transnational attention constitutes a novelty in a panorama that seemed typified by specialization in single-issue movements (from women to the environment, from peace to AIDS).

This structure seems to have undeniable advantages in terms of mobilization, enabling very broad assemblages, with not much pressure for institutionalization, understood also in the sense of prevalence of dynamics of organizational survival over achievement of objectives. The fact that the various groups maintain their separate identities impels broad participation and a search for the common meaning required for joint mobilization.

Without minimizing differences, the movement expands its potential reference groups. There nonetheless remain some difficulties with network structures associated particularly with the high time investment needed to make decisions, assess representativity and implement accountability, and the risk of fragmentation especially at times when mobilization ebbs.

Cross-fertilization in Action Repertoires

Social and political heterogeneity led to cross-fertilization among different action repertoires. The social movements are in general characterized by the adoption of unusual forms of political behavior. Many scholars see the fundamental distinction between the movements and other political actors as lying in the formers' use of *protest*—an unconventional form of action that breaks the daily routine—as a way of applying political pressure (Rucht 1994). Through the mass media, protesters most often turn to public opinion, even before elected representatives or the public bureaucracy. Protesters seek to influence public decision makers using three different types of logic: (a) a capacity to cause material losses, on what may be termed the logic of damage; (b) the spread of support for their cause, on a logic of numbers; and (c) the urgency for action by citizens, on a logic of witnessing (della Porta and Diani 1999, ch. 7).

The global movement has also used forms of protest that come close to the modus operandi of a battle: the logic is that of potential *material damage*. In its most extreme form, not very frequent in democracies, this logic of action is reflected in political *violence,* which tends to be aimed at inflicting material losses on the enemy. Apart from the most extreme cases, however, a certain element of material disturbance is present in the most varied forms of protest in the sense that by threatening disorder they obstruct the normal course of things (Tarrow 1994, 103). They challenge elites by enhancing uncertainty and may thus bring tangible and sometimes even material damage. By naming and shaming boycott aim at reducing the profits of the targeted corporations and support for the targeted politicians. It is clear, however, that the break from routine has symbolic value first and foremost: the damage is not that associated immediately with some specific roadblock or strike, but rather the effect of delegitimization of the state as the monopolist of legitimate force.

A second logic of action followed by many protest forms of the emergent movement is the logic of *numbers*—present in particular at Genoa, but also at Florence. The fate of the movements in great part depends on their number of supporters, since "there is always strength in numbers" (DeNardo 1985, 35). The larger the number of demonstrators is, the greater not just the disturbance and the media coverage produced immediately, but also the potential for loss of consensus by a government refusing to negotiate with them. Just as parties seek to increase their number of voters and pressure groups their number of supporters, so protesters must seek to mobilize the largest possible number of demonstrators. From this point of view, protest acts as a sort of vicarious referendum.

The movement for globalization from below has also used forms of protest based on a logic of *witnessing*. These actions are aimed at demonstrating strong commitment to an objective regarded as of vital importance for the fate of humanity. The activists' chief objective is to show by their own example the possibility of acting collectively on common goals. This logic is perhaps the most consistent with the concept of participatory democracy widespread among the activists, where the right to influence a decision-making process comes not from formal investiture or from intrinsic power, but from strength of commitment. Witnessing is expressed first and foremost through participation in actions involving high costs or personal risks, and permeates, for instance, tactics of civil disobedience based on the deliberate breach of a series of rules regarded as unfair. Moreover, the logic of witnessing implies the use of techniques that enhance the symbolic impact of the actions so as to attract media attention.

While the movement is decisively nonviolent, it is also true that initially the presence of more radical repertoires produced resonance effects. In Seattle, in particular, media attention was drawn by some actions led by a logic of material damage; but this enabled other, nonviolent components of the movement to gain visibility too. In subsequent developments, the logic of numbers and the logic of witnessing have intermingled in many cases, and the relationship with those using violent forms of action has become increasingly problematic. While in Gothenburg the risk of more radical actions leading to a stigmatization of the whole movement emerged glaringly, in Genoa the exclusion from the working agreement of those not ready to renounce offensive implements proved to be an imperfect solution. In Florence the movement decided, especially for the final demonstration, to ban any aggressive manifestation, even in only symbolic forms.

While the link with movements in the south of the world keeps open the debate on the use of violence in nondemocratic contexts, in the world's north the movement has adopted a nonviolent strategy, increasingly stigmatizing the most disruptive forms of protest, both in more pragmatic terms (as unsuited to bringing consensus from outside) and in more substantive ones (as a reflection of the violence in the system). Direct nonviolent action and civil disobedience are instead presented as forms of action capable of simultaneously drawing the attention of public opinion and attesting to the activists' commitment. Additionally, protest seeks to gain efficacy by bringing into action the consumer (through boycotts and critical consumerism) and the saver (through ethical banks) alongside the citizen. In its strategies, the movement attaches value to alternative knowledge and skills, aiming to build up a global public sphere. The relevance of communication is confirmed by the importance assumed in the movement not just by the Internet but also issues connected with it, from copyright to censorship of telecommunications.

Tolerant Identities

Social heterogeneity and network organization are interwoven with particular forms of collective identity. In the past, the movements that referred to homogeneous social groups—in particular specific social classes or ethnic groups—often, especially in the initial stages of their mobilization, developed strong, totalizing, exclusive identities. The need to build up a "we," often by inverting the sign of a stigmatized identity to a positive one (for instance, in the case of workers, Afro-Americans, or women) led to a clear antagonism to the outside, the Other. The search for an emergent collective identity often developed into utopias.

In the case of the movement for globalization from below, the multiplicity of reference bases in terms of class, gender, generation, race, and religion seems to have encouraged composite identities. Concerns with environment, women's rights, peace, and social inequalities remain as characteristics of subgroups or networks in the mobilization on globalization. The definition of "movement of movements" stresses the survival of the specific concerns and the nonsubordination of one conflict to another: if in the socialist ideology women's emancipation was subordinated to the workers' emancipation, in the new global movement there is no hierarchy of conflict.

Through the continuous work of frame bridging, the fragments of diverse cultures—secular and religious, radical and reformist, young and older generations—have been fitted together into a broader discourse that has taken the theme of social (and global) injustice as an adhesive, while still leaving broad margins for separate developments. Although emphasizing pluralism and diversity, in the discourse of the movement the definition of the self stresses a global dimension. The enemy is singled out in neoliberal globalization, which characterizes not only the policies of the international financial organizations (WB, IMF, and WTO), but also the policy choices of national right-wing and even left-wing governments. These are considered responsible for growing social injustice and its negative effects on women, the environment, the south, and so on.

Alongside social justice, the metadiscourse of the search for new forms of democracy emerged as a common basis. At the cost of leaving margins of ambiguity about the movement's proposals—fluctuating in particular between antineoliberalism and anticapitalism, a return to a pure, hard-line old left discourse and innovative development of the "postmaterialistic" themes emphasized by the women's and ecological movements in past decades—the development of a multifaceted, tolerant collective identity allowed very different spirits to be kept together by partly combining them, albeit in very gradual fashion, bringing about a high degree of identification among activists and sympathizers.

A Demand for New Politics

The special delicacy of the theme of violence and of potential stigmatization in the mass media is linked to a further peculiarity of the movement for globalization from below. We have said that as well as social variables the growth in capacity to organize the individuals least endowed with material resources is also associated with political opportunities. From this viewpoint, access channels to political decision making diminish with the growth in power of international bodies, which by their nature do not act transparently and have little responsibility in terms of the procedures of representative democracy. In the nineties, moreover, neoliberal policies were embraced, with greater or lesser conviction, by many national governments (including left-wing ones).

In particular, the closing off of political opportunities was reflected in the broad use of coercive action to limit the right to demonstrate rather than on negotiated strategies to administer public order (della Porta, Petersen, and Reiter forthcoming). In Italy, an exclusive tradition combined with an incomplete reform in police forces in the eighties, specifically, the survival of militarized bodies (such as the carabinieri) and tight political control, might explain the particularly brutal forms of protest control employed at Genoa. However, developments in protest control in recent decades point particularly toward selectivity in techniques used according to the perceived degree of legitimacy of those engaged in the protest. Thus, if some movements (typically the labor movement) were gradually accepted as legitimate, and their organizations considered as "partners" for common implementation of public order, others (especially the social centers) were denied this legitimation, often with ritualization of conflict between demonstrators and police.

In order to explain what looked like the inversion of a trend to moderate protest-control actions, in particular by adopting negotiated strategies, we considered the alliance structures available to the movement. Social movements move within an organizational sphere, interacting with various other actors. They find allies within the public administration, in the party system, among interest groups, and in civil society. While the alliance system supplies resources and creates political opportunities for challengers, the conflict system tends to reduce those opportunities. The outcomes of conflict are defined by the specific *power configuration,* that is, the distribution of power among relevant actors operating either in the party system or among interest groups (Kriesi 1989). Times of electoral instability or division among elites may open up windows of opportunity for social movements, impelling them to mobilize so as to exploit a favorable situation. Renewed consolidation of elites in power, with consequent loss of institutional allies, may discourage mass mobilization and instead radicalize forms of action and the attitudes of those remaining active within the movement (della Porta 1996).

The '68 movement had already criticized the bureaucratization of representative institutions and their isolation from citizens, but left-wing political parties were still regarded as the main potential allies of the movement, managing to channel the protest (Tarrow 1989). At Genoa, the movement seemed devoid of institutional protection, perceived by all the main political parties, on the right and on the left, as a dangerous challenger in both policy content and the very conception of politics. The demonstrations against the G8 expressed a strong demand for political participation the parties no longer seemed able to respond to. As emerged in subsequent mobilizations, protest developed outside the parties and presented strong criticism of the forms of representative democracy. Nevertheless, although very slowly, some of the concerns of the movement started to be debated by the left-wing political parties.

Global Justice and Movement Studies

The mobilizations on globalization seem to be taking on many features typical of the preceding generations of social movements, but also new ones, above all a supranational dimension: they express a conflict defined as "global," getting new collective identities to emerge; they employ protest repertoires in international campaigns innovating on the margins of forms already widespread in the past; they construct transnational networks.

More pluralist, media-oriented, and networked than past mobilizations, they impel a rethinking of some concepts and hypotheses present in social science research. The concepts and approaches of social movement studies provide useful insights for understanding the movements of the new millennium; however, they should be adapted and specified to account for emerging phenomena.

Until the sixties, studies in social movements had been dominated by a functionalist approach interpreting them as responses to system dysfunctions, often reducing them to a pathological, purely reactive phenomenon, in the last analysis irrational (Smelser 1962). Against this representation, during the seventies a trend of study developed that regarded the social movements as part of the normal political process, concentrating analysis on mobilization of the resources needed for collective action. According to this approach, the social movements act in rational, proactive, organized fashion. The protest actions are the outcome of a cost-benefit calculation influenced by the presence not just of conflicts but also of necessary resources for mobilizing these conflicts. In a historical situation where deprivation, contrasts, clashes of interest, and conflicting ideologies seem ever present, the rise of collective action cannot be explained by these factors alone. It is not enough to discover the existence of clashing interests; it is also necessary to study the conditions that allow the transformation of discontent into action. The movements studied using this approach in the eighties and nineties proved rich in both symbolic and material resources, often invested in creating more or less powerful movement organizations active on such single issues as defending the environment or women's liberation. Accordingly, what was chiefly described were the resources available to relatively well endowed groups, while analysis of more marginal groups regarded as incapable of mobilization was neglected. The movement for globalization from below exposes the need to reconsider the capacity for collective action of the powerless. Not only in the south, it involves the poorest classes, like the Brazilian Sem Terra or the Argentine *picqueteros,* but also in the world's north, at least in some countries, it mobilizes groups described as poor in collective resources (like the unemployed or precariously employed) or lacking the most basic rights (like migrants).

The dominant resource mobilization approach focused attention on the dynamics of mobilization, but undervalued the nature of the disputes—they aimed at the how, ignoring the why (for a review, see della Porta and Diani 1999, ch. 1). The latter was an issue taken up in the sixties by scholars who analyzed social changes suggesting the emergence of new social movements (Touraine 1978) and postmaterialist values (Inglehart 1977). They stressed that conflicts over economic equality had been pacified and new demands tied to the defense of individual freedoms against the new technological society emerged instead. The new middle classes were regarded as the main reference base for the new movements, which shared new values—or "other codes" (Melucci 1996). However, the end of the midcentury "compromise" between capitalism and the welfare state (Crouch 2004) brought to center stage the conflicts on social rights—underlined in the definition "movement for globalization of rights"—albeit not without attention to new themes (like environmental sustainability or gender) that had emerged with the new social movements. This explains the encounter between the theme of social justice typical of the Old Left and the defense of cultural differences, gender parity, and the natural environment more typical of the newer movements. Class conflict thus does not—as proclaimed since the sixties, at least for Western societies—appear to be pacified: instead, wealth distribution is again becoming central in the political debate. In this sense, the movement on globalization challenges researchers to reopen the academic debate on the structural nature of the conflicts in a society that can no longer be simply defined as postindustrial. As Kaldor (2000) observed, the traditional cleavage between supporters of the free market and supporters of the welfare state interacts with the one between protectionist and cosmopolitans. How these new strains could be mobilized into new conflicts is one of the main issues we focused on.

The fragmentation brought into the social structure by policies of cutting public expenditure, deregulation, and privatization of public services was reflected in the movement's identity—for it sought to link up different social actors while at the same time respecting their diversity. Through a multifaceted identity positively valuing differences, the movement succeeds in bringing into a common antineoliberalism reference pattern the concerns and demands of trade unions and ecologists, feminists and religious groups, peasants and urban social centers.

The multiple identity of the movement seems to reflect the disappearance of a utopian view of the future, combined with acceptance of broad margins of uncertainty, but does not entail renunciation of the building of "another possible world." Instead, by managing diversities, it enables dialogue and networking of multiple actors, starting from a recognition of the fundamental role of the individual. As Alain Touraine has noted, "The point is no longer, then, to recognize the universal value of a culture or a civilization, but quite differently, to recognize each individual's right to combine, to articulate in their own experience of personal or collective life, participation in the world of markets or technologies with a particular cultural identity" (1997, 50). The creation of collective solidarity presupposes the acceptance of the value of individual subjectivity. The processes of identification and recognition acquire a new centrality for the analysis of the movement that, however, has to recognize the complexity of multiple belongings.

The movement's organizational features reflect this evolution of modernity. Such values as autonomy, creativity, spontaneity, and self-realization are taking on a central role in the movement (Ceri 2003), marking its organizational structure: from the choice of flexible forms of coordination to creating inclusive participation in several groups, from the search for consensus to that of a conception of activism that respects subjectivism. Related to this, the search for new horizontal and participatory organizational formulas is central for the movement, not confined to mere imitation of movements of the past. These characteristics of the movement should lead sociological analysis to employ a conception of organization that is not purely instrumental.

The plurality of actors is reflected in a multiple, innovative repertoire that tends to adapt to certain features of the emergent society. First and foremost, while movements have always needed the mass media as megaphones for their protests, media links are becoming increasingly important in the information society. The very search for media visibility has in fact been presented as a justification for employing forms of violence, albeit limited to violence against things. The literature on social movements had presented protest as an indirect resource that had to be mediated through the mass media. The globalization movement instead impels the study of forms of direct communication through the creation of new public spheres. In this sense, the global movement can build on already developed structures and spaces for communication, inherited from previous waves of mobilization, and also create new causes, exploring new technology.

A last challenge for the literature on social movements comes from the interactions between the global movement and national and transnational political opportunities. The literature on social movements has traditionally developed in the analysis of nation-state and representative democracy: it therefore needs to address all the already discussed challenges to both. Without implying a demise of the nation-state or the end of representative democracy, we have singled out how the transformation in both polity and politics affected the traditional functioning of the democratic state.

In this context, the traditional questions of the alliances in the political and institutional system also have to be reformulated. While emphasizing the differences between the two type of actors, the political process approach to social movements has considered that openness and alliances among institutional political actors are necessary for social movements to be successful. While undoubtedly the interactions between institutional politics and politics from below—between *routine* and *contentious politics* (McAdam, Tarrow, and Tilly 2001)—continue to be important, the more problematic point is the image of a sort of division of labor, especially on the left, between parties and movements. Although the movement stresses the need for political governance of the economy, there is nonetheless an increasing tension between a representative conception of politics and a participatory one—a separation symbolically expressed in the opening slogan for the international parade at Genoa: You G8, we six billion. In the first conception, in a modern representative democracy politics becomes an activity for professionals (the G8 rulers and other professional politicians) who make decisions legitimated by electoral investiture. The second conception articulates a demand for "more" politics but also advances a proposal for "different" politics, that is, for participatory politics carried out in arenas open to the citizens, regarded as political actors themselves.

In summary, social movements are addressing some of the challenges that developed together with the various processes of globalization we mentioned in chapter 1. First, the challenge of post-Fordist society is a weakening of traditional identities, with fragmentation particularly of the social basis of the workers' movement. The deregulation of the economic market, with the spread of "flexible" jobs, has helped to fragment the social reference basis for protest. In the eighties and nineties, even the social movement organization had specialized around single issues. At the same time, there has been a structuring of more or less formal organizations and groups linked to various movements emerging in the seventies and eighties, as well as some belonging to the old left. In these conditions the movement faces the challenge to keep different, heterogeneous groups together by developing tolerant identities.

Second, one element of what has been called postmodernity is the spreading of a culture that emphasizes the role of the individual. Processes of individualization have in fact been seen as obstacles to the development of collective action, taking away the strong identifications of the past. On the other hand, as some scholars of social movements have already indicated (especially Melucci 1989), contemporary societies offer multiple resources for building up complex identities. In some circumstances collective action has been observed even in the presence of a culture marked by personalism, i.e., "ways of speaking or acting which highlight a unique personal self. Personalism supposes that individuality has inherent value, apart from one's material and social achievement, no matter what connections to a specific community or institutions the individual maintains" (Lichterman 1996,

86). The challenge for the contemporary movements is to develop a model of internal democracy able to bring all the subjectivities together, recognizing the role of individuals but at the same time able to sustain collective action.

Finally, neoliberalism, by stressing markets' capacities for self-regulation, has emphasized the difficulties of representative democracies. Globalization as liberalization of movement of goods and capital has in particular spread an image of the growing inability of national governments to intervene in the major economic and social problems (starting with unemployment), with deterioration in particular in policies for reducing inequality. The international financial organizations seem for their part actively involved in favoring free trade, conditioning elected government with a growing democratic deficit in public decisions. If these circumstances seem to be reducing citizens' trust and interest in conventional forms of democratic participation, the new cycle of protest is witness to a growing demand for politics, albeit of a new, unexpected type, in particular from the new generations. In this sense, the challenge for the movement is to build an organizational model that can broaden participation in joint campaigns, thereby promoting cross-fertilization in the course of action.

Notes

1. Globalization and Social Movements

1. Scholars of international relations have coined such concepts as "civil world politics," referring to "that part of associational life that exists above the individual and below the state, crossing national borders" (Wapner 1995, 313), or "world civil society." If these concepts are criticized as being imprecise and ambiguous by including heterogeneous entities, they do nonetheless reflect the growing attention focused on a supranational, nonintergovernmental dimension.

2. From 1909 to 1988, the number of INGOs grew from 176 to 14,518 (Princen and Finger 1994, 1) and, thereafter, to 15,965 in 1997 (Deutscher Bundestag 2002, 427).

3. We selected seminars and workshops of the ESF according to the type of proponent organizations (ecologist, religious, pacifist, feminist, trade unions, left-wing political parties, and anticapitalist groups). Interviewers were asked to distribute questionnaires at random, seeking, however, to respect the balance among gender and age of the respondents present at the ESF. As for the nationality of the organizations at the ESF, we focused on the Italian, French, Spanish, German, and English ones. Of the total number of interviewees, 1,668 were Italian, 124 French, 77 German, 88 Spanish, 118 British, and 309 from other countries. The different sizes of the country samples are proportional to national presence at the ESF.

4. The participants in the two surveys that declared affiliation to organizations were grouped in organizational macrosectors of the movement: ecopacifist, antineoliberalist, and anticapitalist (see chapter 2). The category "ecopacifist" includes environmental and pacifist groups, religious associations, lay volunteer organizations, and NGOs; the category "antineoliberalist" covers ATTAC, trade

unions, and institutional left-wing parties and the youth organizations and student organizations close to them; the category "anticapitalism" includes various kinds of social centers, White Overalls/Disobedients, radical unions, neocommunist organizations, anarchist groups, and autonomous organizations.

5. Although the distribution of most sociodemographic characteristics (education, age, and social situation) was significantly different between the Italian sample and the overall population of Italy (likelihood ratio chi-squared test), the Italian sample was not stratified for these conditions because the distributions of some other countries also differed from those of their respective populations. Varying the Italian sample would have meant reducing it to a median category and foregoing variation. The gender distribution was equal among all the other countries; only the Italian gender distribution deviated from this (with males dominating). Therefore, a stratified reduced sample was drawn from the Italian sample that respected the equal distribution of men and women in the population. Furthermore, the Italian subsample was reduced in numbers; overrepresenting the Italians would have biased the results and made some types of statistical analysis less applicable.

6. The focus groups were run by Elena Del Giorgio with the supervision of Fiammetta Benati, psychologist. The groups included a total of forty-five people, of whom twenty-three were women, and were organized by different age cohorts: (1) from sixteen to eighteen years old; (2) from twenty-two to twenty-seven years old; (3) from twenty-six to thirty-five years old; (4) from thirty-five to forty-one years old; (5) from forty-eight to fifty-nine years old; (6) from sixty-five to seventy-seven years old. Quotations from focus groups will be made using the acronym FG followed by a number (indicating the age cohort) and a letter (indicating the person speaking).

2. The Development of a Global Movement

1. "Social centers" are communities managed by politically engaged young people (mainly students and unemployed) who occupy unused buildings where they organize political and cultural activities.

2. In the text, we shall use the term "mechanism" to describe "a delimited class of events that alter relations among specified sets of elements in identical or closely similar ways over a variety of situations" (McAdam et al. 2001, 24).

3. This phenomenon is well exemplified by what happened in 1968 in Italy when, following a university reform project, students appropriated corporative student union organizations affiliated to the parties to embark on a battle that spread from the university to other sectors of Italian society (Tarrow 1989). Another example comes from the birth of the civil rights movement in the United States: in 1955 a few activists like Rosa Parks brought fairly conservative religious organiza-

tions into the bus boycott campaign in Montgomery, Alabama (McAdam, Tarrow, and Tilly 2001, 47).

4. The Italian trade union rebuilt itself on a unitary basis around the CGIL in 1944 before the end of World War II. The tensions of the Cold War led to it being split into three major trade union confederations in 1948: the CGIL (of socialist and communist inspiration), the CISL (Catholic), and the UIL (laical). Toward the end of the 1960s, these three organizations got closer, forming a confederation, then splitting again in the 1980s.

5. Among others, Tarrow has pointed out (1989) that the student movement of 1968 had an important effect on the churches. In Europe and Latin America, grassroots communities and "political" Christian groups sprang up, drawing theoretical inspiration from the so-called liberation theology developed by grassroots ecclesialbased communities, especially in Latin America, stressing the issues of justice and equality within a "preferential option for the poor" (Eckstein 2001, 30–33).

6. Partly because of the competition between the more radicalized groups of the south and the more institutionalized organizations of the north, Jubilee Research has decided to widen its original mandate: while at the beginning the campaign based its claim for debt relief referring to social and economical exploitation of the third world by richer countries, today it also adds "environmental exploitation" (http://www.jubileeresearch.org).

7. Interview with a White Overalls' activist (Genoa, July 18, 2002).

8. The anticapitalist component in France is represented by Troskyist groups (see chapter 7).

9. On the distinction between politics-oriented and society-oriented groups, see Kriesi 1996.

10. We placed all participants who stated they belonged to NGOs, voluntary or environmentalist associations, or religious movements, or had done so in the past, in the "ecopacifist" category, members of a political party or trade union in the "antineoliberalist" category, and those involved in social center and student collective activities in the category of "anticapitalist left." It is to be remembered that the analysis deals with all those activists who had organizational experience, not only those who belonged to organizations that were formally part of the ESF.

11. The remaining 6.2 percent belong to none of these sectors but to ones less easy to classify, such as sports associations and groups in support of migrants.

12. However, members of the NC of ATTAC–Italy state that they never vote during meetings and that decisions are made by consensus (interview, May 27, 2004).

13. Representation toward the outside is allowed only on highly specific issues and is in any case subject to monitoring and rotation. Lilliput "constantly verifies organizational modes, tasks performed and responsibilities entrusted. Wherever the task of spokesperson, referent, coordinator or such like is entrusted, it is limited

in time defined by the duration of the campaign or initiative and/or by criteria of rotation" (Rete Lilliput 2002).

3. Master Frame, Activists' Ideas, and Collective Identity

1. We refer to a collective action frame as a "schemata of interpretation" (Goffman 1974, 21) for collective action. Snow and Benford provide different definitions of collective frames depending on whether they wish to stress its interpretative or strategic use. In the former, a frame is "an interpretative schemata that simplifies and condenses the 'world out there' by selectively punctuating and encoding objects, situations, events, experiences, and sequences of actions within one's present or past environments" (Snow and Benford 1992, 137); in its strategic function, the frame is "action-oriented sets of beliefs and meanings that inspire and legitimate the activities and campaigns of a social movement organization" (Benford and Snow 2000, 614).

2. For an analysis of the social construction of the working class, see E. Thompson 1980; for a cultural approach to the formation of the working class see Somers 1992 and Steinmetz 1992; and for the importance of symbolic construction in new social movements, see Melucci 1996. Hunt, Benford, and Snow 1994 provide a theoretical framework for the identity formation through framing process.

3. Gerhards and Rucht call this function "cultural integration" (1992, 559).

4. Gamson claims that "collective action frames are *injustice* frames" (1992b, 68).

5. "Schemas" are defined as "participants' expectations about people, objects, events, and settings in the world" (Tannen and Wallat 1993, 60). Since "frames and schemas interact during the course of interaction between two or more individuals, with frames providing an interpretive 'footing' that aligns schemas that participants to the interaction bring with them" (Benford and Snow 2000, 614), we will use "schemata of interpretation" to refer to collective frames (both sectorial frames and the master frame), and "schema" to refer to participants' expectations about what social movements should do or "think."

6. Margaret R. Somers calls this narrative "ontological": "Ontological narratives—she claims—make identity and the self something that one *becomes*. . . . Narrative embeds identities in time and spatial relationships; ontological narratives structure activities, consciousness and beliefs" (1992, 603).

7. We are not referring to an objective coherence, but to the form of argument used, which is logical in the sense that the protest is motivated by showing the cause-problem connection.

8. About 15 percent of the activists did not respond to this open question.

9. In 2003 ATTAC–France had thirty thousand members organized in two hundred local groups (Ancelovici 2002; Kolb 2005).

10. When it was founded in 2001, ATTAC–Germany had only four hundred members, which grew to ten thousand by November 2002, when ATTAC–Germany was one of the largest national branches of that organization in Europe (Kolb 2005).

4. Global-Net for Global Movements?

1. To analyze Web sites no longer extant, we used an online database that periodically downloads Web sites and files them under different dates (http://www.archive.org).

2. Arabic, Greek, and Russian translations were also advertised on the site but were never made accessible to Internet users.

3. Regression coefficient is T statistic, obtained dividing ß unstandardized by the standard error (Urban 1993, 38–39). This coefficient estimates significance and allows comparison among independent variables in a binary logistic regression. Wald coefficient in SPSS is equivalent to (T statistic).

4. Even though there is no law against it, participation in a Net strike is considered by some law experts illegal. Net strikers base the legality and legitimacy of this form of online protest on the right to strike (Freschi 2000).

5. We have used this correlation index according to the level of scale of the variables. This basically means that the classically known correlation index (Pearson) was of little use since it should be applied only if both variables have an interval scale level, in other words, if both variables are truly quantitative. This was hardly ever the case ("Use of the Internet" is a five-point-scale ordinal variable). Even the high number of respondents does not justify its use. Therefore, we used Kendall's Tau ß, which is the usual measure for two ordinal variables.

6. Especially if attention is turned to such factors as the issues of debate, the degree of autonomy of the setting, the technological applications used, the rules of discourse instituted, and the type of discussion management undertaken (Dahlberg 2001; see also Salter 2003).

7. Of 12,787 voters, the three questions were answered affirmatively by respectively 87.3 percent, 72.7 percent, and 79.4 percent. It should be noted, however, that unlike the normal practice in conducting online surveys, more than one vote could be cast from the same computer station.

8. Latent ties are created on the Internet in asynchronous shared communicative spaces, and they can be activated by just sending an e-mail message. If the message stimulates an interactive relationship, a weak tie is activated (Haythornthwaite 2001b).

9. Models were tested using as dependent variables three dummy variables (0, none/a little/somewhat; 1, a lot).

10. Considering that the "use of the Internet" variable is a dummy variable

with only two categories and low variance, the result of the correlation can be considered absolutely acceptable.

11. The analysis was carried out applying an approximate Mann-Whitney U test to our data. This test is similar to a parametric unpaired t-test for explaining the difference between two groups. However, unlike the t-test, the Mann-Whitney U test allows for an ordinal dependent variable (such as trust in institutions). Up to a case number of thirty, an exact test has to be used; as our data set comprises many more cases, an approximation can be used. This also facilitates the interpretation, as the significance is calculated on the basis of the well-known Z values of an (approximate) normal distribution.

5. Media-Conscious and Nonviolent?

1. The principle of investing along ethical lines became increasingly important in the nineties; from 1985 to 2000, investment in socially responsible funds in the United States rose from $40 billion to $3.3 trillion (and one-tenth of U.S. investments overall) (Oliviero and Simmins 2002).

2. Public opinion polls point to a consistently high level of confidence in NGOs and low confidence in governmental ones.

3. Just to give one example, Amnesty International (AI)—which has often adhered to antiglobalization protests—in 2000 could count on the support, including funding, of 1,300,000 members organized in 53,000 sections in 56 nations (Schneider 2000).

4. On the issue of immigration, the EU has, for example, preferred the projects of big, heavily bureaucratized organizations to those of small migrants' groups (Guiraudon 2002).

5. Despite this declaration of intent, it should be pointed out that in Prague (September 2000) the "yellow" march headed by White Overalls used sticks against police lines. In later mobilizations, the promise not to carry objects of aggression seems to have been kept.

6. Interview with Vetriolo, a Sicilian anarchist of the Italian Anarchist Federation.

7. Many documents found on the Web point to a split within the more radical fringes of the movement. For example, one BB press release states, "The bank and multinational corporation windows smashed are symbolic actions. The destruction of small shops and cars does not fit in with what we do. This is not our policy" (BB 2001b).

8. Here and elsewhere, the focus group (FG) participant is identified with a number (for the specific group) and a lowercase letter (for the individual in that group). The last number is the page number of the transcription from which the quote is taken.

9. As one activist said, "Many parts of the movement didn't use violence because there was still some fear, because in my view the specter of Genoa is still
there, there's no doubt about that . . . but there are parts of the movement who are
convinced on nonviolence and there are others that aren't because, the way I see it,
nonviolence doesn't just mean not smashing windows, it means when the police
come along and start beating you up you lie down and don't fight back. It means
a whole load of other things too like how you organize marches. It's not just about
not smashing windows" (FG 1a, 18).

10. In Seattle, the mass media had given ample coverage to the violence staged
by (an estimated) 1 percent of demonstrators, presenting images of an uprising
rather than of a political demonstration, so much so that in December 2001 the
Google search engine showed 104,000 pages in response to the query "Seattle
riots" (Morse 2001). In a research project on the German press coverage of some of
the main protest events organized during international summits, it emerged that
while attention is certainly higher (from 130 articles on Seattle to 398 on Genoa),
little is written about the substance of the protests (from 1.5 percent of the articles
on Seattle to 3.8 percent of those on Genoa), while an increasing number of articles
deals with police action (29.1 percent of the articles on Genoa dealt with this aspect) and the violence perpetrated by demonstrators (from 6.9 percent in Seattle to
10.6 percent in Genoa) (Rucht 2002a, 72–73).

6. Transnational Protest and Public Order

1. For a definition of "protest policing," see della Porta 1995, ch. 3. For a discussion of the various styles of protest policing in Europe and in the United States,
see della Porta and Reiter 1998a.

2. For a fuller discussion of the factors determining police forces' public-
order strategies, primarily police knowledge, see della Porta and Reiter 1998b.

3. According to a recent study, not aspiring to completeness, 109 demonstrators were killed in clashes with the police between 1947 and 1954 (Marino
1995, 169). According to Italian Interior Ministry statistics, from January 1, 1948,
through June 30, 1950, workers killed "on the occasion of public-order duties"
numbered 34 (28 of them Communists), with 695 injured (572 Communists), and
13,609 arrested (10,728 of them Communists) (Caredda 1995, 94ff.).

4. After the clashes during the 1998 soccer World Cup matches, German
passport law was changed to allow hooligans to be barred from leaving the country.
Use of this sanction against neo-Nazis was accepted by the Constitutional Court,
even without final sentences, in the case of offenses committed during trips abroad
resulting in severe damage to the state. Before the G8, the German police issued
injunctions to seventy-nine activists against participation in tumult and violence,
and barred another eighty-one from leaving the country, with an obligation to

report daily (*Der Spiegel,* no. 31, 2001, 24). In some cases these measures were confirmed by the administrative magistracy. After Genoa, this practice and the criteria employed to identify and register violent activists or those presumed to be so (in some cases on the basis of a mere document check during a demonstration) were subjected to growing criticism (see *Der Spiegel,* no. 31, 2001; *Die Zeit,* no. 37, 2001, 4ff.; Griebenow and Busch 2001).

5. See Griebenow and Busch 2001, 64ff.; Council of the European Union 2001a) The joint action of 1997 (Council of the European Union 1997) provided for the exchange of information on "sizable groups which may pose a threat to law and order and security" traveling to "events" from one member state to another. The preamble defined "events" as including "sporting events, rock concerts, demonstrations and road-blocking protest campaigns."

6. For the Gothenburg events, see Peterson and Oskarsson 2002; Peterson 2003; and Wahlström 2003.

7. A proposal to hold the demonstrations between June 27 and July 15, a week before the summit, was formalized on February 8 and communicated to the GSF, which rejected it (IPIC 2001c, 111). On April 4 the movement organized "telegram day"—thousands of telegrams, e-mails, and faxes were sent to the president of the republic and government figures asking for meetings to define the details of the protest—a day after sit-ins in front of the Ministry of the Interior in Rome and dozens of Prefectures throughout the country (IPIC 2001j, 20).

8. After telegram day, the prefect was mandated to negotiate with the GSF, but without new instructions. His attempt ended on April 20, when he told the government that the movement was insisting on its demands: demonstrations during the summit days, and premises and infrastructure to host demonstrators (IPIC 2001e, 101ff.).

9. The group was not consulted or involved when the police, on a decision by the public prosecutor—before the start of the summit and before any violent episode had occurred—cleared the biggest school premises allotted to the demonstrators. The lack of success in searches for improper weapons and violent activists— the justification given for the action—damaged the credibility of the contact group among protest organizers and increased animosity toward the police on the part of the peaceful bulk of the demonstrators. For an English summary of the findings of the Gothenburg commission, see Justitiedepartementet Betänkande av Göteborgs-kommittén 2001.

10. That the police were aware of sending nonverbal signals through certain preventive measures is evident from the statement by the former head of UCIGOS (central political police), La Barbera, according to whom systematic activities of preventive pressure were abandoned in order not to adversely affect attempts at dialogue (ICIP 2001f, 61). In addition to searches, many telephone taps were car-

ried out, along with computer monitoring and a census of the most extremist social centers (64ff.).

11. In Sweden, most of the people facing judicial action were identified after the summit on the basis of video recordings: sixty-six activists have been prosecuted, accompanied by allegations of tampered video evidence and with sentences that have been defined as "remarkably high" (Swedish NGO Foundation for Human Rights 2002, 61ff.).

12. Zinola 2003, 73. For a detailed reconstruction of the three days at Genoa, see Gubitosa 2003.

13. Police chief De Gennaro stated that tear gas "was to be regarded as an ultimate remedy for tackling particularly serious situations that cannot be handled otherwise, given also the heavy impact it has on the crowd. . . . We hear in the reports I have cited that officers were saying: 'Then I also used tear gas.' I think that these are motives for reflection—on my part too—so as to improve, and correct if necessary" (IPIC 2001i, 51).

14. Twenty-eight arrestees were freed directly by the prosecution service, which did not apply for confirmation of their arrest; seventy-six arrests were not confirmed. "Against 225 applications for preventive detention, only 20 people remained in prison, and 29 bans on residing in Genoa were applied. . . . Failure to confirm arrests is an outcome a lawyer hardly ever sees, since the judge has to assess whether the arrest was legitimate on the basis solely of what appears on the arrest report, plus the accused's statements. In this position it is rather hard for the judge to reach the point of saying that there were no elements justifying arrests, essentially disowning the police action; the greatest success is usually to see the accused freed on the grounds that while having committed an offence they are not dangerous" (Genoa Legal Forum 2002, 114).

15. Before the parliamentary investigative commission, police spokesmen long maintained that the demonstrations on July 20 had not been authorized. However, due notice had been given, and police headquarters had taken note by denying the use of particular squares and barring the Disobedients' parade from going further than Piazza Verdi.

16. For the differences between the first draft of the majority report and the final version, see Gubitosa 2003, 304ff.

17. Cf. Gubitosa 2003, 214f. The Disobedients were the only GSF group that did not manage to enter even the yellow zone.

18. Recordings of communications inside the police headquarters that recently emerged at trials connected with the Genoa events indicate surprise and disapproval of the decision to charge the Disobedients' parade.

19. At Gothenburg, the assault on a school being used as a dormitory by demonstrators on the night after the hardest clashes seems to have had similar features,

though with much slighter consequences to demonstrators. It was carried out by a special paramilitary unit and justified by the search for an armed German terrorist.

20. See, e.g., Waddington 1994, on the control of public order in London.

21. A general reference to the law is not enough, since it is a consolidated practice to tolerate minor infractions, nor is a statement like that by the police chief to the GSF that the police would suit the deterrent response to the conduct of those who had broken the law (Gubitosa 2003, 58).

22. For a discussion of how the presence of foreign dignitaries influences police strategy and how extensively their protection can be interpreted, see Ericson and Doyle 1999.

23. Of activists who were present at Genoa, 77.4 percent had no trust in the police (62.1 percent of those not present), and 3.7 percent (6.8 percent) had some or much trust. Of those taking part in movement initiatives in their own countries, 69.5 percent had no trust (against 58.5 percent of nonparticipants), and 4.9 percent (8.9 percent) had sufficient or great trust.

24. Results for the various countries are (as in the case of the question on trusting the police) very similar for Italian, French, and German activists, while a high percentage of the Spanish (34.5 percent) and British (41.1 percent) activists find police presence harmful in all cases. For Britain, one explanation of this result might be that almost all British activists present at the ESF belonged to the Socialist Workers' Party.

25. The demand that police controlling public order should not carry firearms is a constant in the history of the Italian left. In the seventies the trade unions and left-wing parties were asking that the police not be present at trade union or political demonstrations or that they be disarmed for public-order service (della Porta and Reiter 2003).

26. Of activists interviewed at Genoa, 2.9 percent found police presence necessary for opposing violent actions, 48.7 percent found it necessary if confined to guaranteeing the regular holding of the demonstration, 11.4 percent found it unnecessary, and 37.0 percent found it harmful.

27. Looking at forms of actions that activists state they have used in the past, a similar trend emerges for all forms of most direct action (occupations of buildings and also strikes and sit-ins) or the most committed ones (boycotts and party activism).

28. Not only in the media: a note from the general secretariat of the Council of the EU, dated July 3, 2001, contains the proposal to compare the list of potential hooligans, prepared for the 2000 European soccer championship, with a list of names compiled after Gothenburg (Council of the EU 2001).

29. For the organizational confusion during massive personnel transfers, es-

pecially if they also involve carabinieri and financial police, see the interview with a SIULP (police union) leader in Gubitosa 2003 (512). For the burdensome work situation of the policemen deployed in Genoa, see ibid., 501–2, 512; IPIC 2001b, 109s. Problems range from long working shifts, often notified at the last moment, to the unsuitability of accommodation structures. These too have operational repercussions, since the officers often see demonstrators as responsible for the situation. The confusion in police organization for major events is not a purely Italian problem. The Swedish police union has published its own inquiry into Gothenburg based on responses from nine hundred officers in service during the summit days, with the significant title "Kaos."

30. Use of the new truncheons had been authorized by the Amato government (IPIC 2001c, 136). Taken up even before Genoa by the carabinieri—who at Naples were still using the butts of their guns—these truncheons are a fairly widespread weapon among other police forces. The accusation raised after Genoa that the tonfa caused much more serious injuries than the traditional type was rejected by Valerio Donnino, who did, however, admit the risks associated with wrong use of the weapon, documented in some episodes: namely, with the handle the other way around (like a hammer), and used vertically (IPIC 2001i, 35, 45).

31. Specialized units, one of whose tasks is to intervene against violent fringes at demonstrations, exist in most European police forces. They are fundamental to the strategy of *de-escalating force,* which combines commitment to dialogue with targeted action against the violent, to isolate and arrest them without involving peaceful demonstrators. For the polemics accompanying their creation and deployment in Germany, see Sturm and Ellinghaus 2002, 26ff.

32. It requires officers to act aggressively in conditions of relative anonymity: protective armor is worn; a helmet at least partly covers the face; and especially, one acts not as an individual but as part of a group. The target of the action is not other individuals, but an equally anonymous collective—the crowd, "them," which is perhaps insulting and physically attacking "us," the police. If officers' resentment and frustration has been stimulated by demonstrator actions perceived as aggressive, the charges permit retaliation in conditions that minimize individual responsibility (Waddington 1991, 177–78).

33. The mobile operational groups (GOM) of the prison police were set up in 1997 (and then regulated by Ministerial Decree of February 19, 1999) with the task of controlling the most dangerous prisoners, transfers of accomplice witnesses, and intervention in cases of revolt. They were involved in episodes of jail violence—in Milan in 1998 and in Sassari in 2000.

34. As already mentioned, one of the features of protest policing in the 1980s and 1990s was its selectivity: certain "hard" methods survived in opposing small groups,

especially the social centers. Among precedents for certain features of the search at the Diaz-Pertini school were the searches of two social centers, the Leoncavallo in Milan in 1995 and the Askatasuna in Turin in 1999 (Pepino 2001, 892).

35. The requirement for an independent investigative structure cannot be met by the magistracy investigating only facts of criminal relevance. Moreover, the practical conduct of judicial inquiries always remains a task for the police forces.

36. In July 2001, the UN Human Rights Committee underlined that the current system of investigating complaints against the police in the Czech Republic "lacks objectivity and credibility and would seem to facilitate impunity for police involved in human rights violations" (AI 2002a, 2002b). In its concluding remarks on the fifth periodic report of Sweden, the UN Human Rights Committee expressed concern about cases of excessive use of force by the police, for instance, during the Gothenburg summit, and recommended: "The state party should ensure the completion of investigations into such use of force, in conditions of total transparency and through a mechanism independent of the law enforcement authorities" (Human Rights Committee 2002, 2). The 188 charges filed against the police after Gothenburg did not result in any convictions (Swedish NGO Foundation for Human Rights 2002, 61ff.).

37. In his deposition to the parliamentary commission on the Genoa events, ex–minister of the interior Bianco reports on an internal inquiry into the Naples actions that had found "some excessive initiatives by uniformed personnel, not yet identified since they were wearing the protective helmet" (IPIC 2001k, 54). The depositions from some detained demonstrators about brutality and harassment led to a judicial inquiry, accompanied by heavy polemics, more than a year later.

38. According to the communiqué, among the enemies are the "Genoa fire-hydrant thrower, the Agnolettos, Casarinis and our very own Carusos, in no way peaceful little lambs but fomenters of disorder, culprits or promoters of attempted lynching" (*La Repubblica*, August 21, 2001).

39. Margherita Paolini, charged by the Amato government with negotiating with the GSF, added, "I perfectly recall that these were the words pronounced" (IPIC 2001h, 11).

40. The reference to constitutional principles is, moreover, "trapped" between rejection of violence as an instrument of political action, celebration of legality as a fundamental democratic value, and reference to the "necessary protection of citizens' safety and public order" (IPIC 2001a, 246).

41. Because of the disorders around the barracks, the three MPs and Deputy Prime Minister Fini were allegedly forced to continue their presence until the march dispersed (IPIC 2001a, 225). Colonel Graci, commander of the carabinieri operational division, in Genoa for five years, states that this was the first time MPs had come into the operations center (IPIC 2001g, 52).

42. According to a PeopleSWG survey, for instance, 57 percent of those inter-viewed held that "the violence and beatings suffered by the demonstrators on the streets and in the jails were really serious," as against 28 percent regarding them as largely media exaggerations.

43. Before the parliamentary investigative commission, its chair, Paolo Serventi Longhi, mentioned that the police forces wore the yellow press recognition vests, already complained of in a letter to the Ministry of the Interior on Friday, July 20, but still used by policemen even after the questore of Genoa, Colucci, speaking to the journalists' association of Liguria, had ruled out their use. Referring chiefly to the police forces but also to the extreme fringes of the movement, Longhi further denounced "an objective attempt, by those who felt in some sense at risk as regards documentation, to eliminate that risk. That has already happened other times, and at Genoa certainly did particularly obviously; on the street there were widespread attempts to sequester or obstruct video documentation" (IPIC 2001h, 41, 48).

44. Indeed, the coverage of international summits in Seattle, Prague, and Genoa focused on police issues and violence (Rucht 2002c, 72–73).

45. The GdP (German police trade union) president concludes, "countries where the police has military traditions and training and working methods or even depends on the defence ministry have an urgent need of a police reform. Moreover, in all EU countries police staff must be granted trade union rights, and with these the rights to contribute to shaping the features of their own profession" (ibid.).

46. IPIC 2001c, 161. For this reading of the history of public order in Italy, Genoa (and earlier Naples) constitutes a break with a soft line of protest policing consolidated in the seventies. The soft line became established, however, only in the eighties, and always remained selective. For some actions by the Italian police in the seventies that led to deaths among demonstrators, see della Porta and Reiter 2003, 241ff.

47. See Sheptycki 1994; Peers 2000; Denza 2002; Walker 2003. The objective of EU policy for the "area of freedom, security and justice" is defined in Article 29 of the Amsterdam Treaty as "to provide citizens with a high level of safety." Specifi-cally, on the EU's policing response to the global justice movement, see Hayes and Bunyan 2004 (274), who report that after Gothenburg four hundred names were added to the Schengen Information System.

48. According to research by Statewatch in 2003, in the two previous years the Schengen agreement was suspended twenty-six times, at least sixteen of these on the occasion of political demonstrations (Hayes and Bunyan 2004, 274). The report on human rights in the EU for the year 2001 had also asked the Commis-sion and the member states "not to allow any restrictions on freedom of movement in connection with EU summits where this seems appropriate to prevent people from taking part in demonstrations" (Committee on Citizens Freedoms 2002,

23). Other language contained in the handbook leaves one equally perplexed: "The overall policy *can* include policies such as: the right to demonstrate and to free speech is respected, . . . the police should, *at its discretion and when appropriate,* demonstrate a low level of police visibility and a high level of tolerance regarding *peaceful* demonstrations. . . . It is recommended that a single point of contact is appointed for the media to *ensure a coordinated media coverage*" (emphasis added).

49. For an account of the risks the response to international terrorism may present for civil rights (repeatedly emphasized in the European Parliament's reports on human rights in the EU), see the thematic comment "The Balance between Freedom and Security in the Response by the EU and Its Member States to the Terrorist Threats," drafted on request by the European Commission and submitted on March 31, 2003, by the EU Network of Independent Experts in Fundamental Rights (CFR-CDF).

50. "Per Aspera ad Veritatem—Rivista di intelligence e di cultura professionale," no. 21, September–December 2001. At the investigative commission hearings on the Genoa incidents, other officials had already linked the extreme fringes of the movement with the reemergence of terrorist actions in Italy (see La Barbera, in IPIC 2001f, 66; Andreassi, in ibid., 101).

51. "Per Aspera ad Veritatem," no. 22, January–April 2002.

52. On the debate within EU institutions on how to define "terrorism" after September 11, see Mathiesen 2002. In early 2002, the Spanish presidency presented a draft decision calling for the exchange of information on incidents caused by violent radical groups with terrorist links and, where appropriate, prosecuting violent urban youthful radicalism increasingly used by terrorist organizations to achieve their criminal aims, at summits and other events arranged by various community and international organizations. Because of opposition by other member states, the Spanish initiative led only to a nonbinding resolution in November 2002, which, however, allowed governments wishing to do so to exchange information on movement activists in the name of the fight against terrorism. Being a simple recommendation, it was not necessary to consult the European Parliament or the national parliaments (Hayes and Bunyan 2004, 277).

53. As regards the EU, the decision to hold European summits always in Brussels and no longer in the country temporarily holding the presidency will very likely lead to a strengthening of the international police.

54. For the break-in to the Diaz-Pertini school, the Genoa prosecution service officialized the request to try twenty-nine officials and officers, while thirty-nine are being investigated for the Bolzaneto violence (*La Repubblica,* March 4, 2004). A trial for devastation and sacking had begun for twenty-six demonstrators, with a minimum penalty in the civil code of eight years (*La Repubblica,* March 2, 2004).

55. The special antiriot squad of the Roman public-order police unit is to be

dissolved (*La Repubblica,* June 20, 2002); its commander, vice questore Canterini, is under investigation by the Genoa magistracy.

56. Rejection of militarization and organizational fluidity made the movement reluctant to set up stewardship services. On the role of such services in the 1970s escalation that led to terrorism, see della Porta 1995, 90–94, 153–58. At the meeting on June 30 with the police chief, the GSF was informed that the BB would seek to infiltrate its demonstrations. The parties agreed that it was a task for the police forces to deter or isolate violent demonstrators and not a matter for the movement (IPIC 2001j, 54).

57. Prior to the Summit, the Danish police chief Kai Vittrup had declared that under no circumstances would the police accept the anticipated symbolic actions of occupation of multinational concerns and public spaces and that such actions would be regarded as an invitation to voluntary arrest. The Danish police tactics to throw the activists out of balance by preventive detentions (e.g., of Luca Casarini, leader of the Italian Disobedients) and impound material (even pure propaganda) for use in such actions are problematic from not just political and legal but even technical viewpoints: they seem ill-suited to bigger demonstrations (Peterson 2003; Wahlström 2003). In the United States, the ACLU started a lawsuit against the Secret Service for the continuing practice of allowing pro-Bush demonstrators to remain visible to cameras during presidential appearances while corralling anti-Bush protesters into pens or designated areas far from the media.

58. Also without incidents were the demonstrations on the occasion of the EU summit in Copenhagen in December 2002, where police action followed a somewhat different line: a full year before the event dialogue with the movement was actively sought, and a mobile, flexible strategy that was not concentrated on defending certain static places, as at Gothenburg or Genoa, but sought to take and keep the offensive to control all situations regarded as dangerous or wrongful developments (Peterson 2003).

59. At the demonstrations against the EU summit in Copenhagen, situations of tension during demonstrations were successfully defused by direct contact between police and movement figures (Wahlström 2003).

7. Politics, Antipolitics, and Other Politics

1. Similarly, concepts such as associative democracy (Hirst 1994) or radical democracy (Mouffe 1996) also stress the need for complementing representative democracy with alternative forms.

2. Although in Spain, the Socialist Party won the election in March 2004.

3. Led by the Workers Party (Partido dos Trabalhadores), Porto Alegre's city government launched a project of participatory budgetary decision making for the city in 1988 with the aim of getting people involved in political participation by

creating a real forum in which the public could express their views, and developing rules to encourage deliberation (Gret and Sintomer 2002, 26). The decision-making process provides for moments of direct democracy, with decentralized assemblies open to everyone, as well as for moments of representative democracy, with delegates of the assemblies who participate in the sixteen district assemblies with a binding mandate.

4. Among the proposals for an inclusive, nongovernmental management of the summit were, for example, the creation of a Web link between the official Web site and that of the GSF, joint press conferences between government members and INGOs, adequate hospitality structures and places for meeting the press made available to the demonstrators, the setting up of public debates, and throwing parts of the summit open to the public (*Limes,* January 3, 2001, 197–202)

5. See the testimony of Margherita Paolini, charged by the Amato government with the dialogue with the GSF, made before the investigative commission (IPIC 2001h, 10) in which she emphasized that "during this time nothing further was heard concerning the requests" put forward by the GSF. Paolini's testimony was challenged by ex–prime minister Giuliano Amato in a letter he sent to the commission (IPIC 2001i, 3), in which he affirmed a document had been prepared titled *Genoa Non-governmental Initiative* to which a number of GSF exponents had contributed through seminars, and that had been handed to Amato himself on June 5.

6. This judgment was confirmed by the former mayor of Venice and member of the Margherita Party Massimo Cacciari: "Politicians in not understanding a thing about this movement make two mistakes. The first is the attempt to criminalize the so-called no-globals. The second is the belief that you have to divide the movement, imagining that in so doing the extremists will be isolated. This is lunacy that risks losing a whole generation of kids, kids that tomorrow will make their contribution to the political culture of this country" (*La Repubblica,* August 21, 2001).

7. The DS party whip in the Senate, Violante, justified the DS's inattention citing its governmental responsibility and hence the "parliamentarianizing of political life": "from 1995 to 2000, our party contributed to the guidance and support of municipalities, provinces, regions, public bodies and institutions, and now national government. We are talking about no less a commitment to government than that of the Christian Democrats in its much longer history of being the party in government. But above all we are talking about an abrupt need for a massive shift of party staff to the institutions, which sapped the party resources" (in *Micromega,*" April 2001, 113).

8. After Genoa, the New Labour government came under criticism from the British press for not giving their support to demonstrators. The *Independent* noted: "It's looking as though Tony Blair's unswerving support of police repression in

Genoa—more unconditional than that expressed by many Italian politicians—has convinced some Foreign Office officials to be less insistent than they might otherwise have been to gain access to those arrested" (quoted in Notobartolo 2001, 105). This criticism was echoed in the *Observer:* "We British have every right to be worried about our democracy. This government always seems ready to condemn unrest in whatever shape or form but slow to understand it. The Prime Minister Tony Blair and the Foreign Minister Jack Straw had no qualms in showing understanding for the Italian police and they did so with indecent haste. Jack Straw has said he would ascertain whether there were grounds for 'formulating a protest with a capital P.' He should not be surprised if people start expressing their anger with a capital A" (ibid., 109).

9. An Enquete-Kommission is a parliamentary commission of inquiry on long-term policy issues; half of the commission is made up of parliamentarians and half of experts. Its establishment can be demanded by one quarter of parliament. A Bundestag regulation requires that the results produced by an Enquete-Kommission be debated in Parliament before the end of the legislature. The majority decision to present the partial results of the commission on "Globalization of the World Economy—Challenges and Responses" to Parliament was criticized by members of the opposition as instrumental and aimed at contrasting the criticism of the stance of the majority vis-à-vis the movement for a globalization from below that emerged in particular after Genoa.

8. The Global Movement and Democracy

1. For instance, at the international march of December 14, 2001, against the EU summit in Brussels, more than 60 percent of the participants were Belgians, and another 20 percent came from neighboring France and the Netherlands (Bédoyan, van Aelst, and Walgrave 2004).

Bibliography

Note: Unless otherwise specified, online sources were accessed in August 2004.

Agnoletto, Vittorio. 2003. *Prima persone: Le nostre ragioni contro questa globalizzazione.* Rome: Laterza.

AI. 2001. *Italy: Amnesty International Calls for an Independent Inquiry into Actions by Law Enforcement Officers during Global Forum in Naples.* April. At http://web.amnesty.org/library/Index/ENGEUR300012001?open&of=ENG-ITA.

———. 2002a. *Czech Republic: Past Mistakes Must Not Be Repeated: Respect for Freedom of Expression.* November. At http://web.amnesty.org/library/Index/ENGEUR710012002?open&of=ENG-CZE.

———. 2002b. *Report 2002.* May. At http://web.amnesty.org/library/pdf/POL100012002ENGLISH/$File/POL1000102.pdf.

Allum, Percy. 1995. *State and Society in Western Europe.* Cambridge, England: Polity Press.

Ancelovici, Marcus. 2002. "Organizing against Globalization: The Case of Attac in France." *Politics and Society* 30, no. 3: 427–63.

Andretta, Massimiliano, Donatella della Porta, Lorenzo Mosca, and Herbert Reiter. 2002. *Global, Noglobal, New Global: La protesta contro il G8 a Genova.* Rome: Laterza.

———. 2003. *Global—New Global: Identität und Strategien der Antiglobalisierungsbeweung.* Frankfurt am Main: Campus Verlag.

Andretta, Massimiliano, and Lorenzo Mosca. 2003. "Il movimento per una globalizzazione dal basso: Forza e debolezza di una identità negoziata."

In *Globalizzazione e movimenti sociali,* ed. D. della Porta and L. Mosca, 21–47. Rome: Manifestolibri.

ATTAC. 1998. *Platform of the International Movement ATTAC.* December. At http://www.attac.org/contact/indexpfen.htm.

ATTAC–Italy. 2001. *Genoa 2001: Concluding Remarks* [Genova 2001: Considerazioni finali]. July. At http://www.attac.org/italia/genova/attacalg8.htm (accessed on June 2002).

———. 2002. *Associative Statute.* June. At http://italia.attac.org/spip/article .php3?id_article=202.

Ayres, Jeffrey M. 1998. *Defying Conventional Wisdom: Political Movements and Popular Contention against North American Free Trade.* Toronto: University of Toronto Press.

———. 2001. "Transnational Political Processes and Contention against the Global Economy." *Mobilization* 6, no. 1: 55–68.

Barlett, Frederic C. 1932. *Remembering.* Cambridge, England: Cambridge University Press.

Bateson, Mary Catherine. 1990. "Beyond Sovereignty: An Emerging Global Civilization." In *Contending Sovereignties. Redefining Political Community,* ed. R. B. J. Walker and Saul H. Mendlovitz, 145–58. Boulder, CO: Lynne Rienner.

Bauman, Zygmunt. 1982. *Memories of Class.* London: Routledge & Kegan Paul.

———. 1999. *In Search of Politics.* Oxford, England: Polity Press.

BB. 2001a. *International Genova Offensive.* July. At http://www.nadir.org/nadir/ aktuell/2001/07/18/5040.html.

———. 2001b. *Statement.* July. At http://www.infoshop.org/news6/genoa_bb _statement.html.

———. 2004. *Black Blocs for Dummies.* January. At http://www.infoshop.org/ blackbloc_faq.html.

Beati i Costruttori di Pace and Pax Christi. 2001. *Proposal of Hunger for Peace* [Proposta di digiuno per la pace]. November. At http://members3.boardhost .com/GiovaniMission/msg/219.html (accessed on June 2002).

Beck, Ulrich. 1999. *Che cos'è la globalizzazione: Rischi e prospettive della società planetaria.* Rome: Carocci.

Becucci, Stefano. 2003. "Disobbedienti e centri sociali fra democrazia e rappresentanza." In *La democrazia dei movimenti: Come decidono i noglobal,* ed. P. Ceri, 75–93. Soveria Mannelli, Italy: Rubbettino.

Bédoyan, Isabelle, Peter Van Aelst, and Stefaan Walgrave. 2004. "Limitations and Possibilities of Transnational Mobilization. The Case of the EU Summit Protesters in Brussels, 2001." *Mobilization* 9, no. 1: 39–54.

Benenati, Sabrina. 2002. *Storia del Chiapas: Gli zapatisti e la rete sociale globale.* Milan, Italy: Mondadori.

Benford, Robert D. 1993. "'You could be the Hundredth Monkey': Collective Action Frames and Vocabularies of Motive within the Nuclear Disarmament Movement." *Sociological Quarterly* 34: 195–216.

———. 1997. "An Insider's Critique of the Social Movement Framing Perspective." *Sociological Inquiry* 67: 409–30.

Benford, Robert D., and David. A. Snow. 2000. "Framing Processes and Social Movements: An Overview and Assessment." *Annual Review of Sociology* 26: 611–39.

Bennett, W. Lance. 2003. "Communicating Global Activism: Strengths and Vulnerabilities of Networked Politics." *Information, Communication, and Society* 6, no. 2: 143–68.

Bennett, W. Lance, Terry E. Givens, and Lars Willnat. 2004. "Crossing Political Divide: Internet Use and Political Identification in Transnational Anti-War and Social Justice Activists in Eight Nations." Paper presented at the ECPR joint sessions, Uppsala, Sweden.

Bentivegna, Sara. 1999. *La politica in rete.* Rome: Meltemi.

———. 2002. *Politica e nuove tecnologie della comunicazione.* Rome: Laterza.

Béroud, Sophie, René Mouriaux, and Michel Vakaloulis. 1998. *Le movement social en France: Essai de sociologie politique.* Paris: La Dispute.

Berzano, Luigi, and Renzo Gallini. 2000. "Centri sociali autogestiti a Torino." *Quaderni di Sociologia* 22: 50–79.

Berzano, Luigi, Renzo Gallini, and Carlo Genova. 2002. *Liberi tutti: Centri sociali e case occupate a Torino.* Turin, Italy: Ananke.

Bimber, Bruce. 1998. "Toward an Empirical Mapping of Political Participation on the Internet." Paper presented at APSA annual conference, Boston.

Black, Mary. 2001. *Letter from Inside the Black Bloc.* July. At http://www.alternet .org/story/11230.

Boli, John. 1999. "Conclusion: World Authority Structures and Legitimations." In *Constructing World Culture: International Nongovernmental Organizations since 1875,* ed. John Boli and George Thomas, 267–300. Stanford, CA: Stanford University Press.

Boli, John, and George M. Thomas. 1999. *Constructing the World Culture: International Nongovernmental Organizations since 1875.* Stanford, CA: Stanford University Press.

Bologna, Gianfranco, et al. 2001. *La Rete di Lilliput.* Bologna: EMI.

Bonanno, Alfredo M. 1999. *Internazionale Antiautoritaria Insurrezionalista.* Catania, Italy: Edizioni Anarchismo.

Bonet i Martí, Jordi. 2003. "Movimientos sociales y nuevas tecnologias en Barcelona: Potencia y debilidad de una relación." Paper presented at the Graduate Conference on "Globalization, Conflicts and Social Movements," Trento, Italy.

Brand, Ulrich, and Markus Wissen. 2002. "Ambivalenzen praktischer Globalisierungskritik: Das Beispiel Attac." *Kurswechsel* 3: 102–13.

Brecher, Jeremy, Tim Costello, and Brendan Smith. 2000. *Globalization from Below: The Power of Solidarity.* Cambridge, England: South End Press.

Bündnis 90/Die Grünen [German Greens]. 2002. *Organizing Globalization Positively with Green-based Policies* [Globalisierung: Mit grüner Politik positiv gestalten]. March.

———. 2003. *Statement on Neoliberal Globalization.*

Busch, Heiner. 2002. "Vor neuen Gipfeln: Über die Schwierigkeiten internationaler Demonstrationen." *Bürgerrechte & Polizei/Cilip* 72: 53–57.

Cardon, Domenique, and Fabien Granjon. 2003. "Peut-on se liberer des formats mediatiques? Le mouvement alter-mondialisation et l'Internet." *Mouvements* 25: 67–73.

Caredda, Giorgio. 1995. *Governo e opposizione nell'Italia del dopoguerra.* Rome: Laterza.

Caritas Internationalis. 2003. *Guiding Values and Principles.* At http://www.caritas.org/upload/ERSTING.qxd.pdf.

Carlos, Alfonso. 1997. *APC Statement on Mail Bombing as a Method of Political Protest.* July. At http://www.apc.org/english/press/archive/apc_p013.shtml.

Castells, Manuel. 1996. *The Rise of the Network Society.* Oxford, England: Blackwell.

———. 1997. *The Power of Identity.* Oxford, England: Blackwell.

———. 2001. *The Internet Galaxy: Reflections on the Internet, Business, and Society.* Oxford: Oxford University Press.

Ceri, Paolo. 2001. *Movimenti globali: La protesta nel XIX secolo.* Rome: Laterza.

———, ed. 2003. *La democrazia dei movimenti: Come decidono i noglobal.* Soveria Mannelli, Italy: Rubbettino.

Chandhoke, Neera. 2002. "The Limits of Global Civil Society." In *Global Civil Society 2002,* ed. M. Glasius, M. Kaldor, and H. Anheier, 35–53. Oxford: Oxford University Press.

Chatfield, Charles, Ron Pagnucco, and Jackie Smith, eds. 1997. *Solidarity beyond the State: The Dynamics of Transnational Social Movements.* Syracuse, NY: Syracuse University Press.

Chester, Graeme, and Ian Welsh. 2004. "Rebel Colours: Framework in Global Social Movements." *Sociological Review* 52, no. 3: 314–35.

Chiesa, Giulio. 2001. *G8/Genova.* Turin, Italy: Einaudi.

Clark, John. 2003. "Introduction: Civil Society and Transnational Action." In *Globalizing Civic Engagement: Civil Society and Transnational Action,* ed. J. Clark, 1–28. London: Earthscan.

Clark, John, and Nuno Themundo. 2003. "The Age of Protest: Internet-Based 'Dot Causes' and the 'Anti-Globalization' Movement." In *Globalizing Civic Engagement: Civil Society and Transnational Action,* ed. J. Clark, 109–26. London: Earthscan.

Cleaver, Harry. 1995. "The Zapatista Effect: The Internet and the Rise of an Alternative Political Fabric." At http://www.eco.utexas.edu/Homepages/Faculty/Cleaver/zapeffect.html.

———. 1998. "The Zapatistas and the International Circulation Struggle: Lessons Suggested and Problems Raised." At http://www.eco.utexas.edu/Homepages/Faculty/Cleaver/lessons.html.

COBAS Confederation. 2001. *Inflexible against the G8* [Inflessibili contro il G8]. June. At http://www.ecn.org/nog8/italiano/iniziative/cobas.htm.

Colomba, Giampiero. 2003. "Polizia e ordine pubblico: Il controllo della protesta e della violenza negli stadi." Master's thesis, University of Florence.

Committee on Citizens' Freedoms and Rights, Justice, and Home Affairs. European Parliament. 2001. *Report on a Recommendation to the Council on an Area of Freedom, Security, and Justice: Security at Meetings of the European Council and other Comparable Events.* Watson Report. November. At http://www2.europarl.eu.int/omk/sipade2?PUBREF=-//EP//NONSGML+REPORT+A5-2001-0396+0+DOC+PDF+V0//EN&L=EN&LEVEL=3&NAV=S&LSTDOC=Y.

Committee on Citizens' Freedoms and Rights, Justice, and Home Affairs. European Parliament.2002. *Report on the Human Rights Situation in the European Union 2001.* December. At http://www2.europarl.eu.int/omk/sipade2?PUBREF=-//EP//NONSGML+REPORT+A5-2002-0451+0+DOC+PDF+V0//EN&L=EN&LEVEL=3&NAV=S&LSTDOC=Y.

Cosi, Stefania. 2004. "L'informazione sul Fse nella stampa italiana: Tra allarme sociale e sottorappresentazione mediatica." In *Processi sociali e nuove forme di partecipazione politica,* ed. L. Cedroni, 212–32. Milan, Italy: Franco Angeli.

Council of the EU. 1997. *Joint Action with Regard to Cooperation on Law and Order and Security.* May. At http://www.statewatch.org/news/2001/aug/japubord.htm.

———. 2001a. *Conclusions Adopted by the Council and the Representatives of the Governments of the Member States on 13 July 2001 on Security at Meetings of the European Council and other Comparable Events.* June. At http://www.statewatch.org/news/2003/jul/prot09069en2.pdf.

———. 2001b. *Note from the General Secretariat of the Council of the EU.* July. At http://www.statewatch.org/news/2001/aug/10525.pdf.

———. 2002. *Security Handbook for the Use of Police Authorities and Services at International Events Such as Meetings of the European Council.* November. At http://www.statewatch.org/news/2003/jul/prothand12637-r3.pdf.

———. 2003. *Draft Council Resolution on Security at European Council Meetings and Other Comparable Events.* June. At http://www.statewatch.org/news/2003/jul/protests10965.pdf.

Crahan, Margaret E. 1999. "Religion and Societal Change: The Struggle for Human Rights in Latin America." In *Religion and Human Rights: Competing Claims?* ed. C. Gustafson and P. Juviler, 57–80. New York: M. E. Sharpe.

Cristante, Stefano, ed. 2003. *Violenza mediata: Il ruolo dell'informazione nel G8 di Genova.* Rome: Editori Riuniti.

Crouch, Colin. 2004. *Post-democracy.* Cambridge, England: Polity.

Dahl, Robert. 1999. "Can International Organizations Be Democratic? A Skeptical View." In *Democracy's Edges,* ed. I. Shapiro and C. Haker-Cordón, 19–36. Cambridge: Cambridge University Press.

Dahlberg, Lincoln. 2001. "Computer-Mediated Communication and the Public Sphere: A Critical Analysis." *Journal of Computer-Mediated Communication* 7, no. 1.

Dahrendorf, Ralf. 1995. *Quadrare il cerchio: Benessere economico, coesione sociale, e libertà politica.* Rome: Laterza.

Dalton, Russell J. 1994. *The Green Rainbow: Environmental Groups in Western Europe.* New Haven, CT: Yale University Press.

della Porta, Donatella. 1995. *Social Movements, Political Violence, and the State.* Cambridge: Cambridge University Press.

———. 1996. *Movimenti collettivi e sistema politico in Italia, 1960–1995.* Rome: Laterza.

———. 1998. "Police Knowledge and Protest Policing: Some Reflections on the Italian Case." In *Policing Protest: The Control of Mass Demonstrations in Western Democracies,* ed. D. della Porta and H. Reiter, 228–51. Minneapolis: University of Minnesota Press.

———. 2001. *I partiti politici.* Bologna: Il Mulino.

———. 2003a. "Ambiente e movimenti sociali globali." Paper presented at the conference "I Conflitti ambientali nella globalizzazione," Florence, Italy.

———. 2003b. *I new global.* Bologna: Il Mulino.

———. 2003c. "Social Movements and Democracy at the Turn of the Millennium." In *Social Movements and Democracy,* ed. P. Ibarra, 105–36. New York: Palgrave Macmillan.

———. 2004. "Multiple Belongings, Flexible Identities, and the Construction of Another Politics: Between the European Social Forum and the Local Social

Fora." In *Transnational Movements and Global Activism*, ed. D. della Porta and S. Tarrow, 175–202. Lanham, MD: Rowman and Littlefield.

della Porta, Donatella, and Massimiliano Andretta. 2002. "Changing Forms of Environmentalism in Italy: The Protest Campaign against the High-Speed Railway System." *Mobilization* 1: 59–77.

della Porta, Donatella, and Mario Diani. 1999. *Social Movements: An Introduction*. Oxford, England: Blackwell.

———. 2004. *Movimenti senza protesta? L'ambientalismo in Italia*. Bologna, Italy: Il Mulino.

———. 2006. *Social Movements: An Introduction*, 2nd ed. Oxford, England: Blackwell.

della Porta, Donatella, and Olivier Fillieule. 2004. "Policing Social Movements." In *Blackwell's Companion on Social Movements*, ed. David A. Snow, Sarah A. Soule, and H. Kriesi, 217–41. Oxford, England: Blackwell.

della Porta, Donatella, and Hanspeter Kriesi. 1999. "Social Movements in a Globalizing World: An Introduction." In *Social Movements in a Globalizing World*, ed. D. della Porta, H. Kriesi and D. Rucht, 3–22. London: Macmillan.

della Porta, Donatella, Abby Peterson, and Herbert Reiter, eds. Forthcoming. *Policing Transnational Protest*. Aldershot, England: Ashgate.

della Porta, Donatella, and Herbert Reiter. 1997. "Police du gouvernement ou des citoyens?" *Cahiers de la sécurité intérieure* 27: 36–57.

———. 1998a. "Introduction: The Policing of Protest in Western Democracies." In *Policing Protest: The Control of Mass Demonstrations in Western Democracies*, ed. D. della Porta and H. Reiter, 1–32. Minneapolis: University of Minnesota Press.

———, eds. 1998b. *Policing Protest: The Control of Mass Demonstrations in Western Democracies*. Minneapolis: University of Minnesota Press.

———. 2003. *Polizia e protesta: Il controllo dell'ordine pubblico in Italia dalla Liberazione ai "noglobal."* Bologna, Italy: Il Mulino.

della Porta, Donatella, and Dieter Rucht. 2002. "The Dynamics of Environmental Campaigns." *Mobilization* 7: 1–14.

DeNardo, James. 1985. *Power in Numbers: The Political Strategy of Protest and Rebellion*. Princeton, NJ: Princeton University Press.

Denza, Eileen. 2002. *The Intergovernmental Pillars of the European Union*. Oxford: Oxford University Press.

Deutscher Bundestag. 2002. *Schlussbericht der Enquete-Kommission Globalisierung der Weltwirtschaft—Herausforderungen und Antworten*. Berlin: Deutscher Bundestag (Drucksache 14/9200).

Diani, Mario. 1995. *Green Networks: A Structural Analysis of the Italian Environmental Movement*. Edinburgh: Edinburgh University Press.

————. 2001. "Social Movement Networks: Virtual and Real." In *Culture and Politics in the Information Age: A New Politics,* ed. F. Webster, 117–28. London: Routledge.

————. 2005. "Cities in the World: Local Civil Society and Global Issues in Britain." In *Transnational Protest and Global Activism,* ed. D. della Porta and S. Tarrow, 65–67. Lanham, MD: Rowman and Littlefield.

Diani, Mario, and Paolo R. Donati. 1998. "Mutamenti organizzativi nei movimenti ambientalisti europei: un modello di analisi." *Quaderni di Scienza Politica* 5: 376–406.

Dines, Nicholas. 1999. "Centri sociali: occupazioni autogestite a Napoli negli anni novanta." *Quaderni di Sociologia* 21: 90–111.

Donnelly, Elizabeth A. 2002. "Proclaiming Jubilee: The Debt and Structural Adjustment Network." In *Restructuring World Politics: Transnational Social Movements, Networks, and Norms,* ed. S. Khagram, J. V. Riker, and K. Sikkink, 155–180. Minneapolis: University of Minnesota Press.

Donner, Frank. 1990. *Protectors of Privilege.* Berkeley: University of California Press.

Driller, Ulrich. 2001. "'Wir können auch anders'—'Wir aber nicht': Möglichkeiten und Grenzen des polizeilichen Konzepts 'Konfliktmanagement' im CASTOR-Einsatz 2001; Entwicklung, Evalution, Diskussion." *Polizei & Wissenschaft* 3: 29–50.

Epstein, Barbara. 2000. "Not Your Parents' Protest." *Dissent* 47, no. 2: 8–11.

Ericson, Richard, and Aaron Doyle. 1999. "Globalization and the Policing of Protest: The Case of APEC 1997." *British Journal of Sociology* 50: 589–608.

EU Network of Independent Experts in Fundamental Rights (CFR-CDF). 2003. *Report on the Situation of Fundamental Rights in the European Union and Its Member States in 2002.* January. At http://europa.eu.int/comm/justice_home/cfr_cdf/doc/rapport_2002_en.pdf.

European Anti-capitalist Left. 2003. *Europe: A Different Europe Is Possible! A Different European Left Is Necessary!* November. At http://www.scottishsocialistparty.org/international/pariseacl03.html.

European Green Parties. 2003. *Statement on a Sustainable Globalization.*

European Social Movements. 2002. *Call of the European Social Movements.* November. At http://www.movsoc.org/htm/tex_art_euromovsoc_engl.htm.

Evans, Peter. 2000. "Fighting Marginalization with Transnational Networks: Counter-Hegemonic Globalization." *Contemporary Sociology* 29: 230–41.

Farnsworth, Kevin. 2004. "Anti-Globalisation, Anti-Capitalism, and the Democratic State." In *Democracy and Participation: Popular Protest and New Social Movements,* ed. M. J. Todd and G. Taylor, 55–77. London: Merlin Press.

Fillieule, Olivier, and Fabrice Ferrier. 2000. "Between Market and the State:

French Environmental Organisations." In *Environmental Movement Organisations in Seven European Union States*, TEA. Interim Report, EC Environment and Climate Research Programme.

Fillieule, Olivier, and Fabien Jobard. 1998. "The Policing of Protest in France: Towards a Model of Protest Policing." In *Policing Protest: The Control of Mass Demonstrations in Western Democracies*, ed. D. della Porta and H. Reiter, 70–90. Minneapolis: University of Minnesota Press.

Finelli, Pietro. 2003. "Un'idea partecipativa della politica: Strutture organizzative e modelli di democrazia in Attac Italia." In *La democrazia dei movimenti: Come decidono i noglobal*, ed. P. Ceri, 31–56. Soveria Mannelli, Italy: Rubbettino.

Fox, Jonathan A., and L. David Brown. 1998. Introduction to *The Struggle for Accountability: The World Bank, NGOs, and Grassroots Movements*, ed. J. A. Fox and L. D. Brown, 1–47. Cambridge, MA: MIT Press.

Freschi, Anna Carola. 2000. "Comunità virtuali e partecipazione: Dall'antagonismo ai nuovi diritti." *Quaderni di Sociologia* 23: 85–109.

———. 2002. *La società dei saperi: Reti virtuali e partecipazione sociale*. Rome: Carocci.

———. 2003. "Dalla rete delle reti al movimento dei movimenti: Gli hacker e l'altra comunicazione." In *Globalizzazione e movimenti sociali*, ed. D. della Porta and L. Mosca, 49–75. Rome: Manifestolibri.

Friberg, Mats, and Bjorn Hettne. 1998. "Local Mobilization and World System Politics." *International Social Science Journal* 117: 341–60.

Fruci, Gian Luca. 2003. "La nuova agorà: I social forum fra spazio pubblico e dinamiche organizzative." In *La democrazia dei movimenti: Come decidono i noglobal*, ed. P. Ceri, 169–95. Soveria Mannelli, Italy: Rubbettino.

Gadner, Gary. 2002. "Religion and Spirituality in the Quest for a Sustainable World." *WorldWatch Paper* 164. At http://www.worldwatch.org/pubs/paper/164.

Gamson, William A. 1988. "Political Discourse and Collective Action." In *From Structure to Action: Comparing Social Movement Research across Cultures*, ed. B. Klandermans, H. Kriesi, and S. Tarrow, 219–44. Greenwich, CT: JAI Press.

———. 1992a. "The Social Psychology of Collective Action." In *Frontiers in Social Movement Theory*, ed. A. D. Morris and C. M. Mueller, 53–76. New Haven, CT: Yale University Press.

———. 1992b. *Talking Politics*. Cambridge: Cambridge University Press.

Garrido, Maria, and Alexander Halavais. 2003. "Mapping Networks of Support for the Zapatista Movement: Applying Social-Networks Analysis to Study Contemporary Social Movements." In *Cyberactivism: Online Activism in*

Theory and Practice, ed. M. McCaughey and M. D. Ayers, 165–84. London: Routledge.

GdP. 2001. *Press Release.* August. At http://www.gdp.de/fred/content-more.cfm ?Loginauftrag=99999&object=GDP&rubrik=Nachrichten&urubrik=&satz =590 (accessed April 2003).

Genoa Legal Forum. 2002. *Dalla parte del torto: Avvocati di strada a Genova.* Genoa: Fratelli Frilli Editori.

Gerhards, Jürgen, and Dieter Rucht. 1992. "Mesomobilization: Organizing and Framing in Two Protest Campaigns in West Germany."*American Journal of Sociology* 98, no. 3: 555–96.

Gerlach, Luther. 1976. "Movements of Revolutionary Change: Some Structural Characteristics." *American Behavioral Scientist* 43: 813–36.

———. 2001. "The Structures of Social Movements: Environmental Activism and Its Opponents." In *Networks and Netwars: The Future of Terror, Crime, and Militancy,* ed. J. Arquila and D. Ronfeldt, 289–309. Santa Monica, CA: Rand.

Geser, Hans. 2001. "On the Functions and Consequences of the Internet for Social Movements and Voluntary Associations." At http://socio.ch/movpar/ t_hgeser3.htm.

Giddens, Anthony. 1990. *The Consequences of Modernity.* Cambridge, England: Polity Press.

Gill, Stephen. 2000. "Toward a Postmodern Prince? The Battle of Seattle as a Moment in the New Politics of Globalisation." *Millennium* 29, no. 1: 131–40.

Gitlin, Todd. 1993. "From Universality to Difference: Notes on Fragmentation of the Idea of the Left." *Contention* 2: 15–40.

Giugni, Marco, and Florence Passy. 2002. "Le champ politique de l'immigration en Europe: Opportunités, mobilisations, et héritage de l'État national." In *L'action collective en Europe,* ed. R. Balme, D. Chabanet, and V. Wright, 433–60. Paris: Presses de Science Po.

Glasius, Marlies. 2002. "Expertise in the Cause of Justice: Global Civil Society Influence on the Statute for an International Criminal Court." In *Global Civil Society 2002,* ed. M. Glasius, M. Kaldor, and H. Anheier, 137–68. Oxford: Oxford University Press.

Glasius, Marlies, and Mary Kaldor. 2002. "The State of Global Civil Society: Before and after September 11." In *Global Civil Society 2002,* ed. M. Glasius, M. Kaldor, and H. Anheier, 3–34. Oxford: Oxford University Press.

Goffman, Erving. 1974. *Frame Analysis: An Essay on the Organization of the Experience.* New York: Harper Colophon.

Granovetter, Mark. 1973. "The Strength of Weak Ties." *American Journal of Sociology* 78, no. 6: 1360–80.

Grazioli, Marco, and Giovanni Lodi. 1984. "Giovani sul territorio urbano: L'integrazione minimale." In *Altri codici: Aree di movimento nella metropoli,* ed. A. Melucci, 63–126. Bologna, Italy: Il Mulino.

Grefe, Christiane, Mathias Greffrath, and Harald Schumann. 2002. *Attac: Was wollen die Globalisierungskritiker?* Berlin: Rowohlt.

Grenier, Paola. 2003. "Jubilee 2000: Laying the Foundations for a Social Movement." In *Globalizing Civic Engagement,* ed. J. Clark, 86–108. London: Earthscan.

Gret, Marion, and Yves Sintomer. 2002. *Porto Alegre : L'éspoir d'un autre démocratie.* Paris: La Découverte.

Griebenow, Olaf, and Heiner Busch. 2001. "Weder Reisefreiheit noch Demonstrationsrecht in der EU?" *Bürgerrechte & Polizei/Cilip* 69, no. 2: 63–69.

GSF (Genoa Social Forum). 2001a. "Document of Presentation and 'Work Agreement.'" At http://www.arci.it/gsf/doc-eng.htm.

———. 2001b. "Genoa Social Forum Call for Action."

———. 2001c. *The GSF on Forms of Mobilization: We will respect the City and no Persons will be attacked.* June. At http://www.arci.it/gsf/press00.htm#eeng.

Gubitosa, Carlo. 2003. *Genova nome per nome: Le violenze, i responsabili, le ragioni; Inchiesta sui giorni e i fatti del G8.* Milan, Italy: Altreconomia, Ed. Berti.

Guidry, John A., Michael D. Kennedy, and Mayer N. Zald, eds. 2000. *Globalization and Social Movements: Culture, Power, and the Transnational Public Sphere.* Ann Arbor: University of Michigan Press.

Guiraudon, Virginie. 2002. "Weak Weapons of the Weak? Transnational Mobilization around Migration in the European Union." In *Contentious Europeans: Protest and Politics in an Emerging Polity,* ed. D. Imig and S. Tarrow, 163–83. Lanham, MD: Rowman and Littlefield.

Gurak, Laura J., and John Logie. 2003. "Internet Protests, from Text to Web." In *Cyberactivism: Online Activism in Theory and Practice,* ed. M. McCaughey and M. D. Ayers, 25–46. London: Routledge.

Haas, Ernst B. 1964. *Beyond the Nation State: Functionalism and International Organisation.* Stanford, CA: Stanford University Press.

Hampton, Keith, and Barry Wellman. 2001. "Long Distance Community in Network Society: Contact and Support Beyond Netville." *American Behavioral Scientist* 45, no. 3: 476–95.

Hayes, Ben, and Tony Bunyan. 2004. "L'Union européenne face a la 'menace interne' Altermondialiste." In *Forum mondiale des alternatives: Centre Tricontinental, Mondialisation des résistances; L'état des luttes 2004,* 271–83. Paris: Edition Syllepse.

Haythornthwaite, Caroline. 2001a. "The Internet in Everyday Life." *American Behavioral Scientist* 45, no. 3: 363–82.

———. 2001b. "Tie Strength and the Impact of New Media." Paper presented at the Hawaii International Conference on System Sciences, Honolulu.

Held, David, and Anthony McGrew. 2000. *The Global Transformation Reader: An Introduction to the Globalization Debate.* Cambridge, England: Polity Press.

Held, David, Anthony McGrew, David Goldblatt, and Jonathan Perraton. 1999. *Global Transformations.* Cambridge, England: Polity Press.

Hick, Steven, and John McNutt. 2002. "Communities and Advocacy on the Internet: A Conceptual Framework." In *Advocacy, Activism, and the Internet,* ed. S. Hick and J. McNutt, 3–18. Chicago: Lyceum Books.

Hill, Kevin A., and John E. Hughes. 1998. *Cyberpolitics: Citizen Activism in the Age of the Internet.* Lanham, MD: Rowman and Littlefield.

Hirst, Paul. 1994. *Associative Democracy: New Forms of Economic and Social Governance.* Cambridge, England: Polity Press.

Hollande, François. 2002. *Declaration on the Florence European Social Forum.*

———. 2003. *Declaration at the Paris European Social Forum.*

Howard, Philip N., Lee Rainie, and Steve Jones. 2001. "Days and Nights on the Internet: The Impact of a Diffusing Technology." *American Behavioral Scientist* 45, no. 3: 383–404.

Human Rights Committee. 2002. *Consideration of Reports Submitted by States Parties under Article 40 of the Covenant: Concluding Observations of the Human Rights Committee on the Fifth Periodic Report of Sweden.* April. At http://www .humanrights.se/svenska/Concluding%20observ%20MP0204.pdf.

Hunt, Scott A., and Robert D. Benford. 1994. "Identity Talk in the Peace and Justice Movement." *Journal of Contemporary Ethnology* 22: 488–517.

Hunt, Scott A., Robert D. Benford, and David A. Snow. 1994. "Identity Fields: Framing Processes and the Social Construction of Movement Identities." In *New Social Movements,* ed. E. Laraña, H. Johnston, J. Gusfield, 183–208. Philadelphia: Temple University Press.

Imig, Doug, and Sidney Tarrow. 2001. "La contestation politique dans l'Europe en formation." In *L'action collective en Europe,* ed. R. Balme, D. Chabanet, and R. Wright, 195–223. Paris: Presses de Science Po.

Inglehart, Ronald. 1977. *The Silent Revolution: Changing Values and Political Styles among Western Publics.* Princeton, NJ: Princeton University Press.

IPIC (Italian Parliamentary Investigative Commission). 2001a. "The Events Which Occurred in Genoa on the Days 19th, 20th, 21st, and 22nd July 2001 in Occasion of the G8 Summit." *Report I: Final Document.* September 20. At http://www.camera.it.

———. 2001b. "The Events Which Occurred in Genoa on the Days 19th, 20th, 21st, and 22nd July 2001 in Occasion of the G8 Summit." *Report II: Alterna-*

tive Proposal to the Final Document Presented by Deputy Luciano Violante et al.
September 20. At http://www.camera.it.

———. 2001c. "The Events Which Occurred in Genoa on the Days 19th, 20th,
21st, and 22nd July 2001 in Occasion of the G8 Summit." *Report III: Alternative Proposal to the Final Document, Presented by Deputy Graziella Mascia.*
September 20. At http://www.camera.it.

———. 2001d. *Minutes of the Hearing.* August 8. At http://www.camera.it.

———. 2001e. *Minutes of the Hearing.* August 9. At http://www.camera.it.

———. 2001f. *Minutes of the Hearing.* August 28. At http://www.camera.it.

———. 2001g. *Minutes of the Hearing.* August 29. At http://www.camera.it.

———. 2001h. *Minutes of the Hearing.* September 4. At http://www.camera.it.

———. 2001i. *Minutes of the Hearing.* September 5. At http://www.camera.it.

———. 2001j. *Minutes of the Hearing.* September 6. At http://www.camera.it.

———. 2001k. *Minutes of the Hearing.* September 7. At http://www.camera.it.

Jasper, James M. 1997. *The Art of Moral Protest: Culture, Biography, and Creativity
in Social Movements.* Chicago: University of Chicago Press.

Jenkins, J. Craig. 1983. "The Transformation of a Constituency into a Movement." In *Social Movements of the Sixties and Seventies,* ed. J. Freeman,
52–70. New York: Longman.

Jiménez, Manuel. 2000. "Organising the Defence of the Environment: Spanish
Ecologist Groups in the 1990s." In *Environmental Movement Organisations
in Seven European Union States,* TEA. Interim Report, EC Environment and
Climate Research Programme.

———. 2002. "Public Identity and Coalition Building Process: The Antiglobalization Movement in Spain." Paper presented at the "Transnational Processes
and Social Movements" conference, Bellagio, Italy.

Johnson, Victoria. 1997. "Operation Rescue, Vocabularies of Motive, and
Tactical Action: A Study of Movement Framing in the Practice of Quasi-
Nonviolence." *Research on Social Movements, Conflict and Change* 20:
103–50.

Johnston, Hank. 1995. "A Methodology for Frame Analysis: From Discourse to
Cognitive Schemata." In *Social Movements and Culture,* ed. H. Johnston and
B. Klandermans, 217–46. Minneapolis: University of Minnesota Press.

———. 2002. "Verification and Proof in Frame and Discourse Analysis." In
Methods of Social Movement Research, ed. B. Klandermans and S. Staggen-
borg, 62–91. Minneapolis: University of Minnesota Press.

Johnston, Hank, and Aili Aarelaid-Tart. 2000. "Generations, Microcohorts, and
Long-Term Mobilization: The Estonian National Movement, 1940–1991."
Sociological Perspectives 43: 671–98.

Jordan, Grant, and William A. Maloney. 1997. *The Protest Business*. Manchester, England: Manchester University Press.

Jordan, Tim. 2002. *Activism! Direct Action, Hacktivism, and the Future of Society*. London: Reaktion Books.

Jospin, Lionel. 2001. *Managing Globalization*. [Maîtriser la mondialisation]. April. At http://www.psinfo.net/entretiens/jospin/bresil.html.

Justitiedepartementet Betänkande av Göteborgskommittén. 2001. *Betänkande av Göteborgskommittén: Summary*. At http://www.regeringen.se/content/1/c4/38/16/6d1e4dcc.pdf.

Kaldor, Mary. 2000. "'Civilizing' Globalization? The Implication of the 'Battle in Seattle.'" *Millennium* 29: 100–114.

Katz, James A., Ronald E. Rice, and Philip Aspden. 2001. "The Internet, 1995–2000: Access, Civic Involvement, and Social Interaction." *American Behavioral Scientist* 45, no. 3: 405–20.

Katz, Richard, and Peter Mair, eds. 1992. *How Parties Organize: Change and Adaptation in Party Organizations in Western Democracies, 1960–1990*. London: Sage.

Keck, Margeret, and Kathryn Sikkink. 1998. *Activists beyond Borders*. Ithaca, NY: Cornell University Press.

Khagram, Sanjeev. 2002. "Restructuring the Global Politics of Development: The Case of India's Narmada Valley Dams." In *Restructuring World Politics: Transnational Social Movements, Networks, and Norms*, ed. S. Khagram, J. V. Riker, and K. Sikkink, 206–30. Minneapolis: University of Minnesota Press.

Khagram, Sanjeev, Jamev V. Riker, and Kathryn Sikkink, eds. 2002. *Reconstructing World Politics: Transnational Social Movements, Networks, and Norms*. Minneapolis: University of Minnesota Press.

Kidder, Thalia G. 2002. "Networks in Transnational Labor Organizing." In *Reconstructing World Politics: Transnational Social Movements, Networks, and Norms*, ed. S. Khagram, J. V. Riker, and K. Sikkink, 269–93. Minneapolis: University of Minnesota Press.

Kitschelt, Herbert. 1993. "Social Movements, Political Parties, and Democratic Theory." *Annals of the AAPSS* 528: 13–29.

Klandermans, Bert. 1992. "The Social Construction of Protest and Multiorganizational Fields." In *Frontiers in Social Movement Theory*, ed. A. Morris and C. Mueller, 77–103. New Haven, CT: Yale University Press.

Klein, Naomi. 2001. *No Logo*. London: Flamingo.

———. 2002. *Fences and Windows: Dispatches from the Front Lines of the Globalization Debate*. London: Flamingo.

Klotz, Audie. 1995. *Norms in International Relations: The Struggle against Apartheid*. Ithaca, NY: Cornell University Press.

Kolb, Felix. 2005. "The Impact of Transnational Protest on Social Movement Organizations: Mass Media and the Making of ATTAC Germany." In *Transnational Protest and Global Activism*, ed. D. della Porta and S. Tarrow, 96–120. Lanham, MD: Rowman and Littlefield.

Koopmans, Ruud, and Ann Zimmermann. 2003. "Internet: A New Potential for European Political Communication?" Discussion Paper SP IV 2003–402. Wissenschaftszentrum Berlin für Sozialforschung (WZB).

Kriesi, Hanspeter. 1989. "The Political Opportunity Structure of the Dutch Peace Movement." *West European Politics* 12: 295–312.

———. 1993. "Sviluppo organizzativo dei movimenti sociali e contesto politico." *Rivista Italiana di Scienza Politica* 23: 309–33.

———. 1996. "The Organizational Structure of New Social Movements in a Political Context." In *Comparative Perspective on Social Movements: Political Opportunities, Mobilizing Structures, and Cultural Framing*, ed. D. McAdam, J. McCarthy, and M. N. Zald, 152–84. Cambridge: Cambridge University Press.

Kruskal, Joseph B., and Myron Wish. 1978. *Multidimensional Scaling*. Beverly Hills, CA: Sage.

Latouche, Serge. 1989. *L'occidentalisation du monde: Essai sur la signification, la portée et les limites de l'uniformisation planétaire*. Paris: La Découverte.

Lawrence, Elizabeth. 2004. "Trade Unions." In *Democracy and Participation: Popular Protest and New Social Movements*, ed. M. J. Todd and G. Taylor, 135–57. London: Merlin Press.

Lebert, Joanne. 2003. "Wiring Human Rights Activism: Amnesty International and the Challenge of Information and Communication Technologies." In *Cyberactivism: Online Activism in Theory and Practice*, ed. M. McCaughey and M. D. Ayers, 209–31. London: Routledge.

Left European Parties. 2003. *A New Dynamic for Another Europe*. November. At http://www.pcf.fr/docs/telecharger/2227Appel.rtf.

Leonardi, Laura. 2001. *La dimensione sociale della globalizzazione*. Rome: Carocci.

Les Verts. 2000. *De Seattle à Davos: La société civile demande des comptes* [From Seattle to Davos: Civil Society Claim the Bill]. January. At http://www.lesverts.fr/article.php3?id_article=771.

Levi, Margaret, and David Olson. 2000. "The Battles in Seattle." *Politics and Society* 28, no. 3: 309–29.

Lichterman, Paul. 1996. *The Search for Political Community*. Cambridge: Cambridge University Press.

Lipsky, Michael. 1965. *Protest and City Politics*. Chicago: Rand McNally.

Livezy, Lois. 1989. "U.S. Religious Organizations and the International Human Rights Movement." *Human Rights Quarterly* 11, no. 1: 14–81.

Manin, Bernard. 1993. *La democrazia dei moderni*. Milan, Italy: Anabasi.

Marcon, Giulio, and Mario Pianta. 2002. "Porto Alegre-Europa: I percorsi dei movimenti globali." In *Mappe di movimenti: Da Porto Alegre al Forum Sociale Europeo*, Lunaria, 5–33. Trieste, Italy: Asterios Editore.

Margolis, Michael, and David Resnick. 2000. *Politics as Usual: The Cyberspace "Revolution."* Thousand Oaks, CA: Sage.

Marino, Giuseppe Carlo. 1995. *La repubblica della forza: Mario Scelba e le passioni del suo tempo.* Milan, Italy: Angeli.

Marks, Gary, and Doug McAdam. 1999. "On the Relationship of the Political Opportunities to the Form of Collective Action." In *Social Movements in a Globalizing World*, ed. D. della Porta, H. Kriesi, and D. Rucht, 97–111. New York: Macmillan.

Marradi, Claudio, and Enrico Ratto. 2001. *Da Seattle a Genova: Gli 8 non valgono una moltitudine.* Genoa: Fratelli Frilli Editori.

Martínez López, Miguel. 2002. *Okupaciones de viviendas y de centros sociales: Autogestión, contracultura, y conflictos urbanos.* Barcelona: Virus Editorial.

Marullo, Sam, Ron Pagnucco, and Jackie Smith. 1996. "Frame Changes and Social Movement Contraction: U.S. Peace Movement Framing after the Cold War." *Sociological Inquiry* 66: 1–28.

Mathiesen, Thomas. 2002. "Expanding the Concept of Terrorism?" In *Beyond September 11: An Anthology of Dissent*, ed. P. Scraton, 84–93. London: Pluto Press.

Mazey, Sonia, and Jeremy Richardson. 1993. *Lobbying in the European Union.* Oxford: Oxford University Press.

McAdam, Doug, John McCarthy, and Mayer N. Zald, eds. 1996. *Comparative Perspective on Social Movements, Political Opportunities, Mobilizing Structures, and Cultural Framing.* Cambridge: Cambridge University Press.

McAdam, Doug, Sidney Tarrow, and Charles Tilly. 2001. *Dynamics of Contention.* Cambridge: Cambridge University Press.

McCarthy, John. 1994. "Activists, Authorities, and Media Framing of Drunk Driving." In *New Social Movements*, ed. E. Laraña, H. Johnston, and J. Gusfield, 133–67. Philadelphia: Temple University Press.

McCarthy, John, and Mayer N. Zald. 1973. *The Trend of Social Movements in America: Professionalization and Resource Mobilization.* Morristown, NJ: General Learning Press.

———. 1977. "Resource Mobilization and Social Movements: A Partial Theory." *American Journal of Sociology* 82: 1212–41.

McChesney, Robert W. 1996. "The Internet and U.S. Communication Policy-Making in Historical and Critical Perspective." *Journal of Communication* 46, no. 1: 98–124.

McPhail, Clark, David Schweingruber, and John McCarthy. 1998. "Policing Protest in the United States, 1960–1995." In *Policing Protest: The Control of Mass Demonstrations in Western Democracies*, ed. D. della Porta and H. Reiter, 49–69. Minneapolis: University of Minnesota Press.

Melucci, Alberto. 1989. *Nomads of the Present*. London: Hutchinson Radius.

———. 1996. *Challenging Codes*. Cambridge: Cambridge University Press.

Members of International Civil Society. 1999. *Statement from Members of International Civil Society Opposing a Millennium Round or a New Round of Comprehensive Trade Negotiations*. August. At http://www.twnside.org.sg/title/wtomr-cn.htm.

Meyer-Falk, Thomas. 2003. *Genoa 2001 and the Eu Parliament* [Genua 2001 und das EU Parlament]. October. At http://de.indymedia.org/2003/10/63175.shtml.

Micheletti, Michele. 2003. *Political Virtue and Shopping: Individuals, Consumerism, and Collective Action*. New York: Palgrave Macmillan.

Mies, Maria. 2002. *Globalisierung von unten: Der Kampf gegen die Herrschaft der Konzerne*. Hamburg, Germany: Europäische Verlagsanstalt.

Moody, Kim. 1997. *Workers in a Lean World*. London: Verso.

Moravcsik, Andrew. 1999. *The Choice for Europe*. Ithaca, NY: Cornell University Press.

Morgan, Jane. 1987. *Conflict and Order: The Police and Labour Disputes in England and Wales, 1900–1939*. Oxford, England: Clarendon Press.

Morse, David. 2001. "Beyond the Myths of Seattle." *Dissent* 48, no. 3: 39–43.

Mosca, Lorenzo. 2003. "Transnational Protest Activists and the Use of the Internet: Hypothesis and Evidences from a Research on the European Social Forum." Paper presented at the "Transnational Processes and Social Movements" conference, Bellagio, Italy.

Mouffe, Chantal. 1996. "Radical Democracy or Liberal Democracy?" In *Radical Democracy*, ed. D. Trend, 19–26. London: Routledge.

Mowjee, Tasneem. 2003. "Campaign to Increase Access to HIV/AIDS Drugs." In *Globalizing Civic Engagement*, ed. J. Clark, 66–85. London: Earthscan.

Müller, Christoph. 2002. "Online Communities in a 'Glocal' Context." Paper presented at the third international conference of the Association of Internet Researchers, Maastricht, Netherlands.

Myers, Daniel J. 2001. "Social Activism through Computer Networks." In *Computing in the Social Sciences and Humanities*, ed. O. V. Burton, 124–39. Urbana: University of Illinois Press.

Neidhardt, Friedhelm, and Dieter Rucht. 1991. "The Analysis of Social Movements: The State of the Art and Some Perspectives for Further Research." In *Research on Social Movements: The State of the Art in Western Europe and the*

USA, ed. D. Rucht, 421–64. Frankfurt am Main: Campus and Westview Press.

———. 1993. Auf dem Weg in die 'Bewe gungsgesellschaft'? Über die Stabilisierbarkeit sozialer Bewegungen." *Soziale Welt* 44: 305–26.

Nepstad, Sharon E. 1997. "The Process of Cognitive Liberation: Cultural Synapses, Links and Frame Contradictions in US–Central America Peace Movement." *Sociological Inquiry* 67: 470–87.

Neveau, Erik. 2000. *Sociologie des mouvements sociaux.* Paris: La Découverte & Syros.

New Labour. 2004. *Our Policies: Foreign Affairs.* June. At http://www.labour.org .uk/foreignaffairs04.

Nicholson, Michael. 1998. *International Relations: A Concise Introduction.* New York: New York University Press.

Nie, Norman H. 2001. "Sociability, Interpersonal Relations, and the Internet." *American Behavioral Scientist* 45, no. 3: 420–35.

Nord-Süd-Kommission. 1980. *Das Überleben sichern: Gemeinsame Interessen der Industrie- und Entwicklungsländer (Bericht der Nord-Süd-Kommission).* Cologne, Germany: Kiepenheuer & Witsch.

Norris, Pippa. 2001. *Digital Divide: Civic Engagement, Information Poverty, and the Internet Worldwide.* Cambridge: Cambridge University Press.

Notobartolo, Alberto. 2001. *I giorni di Genova.* Rome: Internazionale.

Obershall, Anthony. 1973. *Social Conflict and Social Movements.* Englewood Cliffs, NJ: Prentice-Hall.

O'Brien, Robert. 1999. "Social Change Activism and the Internet: Strategic Online Activities." At http://www.web.net/~robrien/papers/netaction.html.

O'Brien, Robert, Anne Marie Goetz, Jaan Aart Scholte, and Marc Williams. 2000. *Contesting Global Governance: Multilateral Economic Institutions and Global Social Movements.* Cambridge: Cambridge University Press.

O'Connor, Jim. 2000. "Die Konferenz von Seattle und die Anti-WTO-Bewegung." *PROKLA: Zeitschrift für kritische Sozialwissenschaft* 30, no. 118: 157–70.

Offe, Carl. 1985. "New Social Movements: Changing Boundaries of the Political." *Social Research* 52: 817–68.

Oliver, Pamela, and Hank Johnston. 2000. "What a Good Idea! Frames and Ideology in Social Movement Research." *Mobilization* 5: 50–65.

Oliviero, Melanie Beth, and Adele Simmons. 2002. "Who's Minding the Store? Global Civil Society and Corporate Responsibility." In *Global Civil Society 2002,* ed. M. Glasius, M. Kaldor, and H. Anheier, 77–108. Oxford: Oxford University Press.

Olson, Mancur. 1963. *The Logic of Collective Action.* Cambridge, MA: Harvard University Press.

Pagnucco, Ron. 1996. "Social Movement Dynamics during Democratic Transition and Consolidation: A Synthesis of Political Process and Political Interactionist Theories." *Research on Democracy and Society* 3: 3–38.

Park, Euyn. 2002. "'Net' Profit of the Nonprofits." Ph.D. diss., Cornell University, Ithaca, NY.

Party of European Socialists. 2003. *Europe and a New Global Order: Bridging the Global Divides.* May. At http://www.pes.org/upload/publications/74ENPES%20Rasmussen_28_05_2003.pdf.

Passy, Florence. 1999. "Supranational Political Opportunities as a Channel of Globalization of Political Conflicts: The Case of the Rights of Indigenous People." In *Social Movements in a Globalizing World,* ed. D. della Porta, H. Kriesi, and D. Rucht, 148–69. London: Macmillan Press.

Pastor, Jaime. 2002. *Qué son los movimientos antiglobalización.* Barcelona, Spain: RBA Libros.

PCE. 2002. *Neoliberal Globalization: Which Alternatives to Promote from the Left* [La globalización neoliberal: Qué alternativas impulsar desde la izquierda]. March. At http://www.pce.es/xvicongreso/globa_neoliberal.htm.

PCF. 2003. *Statement on Neoliberal Globalization.*

Peers, Steve. 2000. *EU Justice and Home Affairs Law.* Harlow, England: Longman.

Pepino, Livio. 2001. "Obiettivo: Genova e il G8; I fatti, le istituzioni, la giustizia," *Questione Giustizia* 5. 881–915.

Peterson, Abby. 2003. "Contentious Politics and Transnational Summits: Reconnaissance Battles in the Frontier Land." Paper prepared at the Congress of the European Sociological Association, Murcia, Spain.

Peterson, Abby, and Mikael Oskarsson. 2002. "Policing Political Protest: A Study of the Police Handling of Protest Events in Conjunction with the EU Summit Meeting in Göteborg." Unpublished manuscript, University of Gothenburg.

Pfeil, Andreas. 2000. "Lehren aus Seattle." *Blätter für deutsche und internationale Politik* 45, no. 1: 15–28.

Pianta, Mario. 2001. *Globalizzazione dal basso: Economia mondiale e movimenti sociali.* Rome: Manifestolibri.

———. 2002. "Parallel Summits: An Update." In *Global Civil Society,* ed. H. K. Anheier, M. Glasius, and M. Kaldor, 371–77. Oxford: Oxford University Press.

Pianta, Mario, and Federico Silva. 2003. *Globalisers from Below: A Server on Global Civil Society Organisations.* GLOBI Research Report.

Piedmont Regional Branch of the Network for Global Rights. 2001. *Remark: We Don't Adhere to the GSF* [Precisazione: non aderiamo al GSF]. June. At http://it.groups.yahoo.com/group/NetworkcontroG8/message/155 (subscription to mailing-list required).

Pink Silver March. 2001. *Tactical Frivolity "Dance down the G8!!"*. July. At http://www.ngvision.org/mediabase/24.

Piven, Francis Fox, and Richard A. Cloward. 2000. "Power Repertoires and Globalization." *Politics and Society* 28: 413–30.

Pizzorno, Alessandro. 1977. "Scambio politico e identità collettiva nel conflitto di classe." In *Conflitti in Europa: Lotte di classe, sindacati e stato dopo il '68,* ed. C. Crouch and A. Pizzorno, 407–33. Milan, Italy: Etas Libri.

———. 1981. "Interests and Parties in Pluralism." In *Organizing Interests in Western Europe,* ed. S. Berger, 3–46. Cambridge: Cambridge University Press.

———. 1993. *Le radici della politica assoluta.* Milan, Italy: Feltrinelli.

———. 1996. "Mutamentis istituzioni e sviluppo dei partiti." In *La storia dell'Europa Contemporanea,* ed. P. Bairoch and E. J. Hobsbawm, 961–1031. Turin, Italy: Einaudi.

———. 2001. "Natura della disuguaglianza, potere politico, e potere privato nella società in via di globalizzazione." *Stato e Mercato* 2: 201–36.

Price, Richard. 1998. "Reversing the Gun Sights: Transnational Civil Society Targets Land Mines." *International Organizations* 52, no. 3: 631–44.

Princen, Thomas, and Matthias Finger. 1994. "Introduction." *Environmental NGOs in World Politics: Linking the Local and the Global,* ed. T. Princen and M. Finger, 1–25. London: Routledge.

PSF. 2001. *Statement on Genoa's G8 Summit.* [Le sommet de Gênes]. Press release. July 23.

RC. 2003. *Appeal to Alternative Forum "For a Social Europe"* [Appello Forum alternativo "Per un'Europa sociale"]. September. At http://www.rifondazione.it/ad/movimenti/Gats/documenti/Riva_del_Garda_2003.html.

Reimon, Michel. 2002. *Days of Action: Die neoliberale Globalisierung und ihre Gegner.* Vienna: Überreuter.

Reising, Uwe. 1999. "United in Opposition? A Cross-National Time-Series of European Protest in Three Selected Countries, 1980–1995." *Journal of Conflict Resolution* 43: 317–42.

Rete Lilliput. 1999. *Manifesto.* September. At http://www.retelilliput.it/index.php?module=ContentExpress&func=display&ceid=10&meid=.

———. 2001. *Strategies towards Genoa G8 Summit* [Strategie in vista del G8 di Genova]. May. At http://www.retelilliput.org/documenti/GenovaG8/STRATEGIE.rtf (accessed on June 2002).

———. 2002. *Shared Basic Values* [Criteri di fondo condivisi]. January. At http://www.retelilliput.it/index.php?module=ContentExpress&func=display&ceid=34&meid=.

Riddel-Dixon, Elizabeth. 1995. "Social Movements and the United Nations." *International Social Science Journal* 144: 289–303.

Risse, Thomas, and Kathryn Sikkink. 1999. "The Socialization of International Human Rights Norms into Domestic Practices: Introduction." In *The Power of Human Rights International Norms and Domestic Change*, ed. T. Risse, S. Rapp, and K. Sikkink, 1–38. New York: Cambridge University Press.

Ritzer, George. 1996. *The McDonaldization of Society: An Investigation into the Changing Character of Contemporary Social Life*. Thousand Oaks, CA: Pine Forge Press.

Robertson, Roland. 1992. *Globalization: Social Theory and Global Culture*. London: Sage.

Rochon, Thomas R. 1998. *Culture Moves: Ideas, Activism, and Changing Values*. Princeton, NJ: Princeton University Press.

Rodríguez, Mauro. 2003. "The Globalization of Globalizing Solidarity: Setting the Scene for the General Assembly." At http://www.caritas.org/upload/G/Globalis-1ng.9xd1.pdf.

Rootes, Christopher A. 2002. "The Europeanization of Environmentalism." In *L'action collective en Europe*, ed. R. Balme, D. Chabanel, and R. Wright, 377–404. Paris: Presses de Science Po.

———, ed. 2003. *Environmental Protest in Western Europe*. Oxford: Oxford University Press.

———. 2005. "A Limited Transnationalization? The British Environmental Movement." In *Transnational Protest and Global Activism*, ed. D. della Porta and S. Tarrow, 21–43. Lanham, MD: Rowman and Littlefield.

Rootes, Christopher A., Ben Seel, and David Adams. 2000. "The Old and the New: British Environmental Organisations from Conservationism to Radical Ecologism." In *Environmental Movement Organisations in Seven European Union States*, TEA. Interim Report, EC Environment and Climate Research Programme.

Roth, Roland. 2001. "NGOs und transnationale soziale Bewegungen: Akteure einer *Weltzivilgesellschaft*?" In *Nichtregierungsorganisationen in der Transformation des Staates*, ed. U. Brand, A. Demirovic, Ch. Goerg, and J. Hirsch, 43–63. Münster, Germany: Westfälisches Dampfboot.

Rucht, Dieter. 1994. *Modernisierung und Soziale Bewegungen*. Frankfurt am Main, Germany: Campus.

———. 1996. "Multinationale Bewegungsorganisationen: Bedeutung, Bedingungen, Perspektiven." *Forschungsjournal Neue Soziale Bewegungen* 9, no. 2: 30–41.

———. 1999. "The Transnationalization of Social Movements: Trends, Causes,

Problems." In *Social Movements in a Globalizing World,* ed. D. della Porta, H. Kriesi, and D. Rucht, 206–22. London: Macmillan Press.

———. 2001. "Transnationaler politischer Protest im historischen Längsschnitt." In *Politische Partizipation im Zeitalter der Globalisierung,* ed. A. Klein, R. Koopmans, and H. Geiling, 77–96. Opladen, Germany: Leske + Budrich.

———. 2002a. "The EU as Target of Political Mobilization: Is There a Europeanization of Conflict?" In *L'action collective en Europe,* ed. R. Balme, D. Chabanet, and R. Wright, 163–94. Paris: Presses de Science Po.

———. 2002b. "Herausforderungen für die globalisierungskritischen Bewegungen." *Forschungsjournal Neue soziale Bewegungen* 15, no. 1: 16–21.

———. 2002c. "Rückblicke und Ausblicke auf die globalisierungskritischen Bewegungen." In *Transnationale Protestnetzwerke,* ed. H. Walk and N. Böhme, 57–81. Münster, Germany: Westfälisches Dampfboot.

———. 2003. "Media Strategies and Media Resonance in Transnational Protest Campaigns." Paper presented at the "Transnational Processes and Social Movements" conference, Bellagio, Italy.

———. 2004. "The Quadruple 'A': Media Strategies of Protest Movements since the 1960s." In *New Media, Citizens, and Social Movements,* ed. W. Van de Donk, B. D. Loader, P. G. Nixon, and D. Rucht, 29–56. London: Routledge.

Rucht, Dieter, and Jochen Roose. 2000. "Neither Decline nor Sclerosis: The Organizational Structure of the German Environmental Movement." In *Environmental Movement Organisations in Seven European Union States,* TEA. Interim Report, EC Environment and Climate Research Programme.

Russett, Bruce, and Harvey Starr. 1996. *World Politics: The Menu for Choice.* New York: W. H. Freeman.

Salter, Lee. 2003. "Democracy, New Social Movements, and the Internet: A Habermasian Analysis." In *Cyberactivism: Online Activism in Theory and Practice,* ed. M. McCaughey and M. D. Ayers, 117–44. London: Routledge.

Scateni, Luciano. 2003. *Vite disobbedienti: Don Vitaliano Della Sala e Francesco Caruso: Autobiografie parallele.* Naples, Italy: Intra Moenia.

Scharpf, Fritz W. 1997. "The Problem Solving Capacity of Multi-Level Governance." Working Paper, Robert Schuman Center, Florence, Italy: European University Institute.

Schmidt, Hilmar, and Ingo Take. 1997. "Demokratischer und besser? Der Beitrag von Nichtregierungsorganisationen zur Demokratisierung internationaler Politik und zur Lösung globaler Probleme." *Aus Politik und Zeitgeschichte* 43: 12–20.

Schneider, Volker. 2000. "The Global Social Capital of Human Rights Movements: A Case Study on Amnesty International." In *Private Organizations in Global Politics,* ed. K. Ronit and V. Schneider, 146–64. London: Routledge.

Schönleitner, Gunther. 2003. "World Social Forum: Making Another World Possible?" In *Globalizing Civic Engagement: Civil Society and Transnational Action*, ed. J. Clark, 109–26. London: Earthscan.

Seattle Police Department. 2000. *The Seattle Police Department After Action Report: World Trade Organization Ministerial Conference Seattle, Washington, November 29–December 3, 1999.* Seattle, Washington. At http://www.cityofseattle.net/spd/SPDMainsite/wto/spdwtoaar.htm.

Shaw, Martin. 1994. "Civil Society and Global Politics: Beyond a Social Movement Approach." *Millennium* 23, no. 3: 647–67.

Sheptycki, James W. E. 1994. "Law Enforcement, Justice, and Democracy in the Transnational Arena: Reflections on the War on Drugs." *International Jour nal of the Sociology of Law* 24, no. 1: 61–75.

Shoch, James. 2000. "Contesting Globalization: Organized Labor, NAFTA, and the 1997 and 1998 Fast-Track Fights." *Politics and Society* 28, no. 1: 119–50.

Sikkink, Kathryn. 1993. "Human Rights, Principled Issue-Networks, and Sovereignty in Latin America." *International Organization* 47: 411–41.

———, 2002. "Reconstructing World Politics: The Limits and Asymmetries of Soft Power." In *Reconstructing World Politics: Transnational Social Movements, Networks, and Norms*, ed. S. Khagram, J. V. Riker, and K. Sikkink, 301–17. Minneapolis: University of Minnesota Press.

———. 2005. "Patterns of Dynamic Multilevel Governance and the Insider-Outsider Coalition." In *Transnational Protest and Global Activism*, ed. D. della Porta and S. Tarrow, 151–76. Lanham, MD: Rowman and Littlefield.

Sikkink, Kathryn, and Jackie Smith 2002. "Infrastructures for Change: Transnational Organizations, 1953–1993." In *Reconstructing World Politics: Transnational Social Movements, Networks, and Norms*, ed. S. Khagram, J. V. Riker, and K. Sikkink, 24–44. Minneapolis: University of Minnesota Press.

SIULP. 2001. *G8: Siulp to GSF, Necessity to Dialogue but without Prejudices* [G8: Siulp a GSF, necessità di dialogo ma senza pregiudizi]. July. At http://www.siulp.it/sez/flash.asp?TipoFunzione=VisSched&IDOggetto=1177&Anno=2001.

Sklair, Laskie. 1995. "Social Movements and Global Capitalism." *Sociology* 29: 495–512.

Smelser, Neil J. 1962. *Theory of Collective Behavior.* New York: Free Press.

Smith, Jackie. 1995. "Transnational Political Processes and the Human Rights Movement." *Research in Social Movements, Conflict and Change* 18: 187–221.

———. 1997. "Characteristics of the Modern Transnational Social Movement Sector." In *Transnational Social Movements and Global Politics: Solidarity beyond the State*, ed. J. Smith, C. Chatfield, and R. Pagnucco, 42–58. Syracuse, NY: Syracuse University Press.

————. 2001. "Globalizing Resistance: The Battle of Seattle and the Future of Social Movements." *Mobilization* 6: 1–20.

Smith, Jackie, Ron Pagnucco, and Winnie Romeril. 1994. "Transnational Social Movement Organisations in the Global Political Arena." *Voluntas* 5: 121–54.

Snow, David A., and Robert Benford. 1988. "Ideology, Frame Resonance, and Participant Mobilization." In *From Structure to Action,* ed. B. Klandermans, H. Kriesi, and S. Tarrow, 197–218. Greenwich, CT: JAI Press.

————. 1992. "Master Frames and Cycles of Protest." In *Frontiers in Social Movement Theory,* ed. A. Morris and C. Mueller, 133–55. New Haven, CT: Yale University Press.

————. 2000. "Mobilization Forum: Comments on Oliver and Johnston." *Mobilization* 5: 55–60.

Snow, David A., E. Burke Rochford, Steven Worden, and Robert D. Benford. 1986. "Frame Alignment. Processes, Micromobilization, and Movement Participation." *American Sociological Review* 51: 464–81.

Socialist International. 1999. *General Resolution of the Congress* [Resolution generale du congrès]. November. At http://www.socialistinternational .org/5Congress/XXISICONGRESS/resolution-f.html.

Socialist International Council. 1998. *Declarations and Resolutions: To Regulate Globalization and to Globalise Regulation.* November. At http://www .socialistinternational.org/6Meetings/Council/Geneva-Nov98/ SICounGeneva-e1.html#1b.

Somers, Margeret R. 1992. "Narrativity, Narrative Identity, and Social Action: Rethinking English Working Class Formation." *Social Science History* 16: 591–630.

SPD. 2001. *Organizing Globalization in a Human Dimension* [Globalisierung menschlich gestalten]. December. At http://www.spd-berlin.de/FA1/ Dokumente/bpt01a1.htm.

————. 2003. *Comment on the WTO Meeting in Cancún.*

SPD and German Greens. 2003. *Parliamentary Motion on WTO Policies.*

Starhawk. 1999. *How We Really Shut Down the WTO.* December. At http:// www.nadir.org/nadir/initiativ/agp/free/seattle/starhawk.htm.

Steinmetz, George. 1992. "Reflections on the Role of Social Narratives in Working-Class Formation: Narrative Theory in the Social Sciences." *Social Science History* 16: 489–516.

Strang, David, and John W. Meyer. 1993. "Institutional Conditions for Diffusion." *Theory and Society* 22: 487–511.

Strange, Susan. 1989. "Toward a Theory of Transnational Empire." In *Global Change and Theoretical Challenges,* ed. E. O. Czempiel and J. N. Rosenau, 161–76. Lexington, CT: Lexington Books.

Stubbs, Paul. 1998. "Conflict and Co-operation in the Virtual Community: Email and the Wars of the Yugoslav Succession." *Sociological Research Online* 3, no. 3. At http://www.socresonline.org.uk/socresonline/3/3/7.html.

Sunstein, Cass. 2001. *Republic.com*. Princeton, NJ: Princeton University Press.

Swedish NGO Foundation for Human Rights and the Swedish Helsinki Committee for Human Rights. 2002. *Alternative Report to the Human Rights Committee: With respect to Sweden's Commitments under International Covenant on Civil and Political Rights*. July. At http://www.humanrights.se/svenska/MOPrap02.pdf.

Tannen, Deborah, and Cyntia Wallat. 1993. "Interactive Frames and Knowledge Schemas in Interaction: Examples from a Medical Examination/Interview." In *Framing in Discourse*, ed. D. Tannen, 57–76. Oxford: Oxford University Press.

Tarrow, Sidney. 1989. *Democracy and Disorder: Protest and Politics in Italy, 1965–1975*. Oxford, England: Clarendon Press.

———. 1994. *Power in Movement: Social Movements, Collective Action, and Politics*. Cambridge: Cambridge University Press.

———. 1998. *Power in Movement*, 2nd ed. Cambridge: Cambridge University Press.

———. 2001. "Transnational Politics: Contention and Institutions in International Politcs." *Annual Review of Political Science* 4: 1–20.

———. 2002. "The New Transnational Contention: Organizations, Coalitions, Mechanisms." Paper presented at the APSA annual meeting, Boston.

———. 2003. "Global Movements, Complex Internationalism, and North-South Inequality." Paper presented at the Workshop on Contentious Politics, Columbia University, New York.

———. 2005. *The New Transnational Activism*. New York: Cambridge University Press.

Tarrow, Sidney, and David S. Meyer, eds. 1998. *The Social Movement Society: Contentious Politics for a New Century*. Lanham, MD: Rowman & Littlefield.

TEA. 2000. *Environmental Movement Organisations in Seven European Union States*. Interim Report, EC Environment and Climate Research Programme.

Thomas, Daniel C. 2001. *The Helsinki Effect: International Norms, Human Rights, and the Demise of Communism*. Princeton, NJ: Princeton University Press.

Thompson, Edward P. 1980. *The Making of the English Working Class*. London: Penguin.

Thompson, John B. 1995. *The Media and Modernity*. Cambridge: Cambridge University Press.

Tilly, Charles. 1978. *From Mobilization to Revolution*. Reading, PA: Addison, Wesley.

Touraine, Alain. 1978. *La voix et le regard.* Paris: Seuil.

———. 1997. *Eguaglianza e diversità: I nuovi compiti della democrazia.* Rome: Laterza.

UN General Assembly. 2000. *United Nations Millennium Declaration.* September. At http://www.un.org/millennium/declaration/ares552e.htm.

Urban, Dieter. 1993. "Logit-Analyse: Statistische Verfahren von Modellen mit qualitativen Response-Variablen." Stuttgart, Germany: Gustav Fischer.

Van Aelst, Peter, and Stefaan Walgrave. 2001. "Who Is That (Wo)man in the Street? From the Normalization of Protest to the Normalization of the Protester." *European Journal of Political Research* 39: 461–86.

Vegh, Sandor. 2003. "Classifying Forms of Online Activism." In *Cyberactivism: Online Activism in Theory and Practice,* ed. M. McCaughey and M. D. Ayers, 71–95. London: Routledge.

Velena, Melena. 2001. *Il popolo di Seattle: Chi siamo, cosa vogliamo.* Rome: Malatempora.

Vindrola, Michela. 2002. "Tematizzare il G8: Il dibattito sul vertice di Genova nei media." Thesis, Università degli studi di Torino.

Waddington, P. A. J. 1991. *The Strong Arm of the Law.* Oxford, England: Clarendon Press.

———. 1994. *Liberty and Order: Public Order Policing in a Capital City.* London: UCL Press.

———. 1998. "Controlling Protest in Contemporary Historical and Comparative Perspectives." In *Policing Protest: The Control of Mass Demonstrations in Western Democracies,* ed. D. della Porta and H. Reiter, 117–40. Minneapolis: University of Minnesota Press.

Wahlström, Mattias. 2003. "Trust and Performance: Communication between Police and Protesters from an Activist Perspective." Paper prepared at the Congress of the European Sociological Association, Murcia, Spain.

Walker, Neil. 2003. "Freedom, Security, and Justice." In *Ten Reflections on the Constitutional Treaty for Europe,* ed. B. de Witte, 163–85. Fiesole, Italy: European University Institute.

Wallerstein, Immanuel. 1979. *The Capitalist World Economy.* Cambridge: Cambridge University Press.

———. 1990. "Antisystemic Movements: History and Dilemmas." In *Transforming the Revolution: Social Movements and the World-System,* ed. S. Amin, G. Arrighi, A. G. Frank, and I. Wallerstein, 13–54. New York: Monthly Review Press.

Wapner, Paul. 1995. "Politics beyond the State: Environmental Activism and the World Civic Politics." *World Politics* 47: 311–40.

Warkentin, Craig. 2001. *Reshaping World Politics: NGOs, the Internet, and Global Civil Society*. Lanham, MD: Rowman and Littlefield.

Weed, Frank J. 1997. "The Framing of Political Advocacy and Service Responses in the Crime Victim Rights Movement." *Journal of Sociology of Social Welfare* 24: 43–61.

White Overalls. N.d. "What White Overalls Are" [Cosa sono le Tute Bianche]. At http://www.ecn.org/valkohaalarit/italiano/tute.htm.

———. N.d. "White Overalls and Violence" [Tute Bianche e violenza]. At http://www.ecn.org/valkohaalarit/italiano/violenza.htm.

———. 1998. *Charter of Milan* [Carta di Milano]. September. At http://www.ecn.org/leoncavallo/26set98.

———. 2001a. "Declaration of Peace toward the City of Genoa" [Pacto con la ciudad y con los ciudadanos de Génova]. June. At http://www.qwerg.com/tutebianche/it/luglio/contenuti/dichiarazionePaceES.html.

———. 2001b. "Declaration of War against the Powers of Injustice and Poverty." May. At http://www.ecn.org/valkohaalarit/english/g8war.htm.

———. 2001c. "From the Multitudes of Europe, Rising Up against the Empire." At http://www.gvezg.com/tutebianche/it/euyis/contenti/proclamiinglese.html (accessed November 18, 2005).

Winter, Martin. 1998a. "Police Philosophy and Protest Policing in the Federal Republic of Germany, 1960–1990." In *Policing Protest: The Control of Mass Demonstrations in Western Democracies*, ed. D. della Porta and H. Reiter, 188–212. Minneapolis: University of Minnesota Press.

———. 1998b. *Politikum Polizei: Macht und Funktion der Polizei in der Bundesrepublik Deutschland*. Münster, Germany: LIT.

World Social Movements. 2001. *Porto Alegre 2001: Call for Mobilisation*. January. At http://france.attac.org/a2978.

———. 2002. *Porto Alegre 2002 Call of Social Movements: Resistance to Neoliberalism, War, and Militarism for Peace and Social Justice*. August. At http://www.forumsocialmundial.org.br/dynamic/eng_portoalegrefinal.asp.

Zanotelli, Alessandro. 2001. "In piedi, lillipuziani!" In *La Rete di Lilliput*, G. Bologna et al., 76–78. Bologna, Italy: EMI.

Zinola, Marcello. 2003. *Ripensare la polizia: Ci siamo scoperti diversi da come pensavamo di essere*. Genoa, Italy: Fratelli Frilli Editori.

Index

DONATELLA DELLA PORTA is professor of sociology at the European University Institute. She is the coeditor (with Herbert Reiter) of *Policing Protest* (Minnesota, 1998).

MASSIMILIANO ANDRETTA is an assistant professor at the University of Pisa.

LORENZO MOSCA is a research assistant at the European University Institute.

HERBERT REITER is a research assistant at the European University Institute. He is the coeditor (with Donatella della Porta) of *Policing Protest* (Minnesota, 1998)